Swift Potomac's Lovely Daughter

*This volume is part of a series
of publications resulting from the
Bicentennial celebration
of Georgetown University
(1789–1989).
The seminar
on which it draws was
sponsored and supported by
Georgetown University's
Bicentennial Office.*

Sharon Romm
SERIES EDITOR

Swift Potomac's Lovely Daughter

Two Centuries at Georgetown through Students' Eyes

Joseph Durkin, S.J.

Editor

Georgetown University Press

Washington, D.C.

Library of Congress Cataloging-in-Publication Data

Swift Potomac's Lovely Daughter / Joseph Durkin, editor.
    p.   cm.
  ISBN 0-87840-501-1
  1. Georgetown University—History. 2. Georgetown University—
Students—History.   I. Durkin, Joseph.

LD1961.G52S95 1990   89-48744
378.753—dc20   CIP

Contents

Foreword

It is often said that young people do not have a sense of history. If that is true in general, it is not true for the members of the student seminar who produced the historical essays in this volume. They share with us their sense of being part of the living history of Georgetown University during the Bicentennial Celebration of its founding in 1789.

This book has its origin in a meeting of the Bicentennial Committee wherein Father Joseph T. Durkin, S.J., Georgetown's senior historian, suggested as a Bicentennial project that students be invited to explore the University's history. In what has to be some sort of record for a quick response in an academic institution, that suggestion became an oversubscribed student research seminar in a matter of days. We expected about a dozen students to enroll. But Father Durkin, in his Pied Piper manner, welcomed over thirty students to participate in the ambitious project of searching the University Archives for information about students and their varied activities in Georgetown's first two hundred years.

The result is this fascinating study of what today's students find interesting and significant in the historical record of yesterday's students. These reports can stir many a lively debate on whether campus and students are better or worse today—in fact, whether deep down they are all that different. Between the lines, we sense the excitement of discovery and the realization of the importance of the past in understanding the present. And occasionally, we are told of the lessons we might learn for the future. Inevitably, there are gaps in the record and some of our questions are left unanswered, but that merely whets our appetite for Father Emmett Curran's definitive history of the University, the first volume of which will appear shortly.

This student history, a collection of papers from a faculty seminar on the Georgetown experience, and Father Curran's first volume are among the first books to appear as part of the printed record of Georgetown's Bicentennial celebration. At this writing, six issues of the *Bicentennial Almanac* and various commemorative programs have appeared, as well as a pictorial essay *Georgetown: A Meditation on a Bicentennial.* The proceedings of many of the Bicentennial conferences are being prepared for publication. All of these books will form an impressive Bicentennial Series.

I am most grateful to the men and women who have made this Bicentennial year the success it has been. In particular, I wish to thank Father Joseph Durkin, S.J., his student historians, and Father John Breslin, S.J., the director of the Georgetown University Press, for their collaboration on this important Bicentennial publication.

CHARLES L. CURRIE, S.J.
Director of the Bicentennial

Preface

On the premise that no part of a university is more important than its students (with the teaching faculty coming in a close second) the editor of the present book believed that the students should participate prominently, and recognizably, in our Bicentennial celebration.

The editor, in what he has finally persuaded himself was *not* for him an unfortunate moment, suggested that a selected group of students should be let loose—with appropriate direction—in the Georgetown University Archives with the aim of mining those precious records for information about the history of the undergraduate schools. It was agreed that, in this quest, two conditions would be honored: (1) the data excavated would be either in substance or emphasis news, and (2) it would be, as far as possible, relative to student activities such as debating, drama, athletics, social service involvement, student customs, and so forth.

Twofold also were the goals of the editor: besides that of adding important details to the general history of the University, he wished to witness the very special joy in the faces of the young researchers as they realized they had discovered something long lost in the darkness of the past. This deep and even thrilling satisfaction, as every real scholar knows, is inimitable: it is what makes intellectual work a constant celebration of the mind's power to create.

The following were some of the questions which the researchers asked the documents to answer—with, in many instances, unexpected results:

Did student interest in the plight of the needy outside campus begin in the 1960s and not before that time? What were the contributions of our black students to the cultural life of the campus, and, generally speaking, have black students felt "at home" here? What were some of the highlights in Georgetown's athletic history? Was a Hoya quarterback-receiver combination the actual invention of football's forward pass? How did it feel to be a female student at Georgetown after 1969? What was the quality of the student writing in the *Georgetown College Journal*? The response of the Archives to this last query is one of the most surprising of all, as well as the unique manner in which the magazine was created and managed. Which student customs and relaxations of the nineteenth century are particularly interesting, and what do they tell us about the conservatism or radicalism of the student of that time? Did any successful professional playwrights emerge from the Mask and Bauble Dramatic Society of the College? How did the Mask and Bauble members become involved in the production of White House entertainments during the President John F. Kennedy era? By what means did the teaching of chemistry at the Hilltop in the last third of the last century outrival in scope and excellence that of any other American college? What were the reasons for Georgetown's eminence in what at the turn of the century was a successful substitute for football—intercollegiate debate competition? Are there among the dusty Archives files some fascinating examples of really competent poetry composed by students? A handwritten exercise book of a poetry class of the early 1840s answers this query in a most gratifying way. What differences and similarities exist between student attitudes to religion and morals a hundred years ago and those of today? How did it come about that the evolution of student government at Georgetown had its source in the Georgetown University Athletic Association? What about the "military presence" on the campus, including the ancient Georgetown military cadets? Finally, in general, how many historical facts concerning undergraduates at Georgetown have not been discovered until now, and in what directions should we advance in order to find more of them?

The authors of these essays are not professional writers; but neither was any professional writer you might name at an early moment of his or her career. The book began, innocently enough, as a pedagogical exercise, with no publication intended; the work appeared worthy of publication as an afterthought proceeding from on high, that is to say, from the academic administration at the summit.

The editor would have been worried if the authors had agreed with all opinions held by their elders regarding the University. So, he was guided by respect for the inalienable right of youth—within reasonable bounds—to make mistakes. The editor was not looking for panegyrics, but assessments, even when he thought his own were better. If he had not adopted this attitude, he believed, the whole point of the enterprise would have been lost.

It might be said of this offering what, reportedly, a parent said about his son as he deposited him for the first time at the College: Don't expect too much of him and you may be able to like him.

Thanks to that wise, tactful handler of quirky editors and young authors, Father John Breslin, S.J., of the Georgetown University Press.

J.T. Durkin, S.J.

I. The Written Word

"John Carroll" by William A. Wilson (from *The Georgetown Journal*, October, 1938).

"Philosophy Student" (from *The Georgetown Journal*, February, 1949).

History of the
Georgetown College Journal

Christopher Donesa

Some day, when the story of college journalism in this country is written, it will be found that nearly everyone who went through college and made a success of writing afterwards, began his work on a college paper, and looks back on that experience as one of the precious incentives of his life.—James J. Walsh quotation in the *Georgetown College Journal*, 1916.[1]

Journalism at Georgetown has touched almost everyone who has walked the Hilltop since the founding of the *Georgetown College Journal* in 1871. The *Journal* began a century-long tradition by attracting many student writers and editors who gave freely of their time and energy to depict the panorama of Georgetown. Since their appearance on campus, student publications have served not only to chronicle Georgetown's past, but also to look into its future, promoting vision at Georgetown and pushing the University ever upward toward greatness.

The story of Georgetown's journalistic tradition is more than the volumes which line the shelves of the University archives. It is also a story of notable young men, many of whom moved on to literary or other kinds of eminence after spending their early years working on a campus publication. Finally, it is a story of how these publications themselves evolved through the hard work and ingenuity of their editors.

The Founding of the *College Journal*

> It is only after strenuous exertions, and a struggle with many diffi-
> culties, that we have succeeded in establishing this new enterprise
> in our college.—*Georgetown College Journal* 1, no. 1.[2]

The first known student publication at Georgetown appeared in
1820. Known as the *Minerva*, it was a handwritten manuscript
whose few copies were passed from student to student. The obvious drawbacks of this method of publication forced the editors to discontinue publication after only a few issues. A second
and similar attempt at college journalism likewise failed in
1862.[3]

In 1871, the Reverend Edmund Young, S.J., arrived at
Georgetown as a new professor of rhetoric. Young had come to
the Hilltop from Santa Clara College in California, where he
had helped found the successful newspaper, *Owl*, which had
flourished for several years. Surprised at the lack of student
publications at Georgetown, Fr. Young enlisted the assistance of
students in the college to create a new journal.[4]

Young soon found his other commitments too pressing to
continue actively leading the *Journal* Association and handed
over the reins to the Reverend John H. Sumner, S.J., known fa-
miliarly as "Pap."[5] Sumner took control of the *Journal* just as efforts to get the paper started were picking up steam. The first
general meeting to discuss the project was held in the old Philosophers' study on the first floor of the North Building. Each
man was expected to contribute five dollars to start the paper.
"I recollected what a big sum it seemed to me in those days," remembered one of the founders.[6]

The collection did not come close to funding the fledgling
Journal, which had to rely on innovative means to raise additional funds. Although sources differ as to whether it took place
in June, 1872 or in the previous winter, the staff rented an auditorium in Georgetown and staged a benefit concert. The show
consisted of "recitations, readings, songs and music," and the
admission fee went toward funding the newspaper.[7] The concert was a great success, and the venture went forward.

After the concert, the students decided to go ahead with

forming a joint stock company to publish the *Journal*. Twenty-five students subscribed to the company, meeting the final capital requirements of the fledgling publication. The money went toward equipment, including old-style linotype machines, stands, a proof press, and other necessities of a composing room.

The corporation was staffed by students. The editorial and business positions went to members of the joint-stock corporation, who continued to participate enthusiastically in the enterprise. Even the typesetting equipment was run by volunteer students who had had previous experience in the publishing business. What resulted was a *Journal* office of frightening efficiency, punctuated by bedlam, as evidenced by the following account by a student who accidentally blundered into the controlled chaos as the first issue was being prepared:

> Sure enough, there in the room where I had never seen any thing more orderly or useful than broken china and chair legs was a busy office in full swing with an inky press at the center..."You see," said [Secretary W.C.] Niblack when were comfortably seated, "This is going to be an interesting experiment. We are going to edit a paper....No, it's never before been tried at Georgetown and should mean a lot to the school if only they will take the interest which a thing of this sort needs and deserves." Just then we were interrupted by a rolling drum and a very army of small, piping instruments which set up a dis-jointed tune in the next room. "You must try and not hear that," [Vice President] Jim Tracey apologized. "It's Charlie Cowardin and his band-to-be preparing for the drill next week."[8]

The first issue finally appeared in December of 1872. It consisted of eight pages and featured four articles: a letter from Southhampton, England by T.H. Sherman, S.J. describing a reception of the Prince of Wales (Sherman was one of the two sons of Civil War General William Techumseh Sherman; he later became a Jesuit priest), a piece on the benefits of fiction, a criticism of the problem of plagiarism, and an essay entitled "The Three Novelists" dealing with the writings of Dickens, Thackeray, and Bulwer-Lytton. These novelists, in 1872, represented contemporary or, at least, modern literature.

The issue also contained editorials, campus news (hash still holds its own; reading at dinner is abolished), two poems, and two pages of advertising, including a lengthy promotion for a local liquor store.[9] The *Journal* was also read by the local community, and reviewers had mostly positive words for the new venture. The *Washington Star* called the *Journal* "creditable," and the *Baltimore Sun* pronounced it to be "in good taste."[10]

Editorially, at least, the first issue had been a success. However, changes would soon become necessary in the production and business side of the paper. The well-meaning amateur typesetters had let more than a few errors get by them, and the mistakes had shown clearly in the maiden edition. In the midst of a passage informing readers of the novelty and advantages of having all-volunteer typesetters, for example, the paper proudly discussed the virtues of the "opportunito" which the *Journal* had given its workers. Likewise, stories on the completely dissimilar topics of "Earnestness" and "The Greek Verb" became intermixed with one another.

To address this problem, the *Journal* hired an outside firm to set the type. The managers also found local help to solicit advertisements. While the magazine had started with the laudable goal of complete self-sufficiency, the scale of its operations soon made evident the need for outsiders, and employees of the College filled many of the remaining gaps. The College wagoner, for example, carried to the printer the precious plates, held in place by a wooden frame crafted by the College carpenter.

The one part of the *Journal*'s operations that continuously struggled during the early years was its business department, as the publication had continuing difficulties in collecting its subscription revenue. One *Journal* historian speculated later that Georgetown itself actually held much of the publication's stock, although under a different name.[11] "We cannot undertake to send the paper on trust: our past experience forbids it," the exasperated staff told its readers in an effort to collect its subscription money. Other messages finally culminated in the challenge "ARE YOU GOING TO PAY OR NOT?" in large type. By 1877 the money problem almost forced the editors to suspend publication, and a second benefit concert was needed to get the *Journal* back on a sound financial footing.[12]

While the second concert did not match the glitter of the first one, it still more than doubled the money in the *Journal*'s coffers. The financial ledger of the *Journal* shows that 262 spectators paid fifty cents each for a ticket to the show. After subtracting the costs of the auditorium and other expenses such as sheet music, the program had netted $63 for the publication. On its face, this amount seems insignificant, but it more than doubled the publication's revenue.[13]

The Leadership and Organization
of the *College Journal*

The *Journal*'s financial situation may have been precarious, but its talent was a solid asset. The magazine's success was largely due to dedicated and talented young men who carried it from its early days of uncertainty to its days as an established part of Georgetown. We should not underestimate, however, the impact which the *Journal*'s constitution had in enforcing a sense of order and decorum on the organization's often potentially divisive operations.

The "Constitution of the Georgetown College Journal Association" resulted from the work of a committee of Ansel Cook, J. Percy Keating, and J. Caldwell Robertson in 1872. The document itself is not especially innovative, but it did set forth a format so that the *Journal* might be run efficiently and without conflict.[14]

The object of the *Journal*, according to the document, was "the encouragement of literature among the students and maintenance in Georgetown College of a paper worthy of the institution." The emphasis on quality and sophistication which would become the *Journal*'s hallmark was thus as much a part of the publication's official persona as its *de facto* one, embodied particularly in the statement that the magazine would have to live up to the considerable reputation of its parent university.

The constitution went on to clarify other matters, setting the price of stock at $5, with shares not transferable, and then described the magazine's editorial structure. The Board would include ten members: a president, vice-president, secretary, treasurer, censor, and five editors.

This orientation reflected the corporate structure of the *Journal* as well as the role of the faculty. With the exception of the president, the officers had little to say in the day-to-day editorial operations of the magazine. Although they frequently doubled as section editors, their duties focused instead on financial and production matters. The broad powers of the office of the president (a Jesuit) demonstrate the strong influence which the Jesuit mentors had on the early years of the *Journal*.

The constitution noted that the president must be chosen from among the faculty; he presides over all meetings of the *Journal* Association, and serves as an ex-officio editor general of the publication. This provision meant that in practice the *Journal* could be controlled entirely by the faculty. But the issue of censorship, it is interesting to note, never became a serious conflict at this time, although it did arise at later dates. The power also meant that the manuscripts could benefit from the experience of a Georgetown professor.

The other officers filled well-defined roles, with the student vice-president presiding over the association on the not infrequent occasions when the president could not attend, and the secretary and treasurer handling administrative matters and the all-important task of managing the paper's independent and frequently faltering finances. Although the latter two offices had little direct input into editorial decisions, they were prestigious enough to give their occupants additional influence on editorial matters.

The office of censor is unique to the constitution. One might expect from its title that its duties would lie on the editorial side. The true responsibility of the job, however, was "to preserve order in the meetings of the association." In effect, the impact of the censor must have been minor, because there is little mention of the position in historical essays about the *Journal* and no well-known names are associated with the job.

Perhaps more revealing of the structure of the *Journal* are its rules and by-laws, which proved to be an inordinately detailed document providing parliamentary procedures usually used for a legislative body. This is perhaps appropriate when one considers that three of the publication's founders went on to become members of Congress, but it serves also as an indication of the fascination felt by the *Journal*'s founders toward lofty and important institutions.

A recorded vote could be taken on any issue, for example, by a one-fifth vote of the members, and a roll-call could be required for inclusion in the minutes by one-third of the stockholders. Additionally, no member could speak more than twice to the same subject in one meeting without the permission of a majority. Perhaps the most telling indication of their aspirations lay in the official guide for the settlement of parliamentary disputes. The choice was Jefferson's *Manual*, the book used by the U.S. House of Representatives.

The by-laws also better defined the editorial decision-making process at the *Journal*. The document stipulated that one of the five editors would be chosen from each class, with one more elected at large. The five would then elect a chairman who would run what the by-laws termed the "editorial core" of the *Journal*, which would in theory serve to edit and approve all of the stories in the paper. In practice, this worked differently, as evidenced by the following excerpt:

> The ostensible duty of the editorial committee was to revise manuscripts proffered by the other students; but in reality this committee was forced to do nearly all the writing and was often unnecessarily criticised on account of the nature of its work in articles sent to it over pen names, and published in the *Journal* when sufficiently well-written.[15]

To reflect more accurately the workload within the organization, the editors amended the constitution in November of 1877 to provide for a board of ten editors, including the president, to decide on the magazine's content. The president also received the treasurer's portfolio as the custodian of the newspaper's funds.

The meetings held under the by-laws also reflected the editors' wish to obey parliamentary procedure, so the minutes read much like pages from the *Congressional Record*. The first recorded meeting of the official *Journal* organization took place on October 4 of 1872 for the purpose of holding elections. The voters unanimously elected Father Sumner the association's president after an honorary nomination for Father Young, who had planted the seed for the magazine. The other officers were listed as follows, including state affiliations (these allusions to the native states of the students added a touch of dignity to the *Journal*'s directors):

Joseph E. Washington, Tenn.	Vice President
James F. Tracey, N.Y.	Treasurer
Wm. C. Niblack, Ind.	Secretary
Wm. H. Dennis, D.C.	Business Manager
John C. Robertson, S.C.	Censor

The electorate also named two editors for each of the following sections: philosophy, rhetoric, poetry, and 1st grammar. Finally, "a committee of three consisting of Messrs Robertson, Fisher, and Niblack were [sic] appointed to wait upon Fr. Sumner and notify him of his election."[16]

Finally, the regulations furnished a definition of what privileges a stockholder was entitled to: one vote, three copies of the *Journal* and the right to receive a mail subscription for three consecutive years after his departure from the Hilltop. In reality, there was little dispute over the powers of stockholders because there were so few of them. In 1875, for example, each editor held one share, with the exception of John Agar, who had three, and university president Rev. Patrick Healy, S.J., who patronized the *Journal* by holding four shares.[17]

Still, the voting balance held the potential for considerable impact. Agar later claimed that his extra shares had been critical in the history of the publication:

> Another claim I have to fame is that I saved the *Journal* from being strangled by the faculty. We had no faculty moderator then....At this time the Yard suspected that Father Healy had designs upon the editorial page of the *College Journal*. Censorious intentions, suppression of free speech, etc. Liberty was at stake, so I without authority, increased the capital stock of the *Journal* corporation, bought the increased stock issue, gained the increased stock control, and saved many precious things.[18]

The minutes of the *Journal*'s meetings show that Father Sumner called an urgent meeting on November 1 of 1872 to indicate in no uncertain terms that such unauthorized stock issues would not be tolerated, and that all new issues would have to be approved by the president. The students went along without a fight.[19]

Sumner served as the *Journal*'s spiritual heart and soul during his years as its president, and the publication's alumni from the period remembered him as a fine role model, but also a wonderful friend and resource. One alumnus recalled Sumner during the twenty-fifth anniversary celebration of the *Journal*:

> ...first in the line of importance, of course, comes Father John H. Sumner, SJ, more familiarly, if irreverently, known as "Dear Old Pap Sumner." No kinder man nor greater friend of the boys ever walked the corridors of the college. He had some reputation as a man of literary ability, having often contributed to the newspapers and magazines of that day, notably the *Spring Blossom* and *Southern Literary Messenger*....
>
> Father Sumner's popularity was unbounded. No one could tell such interesting and diverting stories; no one could say Mass so quickly, and there was no better friend to the boys when in a scrape than "Pap"....
>
> I remember clearly to this day [an anecdote] he was fond of telling...how Georgetown narrowly missed being the capital of the United States during the War of 1812. When the Capitol at Washington was burnt down by the English, Congress and the Senate found themselves without a place of meeting. There was no house in Washington large enough for their purpose, so they sent up to Georgetown a committee to examine the North building [now Old North]....The committee found it in every way desirable, and so it was resolved to hold the next meeting of Congress there. Early in the morning the Congressmen and Senators started out in carriages...but halfway up what is now the P Street hill, but what was then a most abominable road, their carriages got stuck in the mud. It was impossible to proceed any further, so they were obliged to return to Washington, and leave to Georgetown the meagre glory of an *if*.[20]

The Early Years of the *College Journal*

It should be remembered that although a magazine usually offers little more than glorified journalism it is something very different from a newspaper. No one but a certain sort of historian can stir up in himself any enthusiasm for day-before-yesterday's newspaper;

but a magazine, more tranquilly and carefully prepared, has an audience that extends in time well beyond the subscribers who receive it as it falls from the press. Therefore, while the *Journal* is being written and edited primarily for those who will read it now, it knows that it must not, if ever looked back upon, seem too puerile or ephemeral.—*Journal* editorial, 1932.[21]

Early writing in the *Journal* was knowledgeable, sophisticated, scholarly and provided intellectual challenge for the reader. It was apparent that the editors sought to furnish only the highest level of debate in their forum, and a high moral and intellectual tone pervaded the prose.

Many of the first few volumes of the publication featured essays on current events and trends in society rather than the literary and analytical pieces which later became its trademark. Authors displayed a mature grasp of current events. They did *not*, however, necessarily reach the "right" conclusion each time, as evidenced by the following 1873 passage taken from a highly uncomplimentary essay on a women's suffrage meeting:

One of the most enjoyable of the recreations in which we have lately allowed our editorial gravity to indulge was a visit to the Women's Suffrage Convention while holding its annual session in Washington. The great object of the Convention was to urge on Congress some legislation on behalf of the cause they have at heart, but from the puerile action which characterized the meeting it is highly probable women's right to vote and thereupon to fight, swear, and get drunk like other citizens will be deferred to the Greek Kalends....Miss Susan B. Anthony, President or Presidentess, as you please, of the WSA called the meeting to order and harangued the large, intelligent audience whom motives of curiosity more than anything else had attracted to the hall....A dim-looking female was announced...striking a high key and in a monotone, the effect of which was not altogether dissimilar to the grating of a rusty file on a mill-saw, she ran on in the most harassing manner....[22]

A later (1875) attempt at forecasting political trends came slightly closer to the target:

It seems not a little strange that such a principle as Communism should have found so many advocates even in our country. Where property is every day changing hands, and every industrious man is becoming independent if not rich, it would puzzle even the most accurate reader to account for the existence of such a spirit among us as Communism, unless on the theory that it proceeds from that love of novelty, and distaste for things established which are so characteristic of our age.[23]

The distaste for political change exhibited in such pieces could be attributed to some extent to the editors' respect for the classical tradition, and its accompanying problematic attitude toward change. The initial volumes of the *Journal*, for example, carried articles with titles such as "Horitania" and "Was Caesar's Grief for Pompey Sincere?", and many editorials and space-fillers made masterly use of Greek and Latin phrases, and other essays made references in passing to the writings of Horace and Cicero to support their theses.

Yet, the high regard held by the paper's contributors and editors for the classical past did not preclude yearnings for a better future. In a remarkable forecast of what was to come, the *Journal* printed an essay in 1873 on the prospects for the new technology of air travel. Significant portions are included here to help convey not only the foresight of the writer, but also to show how well he understood an abstract concept:

We are getting too rapid now-a-days to tolerate much longer an impeded progress along the earth. Already impatient glances are turned upward toward the clouds, and brows are knit over the problem of aerial navigation. The era of this mode of traveling may not be as far off as some imagine. All the necessary principles are discovered, and only await the genius who will combine them in a practical machine.

The mistake that many inventors have made has been in attempting to introduce the balloon into their contrivances; or rather they have aspired only to find a means for propelling a balloon...Too little confidence has been placed in the buoyant powers of the air. The force which not only lifts a large and heavy kite into the clouds, but also nearly lifts the adventurous flier off his feet, is the power which it is proposed to take advantage of....The action of the kite in a wind is the same as that of an inclined plane carried horizontally forward in the air. If some apparatus can be designed by which the motion of such an inclined plane can be controlled, so that it may ascend or descend at will, and obey the direction given, the problem would seem to be solved.

It could not, of course, be expected that even with a suitable machine, man should be able to [immediately] navigate the air. To do so will require experience and practice. But there seems no reason to doubt that after outstripping the fleetest animals of the sea and land with his engines he will also surpass the swallow, the pigeon, and the hawk in their flight through the air. What a revolution such an invention would work it is needless to indicate....But in time aerial travel, with its attendant circumstances, will grow a familiar thing and we shall learn to snatch up our valise and parachute and hasten down to the depot to catch the morning air-ship, never doubting that it will land us safely in London by noon.[24]

The publication exhibited also an uncanny ability to analyze passing trends. The *Journal*'s opinions were often quite critical and independent, demonstrating that the editors were not slaves to fashion.

The young journalists were not impressed, for example, with the newfound popularity of cigarettes. "Lately a mania for cigarette smoking has developed itself," noted an 1872 editorial; "These breeders of disease are frequently compounded of refuse tobacco...Those who indulge in the practice 'are easily excited and have a tendency to vertigo, and dimness of vision, besides being troubled by dyspepsia.'" Smokers, they warned, "are also liable to bronchial and throat diseases, and excessive indulgence tends to produce anaemia, which is one of the first steps toward softening of the brain."[25]

In its early years, the attention of the *Journal* to literature lagged somewhat behind its other features. The editors did not include their first short story until the third issue, and the literary criticism seemed to focus on looking at older and classical works (Charles Dickens was the most contemporary writer discussed) instead of providing cogent analysis of new works or trends in the literary community. Early pieces, for example, focused on such abstract subjects as "Poetry: Its Universality" or "The Beautiful."

This limitation did not, however, detract from the overall quality. In addition to its essays on literature and contemporary times, the *Journal* also covered topical events on campus, although usually at the level of a community "bulletin board" marking arrivals and departures of new professors and Jesuits and conveying mundane announcements. The paper also covered Georgetown sports and events at other college campuses. These sections provided highlights equal to the best productions of their journalistic competitors.

In the field of sports, for example, the editors harkened back yet again to their classical models in describing an early rugby match in a literary style that today's sports sections have in all likelihood rarely matched:

> The game, in the surging movements of the combatants, their outcries, and the intensity of the whole action displayed, would have made a fine study for one about to engage in reading an account of the old Homeric battles. We saw Kaiser standing on his head; but whether he was kicked into this position, or assumed it through a momentary impulse of delight, we do not know....Walworth's fair hair streamed in the wind as he followed the bounding ball....[26]

The *Journal* gained wider notoriety through its exchange section. The column quickly became one of the most notable features of the magazine as a verbal contest sprang up with the *Index Niagarensis* published by the female Seminary of the Holy Angels in Suspension Bridge, N.Y. The *Index* had done groundbreaking work in Catholic college journalism, and fancied itself as the clear leader in the field. The high quality exhibited by the *Journal* had set the stage for a memorable print battle.

The first salvo came from the *Journal* against its older and more established counterpart in October of 1873. The New York paper was "edited by a professor, and makes marked improvement," they commented somewhat patronizingly. The *Index* replied that the *Journal* was "one of the best printed of our exchanges." Preliminary sparring continued, until the combat broke into more pointed commentary, the best account of which comes from a 1932 account of the famous exchange:

> The *Index*, weary of such cautious preliminaries, stated disapprovingly that the *Journal* was surprisingly secular in tone for the publication of a Catholic college, and deplored that magazine's vain hab-

it of reprinting flattering notices made about it by contemporaries. The *Journal* sarcastically replied, in regard to the latter fault: "The *Index* must bear with us, by the aid of that 'stable religious principle' which *it* possesses and the *Journal* does *not*," and added that it was trying to keep itself exclusively literary. It ended by saying "The *Index* editor...seems to caper about the field of journalism very much like an untrained colt led out to pasture."

This seems to have displeased the *Index*, and it expressed itself as aghast at hearing that its contemporary was completely uninterested in religious ideas. The *Journal* was indignant; it had been misinterpreted, and demanded that its remarks be reprinted in full. The *Index* reprinted in full, but its comment was still far from complimentary. Quite the reverse, in fact. Accordingly the *Journal* announced the end of the dispute as far as itself was concerned: "We have other and better uses for the space at our command than the protraction of quarrels that are totally useless to us...'Good day, friend!'"[27]

The dispute continued, although with less intensity, into the 1880s. The *Journal* typically held the upper hand in later rounds, as it slung derisive comments left and right toward a clearly less skilled opponent. (In fact, the efforts at a response put forth by the *Index* usually only managed to land them in more hot water as they demonstrated the shallowness of their literary talent.)

The *Journal*, in a few short years, had proved that it belonged among the best of college publications in talent and quality. It suffered, however, with the loss of one of its early driving forces, Fr. Sumner, who unfortunately had to retire, due to poor health, from the *Journal* presidency in 1880 after seven years as leader. In March of that year, the paper was transferred to the Philodemic Society, and the results were not encouraging. "The *Journal*," said one later history of the period, "had a barren season when it printed long accounts of what was going on at the College, with only a reminiscent letter from an alumnus and a rambling essay to an issue to give the magazine a literary semblance. Even this scanty attention paid to literature was too much for one subscriber, who wrote to the editors recommending that its space be filled by still more news of the college."[28]

An examination of a typical issue of the era (October, 1883) confirms the bleak evaluation of the publication's status during the time. The lead was an unimpressive ode to Horace, followed by such stories as a piece on the golden jubilee of former Georgetown president Rev. Charles Stonestreet and a story on the election of the new Vicar-General of the Jesuit order. The lone attempt at a critical or analytical essay came from a lengthy and cryptic piece on the evolution of the word "dude" in popular culture. Although it invoked Latin and Greek traditions in an attempt to analyze the expression of language, the piece did not exhibit the passion or vision of its recent forerunners. Clearly, the publication needed much work to achieve its former success.

A Return to the Past

The beginnings of a return to distinction for the *Journal* came soon afterward, when the publication instituted a new system of selecting its editors from among the best writers in the student body rather than from the stockholders.29 The change brought bright and thoughtful writers back into the organization, and the writing slowly began to improve.

The real impetus for positive changes in the *Journal* came with the modification of its role in the changing campus community. It had started as a literary journal but slowly evolved into a newspaper. The next step was to transform the newspaper into an alumni publication.

"It has been suggested by Justice Martin F. Morris, the recently elected president of the 'society of alumni' to convert the *Journal* into a magazine of review that would serve as an organ of that body," the president wrote in an 1897 letter to alumni. "It is believed," he continued, "that this step will enhance the literary merit of the *Journal*." He went on to propose limiting the space devoted to undergraduate matters so that the magazine might serve as the "voice of alumni," and, of course, to ask for money.[30]

The move may stand as one of the shrewdest in the history of the *Journal*. Not only had the editors tapped the financial resources of the alumni to save the publication; they had also tapped the "old boys'" literary talents. What resulted was not only a return but even an improvement on the quality of the early years of the *Journal*. The paper seemed finally to have met its literary expectations.

Just two months after the format change, in October of 1897, the *Journal* carried two powerful articles in the same issue. Near-legendary *Journal* alumnus Condé Pallen returned with a stunning piece entitled "The Literary Quality" which defined the identity the *Journal* had been seeking for so long. He pointed out that imaginative literature goes beyond mere facts and images to convey the true *essence* of its subject:

"For a moment let us be unusual," wrote Pallen. "...pause and reflect; not to point the pros and cons or the merits or failures of modern quantitative literature, but simply to orient ourselves as anxious travellers in the confusing profession of this haste forward, though not necessarily upward. It is the literary quality we seek; quantity is obvious enough." The conclusion explains further:

> Literature is the exploitation of truth in the freedom of the imagination, and the truth is always more than realism. Truth lies beyond all facts, survives all facts. Not that facts may not be realities, but they never explain themselves; they are contingencies forever disappearing, and their virtue abides only in the soul of truth, which alone holds them in its own imperishable essence. The great emancipator of English poetry from the thraldom of a petty conventionalism, begotten by a shallow religious formalism, sings a line which gives us the complete theory of true literature; he speaks of "The light that never was on sea or land." By this he means the light of idealization, the glory of the imagination making effulgent in the variety of its coloring the white light of truth as it shines out from the intellect....Literature, therefore will find its field in the imagination under the illumination of intellect.[31]

Later in the same issue appeared another essay entitled "Some Views on English Prose of the Last Half of the Nineteenth Century," signed with the pen name of an alumnus, "Atticus." The article looked closely at the literature of the past few years and asked the difficult question whether the writing could meet the standards set by past literary greats. Atticus said no:

> But our prose literature of today, our *fin de siècle* literature, has it not fallen from that stage of excellence? Do its authors not lie some-

where off the line of artistic thought and expression followed up by their worthy predecessors of years past and gone? For fifty years strong, sturdy oaks stemmed the current of the tide of taste, and kept it in proper channels. Now the oaks are down, the floodgates are open, a torrent of worthless literature swoops down us apace. The taste of the age in this, as in all things else, controls supply and demand.[32]

The author reached the conclusion that the "decline" in the literary quality was the inevitable result of an unsophisticated public who had not been adequately educated. Despite the presence in contemporary literature of novels that would soon be considered "great," Atticus remained unimpressed:

The disproportionate success of the novel is precisely what we should expect during the present period. For we live in an age of novelists, of lovers of novelties. The rage for rapid change is now the very atmosphere in which we move—we take it in with every breath. Few, indeed are there who cling sullenly to the old and strive to keep it from the dark night that shrouds the obsolete....Manifold and various, doubtless, are the causes of these deplorable facts; yet may not a partial cause thereof be traced back to the very education that our youth receive? The building up of all the faculties of man must be properly begun, in order that it may be rightly finished. And this important work will never be properly begun until dabblers in pedagogics shall have been ousted from the vantage ground they now occupy, and balked in their endeavors to foist upon the community at large ideas, the whole trend of which is not to build up, but to fill the youthful mind.[33]

The dual questions of education policy and the definition of literature also were the subject of two excellent articles of the *Journal's* late period. In February, 1898, M.F. Morris argued against views that liberal education should be abolished in favor of a scientific one, holding that the development of the ability to *think* (and *feel*) is the most important talent that an educated man could possess:

What is education? It is not knowledge. It is not an accumulation of facts in the mind. It is not the conversion of the human intellect into a storehouse of miscellaneous information, ill-assorted and ill-

digested. It is cultivation; and not alone the cultivation of the intellect, but the cultivation of the heart, the sentiments, the affections,
the imagination as well.[34]

Finally, Daniel Devlin provided a supplement to Pallen's earlier piece on defining literature, explaining *why* its study was a
virtue:

> As art, a literary work must, of course, *please*. But not every and any
> kind of pleasure will do. There are some kinds that are right and
> sound; there are other kinds that are wrong and unsound. How
> shall we discern one from the other? In a matter so wrapped up
> with that inmost striving of our nature—the pursuit of happiness,
> at least under the aspect of pleasure—the solution of this question
> ought to be easy, despite the attempts of writers on "Aesthetics" to
> involve it in hopeless confusion. And the answer is at hand. The
> pleasure derived from the *mere perception* of its *beauty*, is the *only
> true measure* of the artistic worth of a literary production.[35]

Volume 22 of the *Journal* (1898) also featured "Tennyson's
Debt to Theocritus," "The Geniality of Horace," and "Problems
of Catholic College Education in Relation to Present Social
Needs." It was one of the magazine's finest years. The increased
emphasis on literary and critical pieces and the change to an
alumni focus did not, however, completely eliminate accounts
of everyday life at Georgetown. The *Journal* continued its coverage of news and sports in the same somewhat simplistic manner as before.

The news section still served largely as a bulletin board and
chronicle, with little editorial interpretation. Headlined "News
of the Month," the column was devoted to comings and goings
along with academic events, such as the opening of the undergraduate schools. At the beginning of the 1897–1898 school
year, for example, the paper reported that "The genial and well-
liked Rev. Father Coughlan, SJ, has been replaced on the upper
corridor by Rev. Mr. Walter M. Drum, SJ, late of St. Francis Xavier's, New York. Mr. Raley's executive abilities in the Department of Athletics have been recognized. He now adds to his duties of Teacher of Special Classics and of Prefect, the
Directorship of the Varsity Athletics."[36]

Sports also were reported. The games during this period were much more seriously contested. The *Journal's* coverage of the 1894 Thanksgiving football game between Georgetown and Columbia would undoubtedly raise eyebrows today:

> Bahen lay white and motionless on the ground...It is also said that he was struck twice, and that after he was down one of his opponents kicked him in the back, while another jumped upon his prostrate form, planting both knees upon his stomach...Burke twisted his knee, or had it twisted and was carried from the field, making the fourth man who had been injured while playing at the right end.[37]

The player later died, and officials temporarily abolished football at Georgetown.

The *Journal* had successfully weathered an uncertain beginning and a shaky adolescence to mature into a thriving forum for Georgetown's opinions and scholarly work. The founders and early visionaries set the stage for a publication that had the potential to flourish in the future. The question remained as to whether their successors could continue.

The *College Journal* in the Twentieth Century

The *Journal* from the turn of the century to the present can be considered a "mixed bag," depending on the era and the student editors: at times brilliant and, at others, silly. The three- to four-year periods which marked the swings in quality indicate that the changes resulted not by plan or editorial policy, but rather as the result of the differing talents and personal preferences of its changing editors and contributors.

The first example of such a radical shift came shortly after the turn of the century. In the wake of thoughtful pieces such as those chronicled above came another "down" period rivaling the 1880s. The pages of the *Journal* contained mostly short stories designed to amuse but without much lasting value. One such piece, entitled "My Friend, The Dentist," might have been mildly entertaining to its turn-of-the-century readers but today seems silly.

As I said before, the Doctor and I were old friends. We had mutual claims upon each other. I had some of his gold in my teeth and he had some of mine in his pocket, only he had a trifle more than I had. On the strength of old acquaintance I bit his fingers when he hurt me very much, and he evened matters in divers subtle ways—and somehow or other I always got the worst of it....

"Here's a perfectly fair proposition," I continued, ignoring his sarcasm. "If you don't hurt me too much I'll pay my bill."

The doctor chuckled softly and polished his little mirror.[38]

The only development of note during the years from 1900 to 1915 was the rearrangement of the editorial staff from its committee of editors to an editorial board under the control of a single editor-in-chief.[39] The change reflected the gradual evolution of the *Journal* into a more independent publication following its past history of strong faculty influence, although the magazine continued to have a Jesuit moderator.

The reform did not mean that the student writers were entirely free to publish what they wished. Apparently the all-male atmosphere of the College had inspired a great deal of romantic writing in the stories of the *Journal*, prompting Jesuit provincial Joseph Hanselman to take action in a letter to the rector of Georgetown dated August 21, 1911:

Comment has been made that poems and stories in our college journals and annuals deal too much with love as their main motive.

At times the notes have been written in a flippant, worldly spirit, tinged with slang and some vulgarity. Whatever is printed in our journals should elevate the reader.

My intention now is not to advert to any particular instance, but to request Your Reverence to see that the proper censorship is exercised in this respect.

Where not in vogue, let the rector or prefect of studies pass on all that appears in the college journal.[40]

The First World War spurred a thoughtful period in the *Journal* lasting through the 1920s. The magazine contained many of the standard patriotic admonishments for America to move on to greatness against its enemies in the Great War and its files are filled with letters from the infamous "Committee on Public Information" headed by George Creel. Its writings, however, remained somewhat restrained. Authors looked analytically at the events on the continent and the effects which the war might have on foreign affairs in the future. The *Journal* also provided a unique perspective on the war by publishing many letters sent by Georgetown men serving in the military.

The general quality of the magazine during this period was good. Although the editors emphasized poetry, and critical essays on current events in addition to literary works, the articles accurately conveyed the spirit of the decade and stand as a highlight in the history of the *Journal*. Volumes 54 and 55, for the years 1924–1927, for example, featured essays entitled "Why a Separate Air Service?" and "Sea Power of the United States" that reflected questions remaining from the war about the emerging power of the United States on the world front. The newfound cultural identity of the nation received attention in pieces such as "The Great American Audience" and "The Uses of Advertising."

These articles did not overshadow literary works. A regular feature entitled "'Neath the Tum Tum Tree" provided short, bizarre, pieces partly inspired by "Alice in Wonderland." They needed to be read carefully to understand their full meaning, including the following excerpt from 1926 entitled "As Others See Us":

> After searching high and low we finally found the key to Mr. Mythe's single volume, "Essays for Esoterics," under the bath-mat and immediately threw it out the window, laughing uproariously as it jingled through the roof of the green house below.
>
> We liked the essay on the "Gentle Art of Bath Taking." The finely drawn character of the Philosophical Flabtomist got us nowhere, especially when he says "That lady out there in the limousine who bathed daily ignoring the centuries between represents the good boot-black; while the butcher represents the more lax members of that class which includes umbrella menders and the like."
>
> Mr. Mythe answers him subconsciously. "Do you infer that I am a Protestant?"
>
> Thus we see the opaque lucidity of his conclusions.[41]

Understanding the literary art also had not escaped students of the period. In 1928, Arthur Browne echoed the anger of "Atticus" expressed thirty years before, although with much blunter words. "As is everything else in this superficial world of to-day," he groused, "books are judged, not by what is in them, but by what is round them. A flaring jacket with a starting sketch or some grotesque figure or another is bound to become one of our so-called 'best-sellers.'"[42]

An incisive criticism of the plodding form of many short sto-ries came later that year in a piece entitled "Short Stories and How Not to Write Them" by "One Who Does Not Write Them." "Suppose Lord Beverly Beavertop was shot as he sat in his study...," asks the author indignantly. "And suppose Jor-rocks, the butler, in response to the tug of a leaden hand at the bell-rope did rush in in time to find the great man expir-ing....What of it? Don't you think we know who killed him?"[43]

Perhaps the most notable accomplishment was the publica-tion of an issue celebrating the magazine's twenty-fifth anniver-sary as an alumni journal, for which many distinguished *Journal* alumni consented to write.

"I consider it an honor to serve my Alma Mater and I will gladly write the article you mention in your letter," said one busy alumnus.[44] Perhaps the most distinguished contributor was Condé Nast, who had left Georgetown to found his hugely successful chain of popular magazines. "I feel greatly flattered at your invitation to write something for the quarter-century alumni issue of the *College Journal*, to be published next June," wrote Nast; "I am particularly flattered because I haven't writ-ten anything for publication in so many years that I tremble at the thought of becoming an author, as much as I do when I am asked to be an after-dinner speaker."[45]

The *Journal* was permanently changed as a result of competi-tion during the 1920s. In 1919, the Journalism class began publi-cation of a newspaper, the *Hilltopper*, designed to concentrate on campus events and analysis rather than on the predominant literary interests of the *Journal*. By 1920, this publication had mutated into what is now a familiar face on the Hilltop scene.

"A new weekly paper has come into being," wrote the *Journal* in February of 1920. "This is the first issue of the *Journal* to go to press since the *Hoya* made its appearance. In the January num-ber, we hinted at the possibility of the *Hilltopper*'s withdrawal from the field to make room for a larger publication. The editor of the *Hoya*...has succeeded in getting his paper recognized as a force in the College, to say the very least."

The advent of the *Hoya* would subtly change the *Journal* for the rest of its history, with the new publication freeing its predecessor of any responsibility for news coverage and allowing it to focus on being a literary magazine and opinion forum. The older magazine didn't hesitate, however, to remind its readers of the early support which it had given to the new kid on the block. "Newcomers at Georgetown may not be aware of the fact that the *Hoya* is the child of the *Journal*; that the *Hoya* first gazed upon the world under *Journal* auspices and under the direction of *Journal* staff," it wrote in 1922. Moreover, "...the *Journal* does not hesitate to say that it is proud of its child, which has emerged from its infancy and is a lusty three-year old."

While the beginning of the *Hoya* may have pushed the *Journal* from the limelight, it never replaced it. The now old publication had some good years ahead of it.

The Modern *College Journal*

It makes you stop and think. Perhaps in about fifty or sixty years, after solar heating and the Third World War, someone will be chuckling as he thumbs through this *Journal* and finds out what we were doing with our time.—"Abstractions," Spring 1955.

By the 1940s, the *Journal* had become a campus entertainment magazine with a strong emphasis on short fiction and shallow articles of not very high value. Some of the change was due to the heavy drain in talent during the Second World War, but the metamorphosis remained unmistakable at the end of the decade. The magazine included popular departments such as "Movie of the Month." Genuine literary criticism and scholarly pieces had disappeared almost entirely.

The final renaissance came during the 1950s, when the *Journal* returned to a literary focus, perhaps the first time in its history when it consisted almost entirely of critical essays and well-written fiction and poetry, free of the news and alumni sections which had earlier taken up so much of its space.

The short pieces which began each issue are the most memorable feature of the period. "The Caucus Race" provided whimsical observations about modern life, short, amusing parables, and flashbacks to items from the magazine's past. It is difficult to convey the spirit of the column in excerpts, so a short, nearly entire tale follows:

> A mouse who had seen a vision was filled with the wonder of it. He left the house he had been infesting and went to live in the field where he spent his days reflecting on his vision and glorying in it....In fact he was so completely lost in the thoughts of his vision that he paid scant attention to his environment.
>
> And then one day an uncouth cat wandered from the house into the field...Snarling angrily, the cat pounced upon the mouse and quickly killed it.
>
> The cat returned to the house immediately, but it could never wipe away the memory of that afternoon. And for many nights afterward the cat could not sleep well because it had eaten the mouse that had seen a vision.[46]

A slightly different column, called "Abstractions," appeared prior to the somewhat obscure "Caucus Race." Reverend Leo O'Donovan, S.J., who was the *Journal*'s editor-in-chief at the time, said later that the articles were a conscious effort to imitate the sophisticated and witty column "Talk of the Town" which appeared in the *New Yorker*. While providing not much serious competition for its model, "Abstractions" went beyond mere collegiate humor. It succeeded in catching at least some of the easy banter and clever satire of the professionals who inspired it, providing the candid opinions of the editors on a wide range of topics. "We've always thought Ezra Pound to be a very remarkable man," said one early offering. "Besides composing original poetry, he has translated poems from innumerable languages into English verse. He has translated the Chinese, in many different dialects, and has translated many of the other Eastern languages. At the present, he is here in Washington, in Saint Elizabeth's Hospital (mental), translating some obscure work from Confucius."[47]

The *Journal* also featured the well-reasoned literary criticism and essays of the kind which had been absent for a decade. In

1953, for example, Laszlo Hadik presented a strong case for obscurity in poetry in response to a counterargument in the same issue:

> ...one should expect the expression of an idea to be obscure if the idea itself is incomprehensible to the reader. No criticism is made of anyone for finding some conception obscure, except when he insists that the obscurity is unnecessary and inappropriate. The expression of a genius will naturally follow the level of his thought. The average reader will be able to understand the theories of Einstein no more than the poetry of Eliot; yet just as Einstein's mathematical formulae cannot be expressed on a college algebra level, so Eliot's mental meanderings cannot be simplified to Freshman English.[48]

Even without the many other strong *Journal* pieces of the period, one writer alone provided enough material to make the decade a success. In two essays, Kevin Robb fulfilled the earliest goals of the magazine with his detailed analyses of philosophical literature. In "That Individual," published in 1956, he provided a cogent and brilliant analysis of the works and philosophical development of Kierkegaard. In 1958, he moved on to a piece on two other molders of modern thought:

> Both Nietzche and O'Neill were ever contending with their destinies on a brittle edge of destruction; both belong to that rare company of men whose fate it is to suffer out the riddle of human existence tightened to the pitch of a personal torture, a concentrated hell! Yet a fundamental distinction persists. Nietzsche crawled out of the very end of the last path of the earth; with a desperate—almost frenzied—nihilism he drove himself into a euphoria, and the listless night of insanity. O'Neill will muddy his hands in the finite only so long before he seeks to leap up out of it into a transcendental dream of love and beauty rarefied. In the end what distinguishes them is this: O'Neill struggles to salvage a little corner of light and beauty in his blind ally; Nietzsche beats his head against the wall.[49]

It was perhaps fitting that such a developed piece, which represented the ultimate realization of the original goals of the *Journal*'s first editors, would come during the late 1950s. The overall strength of the *Journal* in this decade represented one of the best in the magazine's history. Ironically enough, it also marked the beginning of the end.

By the middle of the 1960s and into the 1970s, the *Journal* slowly underwent its final changes in format until it settled down as a forum to publish student poetry and short stories. Literary criticism had faded from the public consciousness and interest, and the magazine followed the times. The role of public commentator has passed to the *Hoya* and other campus publications, but the *Journal*, now a quarterly, still makes its contribution by offering Georgetown students' work of high quality.

Notes

1. Robert J. Hilliard, "Scattered Thoughts on College Journalism," *Georgetown College Journal* (GCJ) 45 (1916–17), p. 78.

2. *GCJ* 1 (December, 1872), p. 4.

3. Tibor Kerekes and Georges Edelen, "From the Files: The Diamond Jubilee of the *Georgetown College Journal*," *GCJ* 76 (Dec. 1947), p. 4.

4. Ibid., loc. cit.

5. "Recollections of the First Days of the *College Journal*," *GCJ* 26 (1897), p. 100.

6. J. Percy Keating, "Reminiscences," *GCJ* 26 (1897), p. 115.

7. Kerekes and "Recollections" differ on the date.

8. "History of the *Journal*—Its Foundation," *GCJ* 41 (1912), p. 220.

9. Ronald Nelson Harman, "The First Ten Years," *GCJ* 61 (1932–33), p. 83.

10. Kerekes, p. 4.

11. "Recollections," p. 101.

12. Kerekes, p. 5.

13. Ledgers of the *Georgetown College Journal*, Georgetown University Archives.

14. Most material in this section citing the Constitution and by-laws of the *Journal* was obtained from the "Constitution of the *Georgetown College Journal* Association" in the Georgetown University Archives (GUA).

15. "History of the *Georgetown College Journal*," *GCJ* 26 (1897), p. 94.

16. Most material in this section was obtained from the minutes of the *College Journal* Association in the GUA.

17. The early ledgers of the *Journal* are contained in the GUA.

18. *GCJ* 53, pp. 468–69.

19. Minutes of the *GCJ* Association, 11/1/1872, GUA.

20. "Reminiscences," p. 115.

21. "We Begin Again," *GCJ* 61 (1932), p. 49.

22. "The Women's Suffrage Convention," *GCJ* 1 (April, 1873), p. 42.

23. *GCJ* 3 (April, 1875), p. 65.

24. *GCJ* 1 (February, 1873), p. 20.

25. In Kerekes, p. 23.

26. *GCJ* 4 (January, 1876), p. 45.

27. Harman, p. 86.

28. Ibid., p. 84.

29. "History of the *Georgetown College Journal*," loc cit.

30. Unsigned letter to alumni of August, 1897, Box 237.1, GUA.

31. Condé B. Pallen, "The Literary Quality," *GCJ* 26 (1897), p. 2.

32. "Atticus," "Some Views on English Prose of the Last Half of the Nineteenth Century," *GCJ* 26 (1897), p. 44.

33. Ibid., loc. cit.

34. M.F. Morris, "Shall the Basis of Liberal Education Remain Classical or Shall It Become Scientific and Utilitarian," *GCJ* 26 (1897), p. 188.

35. Daniel J. Devlin, "The Literary Conscience," *GCJ* 27 (1898), p. 248.

36. *GCJ* 26 (1897), p. 28.

37. In Kerekes, p. 18.

38. "My Friend, the Dentist," *GCJ* 30 (1901), p. 21.

39. "Turning Back the Pages," *GCJ* 61 (1933), p. 328.

40. Letter from Rev. Joseph F. Hanselman, S.J. of August 21, 1911, records of the *GCJ*, GUA.

41. "As Others See Us," *GCJ* 54, p. 493.

42. Arthur J. Browne, "About These Book Reviews," *GCJ* 56 (1928), p. 235.

43. "Short Stories and How Not to Write Them," *GCJ* 56 (1928), p. 507.

44. Letter from Henry Cortello to J. Edward Coffey, S.J., February 19, 1925, GUA.

45. Letter from Condé Nast to J. Edward Coffey, S.J., March 19, 1925, GUA.

46. "The Caucus Race," *GCJ* 85 (1957), p. 5.

47. "Abstractions," *GCJ* 83 (1964), p. 1.

48. Laszlo Hadik, "The Case for Obscurity in Poetry," *GCJ* 81 (1953), p. 7.

49. Kevin Robb, "Nietzsche and O'Neill: A Story in the Great Renunciation," *GCJ* 86 (1958), p. 11.

Poetry of Georgetown Students Collected by William F. Tehan, S.J. 1845–1850

Andrea Querques

In the decade of the 1840s, when Georgetown was still a college, the tradition of rhetoric thrived throughout this nation. The trend was particularly evident at this Jesuit institution, whose curriculum emphasized the Greek and Latin classics. The students dissected these works into their component parts in order to examine their structures, and, in imitation, compose pieces of their own. They learned what worked, how to make it work, and how to put this into practice. Rhetoric was not, and is not, so much an art of what to say, but how to say it. The rhetorician works with the same tool as the everyday speaker—the language at hand, in this case English—yet he shapes it, and carefully chooses his words, to achieve the proper rhythm, the proper sounds, and the proper tone. By selecting the perfect mix of vocabulary, he expresses himself with eloquence.

This art of rhetoric is showcased in the verse created at Georgetown. The poems of the students of William F. Tehan, S.J., a professor very popular with the students here in the 1840s, have been handed down to us in a handwritten collection. The anthology is one of the few, and certainly the best, of its kind. It displays the talent the young men of Georgetown possessed, and developed through study of the classics. Their skills deserve to be recognized, even if simply for the fact that they were able to write poetry, sometimes as many as one hundred to one hundred fifty lines, with a consistent meter and regular rhyme scheme. While the content of rhetorical matter does not matter as much as does style, the poems of Tehan's students do reflect a continuity of themes. There are five basic ones which recur in the poetry, all of which serve as insights into the lives, thoughts and background of the poets, considered as a body. Subjects include death, patriotism (including death for one's nation), a love of nature, religious topics (especially a devotion to Mary), and poems of a lighter quality.

The attitude towards death, as held by the student poets, reflects their Catholic background. Death is difficult for them to accept. The trial is especially arduous when the individual was special, or young and had not had a chance to experience much of life. Yet in the end, they realize the senselessness of mourning, because the dead rest happily with God, while the living still inhabit a sinful and imperfect earth. They come to accept the grief over their loss as God's will.

John C.C. Hamilton wrote a poem on the occasion of the death of his teacher, and the editor of this collection of poems, William F. Tehan, S.J. Tehan drowned, while swimming in the Potomac, at 7:00 a.m. on July 4, 1850. It appears that his death resulted from an effort to save some students who themselves feared they were in danger of drowning.[1] Hamilton reacted to this tragedy in his "Lines on the Death of William F. Tehan, S.J."[2]

> He is gone! he is gone! the dark spoiler has taken
> The joyest, the noblest, the best of our throng
> And grief, gloomy grief comes again to awaken
> Its loud lamentations these sweet shades among.

> Struck down when the far sounding voice of a nation   (5)
> Was hailing the advent of liberty's day,
> When young hearts were throbbing in quick exultation
> Whilst reckless with sport—Thou wert taken away.

> How quickly each brow was despoiled of its gladness
> How harshly upon us the dread tidings fell   (10)

Each breathing of joy was then mingled in sadness,
   And joined to ring out the deep starting knell.

It is not it cannot be He! we are dreaming
   We are raving by some black delusion misled!
But just now we saw him with cheerfulness beaming   (15)
   Rejoicing and healthful! He cannot be dead.

Yes, gaze on that face once so gentle and smiling
   Those lips were ready with kindness, soft word,
Does its smile still salute you? each labor beguiling
   And those lips are then sweet flowing accents yet heard

Still pallid in death's cold embrace he is sleeping,   (21)
   The kind one that lived in our bosoms so dear,
But he hears not the sighs, and he heeds not the weeping
   Of those that are crowding around his sad bier.

Then why should we weep? that his maker has snatched him
   And borne him his chosen from this fetid earth: (26)
His home was in heaven, for its spirits had watched him
   And guided him thither, e'en from his pure birth.

The fairest of flowers, Religion had cherished,
   In virtue's fair sunshine it opened full and blown   (30)
And thus in its bloom, it was culled ere it perished,
   Before one sweet breath of its fragrance had flown.

Then why should we mourn him from earth early risen
   Why murmur or sink in despair at the blow!
I feel! oh I know, that he's smiling in heaven   (35)
   Whilst we broken hearted here, weep him below.

The friend who delighted in life to caress us,
   Where wisdom shone o'er us, whose life was our guide
Can never forget us, his prayers will oft bless us,
   And will call us at last to rejoice by his side.   (40)

R.I.P.

Hamilton clearly shows how he feels about losing his beloved instructor, utilizing poetic devices to aid in his task. The first stanza, for instance, represents a good example of the use of repetition to augment the flow of words. Not only does he repeat the first phrase, but also the *g*, *l*, and *s* sounds. Also in this stanza, he characterizes death as "the dark spoiler"; this image is common in literature, and will be found in the poems of other students as well.

The poem acknowledges the irony of Tehan's death, that such a tragic thing could happen amid the joy and celebration of the nation's greatest holiday. (The patriotism in the hearts of the students rings out here as it does in other poems as well.) The unexpectedness of the event contributed to the disbelief that Tehan's friends and students experienced; we must be dreaming, thinks Hamilton, or else we have been led astray by some evil being. Remembering the kindness and gentleness of Tehan also adds to their difficulty in accepting "death's cold embrace" (line 21).

Hamilton realizes, however, that it makes no sense to mourn this death; Tehan was taken from this offensive and sinful place to his home in heaven. He takes comfort in the belief that the only pain is that of the mourners, while Fr. Tehan smiles up above. The rhythm of the penultimate stanza reflects these thoughts of the poet; when spoken, it has the sound of a sigh of relief. The poem then concludes with the reminder that someday, this happy fate will come to all. For in reality, death is not grim; it is the life which must continue without the enrichment of those who have been called to God before us which is so odious.

A student, Urbelino De Alvear, also drowned in the Potomac, four years before Mr. Tehan, on May 28, 1846. His death deeply affected his fellow students, testimony of which is the abundance of poems written by his peers. As with Tehan, acceptance of De Alvear's death was hindered by its unexpectedness and by his warm personality. Of the poems which were written, some on the event, some in remembrance on the anniversary, the best was penned by Edmond R. Smith two days after the tragedy, and entitled simply "Death of Urbelino De Alvear."[3]

Smith begins by lamenting the fact that De Alvear had not even the comfort of dying at home. He was "...far far from thy home/Far away from thy own sunny sky" (lines 1–2). Also, its suddenness did not allow for any comforting from his friends, or for any prayers that Smith thinks might have interceded on his behalf, in his passage to heaven. He wrote,

> And without one moment given
> With no hand of care, and no voice of prayer
> That might smooth thy path to Heaven!   (lines 6–8)

As an aside, there might be noted here the difficult rhyme scheme which Smith maintains throughout the poem. Not only does every other line rhyme, but odd-numbered lines rhyme within themselves. To take the above quote as an example: "given" rhymes with "Heaven," and "care" and "prayer" rhyme in line 7 as well as rhyming with "where" and "share" in line 5.

To continue with the content of the poem, Smith, like Hamilton, personified death as a harsh and evil being.

> Death came in his might, like the shades of night
> And with cold icy fetter bound thee.   (lines 15–16)

The students had thought they need not worry about being ravaged by this despicable creature, because their youth had declared them exempt. But they were awakened from this foolish dream with the shock of the death of one among them. And as if to teach them a lesson, death took a second from their midst—apparently, De Alvear was the second student to die in a short while. The poem reads,

> But scarce dried in their bed, were the tears we shed
> When his summons first were spoken!
> And another is dead, Yes the charm hath fled
> For the spell hath twice been broken   (lines 21–24)

Smith creates a simile, likening the death of his friend to the loss of the most fragrant blossom upon the shaking of a branch. Yet, though they must mourn the loss of this noble friend, as beautiful in person as a flower, Smith knows that his soul has been raised to God's care:

Yet we bow Oh God! to thy chastening rod
   And tho' sad we e'er must mourn him
Yet we firmly trust, tho' that form is but dust
   That in spirit on high thou hast borne him.   (lines 29–32)

In "The Widow's Loss,"[4] Smith looks at death from a slightly different perspective. He writes a fairly complex narrative, recounting in verse the story of a widow who has lost her children and taken them for dead. The striking of a clock at twelve becomes a symbol for Smith, for each of the three times the bell tolls, a new episode in the plot unfolds. It is 12 noon when the poem begins, and the village clock reminds the widow that it is time for her children to come in for lunch. When they do not return, she inquires about them, and finds that a fisherman's boat is missing from where they were last seen playing on the beach. The search terminates, for the children are believed dead at sea.

The clock strikes 12 midnight, and the widow turns to prayer for solace. First she asks God, that if He has spared them, not to abandon her children now, but protect them through the night. If He has seen it fit to take them, then she asks for the strength to bear it, as He granted her when she buried her husband. The death of her children would be more difficult for her to bear than her husband's death because, as she rationalizes,

He at least had tasted life! but they—my babes—
Their tender lives not yet to manhood grown   (lines 64–65)

She asks for forgiveness for her weakness and the grace to go on living:

Uphold my little faith Oh Lord and if
Thou hast seen fit to take away my last
My only hope, my all—Thy will be done.   (lines 73–75)

Her petitions are for "me, me me," climaxing to the point when reality calls her back, and she realizes God is of the greatest importance. Whatever the pain she must bear, His will must be done. This is the Catholic mentality speaking, as it did in previous poems; no matter how much easier it would be if the loss of loved ones did not have to be suffered, it always culminates in the simple statement of assent—Thy will be done.

The next morning the townspeople try to soothe the widow's grief, but it is not to be assuaged. Finally, the sail of the missing boat is seen in the distance, and as it nears the shore, the children can be made out on deck. And the clock strikes twelve. The mother does not forget God in her joy—He is not just a God to make requests from, but also one who deserves thanks when things are good. She gathers her children around,

> And by their hearth once more their prayers they raise.
> And lift their thankful hearts to God in praise.   (lines 98–99)

In "'Latantes Imus'—St Aloysius on His Death Bed,"[5] John C.C. Hamilton takes a refreshing view of death. He reverses the characterization of death as the cold, evil, dark creature that comes in the night, and presents death as that which should be given thanks. In other words, he begins his poem from the point at which the three previous poems ended. He realizes from the beginning that it is only through death that we meet God.

"Death! Death! why shrinks man at the word" (line 1) he queries to start. Man acts as though death comes to bring him to eternal night. God does not send death with this wretched purpose, but, rather,

> Thou comest death with gentler hand
> To lead us to that happy land.   (lines 15–16)

He welcomes death as his escape "From this foul sink of misery" (line 22). (This image of earth echoes Hamilton's description in his poem about Fr. Tehan, which reads "fetid earth.") Here, life takes on undesirable qualities, because only life keeps man from his true home with God. Death, and death alone, can unite us with our Father in heaven—and thus is the reason why St. Aloysius beckons it. Note, however, that although the secular is not the final goal in traditional Catholic and Jesuit teaching, it does possess its own joys and value.

These students of Georgetown also wrote poetry about death

related to patriotic actions. Patriotism was also an important theme of their poetry. It was considered noble to die for your country or a just cause and they acted on as well as wrote about this notion. Ten years after the last poems were written, the students had the opportunity to demonstrate their bravery in the Civil War. When they were called upon, the young men of Georgetown rose to the occasion. Besides military service, the patriotic poems relay a simple love of the country, the landscape, its heroes and its history. Throughout the poems it is clear that patriotic attributes are also Christian ones of morality, justice and truth.

The anonymous author of "Death and the Warrior,"[6] a poem about active service, relates a conversation between Death and a soldier. The poet successfully completes the difficult task of writing dialogue in verse. He captures the rhythm of discourse without forfeiting his poetic style; he creates two distinct characters by differentiating their respective voices. The voice of Death is taunting in the attempt to put fear in the heart of the warrior. He advises the soldier to boast to the world about his deeds, and to say good-bye to his love, because soon he would be called to the tomb. As if to rub salt in the wound, Death's lines end with "And she [his love] ere long will forget your name" (line 8).

The warrior replies with courage; the forcefulness of his answer is augmented by its piercing rhythm. He says "I tell thee now I fear thee not!" (line 12). The crispness of the line, its two sharp points, create the emphatic attitude of the warrior. Fear has not gripped him because his fighting in battle will bring praise; the image depicted is that to die in the service of a just cause is to die a glorious and noble death. He says, of his duty,

> I'll strive in the cause that's holy and right
> > On the blood red plains of Palestine. (lines 15–16)

And he imagines that after his demise

> > Then cherished long my name shall live
> And many a sigh and many a tear
> > For my early fate will the fair one give. (lines 18–20)

Death responds with further derision, asking how he can be so sure that his death will be as noble as he imagines. He tells the warrior of dungeons and warns that many

> Have there slept in death that final sleep
> When'er the fatal wish was mine   (lines 27–28)
> ...'Tis thus I tame the stern and bold!   (line 32)

Death is prepared to teach the warrior a lesson, if he is not willing to listen to warnings.

The warrior's courage, however, is relentless. He affirms his conviction that Death can cause him no pain. The truth is, that however God sees fit that he should die, he will accept. This comes in the last stanza, which the poet sets apart from the others by changing the rhyme scheme from *abab* to *aabb*.

> 'Tis him alone, that one above
>   'Tis him I fear, 'tis him I love
> Where ere he wills that I should die
>   Without regret thus will I lie.   (lines 41–44)

The poet purposely alters his rhyme, to draw attention to the moral in this stanza. Again the conclusion is traditionally Catholic: it is not this life that matters, but life hereafter, so however death comes to us does not matter; it is what follows death that is important.

In "The Death of Baron De Kalb,"[7] Edmond Smith also treats the matter of a patriotic death. The poem recounts the tale of the discovery of the fate of this soldier by his foes. He portrays the grossness of death by painting with words this horrible image:

> The film was on his eye
> And drops of purple gore that rolled
> A down his breast too plainly told
>   That brave De Kalb must die.   (lines 9–12)

Notice that the modifier for De Kalb is brave; there was a glory, a compliment in his death. De Kalb himself knew this, he was happy about his death. Smith wrote,

> ...a ray of light
> Came o'er his pallid features bright
>   His dying hour to cheer.   (lines 22–24)

Here Smith highlights the unexpected joyous reaction to this tragic event by playing one off the other; he creates a paradox by contrasting the pallid, lifeless features of death to the bright gaiety of De Kalb's countenance.

De Kalb's expression was prompted by his memories of his life. He recalled how his mother played with his curls, and how he left his noble home to fight for the holy cause of freedom. As he remembered these things, he rejoiced, for this was a good death—his life had not been lost for naught, but for a cause. And so,

> A smile of triumph lit his cheek
> That spoke more plain than words could speak
>   "'Tis glorious thus to die"   (lines 55–57)

The soldiers gathered around De Kalb experienced difficulty in accepting his death. But, it was not the loss of human life they could not handle, but his reaction:

> For as they saw that brow and while
> That lip was curled with scornful smile
>   They could not think him dead.   (lines 64–66)

How could anyone pass from this world so joyfully, they wondered? But that is the phenomenon of a soldier who has served his nation and his cause; in addition, we have the viewpoint of the Catholic author, who, as we have seen before, rejoices in death in hopes that he can meet his Maker.

The students, however, did not concentrate solely on patriotism; they also romanticized the land and the people around them. Smith, in particular, seems to have possessed a great admiration for the Potomac River, and the patriot entombed by her banks—George Washington. In one poem, entitled "To the Potomac River" (pp. 59–60), he praised the river for her beauty and majesty, and what that reflected about the hero enshrined on her banks. He begins by presenting a vivid image of the Potomac, imitating its flow through the use of alliteration and frequent vowel sounds.

> I love to view thy varied scene
> Thy rugged rocks, thy islands green
> And gaze upon thy placid mien
>   Potomac!   (lines 1–4)

After each stanza, Smith uses the simple refrain, "Potomac!" He succeeds in his tribute to the river by hailing her at regular intervals with her name.

The poet feels so strongly the presence of the great Washington in his tomb, that he is convinced that everyone will react in this manner. Even the river recognizes the depth of responsibility she has been given in this charge. Smith humanizes the river by likening her behavior to that of one attending a funeral:

> With reverence past that humble grave
> Where sleep the bravest of the brave
> In silence glides that limpid wave.
>   Potomac!   (lines 13–16)

The Potomac pays its respect with its silence and reserved motion.

Smith continues lamenting the dead hero in "The Monody of the Pilgrim at Mount Vernon,"[8] a lengthy eulogy of the departed forefather. He begins by depicting the simplicity of Washington's tomb, noting that this "Is the noblest of Meccas that nation can boast" (line 21) because it is simply a tomb. No decoration adorns it; thus, nothing detracts from the simple dignity of the one who lies below:

> Tho' here no obelisk proudly doth rise
> In thy bosom a treasure more precious here lies
> Than Earth's richest mine   (lines 17–19)

He also alludes to Westminster and those buried there, not one of whom "can rival a Washington's name" (line 25).

However, it is not the beauty or modesty of the grave which prompts the poet to reflect, but his thoughts each time he visits the sepulchre, the thoughts which occur to everyone who makes the pilgrimage. The soul of Washington hovers around his tomb, and the values which he cherished on Earth are seen at Mount Vernon. Smith advises:

> Oh ye that teach virtue, morality, truth,
> Bring here to this spring of all lessons your youth.
> Here teach them the patriot's virtues and love
> And the duty they owe
> To their fellows below
> And that to their maker above
> For the lesson that's taught by this grave
> Will sink deeply aye deeply with in the young heart
> And leave an impression that never will depart
> Nor be washed by oblivion's dark wave.   (lines 104–113)

Here Smith's explanation of patriotism is similar to what we saw in the poems on dying for the fatherland. Both convey the Christian virtues of justice, morality and duty to God.

Smith concludes by again universalizing the effect the shrine has on him. He declares that anyone who will come to visit—Romans, Russians, Poles, Greeks, Swiss, those from the Rhine, from the Urals, or from the Danube (lines 133–142)—will learn the lessons of Washington and praise him for his service.

> Vernon they shall sing thy praise
> In each clime beneath the sun,
> And where'er their voice they raise
> Shout the name of WASHINGTON!   (lines 146–149)

The last poem examined for its patriotic quality, called "The Indian,"[9] was also written by Smith. The poem shows an early interest in an issue much in our minds today—the place of the Indian in American culture. He employs some difficult devices, including accurate imagery through metaphor and simile, reiteration, onomatopoeia and contrasting images. In addition, he successfully incorporates the difficult Indian names into the rhythm of English verse. The poem reads:

He is gone—but he cannot be forgotten
Ye say that he is blotted
   From the title page of fame
Ye say that he hath perished
   In nation and in name (5)
Ye say that like the melting
   In the spring of winter's snow
He hath vanished, he hath vanished
   From the footsteps of his foes.

Ye say his loud whoop peals not (10)
   But by Ontario's rude shore
Ye say his war song waketh
   Your forest depths no more
Yet tho' his accents never
   May startle you again (15)
His name is on our mountains
   On each river, on each plain.

The Michigan's deep waters,
   His fathers name of yore
And the waves of Naragansett (20)
   Ever chasing with the shore
Tho' the rapids now he braves not
   As when first the white man came
Yet thy thunder O, Niagara
   Is but the echo of his name (25)

By the mighty Mississippi
   His funeral dirge is sung
And Monongahela longeth
   With the accents of his tongue
Our hoary mountains call him (30)
   From their home amid the skies
From Katahdins snowy summits
   To where Appalachia's rise

The red man's bones are gathered
   On each plain and on each hill   (35)
And tho' the shore hath turned them
   His name hangs 'round them still
His sweet wild accents linger
   By grave and mossy spring
As the fragrance of the roses   (40)
   Round the broken vase will cling.

They linger, yes and cursed
   Shall be the vandal hand
That would blot them from amongst us
   That would wash them from our land   (45)
Oh ever in their wideness
   May the red man's names remain
Upon our hoary mountains
   On each river, on each plain

And 'tho 'twas like the melting   (50)
   Of the winter's latest snows
His noble race hath perished
   From the footsteps of his foes
Yet say not he is blotted
   From the records bright of fame   (55)
Oh say not that they have perished
   Both his story and his name.

Smith informs us immediately as to what this poem is about in his concise, first-line thematic statement: we have wiped the Indian from his native land, but we cannot say that he has been wiped from our history. In lines 2–3, a metaphor is created between the Indian and words printed in a book. People simplify things too much, and delude themselves into thinking that the Indian can be erased as easily as words from a page. Next the poet compares the disappearance of the Indian to melting snow (a simile repeated in the last stanza), expressing another facile, thoughtless dismissal. He reminds us that though we think the Indian has been defeated, in reality he has penetrated our nation, leaving his mark everywhere—on our mountains, on our rivers and on our plains.

The presence of Indian names on maps is compared to the scent of roses which remains around a broken vase. It is a paradox in which the sweet hovers over the corrupt; though the white man ruthlessly sought to destroy the Indian race, "his sweet wild accents linger" in recognition of the just ownership of the land by the red man. The paradox is completed by the contrast between sweet and wild, and the mossy spring and the grave; here too Smith presents the pleasant alongside the tragic, as the floral perfume beside the jagged glass.

The poem ends by admitting that the Indian was defeated in battle, but that, as stated in the first line, he has not been eradicated from memory. The Indian is an unforgettable part of our country's history, in spite of the inhumane and immoral manner in which we treated him.

The boys of Georgetown College had a great affinity for the natural world as seen in the continual appeal to nature as a subject of their poems. This concurs with the traditional view held by the Society of Jesus: nature was to be respected, as emphasized in the book of Genesis: "God looked at everything he had made, and he found it very good" (Gn 1:31).

This affection also sheds light on the historical backgrounds of these students. In the 1840s, even those who came to Georgetown from the big cities were not leaving behind today's towering steel skyscrapers and concrete mazes. Georgetown comprised a few buildings and vast acres of tree-filled lands and grassy knolls. Her students did not feel the need to "get back to nature," because they had never abandoned it; but they did deem it necessary to record their love for Nature in poetry.

One example of devotion to nature is Edmond R. Smith's poem, "The Pearl,"[10] written for his Rhetoric class on November 5, 1846. In good poetic style, and with a regular rhyme scheme, Smith extols the beauty of the gems of the earth, and the purity of the pearl. The poem consists of five stanzas of four lines each, with alternate lines rhyming. Smith's aptitude for vivid description shines through; he has the ability to employ words that evoke vivid images:

'Tis not the crystal of light
Sparkling 'mid ice and 'mid snow
'Tis not the diamond bright
Flashing where rivulets flow.   (lines 1–4)

Thus he describes the beauty of the diamond—its luster, its clarity, its iciness, its radiance and its ability to catch the light—all those qualities without which a diamond would be just another piece of glass.

This lovely diamond is not the jewel for his maiden, however, nor is the "brilliant and ruddy" (line 6) ruby. The perfect gem for a fair maiden is the pearl, for only the pearl can match her in purity. The pearl captures beauty without being robust or ostentatious; in fact, its demureness is its strength.

Pure as the fallen snow
Robes not yet in splendor and light
Modesty veiling the glow.   (lines 14–16)

In this manner does Smith convey the purity and modesty which make the pearl the proper ornament for a young lady, and, in so doing, implies his own ideal of womanhood.

G.F. Fulmer and H.D., a writer identified by his initials only, showed affection for nature by identifying a longing for home and those things which belong to the natural world. Fulmer's "My Childhood's Home,"[11] written on November 8, 1848, for First Humanities, was his first original piece. Much of the poem is an outpouring of emotion and expression of nostalgia for the familiar things he left behind. For a beginner, he possessed a keen sense of harmony, for his rhythm and phrasing correspond perfectly to the feelings he wants to convey. In the first three stanzas, when he thinks of home, the pace is slow and the lines seem to coo. The connotations of his words are all positive, recalling happy times. He refers to "pleasant...recollections" and "sweet gentle memory," thus sketching an affable vision of his home. We find that what he is remembering are the hills, mountain paths, ancient trees, lowly rills and verdant banks of his native shore (lines 8–12).[12] It is not the building which serves as shelter, or the people who form his family that his longing is

for, but the intimacy he had formed with his natural surroundings. When he arrives there, in the last stanza, his joy is reflected in the rhythm of the lines. It becomes light and elated as
compared to the sorrowful longing evinced previously. He
writes:

> And now I've reached my woodland home
> My childhoods home forever dear
> I'll pause amongst its shades to roam
> Such pleasant scenes my heart will cheer.

H.D.'s "A Lament,"[13] written in August of 1847, is also an
emotional longing for home. His use of imagery, in drawing his
portrait of home, is well done. He calls on the senses of sight,
sound and smell to aid in the representation. The third stanza is
particularly evocative because it appeals to all three of these
senses:

> Where fountains bright are gushing high
> And pearling brooks are rippling by:
> Where every breeze wafts sweet perfume
> And flowers soft forever bloom: (lines 9–12)

The effectiveness of his imagery is enhanced by the onomatopoeia of "gushing" and "rippling." This is used earlier as well,
in "warblers gay in concert join their melody" (lines 7–8). Other
visual images depend on color—"verdant hills," "forests green"
and "orange groves."

As Fulmer did, H.D. takes comfort in what is native—what is
found in nature. H.D. highlights this by beginning and ending
his poem in petitioning his "native sky." It begins

> Give me again my native sky
> Where Nature wears its richest dye;   (lines 1–2)

and ends

> Oh! beautious South with azure sky.
> My native clime to meet me fly.   (lines 19–20)

Lastly, the students adopt the theme of nature in order to analyze man's life on earth. Following ancient tradition, they use
the seasons as symbols of different stages in life—specifically,
spring represents birth, summer means youth, autumn stands
for middle age and, finally, winter is the symbol for old age and
death. John C.C. Hamilton uses this symbolism in "The Autumn Leaf,"[14] which he wrote for his poetry class in 1848. After
describing the woes of the leaf, Hamilton continues that such is
also the fate of man. He acknowledges the beauty of the leaf,

> When first thy bursting bud was seen
> In May that month of sweet perfume.   (lines 5–6)

But the time for the leaf to live is short. Put simply, "it buds,
it blooms, its life is brief" (line 10). Likewise, man does not
spend long on earth; whoever he may be in life, he still will
meet the fate of death. Hamilton carries along the symbol of the
leaf through lines such as:

> The old, the youth in beauty's prime
> Must wither, fade, and fall with time.   (lines 21–22)

He concludes with his observation that all must come to the
same end:

> With glory wealth and all beside,
> The low in birth, the wise, the brave
> Must sleep forgotten in the grave.   (lines 23–25)

Hamilton was skilled in selecting words that conveyed his
feelings. He also employed the devices of alliteration and of
repetition to help move the poem along, as in "How like to thee,
thou faded leaf!" (line 9) and "And all thy pomp and pride"
(line 18).

E.R. Smith repeats this symbolism between life and the seasons. He does such a fine job that his poem is worthy to be tran-
scribed in its entirety.

Extract—From a Poetical Epistle
Written on a Fine Day of Autumn, October 7, 1845

'Tis Autumn; yet the sky is clear—and clouds
Of snowy whiteness, bathe air
That breathes not:—& the placid river wide
Spreads o'er its glassy brine the fading green,—
The sickly yellow,— and the crimson dye,—   (5)
The dark, rich brown,— the maple's scarlet leaf;—
With all the mingled hues, and varied tints
That dying nature knows:— and over all
The azure depths of Heaven. The mighty hills
Majestic in their silence, rear their fronts   (10)
Dressed in their sombre robes,— yet seem to smile
With decent gravity, and calm await
The approach of winter. And the winds, stir not
The fallen leaf: nor mid the forests moan,
(As is their wont) for Summers dying flowers.   (15)

—Thus nature's works seem to rejoice, that well
They have performed their several parts: and wait
In pleasing contemplation of their end.—

Thus oh my friend! May thus in peace be passed
The Autumn of your life, when age at last   (20)
Shall strip thy brow of raven curls that flow,
And crown thy temples with a wreath of snow.
When those soft eyes that shine with radiance light,
Shall dimmer grow & lose their lustre bright;
And when the cheek with youth that blooms so fair   (25)
Shall fade with age & lips corroding care.—
Then may no adverse winds too roughly blow
And cause the tears of sorrow fast to flow;
Then may those smiles that wreath thy lips with grace
Still cast a pleasing radiance o'er thy face.   (30)
Then may'st thou calmly wait for death to come
To call thee to thy long, long hoped for home;
And seem to wish but for the mandate given,
To leave these earthly realms, and rise to Heaven.

The tone of this poem is peaceful, calm, and conciliatory towards death. Besides his choice of mellow sounds and rhythms, Smith conveys a feeling of acceptance through the stillness of the air. He mentions the "air That breathes not" (lines 2–3) and "the winds, stir not The fallen leaf" (lines 13–14). It is as though a hush has fallen over the world as it awaits the death of winter. The river is placid, the hills are silent and somber, "yet seem to smile," and the forests do not moan as they would like. Nature is quiet in its wait, because all have done their best, and achieved their fullest potential.

Smith uses unspoken metaphors to make his symbolism complete. In lines 23–24, he likens the dimming of human eyes between youth and old age to the dimming of the sun between summer and winter. Similarly, in lines 25–26, he likens the fresh complexion of youth, which fades with age, to the blooming of flowers and leaves in Spring, and their withering by Fall.

Smith goes one step further than Hamilton, in saying there is a lesson to be learned from the natural world. When man reaches the Autumn of his life, he should prepare for and accept death. If he has used the talents God has given him, he will even hope for the call from God to join Him in heaven. This poem, thus, reflects the Catholic Christian background of the student and the University. For the Catholic does not spend his life on earth only in pursuit of worldly pleasures, but rather, in trying to be a good Christian so that he may earn eternal life. His goal is to live forever with God, thus explaining Smith's advice that we greet our death with joy. Essentially, our purpose in life is to live well, so that when death comes we will be in this state of loving acceptance.

The students show evidence of their Catholicism in poems of a religious nature. Most demonstrate their devotion to Mary, a distinctly Catholic phenomenon. They present the image of Mary as mother, yet also as queen; she is familiar, yet inspires awe. She is also frequently depicted by the Georgetown students as being venerated by nature and they draw attention to the tribute that the month of May pays to her.

One poem which deals with a religious subject other than with our Holy Mother was written by E.R. Smith on Christmas Eve of 1845, and is called "A Reflection."[15] Smith wonders what his reaction will be when Jesus comes "knocking at my soul's gate." He shudders to think that he might react as Bethlehem did on the night of His birth, and not welcome Him. Smith's characterization of Jesus is as a humble and unimposing individual. He sought in vain to find a comfortable place in which to be born, as He seeks to find a place in our hearts. Jesus is portrayed as unobtrusive, yet He is all-powerful. His uniqueness is such that He need not ask, but He does. The Baby is "friendless and alone" (line 2) and though He is

> ...the maker of the skies,
> Who clothes the beast, the bird of air
> Now helpless, cold and shivering bare
> In a rude manger lies! (lines 4–7)

In Smith's life, Jesus will search for shelter just the same:

> When meek and patient he doth wait
> Knocking at my soul's gate—my soul pollute with sin
> (lines 10–11)

The metaphor is complete. Jesus, the almighty being, was undemanding in His pursuit of a birthplace and will behave similarly in seeking entrance to our souls. Our free will determines whether He will find shelter there. As Smith realizes, his response might be—as horrible as this sounds, and as much as he would regret it—

> Shall I unmoved my Saviour see
> Nor rise and let him in? (lines 13–14)

Henry P. Tricon of Louisiana composed a poem for his First Poetry Class entitled "The Month of May."[16] He focuses on the glory of Mary, and an observance of how nature sings her praises during the month devoted to her. The poem is not intricate, and Tricon utilizes no poetical techniques except rhyme. But its simplicity works for him, in communicating the purity of feeling that is his purpose in writing.

He begins by enunciating the feeling of joy which wells up

inside him as he looks around at the beauty of God's world. May has called the splendors of the Earth to its surface, and laid them before his eyes. Why is the Earth decked in all her finery, he ponders.

> Why but to make us think
> > Of one than they more fair (lines 11–12)

Tricon proceeds to ask Mary to bring virtue into our lives, so that we can forever live with peace and joy. The last stanza echoes the ending of the "Hail Mary"; the poet seems to have transformed the petition of "pray for us sinners now and at the hour of our death" into a more lyric request. The poem concludes:

> And when our pilgrim course
> > Shall happily be o'er
> Oh! may we not in death
> > In vain thy aid implore. (lines 21–24)

Thus, Tricon succeeds, in his poem, in imparting to us Mary's beauty and his affection for her. He requests her aid and guidance in his life and at death.

In "Ad Beatam Virginem,"[17] H.D. sings the praises of Mary in the same manner as Tricon; however, he writes in a slightly more intricate form. He begins in a similar way, with the recognition of May's rejuvenation of the Earth in Mary's honor:

> May returns and zephyrs breathing
> > Waft the flowers' wild perfume:
> Garlands fair are gaily wreathing—
> > Hill and plain and meadows bloom. (lines 1–4)

Notice, first, the alliteration, the repetition of the soft *w* and *g* sounds which mimic the soft wind, carrying the scent of the blossoms. Also, the use of the phrase "zephyrs breathing" personifies the reaction of nature, making it a rational response to Mary, rather than just what occurs in the Earth after the death of winter. In other words, by giving a human quality to the wind, when he could simply have written—May returns and gentle breezes—H.D. tells us that the world acts upon an awareness of the glory of Mary, and is not just fulfilling the cycles of nature.

The poet then proceeds to tell how the children are picking violets and daisies to give to Mary, and that he too will roam the valleys to find flowers to lay at her feet. He is able to employ alliteration again in the stanza about the children:

> Pluck the violets of the vale
> They those flowers join for thee
> With the daisies of the dale. (lines 6–8)

In the next two stanzas, H.D. addresses Mary directly. First he calls her Virgin Mother, and requests that she hear her children, and smile down on them. Then, he calls her Virgin Queen and asks that she soothe souls with her love, and bless them. It is evident here that the poet envisions a dual nature in Mary. She has the endearing and caring qualities of a mother; he prays that this facet of her will smile on, or encourage, and lend support to her children on Earth. On the other hand, she is regal, and powerful, and mother of Christ Himself; H.D. petitions a blessing from this persona of Mary.

The poem concludes with a reaffirmation of Mary's glory and the praise she deserves. The last stanza is a mandate to the sun to pay Mary her due homage:

> Radiant, hopeful, beaming star;
> Dawn of an eternal day,
> Spread thy genial light afar.
> Bless thy consecrated May! (lines 21–24)

There is another poem entitled "The Month of May,"[18] written by John C.C. Hamilton. He creates an analogy in which he likens the care that the Earth gives to her flowers to the care that Mary gives to us, her children. Stanzas 1–3 correspond exactly to stanzas 6–8, with 4 and 5 serving as the link. They are presented here side by side to facilitate comparison:

1

How bright, how pure, how lovely!
 Fair daughter of the spring!
This earth, when first thou comest
 Thy vernal gifts to bring!

2

The shrub the tender flower
 That shrunk from winter's cold,
By thy kind smile awakened
 Their infant charms unfold

3

They feel when'er encouraged
 And fostered by thy care,
That they may bloom securely
 To deck the budding year.

4

These are thy beauteous children
 They own thy gentle sway,
And thou art ever watchful
 Lest they should waste away.

5

How like to that fond parent
 Who reigns in heaven above,
Whose kind eye watches o'er us
 With   all   a   mother's   love.

6

How bright, how pure, how lovely!
 Is every Christian heart,
When thou dost come in gladness
 Thy favors to impart.

7

The soul whose budding virtue
 Had feared the storm to meet;
In gladness blooms, and safely
 Reposes at thy feet.

8

We are thy tender children!
 Oh! with thy mighty arm
Shield us we pray, sweet mother!
 From danger and from harm.

The world of nature is bright, pure and lovely when Earth brings her springtime gifts. Similarly, Christian hearts are bright, pure and lovely when Mary offers her blessings. As the shrub and the flower shrink from the cold and destructive power of Winter, until the warmth of Spring unfolds, so too does the soul cower in fear of a storm until it recognizes the safety of Mary's presence. Both the flowers and the children of Mary feel that they can only bloom their brightest under the encouragement, security and protection offered by the Earth in springtime and through our Holy Mother. This, in brief, is the comparison drawn by Hamilton in the corresponding stanzas.

In the stanzas that serve as a junction, 4 and 5, Hamilton

makes the linkage clear. He states plainly that the flowers are the children of the Earth, which she watches over to ensure that they will not decay before their time. Then, he states directly how similar this situation is to that between us and our mother above who watches over our souls. It is clear that Mary, in this poem, is portrayed as a caring parent. She inspires no awe, except for the respect due to a parent, but instead, shields us from the brutal harshness of the world.

The student poems of a lighter quality are not particularly notable for their poetic style, but for how they convey the authors' attitudes. They all attempt to make light of some unfortunate circumstance. This provides us with a view of the student body aware of unhappy circumstances but unwilling to let them dominate their lives. It is not that they laugh at the expense of others' misfortunes, but that they are of an active not a weepy nature. These poems also allow us to see the more informal side of the students of the 1840s—their minds were not always on serious subjects like death and religion. The modern student might be able to relate well to these poems, because they address the types of issues we face today.

"The Beggar's Petition,"[19] written by E.R. Smith in January of 1846, informs us by its title that the poem will address an issue we can relate to the contemporary problem of the homeless. The subject matter is serious, but the manner in which it is presented is light and playful, and the beggar himself is a bit laughable. The poet begins by setting the scene, and Smith does so in a way which suggests immediately that he is, at least in some remote way, affected by the atmosphere of Washington—marking time by the calendar of the government:

'Twas winter's season just about
The time that congress meets   (lines 1–2)

At this time, there was a beggar wandering around the streets of the capital. It was cold and windy, and the vagrant "around the gills/was looking rather blue!" (lines 5–6). But the man was not a lazy person, whose life had been spent loafing; he sounds like many of the homeless today who were once wealthy and successful. He wore a hat that had lost its top, and which "had once been jetty black/But now 'twas rather brown" (lines 11–12). Yet the hat had a graceful, somewhat stately quality in the eyes of the poet. It seemed to be saying, to anyone who cared to listen, "'When this old hat was new!'" (line 16). There was an air of dignity about this poor man; the sense of what he used to be remained with him.

The beggar was making his way boldly towards the White House. Arriving there, he found the President, James Polk (Smith only writes J_ P_) sitting by a fire. The beggar humbly introduces himself, and brazenly asks if there is a vacancy in an office. He continues to explain that it can be anything, he will do anything to serve the party—as he already has done:

> I've served the party ev'ry way
>   Let it be right or wrong!
> I've written libels, sworn to lies,
>   Done all that man could do,
> And lastly voted twenty times
>   Most honored Sir for you!   (lines 39–44)

The President interrupts the beggar and tells him that he has arrived too late—the vacancies are filled. The poem ends with the president's command:

> And waiter you will please to show
>   This gentleman the door!!!   (lines 51–52)

This commentary by Smith on his society asks the question of why men who have served their country or their party are being turned away by the government, and literally getting doors slammed in their faces.

The next two poems address a discipline measure. It appears that sometime around January 12, 1851, a Mr. James Tehan forbade the smoking of pipes by students. Both T.M. Quade in "On the Loss of a Pipe"[20] and J. Timmons in "For the Confiscated Pipe"[21] mourn their lost pipes.

Quade begins with Tehan's addressing a student named Peter, asking him why he has been so unhappy, why he does not behave as he used to. With a touch of sarcasm Tehan demands

> Come, Come be quick my Peter dear
> And tell! your hard old case.   (lines 27–28)

Peter answers the prefect unabashed:

> Now Mr. Tehan full well you know
> The cause for which I moan
> You are the one that caused my woe
> My pipe is now your own.   (lines 37–40)

Both poets have fun with the situation, not only through this sarcastic type of humor, but also in the way they portray the boys who wish to win back their pipes. The loss is exaggerated to be as painful as the loss of a loved one. Timmons' student says that his pipe has gone to Pipe Heaven, and other references are also made as to a person. He pleads "Oh! Give my darling back" (line 12) and grieves

> That through the long long winter's eve
> Its kiss I must disdain.   (lines 27–28)

Finally, he concludes by saying that if he could have his pipe back he would love it more. Similarly, Peter assures Mr. Tehan of how attached he was to his pipe, and if he knew how much Peter loved it, he would give it back.

These humorous treatments of this painful situation inform us that the students did not take themselves too seriously. They were able to laugh at their misfortunes, to exaggerate, personify their pipes, and portray themselves as being as distraught over the loss of them as they would be over the loss of a girlfriend.

Lastly, "The Student's Woes!"[22] by Smith recounts the horror of every scholar—oversleeping. A friend requested that Smith tell a tale, so he does, and as he says, this is "a tale of woe!/of horror and of fright!" (lines 7–8).

It was not yet morning, when a dream came upon him in his sleep. The scene was at a banquet with gallant knights and fair ladies; there was laughing and dancing,

And thoughts of joy and youthful love
  Were seen in every glance.   (lines 35–36)

Then a change came over his dream—he heard a ringing sound, and trumpets; that too familiar experience when your alarm clock coincides with a ringing in your dream, and so you go on sleeping. But,

A gentle whispering voice was heard
  Get up! tis time! tis time!   (lines 59–60)

But the student continued sleeping and his dream progressed into a duel among the knights over who had the fairest lady. Again he heard the voice

Whispering—"Arise! Arise!"
I turned and quick my trusty sword
  Forth from my side I drew
And high, I waved it in the air
  And—lo!—It was a—shoe!!   (lines 80–84)

The student woke up then, and then his woes began. His roommate tells him that it is long past time that he should have been up and washing. And further, he tells him he acted impudently in his sleep, murmuring something about dinner. He dressed and went quickly downstairs, only to find the "guard" (probably a Jesuit because he says, "His garb! I shudder as I write!/Was horrid gloomy black!" [lines 113–114]) would tell him he was too late, and he must wash at the pump. Needless to say, this bathing outdoors was not a pleasant experience:

The wind blew chill and cold;
As by the horrid pump I stand
  Cold breezes round me blows   (lines 128–130)
And be assured my washing then
  Was hasty and was brief!   (lines 133–134)
All other woes I well could bear
  E'en hear the martial trump;

But oh ye gods! Avert! Avert!
  This washing at the pump!! (lines 137–140)

The humor in this poem arises out of Smith's ability to pin-point common experiences, and weave them into something fresh and new. It is the familiarity of the situations that makes us laugh. Almost everyone has overslept, talked in their sleep, acted in their sleep on a situation in a dream, and worst of all, been forced to take a cold shower because all the hot water had been used. Smith's recounting of these tales together, under the title of "A Student's Woes!"—which one would expect to be concerning schoolwork—gives the poem its comic quality.

Several things become obvious to the reader of Fr. Tehan's collection of his students' poems. Aside from observing that these young men had a great talent for writing poetry, one finds that they held deep religious commitments, the Catholic mentality shining through in much of what they wrote. In addition, they entrusted themselves to God's hands, and this gave them an optimistic outlook on life, allowing them to live the carefree life characteristic of youth. One last poem serves to summarize this anthology and illustrate the shared qualities of the poets.

"Trust to the Future"[23]

Trust to the Future, Tho' gloomy and cheerless,
  Prowls the dark Past, like a ghost, at thy back,
Look not behind thee; be hopeful, and fearless;
  Steer for the right way and keep to the track!
Fling off Despair—it has strength like a giant—
  Shoulder thy purpose, and boldly defiant,
Save to the right stand unmoved and unpliant—
  Faith and God's promise the good never lack.

Trust to the future then;—Cease from thy weeping;
  Faith and a firm heart are all that you need—
God and His angels have yet in their keeping,
  Harvests of Joy if we'll but sow the seed!
Trust to the future,—all life will be glorious;

Trust for in trusting the [?] is victorious;
Trust, and in trusting be strong and laborious:
Up and be doing and give God the weed!

Notes

1. *Woodstock Letters* 30 (1901), p. 240.
2. Fr. William Tehan, S.J. "Anthology of Poems Written by His Class of Poetry, 1845–1850." Georgetown University Archives, pp. 33–15, henceforth to be indicated as W.T.
3. W.T., pp. 205–06.
4. W.T., pp. 171–74.
5. W.T., pp. 292–93.
6. W.T., pp. 265–66.
7. W.T., pp. 241–44.
8. W.T., pp. 188–94.
9. W.T., pp. 239–41.
10. W.T., p. 259.
11. W.T., pp. 4–5.
12. The significance of the use of the word "native" will be covered in the discussion of the next poem.
13. W.T., pp. 21–22.
14. W.T., pp. 278–79.
15. W.T., p. 177.
16. W.T., pp. 285–86.
17. W.T., pp. 22–23.
18. W.T., pp. 286–87.
19. W.T., pp. 244–46.
20. W.T., pp. 93–96.
21. W,T., pp. 96–97.
22. W.T., pp. 54–59.
23. W.T., pp. 385–86.

The Educated Catholic Gentleman: A Collection of Writings

Josephine Lecraw

"From the lofty position of unbiased inquiry," writes William Willcox in 1876, "with a full sense of the importance of our subject in mind, we should deliberately judge concerning the conditions and tendencies of our enlightened age."[1] If it were only that easy! Each age has its own bias; each mind is affected by contemporary circumstances. My inquiry is by no means unbiased. When I set out to explore Georgetown University student writing, the writing of my peers, I thought of Tocqueville and the idea that democracy may breed mediocrity. I thought of recent indictments of American higher education. Finally, I thought of cultural relativism. Would there be any "values" common to all Georgetown students? Would the quality of writing be consistent throughout?

Coming to any sort of understanding meant wandering through volume after volume of the old *Georgetown Journal* and several other sources of student essays. Often, a crusty issue in my lap, and fluorescent lighting beating down on me in Lauinger Library, the open-ended nature of this assignment pressed in upon me. Certainly, the questions I raise cannot be answered by a student journal of limited authorship, limited publication, limited....But the *Journal* provides occasion for thought. Sometimes, individual writers caught my attention, and I would follow their development for three or four years. I thought about their economic background, family history, personal experiences, and considered each as an individual. There are so many variables in each writer's life. Yet certain aspects in the writing seemed to stand out in front of me, and it is these that I have chosen to write about.

Up in the archives, in a box labeled "old student essays," I encountered William Willcox, author of "Civilisation in its Aspect to Modern Thought." Solid writing and a scathing commentary on "modern" culture caused me to read on. A philosophy assignment written in 1876, the paper reflects cultural dilemmas about theories of evolution; Social Darwinists come under extensive attack. The author's passion for the subject and his underlying fear of societal change inflame his writing:

> All incentives to improve. Nay all incentives to live will be destroyed when moral obligation shall have been removed, and human acts shall have no conformity with divine law.[2]

This indignation is both the source of the paper's greatest strength and greatest weakness.

Willcox begins forcefully by questioning the validity of modern scientific method. He wonders whether it leads toward faith or is "involved in the labyrinths of doubt," and, too, whether it places man in his proper position of subordination to the Creator or instead "ministers unto the pride of man and calls God to account for what is beyond its comprehension."[3] To address this query, Willcox first defines society, the medium through which man moves, as composed of the physical, intellectual, and the moral. The reader should not find it strange that the author chooses to concentrate upon the moral aspects. Firm opinion and true belief characterize this organized piece.

Willcox cites the crippling vice Pride as that "whispering to the Philosopher those errors and atheistical systems by which in overturning the morality of the world, he may render his name a byword on every tongue."[4] From the Pride of the philosophers, the scientists, the false thinkers, springs the Doubt of mankind. The human mind begins to doubt its own nature and that of society: "This is so less from a diminution of the intellectual powers of man than from an advancement in physical sciences"[5] which nurtures Pride.

Willcox acknowledges the existence of some profitable advancements in physical science, though he names none; but in regard to his primary concern, the moral advancement of man, the author's opinions are less ambiguous. He notes a marked improvement in the moral virtue of Catholics, evidence of which can be viewed by the "present exalted state of women," and the "conjugal tie." After all, "she it was who infused into the heart of man those chivalrous sentiments which caused him to loathe the degraded state in which woman was formerly placed."[6] Only Catholic countries, he assures us, display moral qualities. Spain, France, Italy, and Ireland are virtuous in all respects, whereas Germany and England are perfect hotbeds of immorality.

At this point, Willcox's writing begins to weaken. His penmanship grows increasingly angular and slanted. It takes no genius to feel his fury. What begins as a well thought out, if somewhat strong-minded, piece of writing is transformed into a rambling tirade on the evils of Protestantism. People of the Protestant religion disregard the sanctity of marriage, and the people have a "fitting model in the lives of their pastors."[7] Crime governs Protestant countries. In addition, public schools, "where the auxiliaries of Satan are everywhere working their evil,"[8] nurture immorality.

In short, Willcox devotes a full ten pages to the evils of Protestantism and goes so far as to intimate that it corrupts true philosophy and produces theorists like Spencer and Huxley. Fury notwithstanding, Willcox manages to recapture the coherence of his work with his concluding statement:

> Therefore the grovelling mind of the sceptic shall acknowledge a limitation of the human intellect and shall perceive its inability to comprehend the infinite, and shaking off dull and material sense with its yearning to see and to feel, shall rise into pure intelligence. Then, and not till then, shall the aspect of modern thought towards civilisation be fully recognized and to the Eternal shall be assigned his proper place as the infinite first cause.[9]

My modern reaction to such writing is manifold. In one sense, I feel a strong desire to criticize William Willcox. His description of women which now seems offensive, the embellished writing, an unquestioning faith in the Catholic church, and a self-righteous attitude all combine to disturb this reader.

Yet in another almost stronger sense, Willcox intrigues me. He is certainly not the first man to feel threatened by change and a perceived notion of the direction society is taking. I cannot help but think of Henry Adams overwhelmed by the forces which begin to shape modern times. For the student Willcox, the strain of these changes exceeds skills of expression. What begins as a strong, clear piece of writing soon loses coherence and gives way to emotion, passion. Any student should be able to identify with the emotion that controlled this writer's paper. We react, often lacking the balance between passion and reason which enables clear thought. Finally, there is an attractive quality about Willcox's firmness of opinion. This is reinforced by his signature which appears on the last page of "Civilisation in its Aspect to Modern Thought." The signature underneath the last thought which complements the name on the title page, signifies pride and ownership—a small detail, but one which struck me.

I next encountered the work of Denis E. Hendricks, who, writing in 1931, lived worlds apart from William Willcox. His fiction appears in the *Georgetown Journal*, and, though not of superior quality, attracts the reader nonetheless. The intention here is not to overcriticize; Hendricks does write well. He composes a story with all the necessary components; symbolism, imagery, plot, etc. are not lacking. But if the writing of skilled authors and historians relies heavily on context and individual bias, the student's writing is even more likely to do so. I would love to meet Mr. Denis Hendricks. He seems an odd character.

"Beauty's Right," a short story by Hendricks, appears in the November 1931 issue of the *Georgetown Journal*. It is the story of a beautiful but proud young woman, Norma Findley, whose career it was to steal the male companions of other women. On one occasion, at a spectacular dance, Norma tests her powers on the fiancé of a "close" friend. As they dance, she pronounces her philosophy on men:

> I don't know, I always felt that somehow I would never meet anyone who would be my master. There is always something lacking, some little trick of personality or character, and I have always felt the master of the situation and of the person....He would have to

be someone to whom I could bow down as an inferior being, someone whose very touch would thrill me.[10]

This particular man decides to teach Norma a lesson, smiles "disarmingly," and plans to meet her for lunch the following day. When Norma arrives, she sees to her dismay and embarrassment that the gentleman in question has brought his fiancée with him. Furious, Norma drives away, gets into a horrible car accident, and comes dangerously close to losing that beautiful face. She learns from her mistakes, and while recovering in the hospital, finds true love with one of her more persistent admirers. The moral, I suppose, is twofold: Vanity has consequences, and Norma is best carried off and subdued by her "master."

Other stories by Hendricks are similarly curious. In "Cast-Off," John plans to leave home for college, but fears leaving his mother alone with no one to "care for" her. One day in the doctor's office, John spots an orphan girl in the company of a nun. Immediately interested, he suggests that they take her home to live. Although the mother seems hesitant, John receives a letter at college several weeks later, informing him that the orphan girl has a new home. Mother writes:

Now, John, you will probably think that I am crazy, and maybe I am, but the girl, Mary Turner, is now living at home with me. If you are still reading this, read on....I must confess that as of yet, I am not sure I like the idea...but I have enjoyed taking her around to the shops with me.[11]

Again, a happy ending is in order. Not only does the orphan girl find a home, but John and Mary soon fall in love.

Mary! Oh I love you so much! Don't ever go away or be unhappy again. I want to make you so happy that you will forget about that convent.[12]

By 1931, Hendricks edited the *Journal* and wrote many such pieces of fiction as well as some poetry. Certainly, Hendricks was not the most talented writer to attend Georgetown University, nor the most original; but he interests us still. The reader wonders about Hendricks, the themes that run through his writing, and his seeming need to dominate women. Then too, the author's desire for a happy ending (he writes of small disasters with happy endings) speaks quietly of American attitudes during the Depression. Finally, a kind of simple morality pervades Hendricks' work. Vanity will be punished, good deeds rewarded.

There, by way of introduction, are two vastly different student writers. Still, intuition tells us they have much in common. Reactions to "contemporary" living and a desire to preserve certain "values" characterize both. I prefer the writing of William Willcox to that of Denis Hendricks. Willcox is passionate. His writing drips with a brooding seriousness, draws the reader in. I found that on the whole, blatantly moral pieces were better written (if not always more objective!) than those of lighter subject matter; and those pieces were plentiful.

Robert Gannon's short story "The Tree's First Fruit" inspires. Its theme has lost none of its beauty since 1911, and Gannon writes with a skill that the student hopes to equal. He tells us the story of a young boy Phares, who watches his father turn away a young Galilean couple from an inn one damp night. Gannon's prose flows as the story begins:

> A cold damp fog had settled in the narrow streets. Unusual weather this and unused were the people of Bethlehem to its kind. All day, they hurried from brazier to brazier, wrapped in extra heavy cloaks and hoods. As evening lowered on the city, the elements grew more boisterous. Separate, violent blasts of wind broke loose from the all-including storm, and swept through marketplace and alley in search it seemed of adventure. Water jars were overturned, dust blown in every eye. Veils and caps lifted and carried distances on the dirty stone while annoying, teasing paining everything in their several paths the winds rushed on their way with roaring mirth.[13]

On this night, Phares watches uncomprehending as his father denies the two Galileans room. The incident haunts him, as does the face of the young woman, "and he was sure that his mother, though he'd never seen her face, must have looked like her."[14] Lonely and innocent, Phares befriends the couple, finding "A very young mother whose large deep eyes of softest violet seemed to mirror in their depths the serenity of an angel's soul, and a baby who was healthy and normal and quite innocent except that his little stars seemed already to have gathered expression from his mother's."[15] We learn how Phares benefits from the company of the three Galileans, and as if by osmosis, we too sense the importance of family and nurturing. Phares adores the lady, his adopted mother:

> —Ah the mother he worshipped, confessedly worshipped. To work, run, fetch and carry for her, that was happiness indeed, or when every task was done just to sit there at her feet and have her smile at him; that smile would have chastened hell itself.[16]

Finally, when Phares hears by accident of Herod's intention to kill every male child under the age of two, he rushes off to warn his family, only to find them gone.

Years pass for Phares, who grows into a decadent creature. Left at too young an age with his father's fortune, he learns corruption and immorality:

> Pleasure he made his goal and thereby never knew it. He had too much love that was not love to really love, and after all, a loveless world is barren. So more and more it palled him.[17]

It is not long before Phares finds himself sentenced to die by way of crucifixion, two "criminals" at his side. As Gannon retells the story of the Passion, we feel Phares' anguish and are reminded of the humanity of Christ, the pain he suffered.

Phares addresses his fellow prisoner as they hang together with that "rabble-rouser," the "King of the Jews." He says "We receive the due reward of our deeds but this man hath done no wrong." Phares had looked down to see a beautiful woman weeping beneath the three crosses:

> As yet, he did not recognize his God and maker, only his mother's son and a suffering man in need. Out of this bottomless poverty, he gave what alms he had—a charitable word and no more. Yet Solomon from his golden throne could not have made an offering as rich. At his feet, she in return whose prayers are always answered prayed for him.[18]

The rest we know. "In the flutter of an angel's wings this sin-stained soul sped swiftly through the chaos that lay between him and his God."[19]

"The Tree's First Fruit" stands on its own merit. Powerful, well written, and from the hand of a contemplative soul, this story surpasses William Willcox's essay in so far as the two can be compared. Gannon does not yell for attention. He speaks soft-ly, but his voice is clear and strong; I thought of Par Lagerkvist, the Nobel Prize-winning author who published *Barabbas* in 1951. The act of giving words to a historical figure about whom little actual knowledge exists is an effective technique. I am amused that Gannon and Lagerkvist were the same age. It seems reflec-tive of the interconnected development of humanity.

Three months earlier than "The Tree's First Fruit" appeared in the *Journal*, David Waldron published "It Was Ever Thus," a meditative essay on a man's voyage through life. It would be interesting to determine how strongly the faculty guided the subject matter of early *Journal* submissions. In any case, one sees evidence in student writings of a strong Jesuit influence. The traveller in "It Was Ever Thus" searches for happiness. He searches in the company of Pride and Extravagance. He seeks wealth and titles and reputation, all to no avail. Later, he meets Epicure, who tells him "'tis vain to search elsewhere for happi-ness than nature herself has placed it—in the indulgence and gratification of the appetites which are given us for that end."[20] While dining with Epicure, our traveller meets one last man, Ambition, with whom he spends his last bit of energy. The traveller grows weary, his eyes weak. He loses consciousness and awakes alone and in darkness. Off in the distance, howev-er, he can just discern a priest kneeling in prayer. He strains to hear:

> All that savors of earth is mortal, the happiness Thou givest in serv-ing Thee here beyond only is eternal. But our eyes are opened only when it is time to close them forever; bestow upon mankind, I pray Thee, grace to bewail a life of disorder ere it begins; grace to inspire faith the most lively, love the most pure long ere the sun has set and the reason is half eclipsed and all the faculties palsied by the strong grasp of death. Teach us, I beseech Thee, that the dignities, honors, pleasures, glories, happiness of earth are transitory; teach

us that the little space which intervenes between the cradle and the grave is filled with perfect happiness only in communion with Thee.[21]

This writing, like Gannon's, speaks for itself; and Waldron seems to share with William Willcox a certain pride that can express itself publicly. "It Was Ever Thus" addresses the Georgetown student of any age, though with an intensity that might not be found today. We are, as members of a Catholic university, guided by a sense of Christian mission. Yet always, pressures to "succeed" confront us. The tension between the City of God and the City of Men exists in many contexts. The modern reader may be as misdirected as Waldron's traveller.

Flipping once more through volumes of the *Georgetown Journal*, I found an entertaining criticism of "moral" reform. Walter F. Miltenberger writes "Morality by Legislation," indignantly charging reformers with attempts to use their efforts as a means to improve their own standing, to gain distinction. He accuses these people of impure intentions, and then makes a clear argument for the idea that laws should not be made in vain. "Armed with the proper sanction, they will meet with recognition and respect even in the lowest stratum of society, but stripped of their enforcement, they will become the object of mockery."[22] In other words, laws which seek to enforce a certain morality are unenforceable. Yet Miltenberger mentions no specific law. He speaks only generally of the question of moral reform, and herein lies the weakness of his paper.

The author recommends a strong family life to combat the evils of society. Of course, he recognizes that these remedies require time and patience. "Tastes should be cultivated and encouraged which are the least likely to lead to the principal sources of vice; ideas of independence from foolish conventionality and thoughtfulness should be recommended. The mind should be trained to observe."[23] And how to accomplish all this? Once again, the family....Fathers and mothers are either "too busy or too ignorant" to educate their children. If they would only devote as much time to their children as to a lot of "worthless" endeavors, a better society might be forged.

I do sympathize with the original premise of this essay. Without education and comprehension, laws may be worthless. Miltenberger puts forth a strong argument and surely we can, with some objectivity, understand his reaction to Progressivism. However, there remains some unattractive moralistic quality about the tone of this piece. I would be interested to see Walter Miltenberger confront the writings and pictures in Jacob Riis' *How the Other Half Lives*. How would he face impoverished factory workers and their small children, necessarily more vulnerable to vice and corruption? What of these children while their parents are out doing "worthless" tasks? The author's tendency to generalize, and his bias towards the upper class family offend today's modern reader.

The editorial staff of the *Georgetown Journal* often sought to instruct its readers in questions of morality. In many cases, the prose is fine and the message clear. Two outstanding editorials appear in the December 1931 issue. The first, entitled "The Catholic Educated Gentleman," does well in defining just what that man should be, what Georgetown hoped to encourage:

> An active mind is needed. One that will see beneath the superficiality of pseudo-science the steady and unchanging flow of eternal law and reason. Such a mind, when faced with the subtleties of false philosophy must show keen discrimination tempered with common sense. Its knowledge must extend over the whole field of literature, past and present, so that it can boldly and confidently separate the chaff from the wheat. In a general way it should be familiar with history and facts of political and economic significance.[24]

The very fact of this editorial suggests that these issues were not altogether settled. Clearly, every man at Georgetown did not fit the definition of an educated Catholic gentleman. However, there did seem to be a clear consensus about what that man should be. He should possess a critical mind, a firm faith, and a broad knowledge of literature in order to discern Truth.

With this vision of the educated Catholic gentleman in mind, I have decided to print the next editorial, "A Plea for the Individual," in its entirety. Both the sentiments and the structure impressed this Georgetown student:

> We are on the verge of the Christmas holidays. Everywhere the

spirit of Christmas, never new, never old, manifests itself, but during the next few weeks it will receive a practical test. Those of us who live in a large city will meet with a condition never experienced before during this season of cheer and good will to mankind. Hundreds of beggars will be on the streets. We shall see them at every corner, in front of theaters and restaurants, many of them cold and shivering, most starving, all looking for work. They are waiting relief while the representatives of a supposedly prosperous nation convene in a little room to decide what should be done. But while plans are being made, men continue to starve and suffer. What is to be done is the question on everyone's tongue.

This editorial can not answer that question for the nation, but it can for the individual, the student of Georgetown. Here is a splendid opportunity to shed some of that Christmas spirit in a concrete way. We may not be able to help all out of work, but perhaps we know of some one unfortunate person who, through our help will find Christmas much better in reality than it was in prospect. Why is it that those living in small communities are not suffering as much from the evil effects of unemployment? The answer is because they are able to help one another *unobtrusively*. Cannot we do the same although we live in Chicago or New York City? Is Christmas spirit limited only to the postal cards?[25]

The educated Catholic gentleman must take individual initiative and strive to serve others. The editors despised complacency. If helping some unemployed or homeless person meant grappling with the confusion and impersonal nature of modern cities, so be it.

In December 1889, the *Journal* spoke eloquently on the need for action. Far too many of us, they say, rely heavily on hope:

But we do not intend to moralize on the extravagance of human hope. Our intention is far otherwise. We mean to point out to our friends the mistake they made before in leaving all to hope and tacitly awaiting the golden shower without making any effort to deserve it at the hands of fortune. Thus then that our friends, one and all may not only hope for a bright and prospective year but may take the precautions necessary to insure against disappointment.[26a]

So many of the writings address issues of morality. Editorial opinions serve only to reinforce this impression.

In E.A. McCoy's short story "A Sylvan Memory" of 1898, the theme is transgression of boundaries. One split-second decision, irrevocable action, may affect and change one's entire life. I thought of Theodore Dreiser's *Sister Carrie*, and Carrie's impulsive decision to leave her sister's home in search of a more exciting, fulfilling life. McCoy writes simply but effectively. He tells of a Georgetown student who cannot sleep one night. Restless and irritable, the student breaks curfew and goes out into the courtyard where he encounters a bizarre little man. The man speaks to the student, telling of the one transgression which "ruined" his life, made him the "wreck" that he is. Plagued by his conscience, the man has spent "a life long prosecution before whose eloquence I have trembled for forty years."[26b]

It is a dark Georgetown night and the intensity increases. Despite its simple plot, "A Sylvan Memory" is a well-constructed story. The man continues to speak and our student, stricken by his vision and fearful in his own behalf, hears "a loud peal of bells" ring out. He awakens safely in his bed only to learn "'twas the Angelus of Trinity Church."[27] The bells return the student to the firm reality of church and school.

I received the impression that the educated Catholic gentleman should be the typical American and vice versa. Nowhere is this more clearly illustrated than in Norbert McKenna's 1920 essay, "Typical Americans." Riddled with exaggerations about particular American qualities and somewhat naive in its assessment of political figures, McKenna's patriotism seems foreign to the student of the late 1980s. This reader cannot envision a "Typical American" with ease.

McKenna knows no such difficulty. He writes,

> In mentally picturing our type we see a figure which personifies our principles of independence in thought and action, our love of integrity, individual and nation, and our deep rooted sense of duty justice and equality, which is moved by our indomitable strength of purpose.[28]

Even more foreign to my ears is his characterization of Theodore Roosevelt, about whom he writes, "Since Caesar perhaps, no one man has attained such great perfection in so many different fields." I cannot imagine lavishing such praise on any public leader.

I doubt neither McKenna's strong belief in equality nor his love of country. A sense of American moral duty recurs with some consistency in American history, so McKenna does not shock when he writes: "to carry on a torch whose flames of liberty, equality, and simple justice lighten the whole world. Our duty is plain."[29] I would suggest only that the piece provokes all sorts of thought about the meaning and extent of equality and justice. Would McKenna's justice have included women or minorities (or even Protestants) in a way that would satisfy our conscience?

In the same vein of patriotism, a Thanksgiving editorial of the *Journal* urges its readers in 1915 to give thanks that the evil destroying Europe has not reached and will never reach America. With pious certainty, the editors call World War I "The pyre that is slowly but surely extinguishing all that is good in man and which will leave amongst its ashes the charred embers of undying fate."[30] This editorial exhibits moral superiority and is reflective of the spirit of nonintervention. Ironically, the writers have not explored the possibility that America might one day enter the European war. "No silent ships glide to our shores with maimed and sightless men, and for these inestimable boons let us thank the Prince of Peace."[31]

Author Daniel Devlin, writing for an 1899 issue of the *Georgetown Journal*, asks his readers to examine their "Literary Conscience." In 1899, Mr. Devlin criticizes contemporary taste in literature (which he defines broadly). He hopes to establish one unyielding standard by which to judge whether or not a work is "good." In heartfelt prose, Devlin writes,

> We shall cultivate a literary conscience that will enable us to give a just estimate of a literary product that will guide us infallibly to separate the right from wrong, the sound from the unsound.[32]

All should strive to use words beautifully, for "beauty is never untrue, is never hateful, never immoral."[33]

This piece arouses the reader's curiosity. Did the author believe that such a consensus might be possible? Could the majority of student writings meet Devlin's standards? I wonder whether the author would require a certain uniformity, and if this standard would be intolerant of works of an experimental, or "modern," or perhaps unserious nature. The question intrigued me as I looked at the range of ideas and writings in the *Journal*.

"Broken Threads" by James C. Toomey '39 is a fun short story and a distant relative to the Harlequin romance and the television sitcom, with perhaps a small hint of F. Scott Fitzgerald. "Little" Margot, niece of the wealthy and powerful Christopher Sharp, loves a poor struggling man named Martin. Pouting, she speaks to Chris about her love and convinces her uncle to sign a business deal which will help Martin's career. All this takes place in the Eagle's Manse, one of those dark bars with panelled wood and brass fixtures where fortunes, you know, are made and broken each day. Later that evening, Margot waits for Martin, hoping to tell him the good news. He never arrives. By coincidence, at the very same time, Christopher Sharp drove down a highway drowsy and lost in thought:

> He did not see the two headlights racing towards him on the wrong side of the road until it was too late. Chris steeled himself. A crash! A moment's blinding pain then blackness. Glass tinkled to the roadside. Far away an owl hooted and a dog howled plaintively. Along the road there was no life, only a long white stretch of silence. Christopher Sharp was dead.[34]

Margot, now alone with neither her beloved uncle nor lover Martin to comfort her, decides she cannot face a new day. Toomey ends the story with a dramatic flair as Margot enters her bathroom. "Cold creams, perfumes, face powders, and rouges were all brushed aside as the groping hands searched for a small black vial. Inspecting it, she moved to the window. A last flicker of hope sent her eyes searching down the length of the white road. Then, with a swift gesture, she placed the bottle to her lips."[35] If this story is harmful, the harm lies in the fact that Margot cannot exist without Chris and Martin. Daniel Devlin's guidelines for moral literature might not have encompassed such considerations.

Richard Edward Connell Jr. wrote "The Gorilla" for the February 1912 issue of the *Georgetown Journal*. Its structure is imitative of *Moby Dick*, with perhaps a bit of Joseph Conrad; yet Connell's story seeks more to amuse than to enlighten. I print the lengthy first sentence of this story in its entirety.

Having embroidered a bright purple fringe of polyglot profanity on the inky atmosphere of a Chinese night, and having religiously kicked each member of the native crew twice, Captain Slain of the storied and battered bark "Polly O"gave up his attempts to coax power from the warped boilers of that craft and inserting his Missouri Meerschaum with practiced accuracy in a small aperture in his tangled maze of red beard, announced through another similar orifice on the parted side of his prognathous countenance, that the "Polly O" would stop for the night at that precise spot in, or more accurately on, which the aforementioned "Polly O" was then bobbing like some Titanic hewn chip on a ruffled millpond much magnified.[36]

One of the ship's mates, Clancy, settles down to entertain the rest of the crew with the pleasures of his storytelling. Clancy once witnessed the capture of an enormous gorilla, Vaski, and his equally ferocious but smaller mate. It had required over fifty men to subdue the pair and carry them back to "civilisation." In transit, the brute's mate died and Dave, ship's lieutenant, folded her skin away with the intention of one day having a rug made.

Later in the year, Dave received an invitation to a masquerade ball. His fiancée, Hilda, planned to be a rabbit, explains Clancy with a grin, and she suggested he come as "some appropriate beast."[37] With the help of the entire crew, Dave constructed a gorilla suit, finally putting Vaski's mate to some use. All went well until Vaski escaped and was carried in a taxi to the ball, leaving Dave standing in a gorilla costume afraid for Hilda's life.

When Dave, with Clancy, finally entered the ballroom, he watched as "frogs waltzed with Kangaroos, and numerous bears, snipes, lions, ducks, and seals conversed in a most friendly manner."[38] To his dismay, he spotted Hilda and Vaski seated in a cozy corner. Vaski murmured, "urrg warr urrrrrgggg" as Hilda replied "Oh Dave! I know what you mean but say it in English."[39] Furious and frightened, Dave lunged at the pair, causing Vaski to flee. "With great leaps he crossed the ballroom, and in a frenzy of fear, dived through the window to the street below. The ballroom was on the fourth floor. New York pavements are very hard. Vaski never went to another ball." Meanwhile, the *other* gorilla "drove home in a taxi with a rabbit in his arms."[40]

"The Gorilla" is a clever, well-constructed story. I underestimated this author's talent at first and feared a "cute" or trite ending, and I was alienated by his ethnocentric assumption that bringing Vaski from the jungle was bringing Vaski to a "civilized" and therefore superior place. It also puzzled me that Hilda did not notice the difference between her boyfriend and a live animal. Still, I would concede that Connell had a lively sense of humor and a facility of expression.

So did the editors of the *Georgetown Journal* during the early 1950s. In an excellent example of conscious imitation, the editors adopt the urbanity of the *New Yorker* magazine. Each issue ran a column entitled "Abstractions" which mirrored the *New Yorker*'s "Talk of the Town" to the last detail. They print each "Abstraction" in narrow columns, and even go so far as to call one "At the Met." They do a decent job:

> Having worked later than usual one afternoon, we felt very tired and decided to go down to the room and relax awhile before supper. We went down the long hall, slowly climbed the three flights of stairs, went down another hall, came to our door and just stood there a minute listening. Inside they were playing records and the volume was turned up so high that the music blared out into the corridors (they always explain to us and also the prefect that for maximum efficiency hi-fi must be turned up loud). We went in. Everywhere there were people. They were seated on both beds, on all the chairs and even on the floors. No one had even noticed that we had come in so we slipped quietly over to the window and also sat down on the floor. We loosened our ties, took off our shoes and stretched out full length. The floor felt surprisingly comfortable as we lay there, looking up at the ceiling. After awhile, time seemed to have completely stopped and nothing else seemed to matter. We felt completely satisfied with ourselves (for no apparent reason) and just lay there thinking....What is that they're playing?...it's...of course "Il Trovatore" and this baritone so clear, as though he were standing on a cliff calling into the air...so strong and as though he were here. We were there once, and listening and watching. It seemed so alive with the voices everywhere, thundering and piercing the heights of the place.[41]

What a great image, those students captivated, crowded into

a tiny dorm room. The editors manage to capture the style of the *New Yorker*, the detailed accounts, the point of view, the attitude, and the sense of adventure. Even more important, they capture a sense of Georgetown community, of friendship, of education, and of students speechless in the face of excellence.

And then there was that 1930 anonymous review of *Black and White*, a novel by Fr. Thomas Chetwood, who taught psychology at Georgetown. What can I say? It made me smile. The authors write with absolute honesty, "the cloak of anonymity" having inspired them "with a daring frankness."[42] They confess at the outset that they feared "it would be just another one of those things which are so prevalent in Catholic fiction—an anemic plot flavored with a plentiful dash of religion."[43] They then commence to praise Fr. Chetwood's book in a manner which may not have altogether pleased him. "The casual reader (we plead guilty to the charge) will find this book an interesting narrative...It has sufficient worldly appeal to win the general reading public. If we judged this novel solely from the standpoint of 'pleasure' reading, we might rank it with the best-sellers."[44]

The writers admit they do not recognize the larger psychological implications of the novel until midway through, and say further that "there was danger of our abandoning the book at this point (our anonymity aids a frank confession)."[45] With some perseverance, however, the two finished *Black and White*, only to experience a "peculiar feeling in our hearts." They seem surprised that this feeling is far different from the sensations of the best sellers:

> So strange. How shall we describe it? Our soul felt stirred? awed? moved? All these terms have been used to describe far less noble emotions. It was a strange feeling of—well, we give up an attempt to picture it.[46]

We know little of the novel save that it had profound psychological undercurrents, and not the typical happy ending. Yet somehow this book review works. Its candid nature startles the reader, though I am not sure that its technique and apparent lack of "piety" would satisfy Daniel Devlin's "literary conscience." The authors close by suggesting that several readings may be necessary in order for the average person to grasp *Black and White*:

The first trip through its pages is likely to arouse only the romantic interest of the reader. Of course there may be brilliants who fully appreciate all of the psychological undercurrents without re-reading. But we make no pretense to such acute faculties.[47]

The reader is grateful for this admission.

Some students experimented with different structures of prose and poetry. "Tango," the 1931 poem by James Hendrickson, tells of a lover's deceit, and the dramatic, impassioned deaths of "Lily-White Lilita" and "Macabre Juan." They dance one last tango together. Hendrickson experiments by writing in the rhythm of tango music, and explains in his prelude that the six peaks, or stanzas, of the poem indicate the progression from one movement to the next, and that each color corresponds to the "rich thematic tones or colors of tango music."[48]

An unfamiliarity with the tango handicaps this reader in her understanding of Hendrickson's poem. Yet she can faintly hear the music as it might be played, so good is the poet's attempt. Surely, one can note a musical difference between the two following stanzas:

Strings of wire and gut, winds of wood and tin, tympanic crashes of brass—Tango Diavolo! One dance, one tango, the last, the Devil's tango the test. Crush the red glowing point of your cigarette beneath your shiny black heel, Caballero Juan and fold your China white fan Lilita and dance.[49]

There is passion and anger and deceit and evil. One can imagine the sound of the music as it rises to convey these themes. By sharp contrast, the last stanza conveys spent energy, and the meaningful silent instant after the dance ends, and the couple dies. No images of red pervade this last stanza.

One white gardenia is on the mirror floor beside the round black hat and the echoes of the Tango Diavolo linger, but Lily-Like Lilita and Macabre Juan dance no more. Dancing and flickering, the rolling swells of uneasy waters glide and uneasy cast their frail glassy forms on the shining beach in prayerful murmurings.[50]

In reflecting on the writings of these Georgetown students, I have encountered in a sense the "Catholic Educated Gentleman" with his strengths and weaknesses. At his best, he represents the kind of student that contemporary critics of higher education might wish to reincarnate. Pieces like "Civilisation in its Aspect to Modern Thought" and others seem dedicated to certain truths. Even less overtly serious works like "Broken Threads" deal with the issue of broken vows. "Abstractions" discusses community and bonding and the "higher pleasure" of classical music. Admittedly, the writer makes a crucial decision in selecting works to be highlighted; yet she would argue that these pieces were by no means difficult to find. They seem honestly representative of the body of *Journal* writing.

Where does that leave us? People seem to write about what is closest to them, or most familiar. I would suggest that certain unmistakable gaps in the writing of students cannot go unmentioned. The model of the Catholic educated gentleman *in so far as it went* was a positive one; but this model rarely allowed for the model of a Catholic educated woman. Little writing, creative or not, discusses the problems of minorities, or people of different classes. Society has by no one's standards resolved these issues today, and nostalgia for a seemingly "simpler" time is understandable. Today, however, these issues are part of the continued conversation about justice. Today, there is a language which includes them.

The model of the Catholic educated gentleman with all its pitfalls, and the words he brought forth instill in this writer a keen awareness of context in each piece. Almost always, there is some worthwhile notion which transcends the bias of context. And so, this article will end with a profile of three works which illustrate transcendence in significant ways.

Tom Allen's 1959 "A Reflection" on madness equals previous works in its ability to arouse the interest of the reader. We capture the intensity of Allen's mood and can, with no great effort understand this weary soul. He writes,

In twenty-two years, one becomes accustomed to madness...It's a feeling of abandonment, of disappearing in all directions at once, while moving in a circle that is constantly being squared. Or do you understand what I am trying to say?[51]

Weariness is not an attractive quality, especially in the writing of a twenty-year-old. "A Reflection" reveals Tom Allen overwhelmed with the conditions of modern society and afflicted with a distinct sense of self-pity. But somehow "A Reflection" lacks the self-righteousness of Willcox's work or Devlin's, while maintaining their level of confusion and reaction to contemporary society:

> I saw evil little boys chase evil little girls...and what is worse catch them and let them go. I saw funny little people laugh at funny little people, and then laugh together at the funny people in general....I've grown accustomed to the flickering of a neon sign saying that here and only here will the sun set in fifteen glorious colors. And above all, I've seen the buttresses that were formed by myself, in my own private mind, disappear when the rains came and threatened private dykes.[52]

The reader experiences a certain nostalgia for the self-assurance of earlier writers. Tom Allen's weariness continues to offend. In a different sense, however, the author does address the challenge of maintaining one's perspective. By the last paragraph, we forgive the tone of "A Reflection" and respect the facility with which he conveys the feeling of aloneness that overtakes all human minds every now and again.

> So at last I am alone and mad, I presume. At least I can still presume. The world rights itself a thousand times a day, and a weird thought is made not so weird just by remaining still. And that is what I propose to do; remain very still so that when the rain stops and the sky stops turning as it is doing now, I'll be used to the madness again. And I hope you've understood. After all, the panegyrics of one human mind shouldn't be so difficult to understand. To understand. Rather fearsome isn't it?[53]

In a unique way, "A Reflection" calls upon the reader to understand the confusion and despair of other people. It is a reminder of shared experience and of the unity of humanity.

"The Ol' White Boogie Man," Tom Martin's 1959 short story, does attempt an understanding of the confusion of others—in this case, the confusion of blacks. I feel certain that this short story could not have been written much earlier in the history of

Georgetown. Earlier writers might have objected to its theme. In the context of 1959, Tom Martin handles the subject well and writes an excellent short story.

A black mother sends her children to the beach for the day. Mary Lou, Harold, and Julius, twelve, ten, and five, respectively, are the children of a chauffeur/butler who inherited that job from his father. The day begins pleasantly for these children, but Mr. Martin makes known the extent of underlying unrest:

> The sky to the northeast was blanketed with a salt and pepper quilt work of storm clouds. In the distance, towards the peninsular town, they could see the area in which the sand, sea and sky met. Yet the point at which they met always seemed to be elusively shifting with the swell of the sea and the gusts of the sand blown up towards the restless sky.[54]

The children walk to the very end of the beach, past two beach clubs; and the narrator tells of Harold's confusion at having to go to the same spot each time. "Harold had often wondered why they came down here so far away from the rest of the people."[55]

The children laugh and swim, but always a shadow looms overhead. In order to protect little Julius from swimming too soon after eating, Mary Lou concocts the story of the "Ol' white boogie man" who gets little boys who try to swim out too far. Julius, of course, believes this story unconditionally:

> He had learned enough about the sea and had seen enough of it on TV that he was sure that anything could be in it. On TV, he had seen huge monsters destroying whole towns so why shouldn't there be a white boogie man out there waiting to pull him under.[56]

Harold, however, the older of the two and more stubborn, is skeptical of Mary Lou's fabrication. Shortly after lunch, he decides to ignore his sister's warnings and go swimming. Harold soon cries for help, but the children are too far at the end of the beach for any lifeguard to hear. Desperately, Mary Lou tries to rescue him but "the whitecaps lapped eagerly at her white bathing cap until whitecaps and bathing cap were indistinguishable."[57] Both children drown.

The reader sees Julius left standing on the beach crying "Ol' white boogie man got 'em." He runs past the two beach clubs, back to his home. Running into his room, Julius shouts "Ol' white boogie man got 'em, gonna get me!!!"[58], and cowers under the bed.

Joseph Hayes' "Prayer," written in response to the Korean War, inspires an optimistic conclusion to this endeavor. He writes thoughtfully in eloquent verse. Hayes seems to have an objective, even-tempered, critical understanding of actual circumstance, with a firm grasp on ideals. He reacts to violence and confusion by providing a standard for peace and justice. Joseph Hayes' prayer should speak for itself.

"Prayer"
Lord God of War and Police Action,
 Whose terrible sword has open laid the serpent
 So it withers in the sun for the just to see,
Sheathe now the swift avenging blade
 with its names of student writ upon it,
And assist in our peaceful preparation of Curricula.

Lord God of Text Book and Test
 Who walks in the knowing circle of scholars,
Deliver notice to uniformed young men,
  That the chance of a desk and black-board
   will appear again before the hungry mind,
  That the professor will again meet his class
   knowing the students are there,
  That Freedom will stand like the knowledge
   it allows,
  That never again will student's boots march out
   against an aggressor.

Lord God of Diplomas and Medical Students,
  Who has calculated the slide rule for all time,
  And stored the provender of men in every library,
 Do bring sweet influences on our daily assignments,
 Accept the student's paper among the accredited books
  of Genesis,

Fend from ignorance with a book and a lecture, him—
  whom you made in your image,
And permit him to read of the Russian and English,
  That he may learn today without losing tomorrow,
  And clothe himself with the graduate's gown.

Lord God of Inked Paper and Book Binding,
  Who jointed paper and type and shook them
    'til their name was knowledge,
  Who rostered science and letters side by side,
Appear now among the parliaments of educators
  and give instructions to their schemes,
Measure out new liberties, that none shall suffer
  for his father's color or poverty, not of his choice,
Post proofs that wisdom is not so wild a dream as
  those who profit by postponement would pretend,
Sit in the office of our deans and convoy the hope of learning
  through perilous straits,
Press into the final seal a sign that the road of learning
  is not to be cut by the stroke of a sword.

That knowledge shall be a friend for all forever.[59]

Notes

1. William Willcox, "Civilisation in its Aspect to Modern Thought," May 1876, p. 1.

2. Ibid., p. 10.

3. Ibid., p. 2.

4. Ibid., p. 4.

5. Ibid., p. 5.

6. Ibid., p. 17.

7. Ibid., p. 18.

8. Ibid., p. 19.

9. Ibid., p. 26.

10. Denis Hendricks, "Beauty's Right," *Georgetown Journal* 60 (November 1931):38.

11. Denis Hendricks, "The Cast-Off," *Georgetown Journal* 60 (March 1932):305.

12. Ibid., p. 310.

13. Robert Gannon, "The Tree's First Fruit," *Georgetown Journal* 40 (April 1912):240.

14. Ibid.

15. Ibid., p. 241.

16. Ibid.

17. Ibid., p. 242.

18. Ibid., p. 244.

19. Ibid.

20. David Waldron, "It Was Ever Thus," *Georgetown Journal* 40 (January 1912):149.

21. Ibid., p. 190.

22. Walter F. Miltenberger, "Morality by Legislation," *Georgetown Journal* 38 (February 1910):187.

23. Ibid., p. 190.

24. "The Catholic Educated Man,"*Georgetown Journal* 59 (December 1930):147.

25. "A Plea for the Individual," *Georgetown Journal* 59 (December 1930):148, emphasis mine.

26a. *Georgetown Journal* 18 (December 1889):61.

26b. E.A. McCoy, "A Sylvan Memory," *Georgetown Journal* 27 (December 1898):116.

27. Ibid., p. 117.

28. Norbert McKenna, "Typical Americans," *Georgetown Journal* 48 (1920):139.

29. Ibid., p. 146.

30. *Georgetown Journal* 44 (1915):76.

31. Ibid.

32. Daniel Devlin, "A Literary Conscience," *Georgetown Journal* 27 (March 1899):251.

33. Ibid.

34. James C. Toomey, "Broken Threads," *Georgetown Journal* 64 (March 1936):337.

35. Ibid.

36. Richard Edward Connell Jr., "The Gorilla," *Georgetown Journal* 40 (February 1912):180.

37. Ibid., p. 181.

38. Ibid., p. 183.

39. Ibid.

40. Ibid.

41. *Georgetown Journal* 83-84 (Winter 1954):10.

42. *Georgetown Journal* 57 (February 1929):260.

43. Ibid.

44. Ibid.

45. Ibid., p. 261.

46.Ibid.

47. Ibid.

48. James Hendrickson, "Tango," *Georgetown Journal* 60 (March 1932):297.

49. Ibid., p. 298.

50. Ibid., p. 299.

51. Tom Allen, "A Reflection," *Georgetown Journal* 88 (Fall 1959):14.

52. Ibid., pp. 14–15.

53. Ibid., p. 15.

54. Tom Martin, "Ol' White Boogie Man," *Georgetown Journal* 88 (Fall 1959):6.

55. Ibid., p. 7.

56. Ibid., p. 8.

57. Ibid., p. 9.

58. Ibid.

59. Joseph Hayes, "Prayer," *Georgetown Journal* 83-84 (Spring 1956):20. In the last line of the poem, the word "man" has been changed to read "all."

Sources

1876—"Civilisation in its Aspect to Modern Thought," William Willcox, box of student essays.

1889—Christmas Editorial, *Georgetown Journal*, vol. 18, p. 61.

1898—"A Sylvan Memory," E.A. McCoy, vol. 27, p. 116.

1899—"The Literary Conscience," Daniel Devlin, vol. 27, p. 248.

1910—"Morality by Legislation,"Walter F. Miltenberger, vol. 38, p. 6.

1912—"It Was Ever Thus," David Waldron, vol. 40, p. 148.

1912—"The Gorilla," Richard Edward Connell, Jr., vol. 40, p. 180.

1912—"The Tree's First Fruit," Robert Gannon, vol. 40, p. 240.

1915—Thanksgiving Editorial, vol. 44, p. 76.

1920—"Typical Americans," vol. 48, p. 139.

1929—"Black and White," anonymous, vol. 57, p. 260.

1930—"The Catholic Educated Man," editorial, vol. 59, p. 147.

1930—"A Plea for the Individual," editorial, vol. 59, p. 147.

1931—"Beauty's Right," Denis Hendricks, vol. 60, p. 34.

1932—"Cast-Off," Denis Hendricks, vol. 60, p. 300.

1932—"Tango," James C. Hendrickson, vol. 60, p. 297.

1936—"Broken Threads," James C. Toomey, vol. 64, p. 333.

1954—"Abstraction" (At the Met), editors, vol. 83-84, p. 10.

1956—"Prayer," Joseph Hayes, vol. 83-84, p. 20.

1959—"The Ol' White Boogie Man," Tom Martin, vol. 88, p. 6.

1959—"A Reflection," Tom Allen, vol. 88, p. 15.

Religious and Ethical Teachings at Georgetown University —Reflected in Student Writings

Deborah Wallace

College is a time when young adults struggle with questions about who they are, what values they hold, what their beliefs are and in what direction they want their lives to proceed. Their experiences and knowledge of the world, their society, their community, their family and friends and themselves, all have a profound effect on them in their search for answers.

This paper discusses essays on topics in ethics, social justice, and Catholic education from the manuscript student essays in the Georgetown University Archives and from the *Georgetown College Journal*. The oldest essay that I have examined dates back to 1860 and the most recent one is from 1939. I have also used some speeches given by Georgetown's President, Father Timothy Healy, S.J. His statements provide insight into the meaning and purpose of Georgetown University and reflect many of the ideals and values emphasized in the essays.

Using Fr. Healy's addresses, and my own thoughts and perceptions of today's Georgetown student, I compare some of the students whom I have come to know through the essays with the students whom I know today as a Junior at Georgetown in 1988. I also comment on what these essays reveal regarding the concerns held by students and alumni of Georgetown about themselves, their society, and where they stood in relation to their social environment.

It was encouraging to discover in these essays that despite

differences in time and background, many Georgetown students and graduates have demonstrated an appreciation of the values that the Catholic-Jesuit tradition continues to cultivate at this University. The values of social service, responsibility, leadership, and the pursuit of knowledge have long been fostered at Georgetown.

Before plunging into these comments and summaries, I would like to differentiate today's modern age from the time period between 1860–1939 when the essays I researched were written. These differences provide, at least in part, reasons for some changes in student perspectives through the years. Yet the focus of this essay has been on the opinions and values which are constantly expressed among the writers from Georgetown's past. These writers help one to understand better the ideals that Georgetown tries to foster.

The students entering Georgetown today are part of a world of advanced technology and communications. They belong to a world which is considerably "smaller" than the world of 1860–1939. Students of our era are confronted with a more diverse Georgetown, whereas those from 1860 to 1939 formed a student body of white males.

Another marked difference is that anti-Catholicism was a significantly stronger sentiment between 1860 and 1939 than it is today. In reaction to this hostility and prejudice, students may have developed a more defensive mentality (reflecting the stance of the Church of that day) with regard to their Catholicism. Not until 1965 did the reforms and clarifications of the Second Vatican Council diminish the Catholic feeling of being a Church under siege.

What characterized most of the essays I read was a concern for defending the Catholic faith, applying it to the social order correlating Catholic principles with the American polity and a strong sense of patriotism. Despite the varied topics and styles, some basic themes stand out which represent the ideals of Georgetown. Catholic and American values are seen as harmonious. Societal secular values, taken by themselves, are viewed as inadequate guides for directing one's moral outlook. Looking beyond oneself to the responsibilities one has to serve the local, national and world community is a crucial theme in these essays.

In many of the students' essays, the emphasis and enthusiasm accorded to the Catholic faith are striking. "The true Christian home is the highest type and order of domestic happiness," a student remarks in 1907.[1] "A Catholic should stand out in his community without ever needing to label himself,"[2] observed another writer in 1925.

Because the students brought up their Catholic beliefs so frequently and spontaneously and on such a variety of issues, it might be fair to assume that the students of Georgetown's past were more expressive of their faith, at least in writing, than Catholic students at Georgetown are today. Georgetown students in our own era tend to be more subtle in expressing their religious beliefs. They seem to be fearful of alienating others by drawing on principles that are characteristically Catholic or even Christian. Perhaps this is because students today feel less pressure to prove themselves as Catholics to society. They are therefore uncomfortable with, and less practiced in, arguing in defense of their faith.

Although there seem to be fewer direct references to Catholicism in student writings today, many show their concern for strengthening their faith by using the numerous resources at Georgetown. Many students have personal relationships with Jesuits which allow them to give free expression to their questions and doubts as they struggle with their faith. A manifestation of this student desire to learn more about and to increase their love for their Catholic faith is the present popularity among Catholic students of spiritual retreats, periods of silent prayer and meditation.

In a few early essays, enthusiasm for the Catholic faith bordered on the elitist and arrogant. In 1876, a student compared the Catholic and Protestant contributions to the cause of liberty and concluded that "the present social system of America owes its perfection to the grand, solid, accurate and enlightened Catholic faith."[3] He condemns Protestant philosophies as erroneous and degrading. He associates Protestant ideas with the doctrines of Hobbes and Rousseau, where we would "learn that our present state is unnatural and that a social contract alone prevents an eternal warfare among us."[4]

At the time when this nineteenth century student took his

pen in hand, Catholics in this country were under siege because of their religious faith; and a siege mentality is very likely to produce strong assertions of one's tenets. It should also be borne in mind that this student was at Georgetown when defending the faith through reasoned argument was one of the university's prime emphases.

The nineteenth century students seemed eager to express the way in which their faith related to an understanding of society. That faith, they felt, was more than personally fulfilling; it was more than something that would give them inner strength in order to perfect their individual lives. Rather, they viewed their faith as being the element that directed them in their public as well as in their private lives.

One student writes in 1860 that Catholicism orders "social action toward its highest perfection."[5] He describes how important Catholicity is in contributing to the unification of individuals in political organizations, namely states. He then indicates how the Church leads one not only to consider the ordering of one's own life, but to give thought to the ordering of society as well. He emphasizes the value of justice and feels that the latter is encouraged and sustained by his religion: "...to be a man of high station, one must be a man of religious principles," he insists. He expresses "Catholicity" as "an eternal bond of social perfection." [6]

At Georgetown today, some students demonstrate their sense of responsibility for the needy in society by their commitment to all kinds of volunteer work in the Washington area. The practice of students enriching their own lives as well as those of others continues to be central to Georgetown's character.

All of the views in the early essays on government and society were closely connected with the students' religious views. For all of them, the idea of national morality was rooted in religious principles. One's patriotism, they insisted, depended primarily upon religious beliefs.

One student writing in the late 1870s expresses his conviction that belief in God is essential for the preservation of government:"Destroy the idea of God and you sap the foundations upon which government is built:—you break down the barriers which surround the breast of man and give an easy entrance to the vilest passions."[7]

In 1912, Stephen W. Carroll's Bachelor's Oration states that true citizenship consists in Christian fraternity: "In setting forth the attributes of citizenship I stand firm in the belief that the doctrines we have received here in the halls of Georgetown University are the safe and true rules of sound political as well as private morality."[8] Here again is an affirmation that Catholic principles are not merely concerned with personal right and wrong but with public right and wrong as well.

Private and public morality is emphasized or at least mentioned in all the student essays. "Prudence, justice, fortitude and temperance," declared a student writer, "must abide in the civil as well as in the home life of an individual." Carroll, the same author, presents the three principles of civic virtue as "first, a deep respect for and devotion to properly established civil authority; secondly, a spirit of christian fraternity, and thirdly, personal dignity and self respect."[9]

Today's Georgetown students seem more likely to regard their faith as primarily intended for their private lives rather than understanding it to be something that ought to animate their communal lives. They are thus less inclined to apply the principles of their faith directly to the public issues of today. Why is this? Maybe it is simply because the gap between religion and politics has widened so that students feel that drawing on Christian principles to base their political views is not entirely respectable. It may also be due to the widespread conviction today that religion is mainly a private matter. Or perhaps the emphasis on logic and rationality so characteristic of the modern age, which places so much stress on empirical facts, leads people to regard religious beliefs as an invalid and untrustworthy means for arriving at practical truth.

The stock charge, of course, against the "religious approach" to political and social issues is that it minimizes the rational and employs to a dangerous degree the feelings, the emotions, and the intuitive passions of human beings. However, in a world where history has demonstrated all too well the incredibly inadequate work of logic, the way of wisdom might indeed be a touch of Pascal's "reason of the heart." (Recall that Pascal is thinking within a fundamental frame of reason, and is not referring here to anything like the mindless fundamentalism of today's extreme religious right.) As the ancients teach us, "all the world is given to folly, because no man thinketh in his heart."[10]

In most of the essays, the students or alumni shared a strong pride in being Catholic American citizens. William Sands '96 writes that the object of Catholic education in America is "the production of the best possible type of citizen in (potentially) the best type of commonwealth yet produced by Christian civilization." He adds that "...It is the duty of such citizens, not as segregated masses but as individuals to take each his full part in the development of that commonwealth upon the principles which are entirely harmonious with Catholic Theology, which conform so closely to those expounded in the great [papal] encyclicals as to raise speculation on the extent to which certain of our American Founders may have been familiar with, or indirectly influenced by Catholic political thought of the time."[11] Such speculation was popular among Catholics when this essay was written. Like many of the students of his day, Sands sees the influence of Catholic American citizens on America to be of great importance.

Speaking in 1980, Father Healy reiterates the same Catholic American pride and speaks of the responsibilities of the Catholic American student: "Georgetown strives to make its undergraduate colleges making and remaking places for both the Republic and the Church."[12] Fr. Healy continues the idea that Catholic Americans should stand out in society and play a leading role in American civilization. He often brings up the idea of religious beliefs being inseparable from one's integrity as a citizen. "Making citizens," he explains, "is a secular job deeply influenced and conditioned by a belief in God." He emphasizes that there is a moral base upon which Georgetown and America rest. "There is in America, a civic religion, in which we all participate, and it, too, is a gateway for the Spirit."[13]

Georgetown is a place which prepares its students to be American citizens. Fr. Healy explains that America "...makes as serious a set of demands upon its citizens as any ever made in a body politic. This nation calmly expects of its citizens truthfulness, compassion, and hunger for justice." He concludes that "higher professional skill and knowledge must be tied to ethical bonds of conduct, to the way we run our cities and our lives."[14]

The Georgetown President speaks to his faculty as follows: "Given the brains, the energy, and the promise of the young people who come to us, what we do here is likely to have an influence upon the American republic, far deeper and more explosive than our fondest imaginings. For that reason our consciousness of the ethical imperative of our tradition is all the more important. If we ignore this link to conduct we shirk the burden that the talent and promise of these young people lay on us."[15]

Student Carroll's Bachelor's Oration of 1912 states that "When corruption creeps in—and the cause is not the imperfection of human nature but the deliberate design of men—and the instrumentalities, through which civic justice should be done, are diverted and debased to serve private revenge or to promote private gain, he who stays at home or who but lends his voice to denouncing existing conditions or who withholds his hand and brain from their betterment, does not fulfill the highest purposes of citizenship."[16]

The same student, unwittingly speaking a warning most useful for the present age, is conscious of and angered by those who think only of what benefits themselves rather than of what benefits the society in which they live: "A mighty scorn, indeed, awaits and belongs to the man who enters politics in a spirit of pocket patriotism, who prefers personal profit to public benefaction, who seeks power but to cash it and who holds office but to facilitate private schemes." Carroll judges such a person as "the public enemy and not the public servant."[17] This student obviously regards his Georgetown education as being not only for personal gain but for societal benefit as well.

Some statements in "Citizenship" and other essays seem blind to the imperfections in the American system of government. Carroll often is overly content with the laws of our country, some of which need to be reevaluated and at times revised. He does not seem to recognize that we must watch our leaders and the laws they enact with a critical eye. His statement that "he who holds under suspicion the just laws of a country or who resists her officials cannot verily be a law-abiding citizen" exemplifies this criticism[18] and might be regarded as being too simplistic.

In many essays the major focus of social concern was the

problem of materialism. An essay entitled "Progress of the Age" sarcastically attacks the trend toward materialism which was rampant in 1877. The student's characterization of his time as a "money-making age" speaks directly to the problem of today's Georgetown student who is strongly influenced by our culture's concern with financial status and materialism. The Jesuit influence at Georgetown is one that is likely to have moved this student to speak out against such misguided cultural values and directed his attentions to higher values.

In the same *Journal* (1877–78), an essay by a student expressed similar concerns. He is disturbed about the growth of materialism and the erosion of the sense of the transcendent in society. He criticizes the pursuit of wealth and surprisingly goes so far as to reduce luxury to the level of corruption. Simplicity and modesty are encouraged as he assures his readers that material gain is definitely no grounds for respect.

This student is disgusted with the escalation of materialism in the America of his day. His thoughts are insightful and he seems able to understand that what is most valuable in human life becomes secondary for those who become preoccupied with materialistic aims. He sees Georgetown's task as being much more than the preparation of its students for business careers or professions: "In the pursuit of wealth everything else is forgotten. The majority of those who seek it seem to act on the same principle as the general who resolving to obtain possession of a fortress, determines to sacrifice if necessary nine-tenths of his force in the assault. In the same way men often sacrifice health, honor and the esteem of the good in the pursuit of a desired object." [19]

Wealth, he explains, "magnifies a hundredfold the good qualities with which its possessor may chance to be endowed, and it compensates for the absence of education and moral worth."[20] The student concludes that materialism is a "cover up" for that which is lacking in an individual. He feels proud that his time at Georgetown has made him better able to resist the temptation of materialism.

Although the concern for materialism still exists among students today, their arguments used against that evil might be more varied. These Hoyas of the past explain, in a conservative fashion, that materialism damages a person's character. There is no mention of the fact that materialism hurts others in society. Students today seem more inclined to argue that in seeking to accumulate material wealth, one adds to the oppression of those who are not able to get the bare necessities needed for a decent life.

Some essays expressed the conviction of students and alumni that the Catholic education they received at Georgetown would enable them to maintain Catholic ideals amid the "hurly burly of our American material existence." Sands, the alumnus who writes "The Ideal of a Catholic College," praises Catholic education for this in particular: "That is what I mean by Catholic education: the development of our Faith, not as a check, not as a brake upon our natural inclinations, but as a natural, living rule of life, a refinement of our natural daily lives lived fully in our natural surroundings."[21]

Sands attributes the "roughness, lack of consideration, and absence of refinement in the relations of Catholic to Catholic or with his neighbor" to "a matter of education."[22] He feels assured that the Catholic education that he received at Georgetown could not be replaced by any kind of non-Catholic education.

In the late nineteenth century, higher education seems to have been regarded with less respect than it is today. A student of 1893 decries in his essay his contemporaries' view that: "Higher education signifies in their estimation but a blunting of the practical sense." The college man, "they falsely imagine, has been imbued with visionary theories of every kind, in whom principles have been instilled with no instruction as to their practical application."[23]

Sands and others address a "hot issue" at Georgetown today: preprofessionalism. He insists that turning out professionals is not an end in itself at a Catholic college. The primary result of a Catholic education ought to be its "inescapable refining influence."[24] It solidly lays the foundations for life.

The student who wrote "Dangers of the Age" in 1877 praises education as being beneficial not only to the individual but to society as well. Education, he explains, is "that symmetrical training of the faculties both mental and moral, by which alone men can render true and lasting benefit to society."[25]

His education at Georgetown seems to have given this alumnus a strong sense of duty and responsibility: "The children of to-day are to stamp their character on the society of to-morrow. Society will be but the mirror which will reflect back the image of their souls." He states his belief that "the proper remedy for many of the evils of the age is education." The determination to "make use of education" is strong among Catholics.[26]

In these essays that address the negative influences of society affecting the Georgetown student, there is a consistent repetition of the need for moral and spiritual values to replace those encouraged by society. Georgetown still struggles to maintain its values "which point *beyond* those of the culture."[27]

The essays of the early twentieth century which dealt with issues of social justice were refreshing because instead of merely praising American ideals, the students looked at some real-life situations and made critical comments. The students demonstrated genuine concern and knowledge about the issues they chose to discuss.

Edward W. Bodnar's essay, "Black Man's Burden," written in 1938, is a powerfully pessimistic essay which criticizes discrimination against blacks. He writes a short story about a black boy who attends an all-white male Catholic preparatory school. After hoping that the white students would end their cruel and discriminating practical jokes and learn to accept the black student, the reader finds his/her hopes shattered. The conclusion of the story is disconcerting and shocking. It relates how the black student quit school due to the scorn and hatred he was subjected to by his peers: "He could not accept the Catholic doctrine which preached one thing and did another." The boy developed the attitude that blacks can only "rise by hating whitemen, just as the white men hate them."[28]

The story is disturbing because its ending is so harsh. However, such a shock is needed for the powerful and urgent message that the student seeks to communicate. He shows how severe the impact of black discrimination can be. The damage done by the white Catholic school boys to the black student seems irreparable. The story left me feeling angry and disappointed with some Catholics' behavior toward blacks and I believe that this reaction is what the author intended. He successfully portrayed the terrible thing that Catholic hypocrisy can be.

The most impressive essay was "The Individual and the Constitution," written in the 1938–39 *College Journal* by Burke E. Schoense. It also is a denunciation of racism and discrimination against blacks in America. Schoense appeals to the Constitution and its message of "justice and equality before the law for every citizen regardless of race or creed."[29] He has a strong sense of his responsibility as an American citizen to help remedy the situation of black Americans. He is not only addressing those who discriminate against blacks, but also those who display apathy in the face of such discrimination.

Schoense's writing is creative in that he situates his readers on a trolley car where an incident of discrimination occurs. "Without a word, the man next to *us* gets up, seizes the surprised black by the throat…"[30] His story is effective in bringing home the cowardly behavior of the American citizen on the issues of black discrimination. He criticizes us, the trolley car riders, who do not have "sufficient courage, knowledge or decency to protect the constitutional rights" of the black American. His final question is powerful: "Does the individual citizen rejoice that certain priceless natural rights are guaranteed to all Americans or rather that they are guaranteed to him?"[31]

This essay and a few others were patriotic yet critical and aware of the fact that we are a country whose ideals are still in the process of being realized. The essay's creativity and unique style demonstrate the virtue of intellectual freedom that continues to flourish at Georgetown today.

The recalling of American ideals moved a 1924 student to write in angry protest against America's activity in the Philippines. The Philippines had fulfilled the conditions required by Congress for the granting of independence. The student argues that in not granting independence sooner to the Philippines, America was disregarding principles upon which it was founded. He quotes Abraham Lincoln: "Those who deny freedom to others deserve it not for themselves and under a just God cannot retain it."[32] The student's essay shows not only a well-thought-out argument, but expresses his genuine concern for the Filipino predicament and American action related to it.

What has stood out in almost all the essays I have read is that these students of Georgetown felt the need to repeat the basic truths of our American society, truths that lie at the foundations of Catholicism. It was not taken for granted that these truths could be assumed. Students seemed to know that these truths needed to be continually stated and they did so with enthusiasm. The same students, however, were quite vocal (to this author surprisingly so) in their recognition of flaws in American attitudes. They denounced, as we have seen, discrimination against blacks, imperialism with regard to our foreign territorial possessions, and, of course, the pervasive national hedonism. Our young writers' attack on such aberrations is a testimony to their profound respect for a high level of ethical behavior and a mature assessment of what was required for the good life.

Fr. Healy carries on this tradition at Georgetown today. He has continually voiced the ideas that are at the roots of our culture and Christianity. At St. Michael's College seventy-fifth anniversary, he reminds all that "simple things need resaying."[33] He concludes the November 22, 1980 faculty convocation with: "I started by saying that there would be very little new in what I wanted to say. The older I get in time, and I devoutly hope, in grace, the more it seems to me that the things that need resaying are *simple*."[34]

As these essays reveal, the mission of Georgetown is to educate in a way that integrates the life of the mind with social values and social justice. Throughout the history of our university, Catholic moral and religious principles have been maintained, albeit never with complete perfection. Nevertheless, despite the changes at Georgetown in a rapidly changing world, a common set of values has continued to highlight its purpose and meaning. It is to be hoped that the articulation of these ideals is only a step in the process of their fuller realization. After all, "we have to conceive of an idea before we can do it."[35]

Notes

1. Francis P. Sheehy, "College Men in Politics," Bachelor's Oration, in *Georgetown College Journal* 22 (1893–94), pp. 180–82.

2. William Franklin Sands, '96, "The Ideal of a Catholic College," *Georgetown College Journal* 54 (1929–30), p. 543.

3. William Wilcox, "The Catholic Element in the American Revolution," holograph essays, Georgetown University Archives [henceforth to be cited as GUA 1876].

4. Ibid.

5. A. Landry, "Influences of Religious Principles on Society," 1860. GUA 1876.

6. Ibid.

7. L., "Dangers of the Age," *Georgetown College Journal* 6 (1877–78), p. 67.

8. Stephen W. Carroll, A.B. '12, "Citizenship," Bachelor's Oration, *Georgetown College Journal* 40 (1911–12), p. 334.

9. Ibid.

10. W. Edmund Fitzgerald, S.J., Ph.D., "Jesuit Education and the Culture of the West," *Tradition and Prospect*, Washington, D.C., Georgetown University Press, 1949, p. 19.

11. Sands, art. cit., p. 537.

12. Timothy S. Healy, S.J., address to Faculty Convocation, Nov. 22, 1980, T.S. Healy Files GUA.

13. Timothy S. Healy, S.J., commencement speech at St. Michael's College, Nov. 15, 1980, T.S. Healy Files GUA.

14. Timothy S. Healy, S.J., address to Faculty Convocation, Nov. 22, 1980, T.S. Healy Files, GUA.

15. Timothy S. Healy, S.J., address to Faculty Convocation, Nov. 22, 1980, T.S. Healy Files, GUA.

16. Carroll, art. cit., p. 334.

17. Ibid.

18. Ibid.

19. L., art. cit, p. 67.

20. L., ibid., loc. cit.

21. Sands, art. cit., p. 541.

22. Ibid., loc. cit.

23. Francis Stanton Montgomery, "Socialism," dissertation for degree, Ch.D., holograph in GUA, box 1907.

24. Sands, art. cit., p. 541.

25. L., art. cit., p. 68.

26. L., ibid., loc. cit.

27. "The Mission and Goals of Student Affairs," first draft, Sept. 22, 1986, p. 5, Office of Student Affairs, Georgetown University.

28. Edward W. Bodnar, "Black Man's Burden," *Georgetown College Journal* 67 (1938–39), p. 426.

29. Burke E. Schoense, "The Individual and the Constitution," *Georgetown College Journal* 67 (1938–39), p. 409.

30. Ibid., p. 410.

31. Ibid., p. 412.

32. Joseph B. Brennan, '25, "A Case for the Philippines," *Georgetown College Journal* 53 (1924–25), p. 386.

33. Timothy S. Healy, S.J., commencement speech at St. Michael's College, Nov. 15, 1980, T.S. Healy Files, GUA.

34. Timothy S. Healy, S.J., address to Faculty Convocation, Nov. 22, 1980, T.S. Healy Files, GUA.

35. John Lennon (taken from the last interview before his murder).

II. The Spoken Word

"Debate Moderator" (from *The Georgetown Journal*, January, 1911).

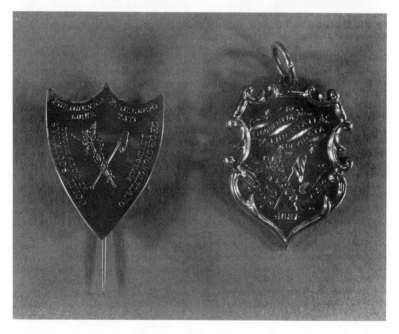

Philodemic Society medals.

The Cultivation of Eloquence at Georgetown College: A History of the Philodemic Society from 1830–1890

Eric M. George

Georgetown's Philodemic Debating Society was born in 1830 in the golden age of American oratory. At the time, kings of debaters—Clay, Webster, and Calhoun—were contending for supremacy in the foremost assembly of free discussion in the world. Railroads were yet to be, the telegraph was but a scientific toy, and one looked to horses as the quickest form of transportation.[1]

Realizing the salient virtues of this historical age, Georgetown's Vice-President James Ryder, S.J., formed an organization to cultivate eloquence among the students of the College.[2] Aside from Ryder, who took the position of president of the incipient debate society, all other positions went to College students. Samuel A. Mulledy was the first vice-president, John H. Hunter the first secretary, Samuel H. Digges the first treasurer, and Eugene H. Lynch the first amanuensis.[3] After three meetings, the members agreed upon a name for the society. "Philodemic" was chosen for its Greek roots, symbolizing "a love of the people."[4] Thus were sounded the chords of patriotism and democracy which were heard long throughout the Society's existence.

At the same meeting, the members resolved to adopt a badge which ultimately took the form of a shield. On one side is an American eagle carrying a trident in one claw while resting its other one upon a globe. Above the eagle is a harp surrounded by rays. The reverse side of the badge portrays Mercury (the god of eloquence) clasping hands with the goddess of liberty (indicated by a staff surmounted by the liberty cap). An inscription runs around one side of the shield, "COLIT SOCIETAS PHILODEMICA E COLLEGIO GEORGIOPOLITANO," and terminates on the other, "ELOQUENTIAM LIBERTATI DE-VINCTAM"—The Philodemic Society of Georgetown College cultivates Eloquence devoted to Freedom.[5]

An original essay of one of the Philodemic's student officials emphasized these coordinate aims:

> in the first place we endeavored to adapt it [the Philodemic] to the peculiar institutions of our country; we went back to the source of all power—to the foundation stone of the republic—the people. As our government is an anomaly in governments—as it is established on principles the reverse of all upon which political institutions have hitherto been based, so must necessarily be every institution [like the Philodemic] which has the same foundation and has for its object the support of that system which grows out of it. Therefore, did we base our infant society upon the same permanent pedestal, by which the stupendous fabric of our government is supported— the people. The object of thus establishing it on an attachment for the people, was a wish at some future time to assist our country-men in watching over and defending the government which guaranteed to all the inestimable blessing of liberty. In cherishing a love for, and identifying ourselves with, the primitive elements of our government, we necessarily blended all our feelings in the government itself.[6]

These patriotic and virtuous aspirations found their way into a Constitution. Although now faded by time, the parchment Constitution set down officer positions, 6 and 1/4-cent monthly dues, 4-cent late fees, and basic procedures.[7] As time passed, an amendment-adding provision written into the Constitution was utilized frequently. (The Constitution became so laden with provisions that it was often rewritten.) Most important, though, were the format for debate, the provision to begin the Philodemic's library, and the establishment of an annual celebration.

"Whether Napoleon Bonaparte or General Washington was the greater man?"[8] This question, debated in October of 1830, was the first posed by the Society. By-laws provided for debate topics and debaters to be chosen two weeks previous to each contest. Two debaters were chosen to support the affirmative; two others, the negative.[9] Each could speak for more than five and less than twenty minutes, or face the penalty of a small fine. When the debate was completed, a vote would be taken among all members present to gauge the results. This democratic method—with decisions almost always resting on the outcome of a vote—marks the procedure of the Philodemic in everything it did.

Debate was not just a means of conveying knowledge. Foremost in its purpose was sharpening logic and oratorical skills. Topics for debate demonstrate this. Questions *presuppose* a working knowledge of history and an appreciation of literature and oratory of epochs past. From 1837 to 1838, Philodemic members debated such topics as "Was the destruction of Carthage beneficial to Rome?"[10] and "Which nation produced the greatest men during the reign of George III and IV, England or Ireland?"[11] An 1842 debate posed the question, "Which was the greater man, Charles XII of Sweden or Peter the Great of Russia?"[12]

The historical subjects were well balanced by current ones. In 1831, Philodemic members debated the beneficience of the tariff to the United States.[13] In 1837, a debate was held on "Can duelling be justified in the United States?"[14]

Often, the imagination of the Philodemic produced topics which jumped the boundaries of time: "Who is the greatest Orator, Cicero or Patrick Henry?"[15] or "Was the age of Augustus Caesar superior to that of Louis XIV in literature?"[16]

If the knowledge necessary for participating in such debates didn't accumulate from College classes, perhaps it came from the Philodemic's library. The money accrued from monthly dues and miscellaneous fines was to be appropriated, according to the original Constitution, to a library for the use of the Society. So diligently did Philodemic members value a well-stocked library, that a "Committee on Books" was established by about

1838.[17] The Committee was to assess (four times each school year) the condition of the library and suggest means for improving it.

In March of 1846, additions to the Library included Webster's *Speeches*, the *Memoirs* of Jefferson, works of Shakespeare, works of Irving, a large quantity of history books, and numerous books of poetry.[18] The "Quarterly Report" from the Committee on Books noted that the "present flourishing state of our library is a source of laudable pride and congratulation to the members..."[19] Yet, two and a half years later, the Committee was to report that it was "somewhat disappointed in [its] survey of the Library. Instead of being the quiet 'sanctum' where old authors may rest in peace, it appeared to...have lately experienced all the horrors of civil dissensions."[20]

In an apparent effort to rectify this regrettable condition, the Philodemic enforced a two-book donation from each member. The Philodemic librarian wrote in 1849 that the Society had "received 40 vols. from the members of the Society. Messrs. ——— have not yet made their contributions of books, and Messrs. Rich, Bryan, and D. O'Byrne have contributed but one volume, consequently another is due from each of them...The amount of fines for the violation of the rules of the library is now $3.00."[21]

The Society's effort to improve its collection obviously fared well; the *College Journal* claimed in 1874 that the Philodemic had a library consisting of over 1,100 volumes.[22]

In addition to setting debate procedure and establishing a library, the Philodemic's laws laid the foundation for an annual meeting of the Society. Minutes of a July meeting in 1831 show that this annual convocation would elect an orator for the approaching July commencement.[23] It seems to have been the custom of the Philodemic to appoint a valedictorian from its members to deliver his address at the College Villa, where the Society and a few guests spent the day and took dinner.

The Honorable Robert Ray, the selected valedictorian in 1854, delivered an oration which aptly put his debating experience in context with his sense of patriotism:

> A long observation has convinced me that an organization of this kind is productive of the greatest good. Here, that diffidence is overcome which the young orator naturally feels in rising for the

first time before the public...Here, that knowledge which is required in wider fields is brought into action. And here that judgment which will more than likely be adhered to afterwards, is given on important subjects...[But] do not view those questions of a national bearing...in the narrow spirit of *sectional feeling*. Do not view them as a Northerner or a Southerner...but as an American, as one whose patriotism embraces the whole country...Remember, that it was in a debating society like this that Henry Clay first manifested that love of country which afterwards showed itself in all his public acts, and caught up that sublime eloquence which afterwards illuminated the world, guiding our own Ship of State, freighted with the dearest hopes of Constitutional liberty, through three of the most violent political storms that have as yet tried the stability of our government...O let but that love of Union which animated a Clay and a Webster, sink into our young hearts, and it will afterwards grow with your growth and strengthen with your strength.[24]

This exuberant nationalism was more the rule than the exception with Philodemic members. In its first year of existence, the Society celebrated Washington's Birthday with an elected orator giving a speech in the presence of the students and professors of the College and the clergy.[25] This February celebration subsequently became a tradition for the Philodemic. At the annual festivities, Washington's Farewell Address would be read, followed by remarks on the Father of his Country.

Similar celebration occurred on Independence Day, with the Declaration of Independence being read, followed by appropriate comments. The *Washington Mirror* wrote in 1835 that "[t]he Address was delivered by the youthful Orator, at the request of the Philodemic Society; and truly it appeared to us, that a more judicious and happy selection could not have been made, for it is not flattery to say, that an Oration more patriotic in its tendency, more felicitous in its matter and style, or more worthy of the elevated institution from which it emanated, could not have been pronounced at our proud anniversary."[26]

In 1888, the *College Journal* reported that the Philodemic celebrated the Fourth of July "with noise of bands and words of flame, in the presence of a select company, composed of authors and statesmen."[27]

After such festivities, banquets were usually held, attended by the members of the Philodemic and their guests. At these affairs, those members who had dutifully been the listeners were now given the opportunity to speak. The result was a torrent of eloquent toasts as patriotic as the public meetings. The banquet on February 22, 1832 recorded forty toasts.[28] The first was naturally to the Father of the United States: "To the immortal George Washington, whose birth was the signal of our freedom and the knell of Tyranny."[29] "*Eloquentia libertati devincta*," began a second, "Eloquence the child, the nurse, and the guardian of liberty." Again: "Liberty is the boon of happiness which Washington left to his countrymen; the eloquence of his countrymen must defend it."[30]

The eloquence of the Philodemic was, indeed, being cultivated, and not infrequently was it manifested in displays of patriotism. An articulate expression of this sentiment originated in 1842 with Fr. George Fenwick. A late arrival from his studies at Rome, he returned determined to make the landing of the Pilgrims at Maryland as famous as the Plymouth Rock landing. The Philodemic Society was willing to assist him in this attempt, and an added clause in the Constitution told of its new obligation.[31]

On May 9, 1842, teachers, students, and a large number of guests—about two hundred in all—left Georgetown for the purpose of making a pilgrimage to St. Inigoes in St. Mary's County. The procession was formed in the College Yard and, led by the College Band, marched through the principal streets of Georgetown, evoking admiration and excitement from the onlooking citizens. The group then embarked on the steamer *Columbia* at one o'clock.

Having arrived late that night, the group loaded small boats and sent them ashore during the morning, whereupon a large procession had formed. High Mass was celebrated by the Most Rev. Archbishop of Baltimore, and was followed by an address by the Bishop of Boston, who spoke of "how beautifully [the] fundamental maxims of Christianity were illustrated in the sentiments and actions of the Colonists of Maryland, who...emigrated to these shores and planted...the standard of civil and religious freedom."[32]

Afterwards, the procession again formed and marched to the

boats with music and banners floating in the air. The steamboats—three in number—were boarded, and proceeded three miles up the St. Mary's River to the spot where the Pilgrim Fathers had first settled. There, the procession was greeted by thousands who had assembled to welcome the pious pilgrimage. [33]

As the march finished, the Philodemic Society was formally given two beautiful banners—the first by the ladies of St. Mary's County and the second by the ladies of the Baltimore Cathedral, who, "deeply sensible of eminent services rendered among them to religion by the distinguished President of the Georgetown College, knew no better mode of testifying their sense of gratitude than to make this offering for a celebration which was intended to honor the establishment of civil and religious freedom, and in which that gentleman was to take so prominent a part."[34]

Once the delegates of the Philodemic Society had responded to the addresses made on behalf of the ladies, the procession moved to the formerly occupied city of St. Mary, where Fr. Ryder, founder of the Philodemic Society and the current president of Georgetown College, invoked a continuation of the blessings which had been imparted to their ancestors. Then, the orator of the day, the able and eloquent William Read of Baltimore, rose to recall the glories of Maryland's natal day.[35]

Using his deep familiarity with history, Read included in his speech a picture of the honorable conduct of the Maryland settlers towards the Indians, and contrasted it sharply with that of the New England colonists, whose early annals were a history of Indian wars. He attributed the peace with the Indians to the influence of the Catholic missionaries:

> Gentlemen of the Philodemic Society, yours is the honor of having instituted this commemorative festival. To your unmerited partiality am I indebted for the part I have endeavored to sustain in it...To you it belongs to exemplify the virtues I have inadequately attempted to portray. Set apart by destiny for the high duty of guiding and enlightening your fellow men, many of your illustrious confraternity have already given precedents which the proudest might rejoice to follow. To such of you as still linger in academic bowers, devoting the "blessed age of admiration" to the contemplation of all that is glorious and good in the history of man, I would say with the

voice of a somewhat more natural experience, you can follow no brighter models than the founders of Maryland.[36]

The oration was followed by an ode written by George Washington's adopted son, George Washington Parke Custis, and sung by a trio consisting of Custis himself, Fr. Fenwick, and a granddaughter of Charles Carroll of Carrollton. As the *College Journal* reminisced at a much later date, "[even] the singers were aware of the historic memories which they called forth."[37]

Such was the first celebration of the landing of the Pilgrims of the *Ark* and *Dove*. As John Shea recorded, the "sacred fire was [then] lighted, and spread from one point to another, like the signal blaze in the Highlands of Scotland."[38] Literary societies across the eastern seaboard had caught the enthusiasm, and began memorializing the landing of the Pilgrims. Unfortunately, the celebration carried out by the Philodemic was not destined to become a tradition. It occurred but once or twice more, and in 1888, the *College Journal* dolefully admitted that "we are allowing too long a time to slip by between our feasts. Could there ever be a better year for another trip to St. Mary's, or could there ever be gathered together a party better disposed to enjoy it? If we need a reason for the celebration, the same old pledge to Fr. Fenwick remains still."[39]

Yet, with the benefits of spirited and eloquent patriotism on Washington's birthday, the Fourth of July, and the occasional pilgrimage celebration came feelings of excessive independence and gradual impatience. In 1850, the Philodemic members began to abuse liberties granted to them such as occasional days at the Villa. On one Sunday they held a meeting in defiance of the express prohibition of the First Prefect.[40] As explained by the amanuensis, William H. Wills, in the Minutes of a January 13, 1850 meeting:

At the end of first studies, a committee of three waited upon the first Prefect to inform him that according to permission granted to the Society...by the President (who was then absent) the meeting would be continued during late studies. The first Prefect, however, positively refused permission, that the Society should meet. The Society somewhat indignant at the imposition of prefect power in contradiction to the authority of the President, met during late studies anyhow. Before resuming the debate, however, considerable debate took place whether it was proper for the Society to meet or not. It was then put to the house and almost unanimously decided in the affirmative.[41]

In further response to what they perceived as excessive "prefect power," the malcontents refused to read in the refectory at supper, disturbances took place in the dormitories, and stones were freely thrown about.[42]

On January 16, three students were expelled. Two left peacefully while the other loitered around until dinner time, when he entered the refectory and made a violent appeal to his fellow students. A great uproar ensued, and many students rushed to the room of Fr. Ward, acting president in the absence of Fr. Ryder. Fr. Ward asked the group who their leader was, and when the group replied that they had none, but were acting unanimously, Ward replied, "If you are unanimous, then walk unanimously out of my room."[43] They did so, rushing back to the dormitory and making general havoc until restrained by the more prudent. Almost the entire student body—a group of forty-four in number—then proceeded into Washington and registered at various Washington hotels.[44]

There the students corresponded with the College, asking that *all* students implicated in the revolt should be received back. The reply was that they were to apply as individuals, and that each case would be judged on its merits.[45] The students then held a meeting and resolved to remain unified. They adapted and forwarded the following:

Washington, *January* 16, '50

WHEREAS, We, the former students of Georgetown College, consider that we have been treated with indignity and contumely, we adopt the following resolutions:

Resolved, 1st. That we, the former students, feeling the contumely imposed by the officers of the College, do not return to the College, unless all those students who were in the College on the 14th day of January be re-admitted.

2d. That no one who has participated in the late proceedings at the College shall be submitted to any punishment proposed by the faculty of the College.

3d. That unless the First Prefect be changed, we shall not return to the College.

REV. SIR—We, the former students at Georgetown College, feeling deeply the measures resorted to by the authorities of Georgetown College cannot retract unless the above resolutions be complied with.

Please answer by 11 o'clock to-morrow.

Respectfully yours,
THE FORMER STUDENTS OF GEORGETOWN COLLEGE.[46]

While the students' latest correspondence was not acknowledged, the hotels were naturally informed that the College was not responsible for any unpaid bills. Moreover, having had enough time for reflection and anxious to avoid angry parents, the students were in a fit mood to listen to proposals when Mr. Maguire and Fr. Duddy sent out to interview them. Mr. Maguire pointed out that the College would do its part and receive back those ready to admit their fault as soon as the students dissolved the league which bound themselves to united action.[47] On January 21 and 22, all students returned after having consented to the conditions.

The "Great Riot of 1850," as this incident came to be known, sets itself in history as an anomaly; more often did the Philodemic use its energies to bring former students back to Georgetown than to disperse them from their Alma Mater. Indeed, it was the Philodemic that was responsible for the first "Grand Re-Union of the Alumni" in 1867. Invitations made their way to numerous alumni bearing the following inscription:

> Dear Sir: The Faculty of Georgetown College, in connection with the Philodemic Society, wishing to renew the ties of association which once bound to the College and the Society their many children now scattered throughout the land, have decided on a Grand Reunion of the Philodemic Society, to be held at the College on the 2d day of July next, at 10 1/2 o'clock A.M., on which occasion, in addition to other exercises, a poem will be delivered by George H. Miles, Esq., of Maryland, and an oration by Richard T. Merrick, Esq., of Washington City.[48]

The invitation further requested that each guest bring a "vignette size" photograph stating the former student's date and place of birth, present residence and occupation, the date of the photograph, and years at Georgetown. The invitation was signed by Fr. B.A. Maguire and Fr. James Clark, presidents of the College and the Philodemic Society, respectively. Thus be it noted, the Philodemic was here laying the foundations for the real beginning of the Alumni Association which would occur in 1881.

In addition to joining together Georgetown sons of years past, the Grand Reunion marked the establishment of the Triennials, celebrations to be held once every three years. Yet after the Grand Reunion in 1867, only the years 1871 and 1874 held the celebrations. Triennials usually featured prominent speakers, a lavish feast, and, of course, the performance of the "Philodemic Grand March," composed by the College's professor of Music, Pedro A. Daunas expressly for the Philodemic in 1854. It was the last Triennial in 1874 which saw the foundation of a prosperous tradition—the Merrick Debate.

The evening proceeded as follows: the Honorable Richard T. Merrick, in a few eloquent words, introduced the Honorable Charles P. James, who addressed the "Orators of the Past and of the Future," including a vivid description of the great Senate debate between Webster and Hayne. Then the poet of the occasion, John G. Saxe, recited his celebrated poem on Love.[49]

In his introductory remarks, Mr. Merrick had suggested that members of the Philodemic Society aim to make themselves great speakers and debaters, especially in light of the great need of eloquent articulation in public, legislative and church assemblies. He continued by saying how the establishment of awards for eloquence among the students would promote these ends.

As President Patrick Healy rose to remark upon the awarding of diplomas (honorary certificates given to members of the Philodemic about to leave the College), he heartily applauded Mr. Merrick's suggestion, and said he was perfectly willing to see the proposal put into practical execution.[50] When the proceedings of the day were over, Mr. Merrick offered to endow the prize which came to bear his name.

Mr. Merrick's project was carried out in the following document:

Know all Men by these presents that I, Richard T. Merrick, of the City of Washington, in the District of Columbia, being desirous of promoting the pursuit of oratory and encouraging the practice of debate among students of the University of Georgetown...do hereby give, grant, assign, and transfer unto Patrick F. Healy, the President of said University, and his successors in office forever, Eighteen (18) Shares of the Capital Stock of the Metropolitan Railroad Company...of the par value of Fifty Dollars ($50) each, and now stand in my name...

In Trust for the following purposes, and none other—that is to say: to hold and manage...and the dividends, rents, issues and profits thereof to apply to the purchase of a suitable gold medal...to be presented to that member of the Philodemic Society, of said University...who shall be deemed to be the best and most competent debater in the Society.[51]

The format for what was meant to be the grandest event each year for the Philodemic was subsequently prescribed; the Society was to select by ballot the four debaters deemed "best," and they in turn were to be judged by a committee of three gentlemen at the Annual Debate.

Grandest event of the year indeed it became. April 22, 1875 marked the first event in which Philodemicians vied for the prized medal. The subject of the debate was chosen by Mr. Merrick himself: "Should the Federal Government grant subsidies to Railway Corporations?" The Washington *Sunday Herald* reported of the debate that "[o]ne does not expect in the undergraduate that directness of argument, or cleanness of analysis or unity of parts which can only be found in the practised debater. Yet we do not hesitate to say that all these were found in the degree of excellence that could be expected under the circumstances."[52]

Many topics later debated for the Merrick Medal foreshadow issues of national importance. Philodemicians debated in 1876 whether it was "expedient that the tenure of the office of President of the United States...be limited to One Term and extended to a period of six years."[53] In 1878 it was debated if "the State should provide the means of education and enforce it by mandatory enactments."[54]

Selection as a debater for the Merrick Medal was indeed so prestigious that "[t]he election in March, where the four contestants are chosen," according to the *College Journal*, "very largely shapes college politics throughout the year and many a future aspirant for congressional or gubernatorial honors takes his first lesson in the mysteries of canvassing for votes, moulding public opinion, not to say log-rolling, during the weeks that precede the selection of the Merrick debaters. The struggle this year for position on the debate, though perhaps neither so violent nor so vigorously contested at every stage of its progress as the famous fight of '81, had its bitterness and the prize was not won *sine pulvere.*"[55]

While the results of the Merrick Debate awaited the sometimes weeks-long deliberation of the judges, the *College Journal* often covered the Merrick Debate with a captious and ever judgmental eye, leaving no secret as to *its* choice. The *Journal* gives the following report of the "Debate of '82," in which the legitimacy of territorial expansion was considered:

> Mr. Madigan's effort on behalf of the affirmative threatened in the beginning to decline to the sophomoric in style and pompous in delivery but, as an eminent critic remarked in our hearing, good, sound sense and closing reasoning speedily redeemed it, and rendered it quite different from the crude, school-boy affair which it promised to become. Not a few considered the speech of the evening.
>
> Mr. Wright's advocacy of the negative side of the question was forcible in manner, clear in statement and division, bold and incisive in argument, and bore less than any of the arguments the appearance of a speech previously written out and committed to memory. There was spontaneity about it in every feature, the language came readily and was both vigorous and elegant, and natural earnestness bore all through to an eloquent and telling peroration.[56]

The Merrick Debate of 1887, questioning the legitimacy of enacting laws which prohibited "the use and sale of intoxicating liquors," brought the following report from the *Journal*:

> Mr. Louis Bush Allain, of Louisiana, was the first speaker on the affirmative, and well that he fill the arduous duty of opening the important question. After a brief exordium this gentleman resorted to facts and solid arguments which stared you in the face.
>
> His arguments showed you the fruit of his observation, they were not clouded with words, but were clearly and pithily put. After proving legality and incidentally refuting all possible arguments, he advanced to the expediency, and proved this in the same

able manner as he did the first part. He showed how revenue would not be lost, but increased, how 40 per cent of crime would be avoided, how three million of years of human life would be saved annually and used with advantage to the States. Having conscientiously proved his side of the question, his eloquence found place in a masterly peroration, picturing man as he should be and man as he is. With this comparison he closed his debate, whose chief and pleasing characteristic was its originality.[57]

Occasionally, a topic was chosen which stifled a potentially excellent debate. Whether "the action of the Senate in refusing to ratify the treaty with Great Britain concerning the Canadian fisheries is to be approved" provoked less than overwhelming enthusiasm from onlookers and debaters alike.[58] One of the faculty remarked to the *College Journal* that "[i]t was impossible with such a subject to rise even once to the dignity of a universal proposition."[59] The *Journal* continued by asking "[h]ow, then, [it was possible with such a topic to] look for eloquence in the speakers?"[60]

More often, criticism from the *College Journal* focused on the more trivial, raising concerns in 1881 that "the habit of drinking water during the delivery of their speeches [is] most pernicious at best, destroying utterly some of the best oratorical efforts."[61]

By May of 1886, the Merrick Debate could be held at the College—as Georgetown facilities could now accommodate it. An article from the *College Journal* describes the setting of the 1894 Merrick Debate:

[Gaston Hall] was tastefully decorated with the National colors, whist on the stage a striking likeness of the Society's beneficient patron [Judge Merrick] reposed beneath the silken folds of the blue and gray. The stage itself never looked prettier. The softened radiance of the electric lights shone on the banks of ferns and palms, illuminating the features of the young orators about to enter upon the culminating contest of their school life in which eloquence was to vie with logic, rhetoric with proof. It is doubtful if a larger audience ever gathered in Gaston Hall. The balcony, even the very aisles, were crowded and the immense audience remained in rapt attention from exordium to peroration.[62]

The crowd for the above Debate included one Supreme Court Justice, and various Senators and Representatives.

In addition to housing the Merrick Debate, the Healy Building (as it soon came to be known) provided a room expressly for the use of the Philodemic Society and the Philonomosian (underclass debating) Society. December of 1881 saw the capacious room occupied for the first time. The first calling to order in the Society's new home was celebrated with a feast worthy of the occasion. "[F]rom Norfolk prime on the half shell to the nuts and chocolate," wrote the *Journal*, "the range was the best that college purveyors and college cooks could furnish."[63]

A year later, a committee was formed by the Philodemic Society to collect photographs of its former members. The *College Journal* wrote of the Committee's task, soliciting contributions of photographs from alumni. Dozens of photographs ultimately found their way onto the now time-stained walls.

Most profound in all the history of the early Philodemic is the serious commitment young men made to their organization and its goals and principles. They worked to preserve the Society and develop their own eloquence. At Georgetown, the Philodemic was an important part of university life.

Notes

1. *Georgetown College Journal* (hereafter *GCJ*), 10 (Jan. 1882), p. 43.
2. *GCJ*, 40 (Nov. 1911), p. 63.
3. Georgetown University Archives (hereafter GUA), Philodemic Box 1.
4. *GCJ*, 40 (Nov. 1911), p. 63.
5. *GCJ*, 1 (April 1873), p. 50.
6. Joseph T. Durkin, *Georgetown University: The Middle Years*, Washington, D.C., Georgetown University Press, 1963, p. 14.
7. GUA, Philodemic Box 1.
8. *GCJ*, 1 (April 1873), p. 50.
9. GUA, Philodemic Box 1.
10. Minutes of Philodemic Society, Meeting of January 7, 1838, GUA, Philodemic Box 2.
11. Minutes of Philodemic Society, Meeting of October 29, 1837, GUA, Philodemic Box 1.
12. Minutes of Philodemic Society, Meeting of November 13, 1842, GUA, Philodemic Box 2.
13. John M. Daley, *Georgetown University: Origin and Early Years*, Washington, D.C., Georgetown University Press, 1957, p. 235.

14. Minutes of Philodemic Society, Meeting of January 28, 1838, GUA, Philodemic Box 2.

15. Daley, p. 238.

16. Minutes of Philodemic Society, Meeting of October 2, 1837, GUA, Philodemic Box 2.

17. Philodemic Correspondence, *circa* 1840, GUA, Philodemic Box 2.

18. Quarterly Report from the Committee on Books, March 1846, Philodemic Box 2.

19. Ibid.

20. Ibid., December 1848.

21. Librarian's Report, 1849, GUA, Philodemic Box 3.

22. *GCJ*, 2 (Aug. 1874), p. 102.

23. *GCJ*, 1 (May 1873), p. 62.

24. *GCJ*, 2 (Oct. 1874), p. 112.

25. *GCJ*, 1 (May 1873), p. 62.

26. *The Washington Mirror,* July 11, 1835, p. 1.

27. *GCJ*, 17 (Oct. 1888), p. 5.

28. Daley, p. 235.

29. Record of Philodemic Celebration on February 22, 1832, GUA, Philodemic Box 1.

30. Ibid.

31. *GCJ*, 17 (Oct. 1888), p. 6.

32. John G. Shea, *History of Georgetown College*, New York, P.F. Collier, 1891, p. 130.

33. Ibid., p. 130–131.

34. Ibid., p. 101.

35. Ibid.

36. Ibid.

37. *GCJ*, 17 (Oct. 1888), p. 6.

38. Shea, p. 133.

39. *GCJ*, 17 (Oct. 1888), p. 6.

40. Shea, p. 165.

41. Minutes of Philodemic Society, meeting of January 13, 1850, GUA, Philodemic Box 3.

42. Shea, p. 166.

43. Ibid.

44. Ibid.

45. Ibid.

46. Ibid.

47. Ibid., p. 167.

48. Invitation to the Grand Reunion, April 1867, GUA, Philodemic Box 7.

49. Shea, p. 255.

50. *GCJ*, 2 (Aug. 1874), p. 103.

51. Shea, p. 255.

52. *Sunday Herald,* April 25, 1875.

53. *GCJ*, 4 (May 1876), p. 92.

54. *GCJ*, 6 (April 1878), p. 78.

55. *GCJ*, 10 (June 1882), p. 115.
56. Ibid.
57. *GCJ*, 15 (May 1887), p. 88.
58. *GCJ*, 17 (May 1889), p. 136.
59. Ibid., p. 144.
60. Ibid.
61. *GCJ*, 9 (June 1881), p. 101.
62. *GCJ*, 22 (March 1894), p. 106.
63. *GCJ*, 10 (Jan. 1882), p. 43.

The Philodemic Debating Society:
The Pursuit of Eloquence and Truth
from 1894 to 1939

David E. Cannella

Whereas all deliberative bodies should be properly organized and constituted and should conduct their proceedings according to such rules as experience has shown to be best adapted to the end of Georgetown College, and desiring to advance in ourselves the love of knowledge and truth and to make progress in eloquence, and wishing to safeguard by means of rules the will of the Assembly, and as to facilitate by them the expression of its deliberative sense rather than obstruct that expression or restrain it unduly, do adopt this constitution.[1]

Preamble to the Philodemic Constitution
Adopted on October 27, 1901

The Philodemic Debating Society adopted its formal Constitution in 1901 in order to "make progress in eloquence" at a time when debating and interest in rhetoric were at an unprecedented high. Gaston Hall was filled to capacity on numerous occasions to hear monthly Philodemic public debates on topics ranging from the contemporary political questions of the day to literary debates over the nature of a character from one of Shakespeare's plays.[2] Whether these debates concerned the annexation of Cuba, a controversial topic of the early 1900s, or the condemnation of Shylock in *The Merchant of Venice*,[3] the Philodemic debates and the society stood for one goal: the furthering of classical education through rhetoric. The Philodemic trained the sons of Georgetown to speak and think in the spirit of the Greeks. When the debating society of Georgetown College searched for a name for the debating union in 1830, "Philodemic," formed from two Greek roots symbolic for *love of oratory* was the natural choice.[4] The activity of the Philodemic followed a wave of interest in debating that was sparked by the rise in intercollegiate debating during the 1890s.

The Society's entry into the intercollegiate debate arena gained momentum with the support of public debates on campus in the early 1890s. The members of the Philodemic and the younger debate society for freshmen, the Philonomosian, impressed faculty and students alike with extraordinary speaking and logical skills during intrasociety debates.[5] An affirmative and a negative team were organized informally at the meetings to discuss topics such as the morality of capital punishment.[6] For the formal public debates, participants were elected by the Philodemic and the debates were extravagantly planned.[7] Songs performed by the Glee and Mandolin Clubs made the public debates both thought inspiring and entertaining.[8] The participants in the debates had a larger audience to persuade than any member of the Philodemic of old and they rose to the occasion. The improvement of the manner in which the debates were prepared and delivered inspired the new members of the Philodemic and earned the respect of the members of the community within and outside of the University.[9] The *Georgetown College Journal* remarked that Father E.I. Devitt, the newly elected director of the Philodemic, had "put new life into the society."[10] More importantly, the success of the public debates in the early nineties gave Philodemic members the confidence to accept unanimously their first major intercollegiate debate challenge from the Fulton Debate Society of Boston College in December 1894.[11]

Apart from the internal development of the Philodemic Society, national interest in college debating affected Georgetown's new intercollegiate stance.[12] By 1894, Yale, Princeton, and Harvard had held intercollegiate debate committees in New York to discuss plans for the formats of their debates for the coming year.[13] They agreed that each side should have three speeches similar to the format of the Yale-Princeton debate of 1893.[14] This became the model for most subsequent intercollegiate debates.

The school spirit and rivalry that had been bred by the increase in intercollegiate athletic contests during the 1880s clearly spilled over into the realm of the intellectual contests.[15] The Law School Society of Georgetown University, not affiliated with the Philodemic but having a profound effect on the Philodemic debates nevertheless, had successfully faced challenges from the Columbia Law School in 1894 and 1895.[16] In the Midwest, the University of Michigan had agreed to debate the University of Wisconsin.[17] The success of a college's debating union was taken very seriously as a measure of the academic quality of the school. Yet, as intercollegiate athletic contests of the 1880s raised the level of athletics, intercollegiate debating was expected to have the same constructive effect on academics.[18] Georgetown, with its traditional emphasis on philosophy and an intercollegiate athletic program in dire straits as a result of the death of a student athlete after an 1894 Thanksgiving Day football game,[19] was an institution likely to be swept up in the tide of debating that had already covered much of the nation. The *College Journal* astutely noted this trend throughout the country:

> And so the fad is on, the epidemic is spreading, and very soon there will not be a university, college, academy or even a bit of a university extension, that will not have its schedule for debates, as it now has for football and baseball contests. The departure is in the right direction...[20]

The "departures" from the emphasis on the intercollegiate athletic contests to the intercollegiate intellectual jousts brought the Philodemic Society into its first confrontation with Boston College on May 1, 1895. Accompanied by Fr. Devitt, seniors James W. Burke, Charles E. Roach, and J. Neal Power made the trip to Boston by train to represent the Philodemic and Georgetown College on the negative side of the question: "Resolved, That the Present Income Tax is Equitable."[21] On an extravagantly decorated stage, these three men elected by the Society to represent Georgetown upheld the Philodemic motto of "Eloquence and Truth" before an appreciative audience. After the first affirmative speaker for Boston College finished, James W. Burke opened the era of intercollegiate debate for the Philodemic with these words:

> Mr. Chairman, Ladies and Gentlemen. Although the time allotted to us for the discussion of this important question is very limited, we trench upon it to thank you for this reception and to express publicly our appreciation...We are deeply grateful to the representatives of Boston College for their hospitality; and sincerely hope these intercollegiate contests may be here after characterized by the same friendly spirit which has been attendant upon their inauguration.[22]

Although the debate was considered a "friendly" affair, it was very competitive. The affirmative's stance was that the present income tax was equitable because it demanded more from those who have the most property.[23] Charles E. Roach, the second negative speaker for the Philodemic, noted that the exemption of incomes of $4000 and under from taxation made the income tax unfair. Roach declared, "The man of moderate means, as the wealthy, must be taxed proportionately without favoritism to individual or class. Are we to exempt $4000, creating thereby a numerous class of fairly well to do, who pay no part of the tax whatever?"[24] The last speaker for the negative, J. Neal Power, demonstrated eloquence and persuasion in the concluding speech of the debate with an impassioned appeal for the American sense of equality:

> Ladies and gentlemen, if our fair country would continue to prosper, it can only be through means that are just and equitable. I say by means that are American! For America's first principle is equality. Equality of privileges, equality of duties, equality of burdens! And if this be the directing and pervading spirit of our laws, all will be well, and this great nation of ours, conceived in the light and spirit of independent equality and nourished upon the bosom of uncompromising justice, will triumph over her enemies and remove any menace that may or can threaten her permanent welfare and continued prosperity.[25]

After the conclusion of the debate, the three-judge panel deliberated for twenty minutes before the chairman, Rev. Fr. Conaty, announced the decision in favor of Georgetown.[26] Fr. Devitt and the debaters received much deserved congratulations from the many Georgetown supporters in the audience and from the Boston College supporters who appreciated the magnificent showing of the Philodemic.[27]

Despite the Philodemic's success in this early intercollegiate debate, the Society would not debate another school again until 1906. The main focus of the Philodemic's activities from 1895 to 1906 were confined to public debates on the campus.

The Merrick Debate was the gem of these latter contests held by the Philodemic. Four debaters, two on each side of a political resolution, were selected by the members of the Philodemic to participate for the high honor of the Merrick Medal.[28] The judges of the debate would select the most outstanding speaker, usually on the winning team, to receive the medal. The prize was founded in 1874 in response to the suggestion put forth by University President Fr. Patrick Healy, S.J., to create an incentive to stimulate the oratorical abilities of members of the Philodemic.[29] The medal was named after its donor, the Honorable Richard T. Merrick.[30] The debate was traditionally held in February, close to Washington's Birthday—a holiday of great importance to the original Philodemic of the 1830s.[31] By Merrick's request, the announcement of the winner was to be made on Commencement Day.[32]

In the middle 1890s, no other event on Georgetown's campus, with the exception of the Commencement, was as prestigious as the Merrick Debate. In February of 1895, the *Georgetown College Journal* introduced its "News of the Month" section with a reminder that "It is the month of the Merrick Debate *and* of Washington's Birthday."[33] The 1897 Merrick Debate over the question of whether we should intervene in Cuba was attended by over eight hundred distinguished people from the nation's capital.[34] The judges, United States Senator Thomas H. Carter, Solicitor General of the United States Holmes Conrad, and Librarian of Congress Ainsworth R. Spoffered, were men of great prestige whose stature added to and reflected the importance of the prized medal.[35] Quite simply, the Merrick Medal was the most prestigious award to be won by an undergraduate student of Georgetown College.[36]

The selection process for the Merrick Debate was not an obligation that the members of the Philodemic took lightly. The four participants in the debate had to be members of the Philodemic, and had to be approved by the members of the Society. The topics selected for the debates were suggested at Philodemic meetings, and mini-debates during the meetings occurred over which topic should be chosen.[37] After the turn of the century, a tradition caught on of selecting two participants for the debate at the last meeting of the Spring and the other two during the Fall.[38]

Those selected to participate in the Merrick Debate were the four most eloquent members of the Society who had not previously participated in the contest. (Note: The four places in the Merrick Debate were usually occupied by seniors although the Junior class occasionally had a member in the debate.)[39] The winner of the medal in 1894, Robert J. Collier of the class of '94, carried his eloquence even further when he penned a poetic verse entitled "Sons of Georgetown" after his graduation.[40] The poem by this medal-winning member of the Philodemic quickly became a favorite of the students and faculty and was adopted as the Alma Mater Song.[41]

Even those participants who did not achieve Collier's preeminence quickly became on-campus celebrities. Their portraits and speeches filled the pages of the *Georgetown College Journal* during the month of the debate.[42]

The importance of the medal seemed to diminish somewhat as more opportunities to attend and participate in debates became available. The founding of the Hamilton Medal in 1909, the formation of the Edwards Douglas White Debating Society in 1912, and of the Gaston Debating Society the following year all contributed to this trend.[43] The Philodemic's emphasis also shifted from the Merrick Debate to intercollegiate debate by 1910. The announcement of the winner during this shift was made immediately following the debate.[44] The enthusiasm for debate was no longer channeled into a single event. The Gaston and White Societies would face each other at the end of the year for a debating contest which undoubtedly took some of the spotlight from the Philodemic's main event. In 1930, the widow of Chief Justice Edward White donated the White Medal to be given to the best individual debater in the contest.[45] This first debate filled Gaston Hall and received the attention of the media.[46] Despite the relative decline in the Merrick Medal's prestige after 1910, the event and the medal were still widely respected until the debates were discontinued in the middle 1970s.

Although the Philodemic was the primary focus of undergraduate debate, the accomplishments of the Law School Debating Society of Georgetown University from 1895–1906 had a profound effect on the history of debating at Georgetown and on the Philodemic. During this era, the Law School Debating Society was more visible than the Philodemic with its frequent intercollegiate and public debates.

The Law School Debating Society was the debating power other schools had to reckon with in the late 1890s. They successfully defeated Columbia University Law School in 1894 and 1895, and they bested the New York University debaters in April of 1897.[47] Unfortunately, the Law School lost to the same New York team on June 5, 1897 in the rematch or "return" debate.[48] In the constructive spirit of the activity, the Law School Debating Society honored the request of New York to debate again. The loss, while on the affirmative side of the question: "Resolved, That the injunction in the Debs case was properly granted," marked the first time a Georgetown team had suffered defeat in an intercollegiate debate.[49]

The preliminary stages of the intercollegiate debate demonstrated the debates' importance and prestige. Both the Law School Debating Society and the Philodemic had an Intercollegiate Debate Committee that considered every invitation from a debating union.[50] During a long negotiation process, representatives from both schools would talk about the date and place of the debate as well as the topic and judges. Disagreements were not easily settled. A rift between the Columbia Law School Debating Union and the Law School Debating Society was so deep that arrangements for a third debate between the two lasted for over four years.[51] In February of 1899, the negotiators from the Law School Debating Society finally received the assurance they wanted from Columbia that the decision of the judges would be accepted as final.[52] After the 1895 debate, Columbia students and faculty "vehemently denounced" a unanimous decision of the three judges despite the fact that one of the latter had been picked by Columbia.[53] The intercollegiate debate was obviously one of high stakes and incidentally one that Georgetown won again from Columbia in April of 1899 with another unanimous decision.[54]

The selection of the debaters to represent the respective schools of the debate was also a tedious process. The procedure which the Law School Society used to determine who would represent them in the Columbia Debate was similar to the process employed by the Philodemic. Those who wished the honor of representing Georgetown in these important contests had to earn it by trying out for one of three slots two months before the actual debate.[55] The prospective intercollegiate debater had to defend Georgetown's side of the resolution in a ten-minute speech before the members of the Society.[56] The Society then voted for the three debaters whom they wished to represent the debating union and Georgetown. In 1899, nine members of the Law School Debating Society tried out for three spots on the affirmative side of the question of the Columbia Debate: "Resolved, That the Right of Suffrage Should be Restricted by an Educational Qualification."[57]

Due to the limited number of intercollegiate debates (at most, Georgetown would debate other schools only twice a year in the late 1890s/early 1900s) the number of members in the Society who participated in these debates was not great. However, the Law School Debating Society kept most of its members involved in active debating, as did the Philodemic, with monthly public debates.[58] These debates, judged by Washington D.C.'s dignitaries such as justices of the United States Supreme Court, were well attended and were often more competitive than the intercollegiate debates.[59]

At the turn of the century, interest in debate was so intense in the Law School that the Debating Society began to hold weekly public debates, several of them in Gaston Hall on the main campus.[60] During this period, success for the Society in the intercollegiate realm was diminishing. Georgetown's debaters fell from good graces with losses to the University of Wisconsin in 1903, to George Washington University in 1904 and 1905, and with a demoralizing loss to Boston University in 1906.[61] The Law School Debating Society was split into the Junior Society for first and second year students and the Senior Society for third and fourth year students when the members adopted a resolution governing the Debate Society passed by the law school faculty in 1906.[62] The emphasis on the rivalry between the two societies soon became the focal point of debate at the Law School.[63] In the wake of the School's lack of extramural activity, the Philodemic had reclaimed its position as the preeminent debating society of Georgetown.

Other factors contributed to the growth in the strength of the Philodemic, most notably the growth of the College in the early 1900s. As the College grew stronger, so did the Philodemic.[64] In 1895, there were twenty-five members of the College who received their bachelor's degree. By 1904, that figure had more than doubled.[65] The members of the Philodemic sought to change major articles in the previous constitution with which they had been dissatisfied.[66] The Constitution, adopted on October 27, 1901, required applicants for membership to receive the approval of two-thirds of the current members and limited the number of members for a given term.[67] Public debates were being held more frequently by the Philodemic and a wider range of topics was being discussed. Another medal was founded in 1909 when alumnus and Law School Dean George E. Hamilton donated the Hamilton Medal to"encourage a more thorough cultivation of extemporaneous speech and debate" among members of the Philodemic.[68] The formation of the Edward Douglas White Debating Society as a debating union for sophomores in 1912, named for the Georgetown alumnus and Chief Justice of the Supreme Court, and the Gaston Debating Society for freshmen, named for Georgetown's first student, William Gaston, provided the Philodemic with experienced juniors who made the Society stronger.[69] In addition to the traditional Gaston-White Debate, the White Society began a three-year series of debates against Holy Cross in 1914.[70] The Gaston and White Societies would, in the 1930s, represent Georgetown University in debates against the less powerful Hughes Debating Society of Fordham and St. Josephs College.[71]

Intercollegiate debate was an activity that soon became the

Philodemic's special domain. A 1906 "Resolution Governing Intercollegiate Debates," approved by the president of Georgetown and the board, was adopted by the university's debating societies in order to establish "university teams" in which representatives of Georgetown University could be drawn from all of the campus debating societies.[72] This resolution was not as revolutionary as one might expect, since the Philodemic generally produced the best debaters Georgetown had to offer during this era. In 1910, a "university team" resumed its debate against Boston College and was defeated, but they defeated Boston College in the following year. By 1912, the annual debates with Boston College's Fulton Debating Society had become completely a Philodemic event.[73]

The most significant factor in the rise of the Philodemic's prestige on and off campus was the direction and guidance of Father Toohey which began in 1912.[74] Under his guidance, the Philodemic became better organized as it held more meetings and became the most prominent debating union in the country.[75] The "golden age" of the Philodemic was about to begin. In April of 1913, the Georgetown University team, two of the three being Philodemic members, defeated Cornell, and the Philodemic was defeated by Boston College in the Fulton Debating Society's first visit to Georgetown.[76] Debating two nonlocal schools during one year, much less in one month, was unprecedented. On May 9, 1915, the judges of the Philodemic debate with the Fulton Society unanimously decided in favor of Georgetown.[77] Less than one week later, the Philodemic defeated the Georgetown Law School.[78]

The Philodemic defeated teams from Lafayette, Johns Hopkins, Pennsylvania State, and Washington and Jefferson College between 1916–18.[79] In 1920, Georgetown defeated the fabled Columbia University debate team that had upset Harvard.[80] With the defeat of Yale on March 22, 1922, the Philodemic began its seventeen-year unbeaten streak under Fr. Toohey.[81] The *Hoya* noted the eloquent style of the Philodemic as the decisive factor in the contest:

> The Georgetown team clearly outargued the Yale team and the decision of the judges was four for Georgetown and one for Yale. The Yale team used a direct conversational style, bringing their

facts in simple, straightforward fashion, with well thought out arguments. Georgetown's debaters, however, were more brilliant, and put over their points with greater polish and thought.[82]

The seventeen-year streak included three more defeats of Yale. The year 1930, the centennial of the Philodemic, was marked by the defeat of Princeton and Harvard within one month.[83] The Philodemic did not lose until March 7, 1939, when the College of Florida won the ballots of two members of the three-judge panel.[84] Even in defeat, the Philodemic emerged from all of their debates under the guidance of Father Toohey as champions in their quest for eloquence and truth.

Although the members of the Philodemic during the Toohey era were perhaps the greatest speech champions Georgetown has ever produced on the basis of their win-loss record, the prestige of the art of eloquence and rhetoric was lessened by the resurgence of popularity of athletics. A *Hoya* editorial cartoon showing an immense monument to college athletics dwarfing the small statue of academia demonstrated how intellectual pursuits had become swallowed up in the "Boola-Boola" of the 1920s and 30s.[85] Fr. William Coleman Nevils, S.J., president of the University in 1930, remarked in a letter to the widow of Chief Justice White who had just sponsored the White Medal to be given to the outstanding debater in the Gaston-White Debate, "our public debates do not usually attract large crowds."[86] Interest in debate had once again subsided. Would it be permanent?

Perhaps not. The impact of the loss of debate's mass appeal must not be overexaggerated. Debate has never regained the popularity it enjoyed at the turn of the century but all this signifies is that debate methods have changed. The one contest against one school per year would evolve into the debate "tournament"—a series of eight debates against eight other schools in the span of two days. We could speculate as to why the debates from 1894 to 1939 were marked by so much eloquence when compared to those of today. Was it because the debaters of the past had fewer intercollegiate debates to prepare for and thus they could afford to devote more time to each speech? Such reasoning is shallow. In many respects, it is unfair to compare debates and debaters of our times with debates and debaters of yesterday since changed conditions demanded new forms. The modern Philodemic need not bow too low to their predecessors. But they and we should admire the Philodemic of old for their commitment to eloquently expressed ideals that should never be forgotten.

Notes

1. *Constitution of the Philodemic Society Adopted in 1901 (Revised 1911)*, Georgetown University Archives (hereafter GUA), Philodemic Debating Society, Box 8 of 11.

2. "College Notes," *Georgetown College Journal* (hereafter *GCJ*), vol. 30, December 1902, p. 139.

3. Ibid., loc cit.

4. James K. Lynch, "The Philodemic Debating Society," *GCJ*, vol. 39, October 1911, pp. 63–64.

5. *GCJ*, vol. 23, December 1894, p. 29.

6. *GCJ*, vol. 23, January 1895, p. 42.

7. "College Notes," *GCJ*, vol. 31, March 1903, p. 275.

8. Ibid., loc cit.

9. *GCJ*, vol. 23, December 1894, p. 23.

10. Ibid., loc cit.

11. Ibid., loc cit.

12. "Intercollegiate Debates," vol. 23, January 1894, p. 65.

13. Ibid., p. 66.

14. Ibid., loc cit.

15. Ibid., p. 65.

16. "Columbia Debate," *GCJ*, vol. 27, April 1899, p. 322.

17. "Intercollegiate Debates," p. 66.

18. Ibid., loc cit.

19. *GCJ*, vol. 26, January 1898, p. 177.

20. "Intercollegiate Debates," p. 66.

21. "Intercollegiate Debate: Georgetown–Boston College," *GCJ*, vol. 23, May 1895, p. 83.

22. Ibid., loc cit.

23. Ibid., p. 84.

24. Ibid., p. 85.

25. Ibid., p. 86.

26. Ibid., p. 86.

27. Ibid., p. 86.

28. "News of the Month," *GCJ*, vol. 24, January 1896.

29. Lynch, pp. 64–65.

30. Ibid., loc cit.

31. Ibid., loc cit.

32. Ibid., loc cit.

33. "News of the Month," *GCJ*, vol. 23, February 1895.

34. "Merrick Debate–1897," *GCJ*, vol. 25, March 1897.

35. Ibid., loc cit.

36. *GCJ*, vol. 27, December 1898, p. 149.

37. "Merrick Debate," *GCJ*, vol. 24, January 1896.

38. Lynch, pp. 64–65.

39. "Merrick Debate," *GCJ*, vol. 26, December 1897, p. 133.

40. *GCJ*, vol. 31, June 1903.

41. Ibid., loc cit.

42. The *College Journal* from 1895 to 1915 carried the full text of the Merrick Debate. Many times, portraits of the debaters accompanied the texts.

43. See notes 67 and 68.

44. "Robert J. Riley Wins Highest of Georgetown's Debating Honors," *The Hoya*, vol. 1, February 19, 1920, p. 1.

45. "Edward R. Glavin Wins First White Debate," *The Washington Star*, February 28, 1930, GUA, White Society, Box 1, folder 4.

46. "White Medal Given to Albany Student," *Washington Post*, February 28, 1930, GUA, White Society, Box 1, folder 4.

47. "The New York Debate," *GCJ*, vol. 25, April 1897.

48. "The Second New York Debate," *GCJ*, vol. 25, June 1897, p. 111.

49. Ibid., loc cit.

50. "Law School Notes," *GCJ*, vol. 27, February 1899, p. 245. This article demonstrates the considerations of the committee very well. Most articles submitted to the *Journal* announcing Philodemic or Law debates were submitted by such committees.

51. Ibid., loc cit.

52. Ibid., loc cit.

53. Ibid., loc cit.

54. "Law School Notes," *GCJ*, vol. 27, June 1899, p. 415.

55. "Columbia Debate," *GCJ*, vol. 27, April 1899, p. 322.

56. Ibid., loc cit.

57. Ibid., loc cit.

58. "University Notes," *GCJ*, vol. 30, December 1901, p. 198.

59. Ibid., loc cit.

60. "Law School Debate," *GCJ*, vol. 35, February 1907, p. 231.

61. "Wisconsin Debate," *GCJ*, vol. 31, May 1903, p. 429. Wisconsin defeated Georgetown on the negative side of the question: "Resolved, That Compulsory Arbitration Between Capital and Labor is Expedient."

"Law School Notes," *GCJ*, vol. 33, January 1905, p. 176. After winning six straight debates against George Washington, the Law School lost two in a row.

"Debating Society," *GCJ*, vol. 34, May 1906, p. 408. Boston University won a unanimous decision of the judges.

62. "Resolutions governing Law School Debates," reprinted *GCJ*, vol. 35, December 1906, p. 140.

63. "Law School Debate" (see note 60).

64. Lynch, p. 63.

65. *GCJ*, vol. 29, October 1900, p. 24. Over one hundred members of the class of '04 entered the Hilltop at the beginning of the '00–'01 term.

66. *GCJ*, vol. 26, January 1898, p. 177.

67. Rev. Mark McNeal, S.J., "The Philodemic Society," *GCJ*, vol. 39, October 1910, p. 29.

68. "Philodemic Society," *GCJ*, vol. 41, December 1912, p. 197.

69. John G. Masterson, "Georgetown 1912–1939," *GCJ*, vol. 67, May 1939, p. 475.

70. "Holy Cross Debate," *GCJ*, vol. 45, February 1917, p. 289.

71. "White Society to debate Fordham," *Washington Post*, March 10, 1935. GUA, White Debating Society, Box 1, folder 4.
Program for the Intercollegiate Debate between St. Josephs College and Georgetown University as represented by the Creation and Gaston Debating Societies, GUA, ibid., loc. cit.

72. "Resolutions Governing Intercollegiate Debates," reprinted in *GCJ*, vol. 35, December 1906, p. 139.

73. "The Boston College–Georgetown College Debate," *GCJ*, vol. 40, April 1912, p. 369.

74. Don Bertaut, "Father Toohey, G.U.'s Grand Old Man," *The Hoya*, vol. 29, May 7, 1948, p. 2.

75. "Philodemic Society," *GCJ*, vol. 42, January 1913, p. 270.

76. "Debating with Cornell and Boston," *GCJ*, vol. 42, May 1913, p. 525.

77. "The Boston Debate," *GCJ*, vol. 43, May 1915, p. 524.

78. "The Law Debate," ibid., p. 525.

79. "Johns Hopkins Debate," *GCJ*, vol. 44, March 1916, p. 373. "Philodemic," *GCJ*, vol. 45, February 1917, p. 289. "Washington and Lee Debate," *GCJ*, vol. 45, May 1917, p. 430. "Double Debate with Lafayette," ibid., p. 432.

80. "Georgetown Wins Debate against Columbia University," *The Hoya*, vol. 1, March 17, 1920, p. 1.

81. "Yale Debating Team Defeated," *The Hoya*, vol. 3, March 23, 1922, p. 1.

82. Ibid.

83. *Philodemic Results under Father Toohey*, GUA, Philodemic Debating Society, Box 9, folder 1.

84. Ibid., loc cit.

85. "A Slighted Demigod," *The Hoya*, vol. 1, February 26, 1920, p. 3.

86. Letter from William Coleman Nevils, S.J. to the widow of Chief Justice White, GUA, White Debating Society, Box 1, folder 4.

A Glimpse of the Philodemic Debating Society (1938–1968)

Marc B. Stahl

I. The State of the Philodemic in 1938

In 1938, Georgetown University's Philodemic Debating Society was experiencing its "golden period." Fr. John J. Toohey had served as the Society's moderator for over twenty-five years, leading Georgetown debaters to unparalleled levels of success.[1]

The traditions of the Society remained intact. A formally elected set of officers, yearly banquets, selective membership, adherence to parliamentary procedure, and an array of expensive awards characterized the Philodemic.[2] Its activities at this time could be divided into two primary areas: intrasociety debates and intercollegiate debates.

The intrasociety debates were usually part of the proceedings of the Philodemic Debating Society. On Tuesday evenings, between 7:00 P.M. and 7:30 P.M., the students and Fr. Toohey would meet in the Philodemic Room on the second floor of the Healy Building. These meetings were governed by parliamentary procedure. The president of the Society would call the meeting to order and the secretary read the roll call.[3]

Approximately twenty-five students attended each meeting. Occasionally, members were "dropped for excessive absences,"[4] but few students missed more than a meeting or two a year.[5]

After roll call, the secretary reported the events of the last meeting. Additions to or corrections of the minutes were approved by the Society as a whole. On the last Tuesday of the month, the treasurer reported on financial matters.[6] After the Society dealt with this business, the weekly debate took place.

Fr. Toohey appointed four debaters divided into two member teams, one affirmative and one negative, and suggested and approved a topic at least a week in advance. He might choose an official critic, although the entire Society was involved in commentary after the debate.[7]

Debates usually centered on current affairs. Options for government action were discussed. As events in Europe steamed up prior to and during World War II, the resolutions often prescribed courses of action for the United States in its foreign policy. Some of the topics debated included "Resolved: that in the case Germany declares war; the United States should join forces with England and France," "Resolved: that the United States government control [its foreign exchange of] munitions," "Resolved: that collective security should be revived by the leading powers in the world today," "Resolved: that the government's line of actions in the sale of airplanes to France was justified," "Resolved: that Congress should lift the embargo on the shipment of arms to the belligerents in the present European war," "Resolved: that the United States should have an independent air force, coordinated with the Army and Navy," "Resolved: that after the present war there should be an international police force to preserve the peace of the world," "Resolved: that post-war Germany should be divided into three parts according to the plan of Mr. Sumner Welles," and "Resolved: that the Lend Lease policy should be continued with Great Britain after the defeat of Germany."[8] Some of these topics were debated more than once. Many similar topics were also discussed.

Despite the importance of the war, however, the Philodemic did not limit itself to foreign affairs issues. Domestic policy provided fertile ground for many debates. "Resolved: that the United States should cease to spend public funds for the stimulation of business," "Resolved: that the tax on payroll should be repealed," "Resolved: that the president of the United States should be elected for a single term of six years," "Resolved: that the United States government should own and operate the railroads," "Resolved: that chain stores are detrimental to the best interests of the American public," "Resolved: that the Wagner Labor Act should be radically amended," "Resolved: that the tenure of office of the president be limited to two terms by amendment," and "Resolved: that medicine should be socialized" were some of the topics discussed between 1938 and 1945. [9]

The affirmative would initiate the debate with an eight to ten minute speech outlining the harms incurred by the present system and explaining how the resolution could redress those difficulties. The first negative speaker would then respond with another "constructive" of eight to ten minutes. The second affirmative and second negative constructives followed. The first negative rebuttal occurred immediately after the second negative constructive. All rebuttals were limited to five minutes. The first affirmative, second negative, and second affirmative rebuttals followed the first negative rebuttal.[10] The speeches can be charted out as follows:

1st affirmative constructive 8–10 minutes;
1st negative constructive 8–10 minutes;
2nd affirmative constructive 8–10 minutes;
2nd negative constructive 8–10 minutes;

1st negative rebuttal 5 minutes;
1st affirmative rebuttal 5 minutes;
2nd negative rebuttal 5 minutes;
2nd affirmative rebuttal 5 minutes.

Sometimes the procedure was altered. Occasionally, only two debaters would face each other. Sometimes three debaters would participate on each team. Speeches could be shortened or lengthened at will. The procedure remained standard throughout these years.

A debate might last an hour, after which critiques were given. Formal procedure called for a standing vote on the merits of the question, to be followed by a secret vote on the merits of the debaters. After the votes, open discussions took place. After these discussions, Fr. Toohey frequently made concluding remarks on the style and substance of the debate.[11]

The proceedings did not conclude with the debate. Proposals for new members were offered at this time. Sometimes proposals and elections occurred at the same meeting and sometimes they were separated by a week.[12] As most members were selected at the beginning of the year, membership elections usually did not follow debates.

After membership issues were decided, Fr. Toohey selected the next topic and the speakers to participate in that debate. Then various committees might report on their activities. Intercollegiate debates, fund-raisers, social events, and other miscellaneous business were considered by the entire Society.[13] Finally, the president declared: "All in favor of adjournment, please rise!"[14] With these words, the meeting officially ended.

This procedure for the conduct of meetings continued for decades. Parliamentary debates served as a foundation for the Philodemic. These sessions, however, were not the only activity in which Philodemic members participated. The program of intercollegiate debates was extremely important and probably more visible. At Georgetown, the debates took place in Gaston Hall. These competitions often received major publicity in national newspapers.[15] The judges were respected community leaders. For example: Justice Harold Stevens, Paul D. Spearman (an assistant on Capitol Hill), and G. Gould Lincoln (a political writer for *The Washington Star*) judged the 1940 Georgetown–Princeton debate. Chief Justice D. Lawrence Groner (U.S. Court of Appeals), Judge Charles S. Hatfield (U.S. Court of Customs and Patent Appeals), and G. Gould Lincoln judged a 1941 competition between Georgetown and Harvard.[16] The debaters dressed in black tie and the events opened with "The March of the Philodemic Society." The emphasis on eloquence and dignity overwhelmed all else.

Three to eight intercollegiate competitions occurred yearly. In 1938, Georgetown debaters defeated teams representing Bates, Bucknell, Princeton, and South Carolina. In addition, some no-decision debates were held. In 1940, Georgetown defeated Harvard, Pennsylvania, Princeton, and Vermont. In 1942, Georgetown teams defeated Bucknell, the College of Florida, Princeton, Virginia, and William and Mary and lost to Harvard University and the University of Pennsylvania.[17] Sometimes these teams competed against Georgetown twice in one year, once at Georgetown and once at their own campus.

Fr. Toohey excelled as a debate coach for public competitions. Between 1924 and 1938, Georgetown University's Philodemic Debating Society went without a single defeat in approximately forty events. Even after a loss to the College of Florida in 1939, the Philodemic continued to rack up victories.[18]

In January of each year, Fr. Toohey selected his intercollegiate debating team from the members of the Philodemic. As many as twenty students would try out for the varsity team. In a series of intrasociety competitions, they were given a subject and half an hour to prepare a short speech. After Fr. Toohey had satisfied his interests, eight students would be chosen to face opponents from other schools.[19]

The debates usually occurred during the spring semester. One resolution was selected for a series of competitions between various schools, and Georgetown students rarely debated other topics. As was true with the intrasociety debates, most resolutions could be described as policy options in the arena of current events. Examples of topics debated include "Resolved: that the United States should follow a policy of strict economic and military isolation towards all nations outside the Western Hemisphere engaged in armed international or civil conflict," "Resolved: that the United Nations should form a permanent union," "Resolved: that the nations of the Western Hemisphere should enter into a permanent alliance," and "Resolved: that the federal government should regulate by law all labor unions in the United States."[20]

The Society participated also in public, intrasquad debates. The most notable among these was the annual Merrick Debate, the winner of which received the Merrick Debating Medal. The award was established in 1874 by Richard T. Merrick, L.L.D. '73, a former Philodemic debater. The competitors were selected solely from the Society. The debate took place in Gaston Hall.[21] Although it was usually a November or December event, the 1939 Merrick Debate was postponed until January due to the wishes of students.[22] From that year on, the Merrick Debate became a second semester event.

The individual declared winner received the five-ounce gold

medal and was recognized as the best debater at Georgetown University. The debate occurred in Gaston Hall. The intercollegiate resolution served as the topic, as the participants' familiarity with it produced the best possible competition. The format involved ten-minute constructives and five-minute rebuttals, the whole debate lasting a little over one hour.[23]

Another intrasociety, public debate was established in 1909 by George Ernest Hamilton, former dean of the Georgetown University Law School and former Philodemic member. The Hamilton Medal was awarded annually to the member with the best "facility of speech, delivery and self-control" in an extemporaneous debate competition.[24] Three students were on each team and policy questions were debated, but the resolutions differed from the intercollegiate topic. The topic discussed in the 1940 Hamilton Debate, for example, was "Resolved: that the Committee for Investigation of Unamerican Activities should be abolished." The debate occurred in Copley Formal or Gaston Hall, depending on the year, and was not nearly as popular as the Merrick Debate.[25]

II. The World War II Lapse in Activities

As the United States entered World War II, the activity of the Philodemic Debating Society declined. Many students left Georgetown and fought in the war. Students who remained became part of an irregular and accelerated curriculum. Opportunities for the development of the Society decreased. Intercollegiate competitions became less frequent and the Hamilton Debate was temporarily halted after 1942.[26]

After May 1943, the Philodemic did not meet until November 16, 1943. This gap is especially significant in light of the accelerated academic calendar, by which students remained at Georgetown throughout the summer.[27]

Finally, on November 16, 1943, the Philodemic experienced a formal reorganization. Most of the members had graduated in 1943, leaving only a handful to conduct Society events. The vice-president, serving as president pro-tempore, personally nominated and signed petitions of membership for a few new members. In desperate need of participating students, the Philodemic accepted members from all classes. The war-time crunch squeezed out the Gaston and White Debating Societies.[28]

The November 16 reorganization did not last long. Few students joined the Society and after a short meeting on November 23, 1943, it did not meet until January 11, 1944, when the Philodemic formally initiated the year's proceedings.[29]

Membership problems continued and Fr. Toohey asked debaters to contact "interested individuals who would be prospective members of the Philodemic Society."[30] Two new members were unanimously accepted at the January 18 meeting, and Fr. Toohey announced a topic and four participants for a debate on January 25, 1944.[31] Despite expectations, Georgetown did not witness the scheduled debate.

The plans fell through and the Society remained out of session until March 21, 1944. After March, however, the Philodemic met for sessions biweekly through August. During that summer, at least seventeen new members were admitted. Not a single scheduled debate was cancelled and the 1944–45 academic year commenced with normal. weekly meetings.[32]

Fr. Toohey became ill in early 1944, and this contributed to the break in activities between January and March 1944. The war, however, was the major reason for delays in Philodemic activities.[33] The conflict caused membership problems by pulling away students and shifting academic schedules. As *The Hoya* lamented in 1944:

> The tradition of the Philodemic Society is a proud one of great achievement through slightly less than a century of our nation's history. It is venerable with names and illustrious Georgetown men throughout the entire period of its history....Georgetown men owe something to those other Hilltoppers of days ago. It is our duty during these terrible days when all things seem to crumble to hold together what we have and hand it to our successors. Georgetown men have met and mastered worse days and the least that can be expected of G.U. during World War II is that we will not let them down.[34]

Eventually, the Philodemic did come together. No intercollegiate debates and no Hamilton Debates occurred through the end of the war, but parliamentary debates continued. By the beginning of the 1945–46 academic year, membership had risen to such a level that freshmen were again excluded and a Gaston-White Debating Society was reformed.[35]

Even the Merrick Debate continued. In fact, after the 1944 Merrick, one of the judges publicly congratulated Fr. Toohey and the entire Society for continuing the tradition under pressing wartime conditions.[36] The Philodemic Debating Society had recovered from the war.

III. Intercollegiate Tournaments

Despite a resurgence in Philodemic activities, Georgetown did not participate in any more intercollegiate debates during the remainder of Fr. Toohey's tenure as moderator. On October 14, 1947, for the first time in thirty-five years, the Philodemic Debating Society convened without Fr. Toohey. He continued as a philosophy professor at Georgetown, but he was no longer involved with the Philodemic.[37]

Fr. Lawrence C. McHugh served as moderator of the Society during the 1947–48 academic year. Weekly meetings and parliamentary debates continued as they had before.[38] Additionally, Georgetown participated in its first intercollegiate debates since 1943. Teams from Columbia and Princeton debated Georgetown on the topic "Resolved: that a federal world government should be established."[39]

Despite the worthwhile nature of these events, debate was changing. The grand, traditional one school versus another standoffs were being phased out in favor of a different form of competition—the tournament. Traditional intercollegiate debates were occasions of great formality. Large audiences would view only two teams, dressed in black tie, in one debate. A tournament, however, may involve hundreds of schools and hundreds of debates over the course of several days. Each two-member team participates in six to eight preliminary debate rounds. The teams with the best records in the preliminary rounds go on to elimination rounds (e.g., quarterfinals, semifinals, and finals).[40]

As a result of the change in format, intercollegiate debate shifted from being a public to a private event. At first, the final rounds of tournaments replaced the traditional debates. Major newspapers carried stories about tournaments and participants in final debates, the impressive nature of the judging panels for final rounds matched that of previous intercollegiate debates, and the general focus of attention from the community was the final round.[41]

A tournament has so many debates occurring at once, however, that it becomes more of a private function. There is no large audience in the preliminary rounds. In most of these debates there are only four debaters and one judge. Only occasionally are there observers for preliminary rounds. If there are thirty teams, fifteen debates are occurring at any one time. Multiply this by eight rounds and there are 120 debates at a small to medium tournament in the preliminary rounds alone. The debate tournament does not occur before the general public.

As a result, style is deemphasized for substance. The students are not persuading a large crowd; they are arguing in front of a judge who is usually a debate coach well versed in the topic. The debate becomes extremely technical as the judge is concerned with the substantive issues.

Eventually, the entire activity, including attire, social events, final rounds, became more casual and more issues-oriented. Delivery was never ignored, as a basic level of clarity and persuasion is essential to a good debate. Today, however, debaters are more concerned with the substance of arguments such as valuing research and critical thinking skills, than were past debaters. [42]

As evidence of the transformations, an observer can examine research efforts made by debaters. In the late 1940s and the early 1950s, the Philodemic purchased debate manuals from a national debate organization in order to acquire evidence. In October 1950, Fr. Gallagher "suggested that members not rely on the debate manuals, but that they should do their own independent research."[43] It was not until November of that year, after the Philodemic had competed at tournaments at Vermont and South Carolina, that the Society formed a central research file on the national topic, integrating their efforts.[44] The topic, "Resolved: that the non-communist nations should form a new international organization,"[45] was certainly a hot issue in 1950. Much was written on the matter and many possibilities for different types of international organizations existed.[46] The extremely tardy and limited research effort indicates that a solid understanding of the issues was deemed unnecessary. This is one indication of how intercollegiate debate has evolved since the 1950s.

The Philodemic Society has slowly evolved with the rest of the intercollegiate forensics community. In the fall of 1948, Fr. Eugene Gallagher succeeded Fr. McHugh as moderator of the Society.[47] It was under Fr. Gallagher that the Philodemic first participated in tournament competition. In December 1948, Society members participated in tournaments at Tufts and Old Dominion.[48]

Georgetown also hosted its own intercollegiate tournaments. On the dates of April 8–10, 1949, Georgetown sponsored the first annual Cherry Blossom Intercollegiate Debate Tournament. Thirty-two teams from sixteen schools competed at this contest. American, Boston University, Columbia, the University of Florida, Fordham, George Washington, the University of North Carolina, Richmond University, St. Peter's, Tufts, the U.S. Military Academy, and the U.S. Naval Academy were among the schools competing. Georgetown also entered teams from the Philodemic and Edmund Campion (from the School of Foreign Service) Debating Societies. The tournament culminated in one elimination round.[49]

The final round was judged by Philip Perlman (Solicitor General), Judge Joseph Raymond Jackson (U.S. Court of Customs and Patent Appeals), and Chief Judge Bolitha L. Laws (U.S.District Court)—all respected men in the community. The final round was advertised in the press and the public was welcome.[50]

In addition, the Philodemic continued to participate in traditional intercollegiate and public debates. Between 1948 and 1950, the Philodemic sponsored debates with the Georgetown University Nursing School, Johns Hopkins, Lynchburg, St. Joseph's, Trinity, and Georgetown Visitation. The events with the Nursing School, Trinity, and Visitation were debates over the worth of men and women, which occurred in Gaston Hall and which were very popular among the students from all schools involved.[51]

The grand event of the year was still the Merrick Debate. The parliamentary debates at the weekly meetings also continued, as did the annual Hamilton Debate.[52] These programs continued into the 1950s with intercollegiate tournaments, the Merrick Debate, and parliamentary debates forming the core of Philodemic activities.

During the 1954–55 season, the national resolution caused some controversy. Because they were debating the topic "Resolved: that the United States should extend diplomatic recognition to the communist government of China," many students would "defend Red China and therefore, all the criminal acts of Communists throughout the world."[53] Fortunately for the Philodemic, the University valued open debate on these issues and responded to inquiries with a distanced understanding.[54]

Debating the Red China topic, Philodemic teams attended tournaments at Dartmouth, Harvard, Johns Hopkins, Massachusetts Institute of Technology (MIT), New York University (NYU), Notre Dame, Vermont, Wake Forest, and William and Mary. At many of these tournaments, Philodemic members participated in elimination rounds and won awards for Georgetown.[55]

During the 1955–56 season, Philodemic debaters participated in tournaments at Brooklyn, Harvard, MIT, Muhlenberg, NYU, Temple, Wake Forest, and Williamsburg. By February 1956, Philodemic teams had placed first at MIT and NYU, second at Temple, and third at Wake Forest.[56]

During the 1958–59 season, Philodemic teams participated in tournaments at American, MIT, NYU, St. Joseph's (Philadelphia), and the U.S. Naval Academy. Philodemic debaters won the American tournament and were undefeated at MIT.[57]

In the mid-1950s, intercollegiate tournaments emerged as the dominant activity of the Philodemic Debating Society. Members expressed more interest in intercollegiate competition at tournaments than they did in any other aspect of the Philodemic, and allocated their efforts appropriately. "[D]espite the fact that they are far removed from us in space, and are only attended every other week during a two-month stretch at the middle of a semester," Fr. William Hunt wrote in 1956, intercollegiate tournaments "are paradoxically the chief integrating and motivating factor for debating back here on campus. Apart from the fact that these tourneys bring together the best thinking and best speaking [debaters] from the finest colleges and universities within our Eastern area, they also serve long before and after the actual event to bring the debaters together in prospective and retrospective research into the problems and practice in public speaking."[58]

Involvement in the tournaments, however, was restricted. With a set number of competitions and limited finances, not every member of the Philodemic could attend as many tournaments as desired. In addition, not every member was willing to make the effort necessary to be successful at national-level tournaments. To supplement the schedule, therefore, the James Cardinal Gibbons Debate League fostered competition among Baltimore and Washington area schools. Teams from Catholic, Georgetown (Philodemic and Campion), Georgetown Visitation, Loyola, Marymount, Mount St. Mary's, Notre Dame College, and Trinity participated in the Gibbons League. Schools hosted a single intercollegiate debate every Tuesday afternoon. A nine-week round of debates occurred every semester, and schools faced each other at least twice each year. Teams from these schools also gathered for occasional one-day tournaments. [59]

The Philodemic, in conjunction with the Campion Society, continued to sponsor the Cherry Blossom Intercollegiate Debate Tournament in March of each year. This event was one of the last tournaments of the year, and it involved social events as well as the debate tournament. In 1954, for example, the two rounds of debate on Thursday were followed by a banquet. Friday morning was kept open for sightseeing, the third round beginning at 3:00 P.M. After the fourth round, a dance was held in McDonough Gymnasium. Girls from Washington area colleges were invited to attend this dance. Saturday involved three more debate rounds and then a final round in Gaston Hall. A reception followed in Copley Formal.[60]

Throughout the 1950s, the Cherry Blossom Tournament grew in size and reputation. Notable community figures such as Judge Walter Bastion (U.S. Court of Appeals), Judge Edward A. Tamm (U.S. District of Columbia Circuit Court), and Judge Joseph C. McGarraghy (U.S. District of Columbia Circuit Court) judged final rounds. Teams from New England, the Midwest, and the South regularly attended.[61]

After a few years, the Society considered holding a tournament for high schools. The Philodemic could provide a service for high school forensics while increasing the popularity of intercollegiate debate and, in particular, increasing the popularity of debate at Georgetown.[62] On Saturday, February 5, 1955, the Philodemic Society sponsored the first annual Georgetown University Debate Tournament for High Schools. Fourteen schools from the East coast participated, including Archbishop Carroll (Washington), Boston College High School, Brooklyn Preparatory School, Fordham Preparatory School, and St. Joseph's High School (Philadelphia).[63]

During the day, there were four rounds of debate. A banquet and an awards assembly were held in Maguire Dining Hall in the evening. Senator Joseph C. O'Mahoney, from Wyoming, spoke at the banquet.[64]

In the next year, sixteen high schools participated in a similar one-day tournament. By 1958, the contest had expanded into a two-day event, with several elimination rounds.[65]

As intercollegiate tournament competition rose in popularity, single intercollegiate debates became less frequent. With the exception of Gibbons League debates, such events were virtually nonexistent.

Interest in intrasociety debates also declined, although parliamentary debates continued. Sometimes it was difficult to motivate debaters participating in these events. Without the intercollegiate aspect, much of the rivalry and sense of competition was lacking. At the beginning of the 1958–59 school year, however, the Philodemic Society introduced an award for the best parliamentary debater of the year, as voted by the entire Society. During that year, topics such as "Resolved: that the process of desegregation in the South thus far has been too hasty," "Resolved: that the federal government should place a ceiling on the capital assets of corporations," and "Resolved: that the requirement for reading 'classics' in the original should not be a requirement for an A.B. degree" were debated by members of the Society. Parliamentary debate was hardly dead, as such meetings occurred weekly.[66]

IV. Transition Years of the 1950s

Despite the apparent progress made by the Society during the 1950s, major organizational difficulties prevented true success in intercollegiate competition as well as in other activities. In 1953, Fr. E. Paul Betowski succeeded Fr. Gallagher as moderator. Betowski had been a member of the Philodemic when he attended Georgetown. As the Society's moderator, he continued the previously established programs. In 1954, Fr. McHugh came back to replace Fr. Betowski.[67]

At the beginning of the 1954–55 academic year, Thomas V. Fitzmaurize served as a debate coach, although he was eventually replaced by L. Connor.[68] As the 1955–56 year began, Fr. McHugh continued as moderator and Edward Cashman became debate coach. McHugh served at weekly meetings and assisted on campus, but he was not a formal debate coach and did not travel to tournaments. Cashman was a speech professor who was not trained to be a debate coach. Philodemic members turned to Fr. J. William Hunt, the moderator of the Gaston–White Society, for help. Hunt did the best job he could, but he was an inexperienced coach and realized his own shortcomings. Hunt led the Philodemic through a moderately successful season while he tried to arrange for a full-time experienced coach.[69]

In 1958, the situation did not improve. Another temporary arrangement began when Fr. D. Gilbert Sweeney was appointed moderator of the Philodemic Society and Leonard H. Thornton became debate coach.[70]

Here a true weakness of the Philodemic was revealed. With the exception of a short stay by Fr. Gallagher, the Philodemic had no stable coach directing its activities after Fr. Toohey's departure.

While Fr. Sweeney was moderator, however, the coaching situation stabilized. Sweeney contacted various deans and finally received a response. By May 1960, Dr. William Reynolds had been hired as a full-time debate coach. Sweeney put in a lot of time securing office space for Reynolds and for the Philodemic and trying to ease the transition to a new coach.[71]

Another major change occurred during these years. Both the Philodemic and the Campion Debating Societies were suffering from coaching and financial deficiencies. Some observers, including Fr. Fadner and Fr. Arthur E. Gordon (Director of Student Personnel), suggested that the problems could be alleviated if the two societies merged.[72]

Initially, both of the societies rejected the concept. Each argued that a merger would result in intrasquad tensions and would reduce the competitive spirit on campus. The Campion Society even offered to withdraw from Cherry Blossom Tournament activities to use their portion of the funds to hire a coach.[73]

Despite these wishes, Fr. Gordon and Fr. McGrath decided that a merger of the two societies would serve the best interests of the University. It was decided that the Gaston–White Society remained for freshmen in all schools and that the Philodemic Society was open to all qualified undergraduates. Fr .Sweeney and Mr. Cunningham (the coach of the Campion Society) were instructed to work out the details for the transition. By the time Dr. Reynolds arrived on campus in the fall of 1960, the Philodemic Society was the sole debate organization for upperclassmen at Georgetown.[74]

V. The Philodemic
under the Direction of William Reynolds

Dr. William Reynolds was the first true tournament-style coach for the Philodemic. Fr. Sweeney continued as moderator of the Philodemic for a few years and by 1962, Fr. John Ryan replaced Fr. Sweeney. Reynolds, however, was the real coach.[75]

No other instructor inspired debaters to do as much work and no other coach was as successful. Looking back on Reynolds' short tenure at Georgetown, Thomas McClain, then a professor at Northwestern University, commented that William Reynolds was "...the person who has contributed more than any other to intercollegiate debate in the last decade."[76]

Reynolds' team consistently displayed excellence. During his first season, he won a post for his team in the National Debate Tournament—the final tournament of the year which is limited to teams qualifying through district tournaments or at-large bids. Georgetown had not been offered such a bid during the previous five years until Philodemic debaters compiled a record of eight wins and no losses (fifteen ballots to one ballot) to win the District VII Regional Debate Tournament on March 24–5, 1961.[77]

In 1963, Georgetown debaters placed second at the Harvard tournament, and won the U.S. Naval Academy, Notre Dame, and Wake Forest tournaments. By 1964, a Georgetown team placed third at the National Debate Tournament. In the Spring of 1965, the Philodemic Society again placed third at the National Debate Tournament and one of its members was declared first-place speaker. During the fall of 1965, Georgetown won the Dartmouth, Emory, U.S. Naval Academy, and Rosemont tournaments; placed second at the Princeton and Wake Forest tournaments; and placed third at Brandeis, Chicago, Harvard, and North Carolina.[78]

In concert with tournament competition, the Philodemic continued to sponsor intercollegiate and high school tournaments, both of which expanded remarkably. The 1962 Cherry Blossom Tournament attracted teams from over sixty schools. By 1964, the tournament became too large to hold while normal classes were meeting. The Georgetown University National Invitational Debate Tournament occurred on Thanksgiving weekend from that year on. By 1965, ninety-two schools were participating at the Thanksgiving tournament, making it the largest intercollegiate tournament of the year.[79]

The Georgetown high school tournament also grew. By 1965, it had attracted over 180 teams from more than thirty states for three days of debates.[80]

The Hamilton and Merrick Debates also continued under Reynolds. On December 13, 1965, for example, the topic of the Hamilton Debate was: "Resolved: that American troops should be withdrawn from the Dominican Republic ."[81] The 92nd annual Merrick Debate occurred on March 31, 1966. The debate topic was: "Resolved: that a national system of compulsory wage-price controls should be established in basic industry." Senator Len B. Jordan (Idaho), Representative William B. Windall (New Jersey), Representative Thomas B. Curtis (Missouri), Representative Martha Griffiths (Michigan), Representative Robert F. Ellsworth (Kansas), Arthur M. Okun (member of the president's Council of Economic Advisers), John F. Henning

(Under-secretary of Labor), Dean Richard A. Gordon (Georgetown University Law School), and Professor George Henigan (Director of Debate at George Washington University) served as the judges of the debate. The Chimes performed during an intermission and a reception for alumni was held along with the traditional events surrounding the Merrick.[82]

General membership in the Society was also up. During the 1965–66 academic year, eighteen members held elected positions. There were twenty-three debaters participating in tournament competition alone. Overall, nearly forty students were involved in Philodemic activities.[83]

Weekly meetings with parliamentary debates continued throughout the 1960s. For example, the topics "Resolved: that Congress include provisions for the protection of all citizens in their right both to register and vote" and "Resolved: that the United States should immediately open peace negotiations with North Vietnam, Russia, and Red China" were discussed in 1965.[84]

The Society also extended its range of activities during the 1960s. An alumni relations committee was established to compile the names and addresses of alumni and to keep the alumni informed about current Philodemic events. To supplement this effort, *The Philodemic Roll* was established. Published three times yearly, the first edition appeared in January 1966. Chief Editor Robert Mannix ('67) announced: "This newsletter is designed to serve as a means of communication with Philodemic alumni, and is entirely the work of Philodemic members. The writing, editing, and layout are all done by students."[85]

The Philodemic also incorporated its talents with the campus radio station, WGTB FM. During the 1965–66 academic year, members of the Philodemic discussed current events over the radio. The Philodemic Forum lasted half an hour and was aired weekly.[86]

In addition to debate tournaments, the Philodemic hosted the National Invitational Model General Assembly every year at Georgetown. Delegates from over fifty high schools visited the University and participated in a model United Nations. Each delegation was assigned a country to "represent." The events lasted for three days during the last weekend in April.[87]

Notable among the new programs was a summer debate workshop for high school students. Georgetown's summer forensics institute was highly regarded in the debate community. It assembled a top notch faculty and hundreds of talented students for sessions of three weeks.[88]

The Philodemic Debating Society was on the rise. Its performance was impressive to all observers. Dr. Reynolds revitalized debate at Georgetown to a level that had not been attained since Fr. Toohey's prime. Unfortunately, he was gone after six years, leaving after the 1966–67 season to conduct federally funded experiments gauging the impact of speech patterns on social mobility.[89]

Reynolds' last season was perhaps his most successful, as Georgetown debaters won tournaments at Brandeis, Dartmouth, and Northwestern and finished second at Emory and Harvard.[90]

Notes

1. *Philodemic Results under Fr. Toohey*, Georgetown University Archives (hereafter GUA), Philodemic Debating Society, box 9, folder 1.

All future references to Georgetown University Archives boxes and folders are Philodemic Debating Society boxes and folders, which are kept in the GUA.

2. "Debating Society at Georgetown U. Arranging Schedule," *The Washington Star*, November 16, 1939, GUA, box 9, folder 1. *The Philodemic Society of Georgetown University Minutes and Records: October 17, 1939–May 6, 1947* (hereafter Minutes and Records), p. 6, GUA, box 10.

The Proceedings of the Philodemic Society: 1933–1939, pp. 131, 146, GUA, box 9, folder 5.

3. *Order of Business*, in Minutes and Records, loose sheet between pages 196–97, GUA, box 10.

Minutes and Records, pages 5–8, GUA, box 10.

4. *The Philodemic Society Attendance: Fall, 1930–Spring, 1949* (hereafter Attendance), page 72, GUA, box 9, folder 6.

5. Attendance, GUA, box 9, folder 6.

6. See note 3.

7. Ibid., loc cit.

8. Minutes and Records, pp. 117, 143, 194, 196, GUA, box 10.

Proceedings of the Philodemic Society: 1933–1939 (hereafter Proceedings), pp. 136, 138–39, 142–43, 148–49, GUA, box 9, folder 5.

9. Minutes and Records, pp. 7, 28, 36, 190, 215, GUA, box 10.

Proceedings, pp. 136, 138–39, 144, GUA, box 10.

10. Minutes and Records, p. 167, GUA, box 10.

Although this is one place where the procedure is specifically mapped out, references to such debates are made throughout Minutes and Records, GUA , box 10, and Proceedings, GUA, box 9, folder 5.

11. See note 3.

12. Ibid., loc cit.

13. Ibid., loc cit.

14. Order of Business.

15. "Debate Team Wins," *The Washington Star*, March 8, 1942, GUA, box 9, folder 1.

"Debating Society at Georgetown U. Arranging Schedule," *The Washington Star*, November 16, 1939, GUA, box 9, folder 1.

"Georgetown U. Debaters Meet W. & M. Team," *The Washington Post*, March 15, 1942, GUA, box 9, folder 1.

"Georgetown U. Debating to Open Jan. 5," *The Washington Post*, November 16, 1939, GUA, box 9, folder 1.

"Girl Debate Team Trounces Men in Contest at G.U.," *The Times Herald*, March 7, 1940, GUA, box 9, folder 1.

"G.U. Debaters Due Back Today from Tour," *The Washington Post*, March 3, 1940, GUA, box 9, folder 1.

"G.U. Debaters End Undefeated Season by Beating Harvard," *The Washington Star*, April 6, 1941, GUA, box 9, folder 1.

Philodemic Results under Fr. Toohey.

Minutes and Records, p. 111.

16. "Georgetown Debaters Meet Princeton," *The Washington Post*, March 15, 1940, GUA, box 9, folder 1.

"G.U. Debaters End Undefeated Season by Beating Harvard," *The Washington Star*, April 6, 1941, GUA, box 9, folder 1.

17. See note 15.

18. *Philodemic Results under Fr. Toohey.*

19. *The Washington Star*, January 25, 1942, GUA, box 9, folder 1.

20. "G.U. Society to Hold Debate Contest Tonight," *The Washington Star*, January 15, 1940, GUA, box 9, folder 1.

"Merrick Debate Held at Georgetown U.," *The Baltimore Catholic Review*, 1940, GUA, box 9, folder 1.

The copy in the Archives was not dated, but the by-line was dated December 12, 1940.

"Philodemic Debate Set," *The Washington Post*, November 15, 1942, GUA, box 9, folder 1.

Minutes and Records, pp. 42–43, 111.

21. "Debating Society at Georgetown U. Arranging Schedule," *The Washington Star*, November 16, 1939, GUA, box 9, folder 1.

"Philodemic Society Reorganized after Brief Discontinuance," *The Hoya*, December 1, 1943, p. 8.

Minutes and Records, p. 179.

22. "Debating Society at Georgetown U. Arranging Schedule," *The Washington Star*, November 16, 1939, GUA, box 9, folder 1.

23. See note 21.

24. "DeFrancis Debates; Gets Hamilton," *The Hoya*, May 21, 1948, p. 5.

"Hamilton Debate," *The Hoya*, May 23, 1947, p. 6.

25. Minutes and Records, p. 43.

26. "Hamilton Debate," *The Hoya*, May 23, 1947, p. 6.

The Washington Star, February 1941, GUA, box 9, folder 1.

27. Minutes and Records, pp. 160–68.

"Philodemic Society Reorganized after Brief Discontinuance," *The Hoya*, December 1, 1943, p. 1.

28. Ibid., loc cit.

29. "Philodemic Society Holds Meeting to Plan for Future Debates," *The Hoya*, January 26, 1944, p. 7.

Minutes and Records, pp. 160–68.

30. Minutes and Records, pp. 165–66.

31. Minutes and Records, pp. 167–68.

32. Minutes and Records, pp. 169–76.

"Philodemic Society Holds Meeting to Plan for Future Debates," *The Hoya*, January 26, 1944, p. 7.

"Philodemic Society Reorganized after Brief Discontinuance," *The Hoya*, July 16, 1944, p. 1.

The Hoya reports that the first intrasociety debate of the year occurred on January 25, 1944; but Minutes and Records reports that Mr. Loving, one of the members scheduled to debate, was absent and that the debate was postponed. The next recorded meeting of the Philodemic in Minutes and Records occurred on March 21, 1944. It is possible that the official minutes are incomplete, in which case debates might have occurred prior to March 21, 1944. There were no intercollegiate debates during this period, however, and the official minutes report no intrasociety debates until March 21, 1944.

33. "Philodemic Society Holds Meeting to Plan for Future Debates," *The Hoya*, January 26, 1944, p. 7.

34. Ibid.

35. "Old Gaston and White Debaters Reorganized as Single New Society," *The Hoya*, November 2, 1945, p. 1.

36. "Annual Merrick Debate Won by Loving and Stenger in Gaston Hall May 4th," *The Hoya*, May 31, 1944, p. 6.

37. *Debate at Georgetown*, 1954, p. 1, GUA, box 10, folder 2.

"Fr. Toohey Resigns; Gave Philodemic 35 Years Service," *The Hoya*, October 17, 1947, p. 7.

"The Philodemic Society," *The Hoya*, October 3, 1947, p. 6.

"Geo. U. Sponsors Debate Tourney," *The Baltimore Catholic Review*, April 8, 1949, GUA, box 9, folder 1.

Philodemic Society Minutes: February 3, 1948–February 3, 1951 (hereafter Minutes), p. 17, GUA, box 10.

Minutes and Records, p. 261.

Some sources report that Fr. Toohey was replaced by Fr. Eugene Gallagher. Although Fr. Gallagher did assume the role of moderator in 1948, Fr. McHugh also served in that capacity between 1947 and 1948.

38. Ibid., loc cit.

39. "Held and DeFrancis Debate Columbia U. Here Tomorrow," *The Hoya*, April 28, 1948, p. 5.

"Philodemic Meets Princeton," *The Hoya*, February 13, 1948, p. 1.

40. *Georgetown University Invitational Debating Tournament—Tournament Bulletin*, 1954, GUA, box 10, folder 2.

"Geo. U. Sponsors Debate Tourney," *The Baltimore Catholic Review*, April 8, 1949, GUA, box 9, folder 1.

"Philodemic in Tourney Today; N.Y. Series Soon," *The Hoya*, December 3, 1948, GUA, box 9, folder 1.

"Philodemic Places Third in National Tournament," *The Philodemic Roll*, January 1966, p. 2.

41. Ibid., loc cit.

42. This statement is obviously a personal judgment of the author and there are certainly coaches and debaters who might disagree.

43. Minutes, p. 117.

The October date is especially interesting in light of the fact that current Philodemic debaters begin their research efforts in July.

44. Minutes, p. 125.

45. Minutes, p. 115.

46. The author will grant that this is his mere assertion. A general understanding of the history of U.S.–Soviet relations and events in Korea indicate that this analysis is probably accurate.

47. "Geo. U. Sponsors Debate Tourney," *The Baltimore Catholic Review*, April 8, 1949, GUA, box 9, folder 1.

"Philodemic Debaters Start 119th Year of Activity," *The Hoya*, October 8, 1948, p. 4.

Minutes, p. 57.

48. "Philodemic in Tourney Today; N.Y. Series Soon," *The Hoya*, December 3, 1948, GUA, box 9, folder 1.

49. *Debating at Georgetown*, 1954, p. 1, GUA, box 10, folder 2.

"Geo. U. Sponsors Debate Tourney," *The Baltimore Catholic Review*, April 8, 1949, GUA, box 9, folder 1.

"Philodemic Society Rooted in Rich History," *The Hoya*, November 4, 1983, p. 10.

50. "Geo. U. Sponsors Debate Tourney," *The Baltimore Catholic Review*, April 8, 1949, GUA, box 9, folder 1.

The Georgetown University Archives have various newspaper clippings reporting on the event and inviting the public to a final debate at 7:00 P.M. on Sunday, April 10, 1949. Unfortunately, no specific references are attached to these clippings. See box 9, folder 1.

51. "Georgetown Debaters Meet Girls' Team," *The Washington Star*, March 6, 1940, GUA, box 9, folder 1.

"Girl Debate Team Trounces Men in Contest at G.U.," *The Times Herald*, March 7, 1940, GUA, box 9, folder 1.

"Philodemic in Tourney Today; N.Y. Series Soon," *The Hoya*, December 3, 1948, GUA, box 9, folder 1.

Minutes, pp. 125, 129.

52. "DeFrancis Debates; Gets Hamilton," *The Hoya*, May 21, 1948, p. 5.

Letter from Thaddeus S. Zolkiewicz (corresponding secretary of the Philodemic Society) to Fr. Bunn (President of Georgetown University), February 23, 1956, GUA, box 10, folder 3.

"Hamilton Debate," *The Hoya*, May 23, 1947, p. 6.

Minutes, GUA, box 10.

53. Letter from Harold J. Thompson (National Coordinating Committee to Defeat Communism) to Fr. Bunn (President of Georgetown University), December 8, 1954, GUA, box 10, folder 2.

See also *Georgetown University News Service*, March 14, 1955, GUA, box 10, folder 2.

54. Letter from Fr. Bunn to Harold J. Thompson, December 16, 1954, GUA, box 10, folder 2.

Letter from Margaret M. Sweetmer (secretary to Fr. Bunn) to Maurice H. Johnson, June 3, 1955, GUA, box 10, folder 2.

55. *Debating at Georgetown*, p. 2.

56. "G.U. Triumphs," *The Catholic Standard*, December 7, 1956, GUA, box 10, folder 3.

Hunt, J. William. *Memorandum: Debating*, 1956, pp. 6–7. GUA, box 20, folder 3.

The *Standard* reported that Georgetown won the NYU tournament while Fr. Hunt's memorandum claimed that the Philodemic debaters placed second at the NYU tournament.

57. *Philodemic Society Minutes: 1958–59* (hereafter PSM), October 14, 1958, and February 24, 1959, GUA, box 10, folder 6.

58. Hunt, p. 4

59. *Georgetown University News Service*, April 12, 1956, GUA, box 10, folder 3.

Hunt, pp. 3, 6.

60. *Georgetown University Invitational Debating Tournament—Tournament Bulletin*, 1954, pp. 2–3. GUA, box 10, folder 2.

61. "G.U. Debate Tourney Planned This Week," *The Catholic Standard*, March 15, 1957, GUA, box 10, folder 3.

Georgetown University Invitational Debating Tournament—Tournament Bulletin, 1954.

Georgetown University News Service, March 14, 1955, GUA, box 10, folder 2.

Letter from Walter J. Nicgorski (President of the Philodemic Society) to Fr. Bunn, December 3, 1958, GUA, box 10, folder 3.

"Philo and Campion Host Top Debaters for Major Tourney," *The Hoya*, March 12, 1959, pp.1, 5–6.

62. Letter from Arnold Donahue (Chairman of the Georgetown University Tournament for High Schools) to "Debate Moderator" (at that time, Fr. Sweeney), November 15, 1958, GUA, box 10, folder 3.

63. *Georgetown University Debate Tournament for High Schools* (tournament bulletin), February 5, 1955, GUA, box 10, folder 2.

"180 Teams Attend High School Tournament," *The Philodemic Roll*, January, 1966, p. 4.

64. Ibid., loc cit.

65. *Georgetown University News Service*, March 1, 1956, GUA, box 10, folder 3.
Letter from Arnold Donahue to "Debate Moderator."
Misuraca, Malcolm. *Georgetown University Invitation Tournament—Memo*,
March 1–2, 1957, GUA, box 10, folder 2.

66. Hunt, p. 3.
PSM, September 23, 1958, October 14, 1958, November 4, 1958, GUA, box
10, folder 6.

67. *Debating at Georgetown*, 1954, p. 1, GUA, box 10, folder 2.

68. *Debating at Georgetown*, 1954, p. 1.
Hunt, p. 11.

69. Hunt, J. William. *Memorandum: Debating*, pp. 2, 10–11.
Letter from Fr. J. William Hunt to Fr. Bunn, GUA, box 10, folder 3.
Letter from Fr. Joseph A. Sellinger (Associate Dean) to Fr. Bunn, April 24,
1956, GUA, box 10, folder 3.

70. "Fr. D.G. Sweeney Chancellor of Philo," *The Hoya*, March 12, 1959, p. 6.
PSM, September 23, 1958, GUA, box 10, folder 6.

71. Letter from Fr. Gilbert Sweeney (moderator of the Philodemic Society)
to Fr. Brian A. McGrath (Academic Vice President), May 1, 1959, GUA, box 10,
folder 3.
Letter from Fr. Sweeney to Fr. T. Byron Collins (Vice President of Business
Management), February 2, 1960, GUA, box 11, folder 1.
Letter from Fr. Sweeney to Fr. McGrath, February 10, 1960, GUA, box 11,
folder 1.
Letter from Fr. Sweeney to Fr. McGrath, May 15, 1960, GUA,   box 11, folder 1.

72. Letter from Henry M. Cunningham (moderator of the Edmund Campi-
on Debating Society) to Fr. Sweeney, April 6, 1960, GUA, box 11, folder 1.
Letter from Fr. Sweeney to Fr. Joseph A. Sellinger (Dean of the College of
Arts and Sciences), April 10, 1960, GUA, box 112, folder 1.

73. Ibid., loc cit.

74. Letter from Fr. Arthur E. Gordon (Director of Student Personnel) to Fr.
McGrath, May 2, 1960, GUA, box 11, folder 1.
Letter from Fr. Gordon to Fr. McGrath, May 10, 1960, GUA, box 11, folder 1.
Letter from Fr. Sweeney to Fr. McGrath, May 15, 1960, GUA, box 11, folder   1.
Letter from Fr. McGrath to Fr. Gordon, May 17, 1960, GUA, box 11, folder 1.

75. "Cool Logic, Hot Debate Flourish at G.U.," *The Washington Post*, October 7, 1962, section F, p. 14, GUA, box 11, folder 1.

76. McClain, Thomas, in "Hoya Debating Coach Faces Final Test," *The
Washington Post*, April 16, 1967, GUA, box 11, folder 3.

77. *Philodemic Wins Regional Debate Tournament*, March 25, 1961, GUA, box
11, folder 1.

78. "Debating Duo Loses to BC in Nationals; Finish in 3rd Place," *The Hoya*,
May 1, 1964, GUA, box 11, folder 2.
*The Philodemic Debating Society of Georgetown University: 1965–1966 First Se-
mester Tournament Results*, 1966, GUA, box 11, folder 3.
"Philodemic Sweeps Eastern Seaboard in Three Contests," *The Hoya*, De-
cember 19, 1963, GUA, box 11, folder 2.

158 / Marc B. Stahl

"Philodemic Team Places Third in National Tournament," _The Philodemic Roll_, January 1966, p. 3.

79. "Georgetown Hosts Largest College Debate Tournament in Nation," _The Philodemic Roll_, January 1966, p. 3.

Letter from Peter V. Handal (Chairman of the Georgetown University National Invitational Debate Tournament) to Fr. Bunn, February 20, 1962, GUA, box 11, folder 1.

"Philodemic Society Sponsors Eighteenth Annual G.U. Invitational Debate Tournament," _The Georgetown University Record_, December 1965, GUA, box 11, folder 3.

80. "Coral Gables Sweeps Debate Tournament," _The Hoya_, February 26, 1965, GUA, box 11, folder 3.

Letter from Joseph S. Clark (U.S. Senator) to William Reynolds, January 23, 1963, GUA, box 11, folder 1.

"180 Teams Attend High School Tournament," _The Philodemic Roll_, January 1966, p. 4.

81. Morelli, Carl J., _The Philodemic Debating Society of Georgetown University: 1965–1966 President's Report_, May 1966, p. 13, GUA, box 11, folder 4.

82. Letter from Robert E. Morris (Co-Chairman of Merrick Debate) to Fr. Gerard J. Campbell (President of Georgetown University), March 20, 1966, GUA, box 11, folder 4.

Morelli, pp. 14–15.

83. Morelli.

The Philodemic Debating Society of Georgetown University: 1965–1966 First Semester Results.

84. _Philodemic Society Minutes: 1964–65_, March 8, 1965, and March 15, 1965, GUA, box 11, folder 8.

85. Mannix, Robert, _The Philodemic Roll_, January 1966, p. 1.

Morelli, p. 16.

"Philodemic Launches Alumni Committee and Newsletter," _The Georgetown University Record_, February 1966, GUA, box 11, folder 4.

86. Morelli, p. 16.

87. Morelli, p. 12.

"Philodemic and IRC Sponsor NIMGA II," _The Philodemic Roll_, January 1966, p. 2.

88. Conversation with Professor David M. Cheshier.

89. "Hoya Debating Coach Faces Final Test," _The Washington Post_, April 16, 1967, GUA, box 11, folder 3.

90. Ibid., loc cit.

Dramatics at Georgetown: The Mask and Bauble Society

Thomas Steinthal and Daniel Hood

In the same year in which Georgetown University celebrated its two hundredth anniversary, the Mask and Bauble Dramatic Society celebrated its 136th season on the university campus. Begun in 1853, Mask and Bauble or, as it is often called, the M&B, is the oldest active college theater group in the nation.

Mask and Bauble has a rich and varied history, of which any member, past or present, can describe some portion (with proper dramatic embellishments, of course). Baublers quickly learn of M&B's prominence in Washington theater in the 1920s and '30s, of the tradition of the Calliopes directed by Donn Murphy, and of the student revolt that almost, but not quite, produced M&B's present home, Stage III in Poulton Hall. Club members know the names of the Tony and Oscar Award-winning directors, playwrights, actors, and actresses trained at Georgetown University theater: John Guare, Jack Hofsiss, Don Ameche, Eileen Brennan, George LaGuerre, Wilton Lackaye, Willard Mack and John Barrymore are part of Mask and Bauble's past. Some, though, have won acclaim outside the theater, such as Justice Antonin Scalia of the Supreme Court and William Peter Blatty, author of *The Exorcist*.

Mask and Bauble's archives date from the turn of the century to the present and provide an interesting picture of student life at Georgetown for the past nine decades. Along with the University Archives, they document the development of the dramatic arts at Georgetown.

Dramatics at Georgetown can be traced to the early nineteenth century. A presentation of *Julius Caesar* by William Shakespeare at the commencement exercises of 1821 was the first dramatic production on record.[1] As an integral part of Jesuit education dramatics, different from today's student activity, existed before the first organized dramatics troupe was formed in 1853. On February 27 of that year, the first constitution was signed in order to create a dramatic society at Georgetown. Its first article declared: "This association shall be called the Dramatic Association of Georgetown College. It professes to hold Elocution as the primary object of its cultivation."[2]

The 1853 constitution consisted of twenty-six articles which defined the rules and regulations of the Association and provided for a president, assisted by a vice-president, treasurer, recording secretary, corresponding secretary, and censor. The officers were elected for one-year terms at the first regular meeting of the Association. The first president, Rev. Charles King, and his successors, selected and cast the plays, as well as set times and locations for rehearsals, performances, and regular meetings of the group. In order to become a member of the Association, an applicant had to receive a two-thirds vote of members present at a meeting. No one objected to inviting students to join the company if the president cast him in a production. The Dramatic Association, in keeping with similar societies of that era, was a highly democratic organization.[3]

The job of censor was important because he had to enforce the collection of fines that the constitution specified. The penalties were levied regularly. For example, if a student was cast in a show and he accepted the part but at a later date decided to leave the cast, he was fined one dollar. If a member was late for a meeting, he was fined ten cents; failure to arrive incurred a fine of twenty-five cents. Actors were penalized ten cents if they used their scripts after the fourth rehearsal. Loud talking or disorder resulted in a ten-cent fine, and chronic abusers were fined twenty-five cents. On the day of a performance, no member of the cast could leave the College grounds; if he did so, he had to pay a fifty-cent fine. Actors faced a twenty-five-cent fine if costumes were not returned to the president two days after a performance. Leaving a meeting for more than ten minutes cost the member ten cents. And if a member discussed the business of a meeting with a nonmember and two members could verify his action, he would be fined fifty cents.[4]

The first shows of the Dramatic Association were seen by invitation only—no tickets were sold. The president appointed an invitation committee to compose the guest list and to make and send invitations.[5]

Sheridan's *Pizzaro* was the first show of the new organization. In the first season, the troupe also presented Bamin's *Damon and Pythias* and Shakespeare's *Hamlet*. In their second year they performed *Brutus, Richard II, Marino Faliero,* and *Richard III*. In their first six years the Dramatic Association produced Shakespeare's *Hamlet* three times; *Richard II, Richard III, Julius Caesar,* and *The Merchant of Venice* twice each; and one showing of *Macbeth, King John,* and *Henry IV Part I*. These fourteen plays were produced in addition to the other work the student players did during the 1850s.[6] M&B's 1854 production of *Richard II* was the first performance of that play in the United States.[7]

Robin Ruff, a member of the class of 1860, "recalls the existence of over fifty years [prior] of the Dramatic Association of Georgetown College, membership in which was held in high esteem in those far-off days."[8] When the organization was founded, its leading actor was Harvey Bawtree, a man whose performance "lingers as a memory over half a century."[9] Ruff also recalls that:

> During the Pentecost holidays what was regarded as a great dramatic revival took place. Former students, who in their college days had gained fame before the footlights, returned for the presentation of three plays on three successive days in which they had earlier starred.[10]

The three plays—*Richard II, William Tell,* and *Hamlet*—were "expertly performed" by men who, after graduation, received recognition in the Civil War, in law and in politics. A mayor of Philadelphia is among the notables.[11] Several alumni of G.U. Theater lost their lives in the Civil War.[12]

Following the Civil War, the Dramatic Association of George-town College became less active. During this time minstrel shows, bal masques, evenings of dramatic scenes followed by a formal dance, held each year as a Mardi Gras celebration,[13] and dramatic readings were popular. These readings became espe-cially popular in 1868 with the establishment of the "Dramatic Reading Association of George Town College, D.C.," whose ob-ject was "the study of Dramatic Reading, and the cultivation of Elocution."[14] Edgar Allen Poe's "The Raven" or excerpts from *Hamlet* were typical selections at Reading Association presenta-tions.[15] Another group, the Bononian Minstrels, were formed in 1866 for "the sole object of...an evening's frolic,...not at lofty outbursts of tragic eloquence, [but rather] the simple role to amuse—to create a tiny oasis in the monotony of our daily life."[16]

In 1898 the Dramatic Association once again gained public acclaim for its work. During that season, the students per-formed *Richelieu*, which was acclaimed by critics as "the best amateur performance of its kind ever given in Washington."[17] Shakespeare's *Henry IV Part I*, which followed, was described by the local press as "the best of its kind ever produced in the theatrical history of the college...The scenery and costumes were such as only seen on a professional stage."[18] Credit for the noticeable increase in quality of Georgetown theater was given to two Jesuits, Fathers Whitney and McCarthy.[19]

After several successful years, Georgetown theater again fad-ed into obscurity. In 1910, Father Edmund Walsh and several students reorganized the Association after seven years of lethar-gy, and the group again became prominent. According to the *Georgetown College Journal* of January 1910:

> The art of acting is praiseworthy and its study has great education-al value. It demands keen powers of observation, complete self-abandonment and the ability to impregnate one's self with the thoughts, feelings, and sentiments of the personality portrayed.[20]

On January 16, 1910, Daniel Bradley Murray, the manager of the football team, was elected president of the reorganized society.[21]

The first show of the revamped group was a farce by William

Gillette called *All the Comforts of Home,* performed at the Columbia Theater in Washington on January 19, 1910 with admission prices in the range of $1.50, $1.00, to $0.75.[22] The play netted $980.00, with all the receipts going to the Christ Child Society, a local charitable organization.[23] Washington and campus critics believed that:

> The universal success [of] the production of *All the Comforts of Home* proved that the cast not only had expert and persistent supervision, but that each and every member of the cast trained and studied with such faithfulness that all were benefited by the instruction they received.[24]

The show was such a success that Father Walsh arranged, with the help of the Alumni Association, to bring it to New York. On March 31, 1910, the Georgetown Dramatic Association performed *All the Comforts of Home* in the Astor Room of the Waldorf-Astoria Hotel.[25]

The costs associated with taking a show to "Broadway" included rental of the ballroom at $150.00 for the night. The orchestra was paid $45.00, and the cost of costumes and wigs was $40.00.[26] *All the Comforts of Home* was originally written with several women's parts, but because women were not allowed to perform in Georgetown productions, the script had to be rewritten. "Those who witnessed the play in Washington," reported a campus publication, "were unanimous in declaring that they were at a loss to see where women characters would fit in."[27]

During the years prior to the First World War, the society performed one show each year in Manhattan, with all the costs being assumed by the Alumni Association. All activity halted, though, with the outbreak of World War I. After the war, the association reorganized and adopted a new name, the Mask and Bauble Dramatic Society, a title chosen to indicate the types of productions in which the group would specialize—serious drama and light farce. In 1922, the Society performed Shakespeare's *Julius Caesar.* In the following years it produced *The Merchant of Venice* and *Hamlet,*[28] in each of which the female parts were performed by men in female garb. After this performance of *Hamlet,* the Society decided not to perform shows with female impersonations. This unprecedented decision set a new standard in college theater, and eliminated Shakespeare for three decades.[29]

On February 25, 1928, Mask and Bauble staged a special production in honor of the noted author and French Ambassador to the United States, Paul Claudel. The group performed two one-act plays, *Allison's Lad* and *The Golden Doom*, and the ambassador commended the players.[30] Later in the same year, *Manhood*, the classical drama written for the Mask and Bauble Club of Georgetown University by the Rev. Thomas B. Chetwood, regent of the Law School, proved a highly successful vehicle to initiate the club's season.[31]

One-act plays became the focus for Mask and Bauble during the 1930s, and their performances have continued to the present. Georgetown and other Jesuit universities held an annual one-act play competition beginning about 1930 and lasting into the 1960s. Georgetown won the competition in 1931 with a production of *The Valiant*.[32] Often, Georgetown entered original plays in this annual contest. In order to encourage playwriting, the University held a one-act play competition among the various schools on the campus.

Mask and Bauble gained such prominence during the twenties and early thirties that its list of patrons rivaled the roll call at a White House reception. Among those who came to the Hilltop to see plays were foreign ambassadors, congressmen, Supreme Court justices, and even the First Lady, Eleanor Roosevelt, who attended many M&B productions.[33]

In 1934, Mask and Bauble decided to break its own rule to produce a musical with female players. After obtaining approval from the University administration, M&B cast women from Visitation Convent, the girls' school next to Georgetown, making this production of George M. Cohan's *The Tavern* the first show in Georgetown's history with women on the stage. However, *The Tavern* is notable for another reason. During a rehearsal, a man arrived at the stage and asked the director if he could watch and lend a hand.[34] The director welcomed any assistance from the stranger, who turned out to be George M. Cohan himself. Cohan did not usurp the director's prerogative, but instead diplomatically coached and advised the actors. After the presentation, Mr. Cohan praised the quality of the performance.[35]

During World War II, Mask and Bauble was much less formally organized than during the 1920s and 1930s. With the disruptions caused by war and some military training on campus, rules for membership were dropped and productions were organized at the discretion of the students. The name of the club was parodied in the "Flask and Bottle" club, which was the name given to a group of participating Hoyas. According to Donn Murphy, the club's moderator from 1956, theatrically inclined students would gather in any convenient place to create a series of sketches or brief musical revue. Then, at their own initiative, they rehearsed and performed the show. Each time they had an idea for a show, the process was repeated.

There was naturally little official structure to "Flask and Bottle," but the desire to perform and the interest in theater remained, despite the lack of a proper forum. Throughout the days when "Flask and Bottle" stole most of the headlines, Mask and Bauble still existed, but on a less formal basis. It produced fine productions, but declined to try Shakespeare and other more difficult plays. After the war director Anthony Manzi brought some stability back to M&B. For a time, the club had two part-time paid directors as well as a Jesuit moderator.

In the early 1950s Mask and Bauble began its productions of an original senior class musical revue. Several seniors gathered to write sketches to original music or to parody well-known music. M&B performed the revue during Parents' Weekend in the spring. The early fifties marked M&B's return to Shakespeare after a thirty-year break. The 1952 version of *The Taming of the Shrew* was Mask and Bauble's first attempt at Shakespeare since 1924. This production is also notable because it represents the first time one of the Bard's classics was staged at Georgetown with women in the cast.

In 1953 the moderator of Mask and Bauble resigned because of a conflict with the Student Personnel Office (SPO). The moderator, Father Albert F. Grau, S.J., felt that the SPO was making his job difficult by prohibiting ticket sales in the cafeteria, thereby diminishing revenue. Also, the SPO hired only one director in 1951 and 1952, a fact which limited the club's dramatic activity.[36] Rev. Paul Betowski, S.J., became moderator, and a Georgetown Law student was hired to direct the productions. Outstanding among his efforts were a student-written musical called *Heir Unapparent*, and a production of *Arsenic and Old Lace*, featuring Eileen Brennan, an employee in the University Treasurer's office who later starred on Broadway, in television and in films.[37]

It was into this atmosphere of somewhat inconsistent student creativity that Donn Murphy entered in 1956. He has led Mask and Bauble into one of its most creative and theatrically successful periods. In 1956, Murphy, fresh from Catholic University with an M.F.A. in Speech and Drama, became director of Mask and Bauble, with Rev. Eugene Lawler, S.J., as moderator. Murphy had toured in the Far East when in the Army, participating in military theater productions.[38]

Murphy found that M&B had no written rules for membership, nor was there a formal body of members. He designed a seal to identify the group and had it printed on all stationery and programs, and encouraged the drafting of a club constitution. He also established weekly Monday evening meetings for the entire membership. In addition, he created a point-system for attaining membership in the club, and made this known to prospective members by publishing what came to be known as the "Bible" of Mask and Bauble: a little black booklet which described club and membership rules, as well as Mask and Bauble's general goals. The preamble of the 1958 constitution proclaims M&B an organization

> ...that will continue the Jesuit tradition of the use of dramatics as a complement to the education of a man, that will provide for its members experience and training in the dramatic arts, and that will bring to the University community the cultural and social benefits of the theater.[39]

The rules of M&B, compared to those of a century before, reflect a return to strict guidelines designed to maintain an atmosphere conducive to high-quality performance.

As Murphy conceived it, the purpose of Mask and Bauble was to provide an artistic outlet and to give the entire campus quality theater. Today, Mask and Bauble still upholds this aim. In any given year, Murphy recalls, there were approximately 100 official club members, with from 300 to 400 students involved in the season's productions. During Murphy's twenty years with Mask and Bauble there was tremendous student body support for the club, and he and the club turned this to their advantage.

Mask and Bauble has attained a high degree of respect in the theatrical community of Washington, though they did not receive the administrative or general social support they had enjoyed in the first half of the century. Even though the general public was not supporting M&B as it had in the past, First Lady Jacqueline Kennedy personally sent Donn Murphy a letter of thanks "for the tremendous effort you put into the production of *The Magic Flute*. As always you did a wonderful job."[40]

Indeed, one of the more glamorous aspects of M&B's activity can be traced to a Sunday when then Senator and Mrs. John F. Kennedy were leaving Trinity Church and saw an industrious group of M&Bers toiling away. Impressed, Mrs. Kennedy asked why they were working on a Sunday morning, and the club members enthusiastically told the couple about M&B. The event remained in Mrs. Kennedy's mind, because a few short years later her social secretary called to seek Mask and Bauble's help. According to Tony Hope, M&Bers went down to the White House to prepare the lighting, the sound system, and the sets for the Stratford Connecticut Shakespeare Players. Until the end of the Johnson administration, Mask and Bauble was the official provider of lighting for opera, ballet, and theater in the East Room and on the White House lawn. The club loaded lights, light stands, cable, and a portable dimming board into a University truck and would spend a day or two setting up under the watchful eye of the White House staff. After the performance, the students, now in black tie, would mingle with the guests at the Chief Executive's Mansion.

One aspect of Mask and Bauble deserves special mention: the establishment of the Calliope, a tradition that continued throughout Murphy's tenure as moderator. Calliope was a series of student-written musicals, performed each spring as major productions. In the previous spring, Murphy and the club selected a student-submitted script for the following season, and then the playwright(s) reworked and edited their show for the next spring. This placed a great deal of stress on student writing and creativity. Having a new Calliope every year, always student-written, demonstrated considerable student interest and talent. The shows were technically elaborate and provided excellent experience for the members. Student creativity was high.

Calliope I was *The Thirties Girl*, written by John Guare, who later went on to write the Tony-award-winning play, *The House of Blue Leaves*. ("I'm Here With Bells On," one of the song in Guare's Calliope, reappears in *Blue Leaves*). Guare also wrote *The Toadstool Boy*, which won first prize for Mask and Bauble in the District of Columbia Play Tournament.

The Calliope champion, according to Murphy, must be Bryan Williams. He created the book, music, and lyrics for Calliopes VI, VII, VIII, and XI, *They Went That-a-Way, One Sleepless Knight, Come Back Little Phoenix*, and *If I Had a Yardstick, I Could Rule the World*.

It was during these highly creative years that Murphy established an annual campus one-act play competition, and eventually a playwriting course. Three original one-acts, produced each year, paved the way for aspiring authors to prepare for the larger demands of writing a Calliope. John Guare felt that this competition offered a wonderful opportunity to experiment with his playwriting. The directors of the one-acts often went on to direct a larger work the following season.

Jack Hofsiss, winner of a Tony for directing *The Elephant Man*, also wrote a Calliope called *The Senior Prom*. This production transferred from campus to the Washington Theater Club, where it ran on weekends for seven months. According to Murphy, this established a longest-run record of sorts in Washington.

The last Calliope was *Leonardo!*, a "tongue-in-cheek" life of DaVinci. (*Bonaparte!* was featured in an earlier Calliope.) Many of the original scripts and cast recordings are still extant in the University Archives, and Mask and Bauble is exploring the possibility of resurrecting an old show for performance during the University's Bicentennial.

The people who viewed the Calliopes year after year marveled at the quality of the student-written productions. About Calliope II, written by William Gargaro, the *Washington Post* enthused: "Georgetown University students all but tore the roof off the Holy Trinity Auditorium....As student musicals go, this is a good one, building into a classy Act III."[41]

The audience could not have imagined the odd methods by which these annual sensations were written and produced. Tony Hope (son of the entertainer Bob Hope) wrote Calliope III—*Show Me the Way to Go Homer*. According to Hope, at the end of their junior year he and his roommate flipped a coin to decide which of the two would write Calliope III and who would be the next president of Mask and Bauble. Hope got the unenviable task of writing the show. The "rules" said that Hope as author would take the summer to write the music and the book for the play, then in September he would present the finished product to Donn Murphy, who would help him edit the play and ready it for production the following spring. But reality, in Hope's case, differed vastly from the rules.

He returned to Hollywood for the summer and scrounged for an idea for the play. After the show was performed, someone came up to him and told him that it was one of the greatest jokes ever. The story line was identical to that of *The Prisoner of Zenda* by Antony Hope Hawkens (no relation of Tony's). Hope denied the allegation since he knew whence he had lifted the story and it certainly was not *The Prisoner of Zenda*. He later read that novel and was amazed that the plot was in fact exactly the same as his. In fact, he stole most of the plot and even some of the jokes from Billy Wilder's movie, *One, Two, Three*, starring James Cagney. Hope did not worry about getting caught stealing from this movie since it flopped and he was "one of its only viewers." But he did worry about borrowing his ideas from a movie that had failed, because it must have done poorly for *some* reason.

Upon arrival at Georgetown in September, Hope had nothing in the way of script for his play. Murphy did not pressure him too much until November arrived and Hope still was not finished. Eventually, with a lot of help from several friends, Hope got the show ready to cast. Being the writer, Hope cast the entire show and was the producer. Murphy himself directed.

Problems arose as the rehearsals began. This scene needs work...That scene must go...This character must be added...

Hope remembers writing songs for a new lead character three nights before opening, and changing the leading lady's lyrics during the final dress rehearsal. He was glad she was a talented lady with a quick ear, for had she not been, the play would have died. Hope believes Murphy must have been "a saint" to deal with all the changes and still keep a high level of quality in the performance. According to Hope, "It must have been a very trying experience for anyone with any sense of professionalism....It's one of those situations where you say it's not remarkable that it was done well, it was remarkable that it was done at all."[42]

Show Me the Way to Go Homer, for all its problems, proved to be light, fast-paced, and funny, as one reviewer commented:

> *Calliope III* followed in the tradition of its predecessors. It is a fine tradition, and in some ways getting finer every year....The reason for this success was not only the excellence but the depth of the performances....Apart from performance, *Calliope* was distinguished by the excellence of its physical production. There was a great deal of spectacle, employing all the resources of lighting, sets and costumes...Final credit, and a great deal of it, must go to Mr. Donn Murphy. Supervision of the overall production is the responsibility of the director, and the unity and tightness which was exhibited...is a monument to his ability.[43]

The Calliope tradition marks the high-point in Georgetown theater since World War II.

Another institution of importance was Midnight Theater, the brain-child of Louis Scheeter, now a producer on Broadway. This was a forum for short, experimental, innovative, avant-garde productions, designed to challenge student directors. Midnight Theater was presented on Friday and Saturday evenings. A "major production" was performed at eight o'clock, and then the set struck, and another put up for the midnight show. One Midnight Theater musical, *Hang-up!*, ran for seven months. The many changes in the cast during the run allowed many performers to try their hand.

As usual, throughout its long history, Mask and Bauble had to make do with a variety of interesting spaces for performance. Murphy inaugurated his position at Mask and Bauble with a production of *Stalag 17* on the stage (subsequently walled in and made into exercise rooms) in McDonough Gymnasium, and ended his first year as director with the production of an original musical, *Banned in Boston*. According to Murphy, an enormous tarpaulin was hung midway back from the stage to divide the gymnasium and create space for a larger audience. After that season, M&B stopped producing in McDonough and moved to Gaston Hall. Gaston had been the scene of many performances earlier in the century, and adventurous students found in the attic above the lecture platform a long-abandoned set of cable and winches which provided the means of rigging pipes and hanging curtains up over the stage, thus creating wings and a backdrop. This system was used many times in the 1950s.

During the 1960s M&B's office, equipment and costumes were housed in the "Old Annex," a "temporary" structure left over from the Second World War. A fire of mysterious origin in "Old Annex" forced M&B to use the basement of Poulton Hall as storage space. Frustrated by scheduling conflicts at Trinity Theater and the time it took to prepare McDonough or Gaston Hall for a performance, Murphy and the students decided to transform their new storage room to a "black box" theater. With student-built risers and canvas director chairs, M&B created an "intimate 75-seat playing space." One problem that this new performance space (it could not be honestly called a stage or theater) had was that it contained a steel support column at its center. According to Dr. Murphy, M&Bers of that era "joked that they would not know how to put on a show without having in the center of their stage a column disguised as a tree, maypole, flag-staff, signpost, or doorway frame."

In 1964 the Belgian Ambassador to the United States cut the ribbon, formally opening "Stage One" for the performance of *Pantagleize* by Belgian playwright Michel de Ghelderode. The "theater" was so popular that M&B moved a wall to increase seating capacity. The list of shows performed in this tiny room is impressive: *The Duchess of Malfi, Man of La Mancha, Death of a Salesman, Stop the World, I Want to Get Off, The Skin of Our Teeth,* and *Arturo Ui*.

The seminomadism in terms of theater space—plays now being performed at Trinity, in Stage One, and on occasion in Gaston Hall, Copley Crypt, and the Hall of Nations—led to one of the better-known aspects of Mask and Bauble history. If you ask a Baubler how the club came to use Stage III, its present facility, he will tell you that in the seventies some wild students staged a sit-in and forced the University to give them the space. This is, however, not the full story. The full story did indeed involve some wild "kids," and one may suspect that they led to the club's acquisition of Stage III, but from there the real story and the rumors diverge greatly.

By the beginning of 1975, there developed among the club membership a greater-than-usual dissatisfaction with its limited performance space. So, a large group of members planned a coup and they named their "secret" plan "Operation Tortoise" because "you have to stick your neck out" to get what you want.[44] With stealthy care, they placed orders for all the materials needed to create a 200-seat black box theater, concealing their plan even from Dr. Murphy until the very last moment. They stayed on campus over spring break in 1975, as curtain riggers arrived and new chairs were delivered. They commandeered room 57 of Poulton Hall, a large classroom on the first floor, once a language lab and now the Hoya Station Post Office, and in the space of a week, they created an excellent little black box theater, complete with a built-in tech booth. They named the space Stage II.

Once school resumed after break, the club could present the University with a *fait accompli*, and indeed, the following Friday, a performance was given in the newly constructed theater. The administration was, regrettably, not amused at this bold stroke of student initiative, and forced the club to dismantle the entire installation. This they did, albeit with a great deal of grumbling. By 1976, however, the University built the club a new black box theater, of almost identical design to the one the students themselves had built. Located in the center wing of Poulton perpendicular to the student-built project, Stage III, as the new theater space was christened, became the place where most Mask and Bauble shows have been produced since. Unfortunately for the organization, in order to gain theater space, M&B had to give up their rehearsal space, costume and makeup space, and storage space. Ten years later, the effects of this "necessary" sacrifice can still be felt.

In the early 1960s M&B had one of the most exciting periods in its history, but the men who made that history, for the most part, do not have fond memories of their college days. Many of the writers of original plays, like John Guare, remember that the only high point of their Jesuit education during a stormy period of protests and confrontations was the opportunity to write and produce original plays. This endeavor was facilitated by the University's original one-act play competition. John Guare believes that this opportunity was unique at the time and a precious opportunity to see one's work actually performed. For anyone interested in playwriting, the competition served as an unequaled chance to learn.

The years of Donn Murphy were high-water marks for creativity and a stress on student involvement in the dramatic arts. Under him, Mask and Bauble took great risks, but also had great successes. They produced shows by authors as diverse as Shakespeare and Brecht and received reasonably consistent positive critical acclaim. Murphy's Mask and Bauble produced some of the first Sam Shepard plays in Washington, as well as a new, original musical every year, and filled the academic year with continuous theater. Unfortunately, in 1976, Dr. Murphy, who had completed his Ph.D. in theater ten years earlier, resigned his directorship of the club.

Following Murphy's departure for full-time teaching in the Fine Arts Department, Mask and Bauble experienced a brief decline. It passed into the moderatorship of Father Denis Moran, S.J. Father Moran was the last full-time Jesuit moderator of the club. With this change, gone were the Calliopes, gone was Midnight Theater, and gone, to a large extent was widespread campus involvement. Moran ruled M&B with an iron hand until 1981, and in the year following his departure the moderator's position was left unfilled. Dennis Healy then directed the organization for a year, and next Camilla David was hired as moderator. She soon changed her title to artistic director, but left shortly thereafter to form her own theater company.

In 1977, Mask and Bauble's present constitution was ratified and provided for six positions on the Executive Board (in order of importance): Executive Producer (E.P.), Associate Producer (A.P.), Business Manager, Technical Director (T.D.), Sales Director, and Marketing Director. The E.P. and A.P. correspond roughly with the old president and vice-president, but the other positions were added because the old secretary and treasurer posts could not carry on Mask and Bauble's increasingly complex everyday business. The new membership prerequisites required only that a person work on two shows in one season, at least once in a technical capacity. M&B now dedicates itself to "providing an educational experience for the student and a series of high quality productions for the general public," a far cry from its original intent to foster elocution![45]

Mask and Bauble's activities declined in the years after Murphy's resignation. The present artistic director, Mary Mitchell-Donahue, found the club in dire straits when she arrived to work at Poulton in 1983. M&B had a bad reputation around campus, as a closed, inbred group. The administration was hostile, the students mistrustful and rebellious, and the moderators/artistic directors did not wield the same power that Donn Murphy had earlier. The tradition built for over a hundred years was dwindling and if it had not been for a small core of dedicated students, the club would have withered to nothing. This small group was so tightly knit that they often alienated the rest of the campus. The quality of the shows varied, with occasional flashes of M&B's past greatness. The resources of the club were also small—Stages I and III for storage and performance, a small budget, and no power tools to build sets. While there was generally a good turnout for auditions, it was difficult to motivate people to stay and help backstage. The inner core of M&B, the "clique," seemed to do everything.

It was into this atmosphere that Mary Mitchell-Donahue arrived in 1983 with a bachelor's degree in Communications and Theater Arts, and a master's in Directing and Acting, both from the University of Maryland. She discovered Mask and Bauble through an ad in the classifieds, responded, was accepted, and took over the position of artistic director of a club that was "disorganized, disoriented, and inconsistent."[46] It was an unpopular club on campus, with what basically amounted to its own ruling oligarchy of students. Mitchell-Donahue has been at M&B

since 1983, and has provided a consistency of administration that was sorely lacking after Moran's departure.

The differences in the club between Mask and Bauble in 1983 and 1988 are considerable. The club now has a full range of modern power tools, a better technical capacity and support from its members, a wider membership, and a higher reputation for quality productions. Shows that would have attracted no one in 1980 now sell out rapidly, and a complete run of standing-room-only performances is not unusual. The productions are better organized, and M&B's publicity department is much improved. The membership has grown and continues to do so at a rapid pace, and the society's relations with the administration are excellent.

What remains for Mask and Bauble is to regain the level of creativity that it enjoyed under moderator Murphy. Perhaps it will soon—it has scheduled for its 1988–89 season a one-act play contest, much like the ones that inspired the Calliopes of the 1960s and 1970s.

Mask and Bauble has grown from a club dedicated to the promotion of eloquence to a very important artistic outlet that also adds art and theater to campus life. The road has had its ups and downs, but always, Mask and Bauble has come back to produce high quality theater, well worth the effort of cast, crew, and audience.

At present, Mask and Bauble is not the only theater group on campus. By the early seventies, M&B had become so professional and demanding, that several theater groups have since formed in order to provide a less demanding outlet for theater. In 1982, an estranged group of M&Bers created Dead Bunny Productions, dedicated to staging the small-scale shows M&B would not put on. In recent years, they have changed their name to Nomadic Theater and have produced a number of shows, including *Evita*, *Sweeney Todd*, and *Deathtrap*. In addition, there is Friday Afternoon Theater (FAT) begun in 1983, a group more closely related to academics. It fosters a closer relationship between director and actors due to its lack of technical complexity and its classroom setting. FAT produces only plays written within the last ten years. It has a good working relationship with Mask and Bauble; many M&B directors start by directing a FAT show. Theatrical opportunities continue for all Georgetown students, and Mask and Bauble may also one day celebrate its bicentennial!

Notes

We would like to thank the following people for their immeasurable assistance: Father Joseph Durkin, S.J., Father Jerome Hall, S.J., Dr. Donn Murphy, Anthony Hope, Mary Mitchell-Donahue, John Guare.

1. Program of *Twelfth Night* by William Shakespeare, May 26, 1921. Georgetown University Archives (hereafter GUA): folder—Mask and Bauble 1919–28; box—Dramatics 1900–35.

2. Article I of the 1853 Constitution of the Dramatic Association of Georgetown College, in the Secretary's Book of the Dramatic Association (hereafter DA) 1853–1863. GUA: folder—DA Minutes 1853–63; box —DA 1853–1903.

3. Article XI of the 1853 Constitution.

4. Article XVII–XXVII of the 1858 revised Constitution of the DA of Georgetown College, in the Secretary's Book of the DA 1853–1863.

5. DA Minutes of December 3, 1853, in the Secretary's Book of the DA 1853–1863.

6. List of plays, pp. 2–3 of the Secretary's Book of the DA 1853–1863.

7. *Julius Caesar* Playbill, 1921. GUA: folder—Mask & Bauble 1919–28; box: Dramatics 1900–1935.

8. Ruff, Robin, "Reminiscences of Former Dramatic Productions," *Georgetown College Journal*, vol. 38, no. 5, February 1910, pp. 173–74. GUA: folder—Dramatics 1910; box—Dramatics 1900–1935.

9. Ibid.

10. Ibid.

11. Ibid.

12. Playbill of *The Last of the Gladiators*, February 28, 1911. GUA: folder—; box—Dramatics 1900–1935.

13. In this folder there are "Mardi-Gras" programs dating from 1876 to 1896. GUA: folder—Dramatic Programs 1853–1859; box—DA 1853–1903.

14. Article I of 1868 Constitution of Dramatic Reading and Elocution Society (hereafter DRES), in Secretary's Book of DRES 1868–1870. GUA: folder—DRES Secretary's Book 1868–1870; box—DA 1853–1903.

15. Program—"Public Readings given by the Dramatic Association of Georgetown College," December 10, 1859. GUA: folder—Dramatic Programs 1853–1859; box—DA 1853–1903.

16. For a typical reading by the Reading Room Association, see unidentified newspaper clipping, May 1, 1870, file "Varia," box 18, folder 2105.

17. Page of clipping from unnamed newspapers dated April 25, 1889. GUA: folder—Dramatics 1860–1901; box—DA 1853–1903.

18. Ibid.

19. Ibid.

20. "The Revival of the Dramatic Association," *Georgetown College Journal*, January 1910, p. 149. GUA: folder—Dramatics 1910; box—Dramatics 1900–1935.

21. Clipping from unnamed newspaper dated January 16, 1910. GUA: folder—Dramatics 1910; box—Dramatics 1900-1935.

22. Program of *All the Comforts of Home* by William Gillette, January 19, 1910. GUA: folder—Dramatics 1910; box—Dramatics 1900–1935.

23. Walsh, Father Edmund, S.J., handwritten expense report. GUA: folder—Dramatics 1910; box—Dramatics 1900–1935.

24. Dailey, Vincent ('12), "A Thespian Triumph," *Georgetown College Journal*, vol. 38, no. 5, pp. 180–85.

25. Typed letter from Mr. Pallen, Manager of the Play *All the Comforts of Home*, on Alumni Association stationery. GUA: folder—Dramatics 1910; box—Dramatics 1900–1935.

36. Typed "Expense Report" from *All the Comforts of Home*. GUA: folder—Dramatics 1910; box—Dramatics 1900–1935.

27. "Dramatics at Georgetown," *The Intercollegiate*, June 1910, pp. 161–63. GUA: folder—Dramatics 1909; box—Dramatics 1900–1935.

28. Programs of Shakespeare's *The Merchant of Venice* and *Hamlet* dated March 23, 1923 and May 10, 1924 respectively. GUA: folder—Mask and Bauble (hereafter M&B) 1919–28; box—Dramatics 1900–1935.

29. *New York Telegraph*, March 14, 1928. GUA: folder—M&B 1919–28; box—Dramatics 1900–1935.

30. Program of February 25, 1928. GUA: folder—M&B 1919–28, box—Dramatics 1900–1935.

31. Clipping from unnamed newspaper dated December 1928. GUA: folder—M&B 1919–28; box—Dramatics 1900–1935.

32. "Georgetown Awarded Intercollegiate One-Act Play Trophy for Best Play," *The Fordham Ram*, May 7, 1931, p. 1. GUA: folder—M&B 1929–35; box—Dramatics 1900–1935.

33. Program of *The Tavern* by George M. Cohan, December 4, 1934. GUA: folder—M&B 1929–35; box—Dramatics 1900–1935.

34. Clipping from *Washington Tribune* dated November 11, 1934. GUA: folder—M&B 1929–35; box—Dramatics 1900–1935.

35. "Cohan Lauds GU Group," *Star*, December 2, 1934. GUA: folder—M&B 1929–35; box—Dramatics 1900–1935.

36. Office memo from Rev. Albert Grau, S.J., to V. Rev. Father Edward Bunn, S.J., President, dated March 4, 1953. GUA: folder—M&B 1953–54; box—Dramatics 1936–1959.

37. According to Donn Murphy, January 1988.

38. Program of Shakespeare's *Macbeth*, March 8, 9, 10, 1956, in Mask and Bauble Archives.

39. Preamble to 1958 Constitution in *Handbook of the Mask and Bauble Club*, p. 20. GUA: folder—M&B 1957–58; box—Dramatics 1936–59.

40. Personal letter from Jacqueline Kennedy to Donn Murphy dated June 4, 1963. GUA: folder—M&B 1963; box—Dramatics 1960–1971.

41. "Georgetown Has Happy Musical Hit," *Washington Post*, April 29, 1961.

GUA: folder—M&B 1961; box—Dramatics 1960–1971.

42. Interview with Anthony Hope, September 29, 1987.

43. Tom Scheye, "The Wicked Stage," in unnamed newspaper on April 5, 1962. Found in Anthony Hope's personal album.

44. Interview of John O'Connell by *Hoya*.

45. Preamble, Charter of the Mask and Bauble Society, 1977.

46. Interview with Mary Mitchell-Donahue, December 1987.

III. Students' Lives

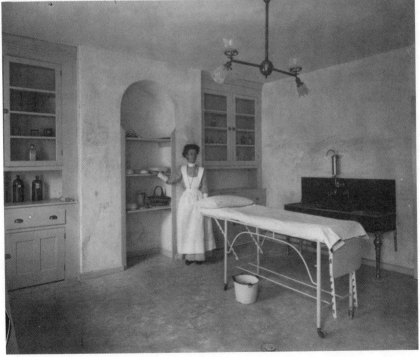

ABOVE: "Girl's Head" by J.E. Sheridan (from *The Georgetown Journal*, December, 1901. BELOW: Emergency room, Georgetown University Hospital, 1910.

Georgetown University Hospital nurses, 1910.

The Yard President, Symbol of Tradition and the Conservative Stance: A True Georgetown Gentleman

Mark Johnson

Although student organizations existed at Georgetown prior to 1891, the first one to serve in the capacity of a representative body was not formed until that year. For example, the College Catalog of 1888 listed the Toner Scientific Society, the Sodality, the Dramatic Association, and the Philodemic Society as student clubs. Yet each of these groups had a limited purpose and scope of interest; the Philodemic fielded a debate team, the Dramatic Association presented theatrical productions. The first club to unite a body of student representatives with a variety of interests for a broad purpose was the Georgetown University Athletic Association.

The Athletic Association was formally organized in 1891 to oversee all sporting and leisure activities at the University. The College Catalog for that year stated:

> The Athletic Association or "The Yard" comprises under one general direction all the organizations existing among the students for the purpose of amusement and exercise such as Baseball, Football, Track Activities, Rowing, Glee Association, Lawn Tennis, and Billiards. These associations which previous to 1889 were independent

of one another, since that date have been regulated by the Yard Committee.[1]

The Association at that time was open to "any student of any department of the University...provided he pay the Yard assessment."[2] The executive Yard Committee consisted of a president, a vice-president, a secretary, a treasurer, and the managers of the baseball, football, track and field, tennis, billiards, and musical clubs. A Jesuit moderator initially served as president, while a member of each year's senior class was elected to the vice-presidency.

Despite his designation as the vice-president, the student leader of the Athletic Association was the functioning head of the organization. The *Journal* of March 1892 reports that after Father Murphy opened the meeting with a prayer, "Vice-President Denver, '92, taking the chair...business was proceeded with."[3] The student vice-president actually presided over the meetings. The Jesuit "president" served in an advisory role, much like the moderators of the other student organizations. By 1901, *The Hodge Podge* (the early yearbook) and the College Catalog listed the elected student leader as the Yard President and the Jesuit moderator as the Faculty Director.

The duties and responsibilities of the early Yard Presidents centered almost solely around athletics. For many years, the Yard Presidents oversaw the actual formation and function of the major sports teams. The *Journal* of February 1893 states, "The Yard officers...have begun the selection of the baseball team."[4] In February 1899, "The news that the yard would hold an indoor athletic meet...[was] welcomed with great enthusiasm."[5] Therefore, the fate of one's presidency often depended on the success of the athletic teams. In praising a president in 1898, the *Journal* stated, "We can recall no time in the history of Georgetown when athletics awakened a greater interest than during the season just closed."[6]

A far greater burden on the Yard President than fielding successful athletic teams (for Georgetown has always attracted men of great athletic prowess), was ensuring the financial stability of the athletic budget. As early as 1891, "At the Yard meeting...the report of the Treasurer showed...a very small margin to open the baseball season."[7] Therefore, the Yard President was constantly devising schemes to raise funds. The first Yard President, Henry P. Wilson, sponsored concerts, while later presidents resorted to season ticket packages and even Mardi Gras parties. To guarantee that the athletic teams were well equipped and financed, the students demanded much of the Yard President. Those who voted believed that "The man that occupies the chair of the Athletic Association at Georgetown should be the most able man at the school."[8]

This requirement that the Yard President possess the skills and talents of a true leader was the most important characteristic of the formative years of the Yard. Editorials implored students to use their votes to do "the right thing for Georgetown and for the future of athletics at the Hilltop."[9] Without "able and forceful speakers" as presidents, the Yard might not have lasted beyond 1900.[10] Facing a financial crisis, Yard President Henry P. Wilson "delivered a speech that had the true ring of Demosthenes and was the very stimulus needed" to raise adequate funds.[11] A later president, H. Murray MacElhinny, was "born a businessman, tactful and courteous...the elements that make for a success."[12]

The Yard President was elevated to his leadership position each May by his peers because of his "ingenuity, his business ability, and his enthusiasm to aid Georgetown."[13] Once in that position, the Yard President became the focal point for raising "the morale and spirit of the men of the University."[14] He had the responsibility of conducting and presiding over huge pep rallies held in the Old North courtyard prior to major athletic contests.

As Georgetown entered the twentieth century and the student population continued to expand, the Yard Presidency began to incorporate responsibilities outside of a purely athletic nature. In 1915, John C. McNamara, hoping to improve Georgetown's social atmosphere, "held many gatherings of good fellowship."[15] By 1920, in addition to the athletic platform, candidates for the office were promising "to form advisory committees...to confer on matters affecting the entire student body...and to see that Freshmen rules were strictly enforced."[16]

This assumption of a social and student advocacy role by the

Yard President increased the demands of the office. In 1919, recognizing that his responsibilities encompassed much more than those of the original Athletic Association presidents, Robert J. Reiss helped form the first Student Council at Georgetown. Its original stated purpose was "to act as a medium of communication between the faculty and the student body."[17] The body consisted of two representatives from each class, with the Yard President presiding as chairman.

In the same year that the Student Council was formed, the Athletic Association adopted a new constitution, creating a Board of Control of Athletics consisting of three students, three faculty members, and three alumni. Presiding over the new board, in "the highest level of executive activity in which the students can engage," was the Yard President.[18] The constitution delegated all powers of athletic scheduling, the awarding of varsity letters, the hiring of coaches, and the budgeting of the teams to the Board of Control.

Thus, in the year 1920 the office of President of the Yard expanded to include the key leadership roles of the Student Council and the revised Athletic Association. During this time period, the *Hoya* began to refer to the Yard President as "the official head of the student body" and to his office as "the greatest honor that can be conferred on any Georgetown student."[19] The Yard President became "a man who is representative [of Georgetown] both on and off the campus."[20] At the same time, the *Hoya* wrote: "We venture to assert that there is probably not more than one man [in each class]...capable of filling the office."[21]

As the glory of the office of Yard President increased, so did the burden. His duties included introducing the freshman class to Georgetown and arbitrating their disputes with the sophomore class, "an almost impossible task."[22] The role further demanded that "he be on hand at every major athletic contest, and be master of every situation that may arise."[23] As head of the Student Council, the Yard President was further charged with improving the general state of student affairs and relations with the administration and functioning as the official representative of the student body. For example, in 1921, President McElhinny traveled to the Chicago funeral of an undergraduate to pay respects to the family on behalf of the student body. For all the praise it heaped on the office in the 1920s, the *Hoya* also labeled the job "a dual responsibility and a very heavy one."[24]

Despite the duality of his role in the 1920s, the Yard President's most important duty continued to be conducting the presidency of the Athletic Association. The spirited Yard campaigns, held annually in May, were still primarily characterized by promises of "bringing big teams here for the athletic schedules,"[25] and "keeping all the athletic activities of the University on the high plane."[26] Only secondarily did the candidates mention other goals such as the "installation of individual mailboxes on the Hilltop."[27]

At the same time, the campus press continued to evaluate the success or failure of a Yard President by his contribution to Georgetown athletics and not by those to the Student Council. Robert J. Riley, '20, "succeeded...in doing his part toward ensuring Georgetown's brilliant athletic successes of the year."[28] In 1924, outgoing President J. Hanway Grasty was praised as "a success if his accomplishments in life are but one half of those he has achieved for the Athletic Association."[29] In 1927, *Ye Domesday Booke* noted Yard President Dennis Shea's "untiring activity...and wholehearted devotion to the interests of Georgetown...[which helped] the Blue and Gray attain its present position in college athletics."[30]

In 1925, the Athletic Association created the office of the Director of Athletics. Up to that point, much of the Yard President's time had been spent on administrative athletic functions, such as scheduling and budgeting. The new Director assumed those job responsibilities. While it might seem that after this change the Yard President lost some of his power or prestige, the opposite is in fact the truth. Without the time-consuming burden of acting as an athletic administrator, the Yard President began to place more attention and effort into the Student Council. By 1925, this organization had "grown in strength and prestige...working for the achievement of the ideals and the perpetuation of the traditions for [sic] which Georgetown is justly proud."[31]

The original Athletic Association founded in 1891 and reconstituted in 1920 disappeared from the records in 1932 as full-time administrators took over its functions. After that time, the President of the Yard was no longer referred to as President of the Athletic Association. Yearbook photographs of the Athletic Association did not include him.

Despite the loss of this administrative role, the Yard President maintained connections with his original roots in athletics. After 1930, Yard Presidents used athletics as a rallying point for unifying the student body and creating a sense of school spirit. The Yard President "was expected to preside at the varsity contests...[as] the recognized cheerleader of the University."[32] His leadership at these events was vital to Georgetown's success. Criticizing Yard President Kiernan Hyland, '40, the *Hoya* stated, "he isn't out there leading the cheers, and the crowd is like a ship without a rudder."[33] For the Yard President in the 1930s–1940s was "a man who tipify[ed] the spirit of the Hilltop."[34]

During the time period between the Yard President's disassociation from the Athletic Association and World War II, the Yard President was recognized as the leader of the student body by students and administrators alike. Although students proclaimed him the "epitome of the Georgetown gentleman, the 'front man' for the College in its dealings with...the outside world," the real affirmation of his importance came with administrative recognition.[35]

Several times during the 1930s, the administration demonstrated its respect for the Yard Presidency. The first paragraph of the lead *Hoya* story on March 9, 1932, reporting on a George Washington bicentennial ceremony, reads, "The Rev. Coleman Nevils, S.J., Mr. Gerard J. O'Brien, President of the Yard, and the Vice-President of the United States, Charles Curtis...received a brilliant reception here in the Hall of Cardinals."[36] Later in that same year, in honor of Founder's Day, "a colorful and distinguished assemblage of the diplomatic and education circles of Washington...[gathered at Gaston Hall] ceremonies opened with greetings from the President of the Students."[37]

Perhaps the greatest testimony ever to the universal respect accorded to the Yard President came during the 1936 Hilltop visit of His Eminence Eugenio Cardinal Pacelli, the Papal Secretary of State to Pope Pius XI and himself a future pope. At the ceremony honoring the Cardinal, Yard President Peter Brennan extended the greetings of the student body in an address delivered in Latin. The *Hoya* reports that Brennan's remarks "evidently appealed to His Eminence, who listened attentively to every word."[38]

In 1940, the studentry voted to restructure the Student Council constitution. The new Council incorporated the heads of major student activities such as the Philodemic, the Sodality, and the *Journal* into the voting body. This change led to a better regulation of student organizations by the Council and actually to a stronger student government. Student leaders were united in the same body for the purpose of serving Georgetown. Showing their respect for the tradition and prestige of the Yard Presidency, the students placed the Yard President at the head of this new assemblage.

As previously stated, the respect engendered for the Yard President stemmed from his ability to lead and represent the student community at Georgetown in a gentlemanly fashion. During the period immediately preceding United States involvement in World War II, the Yard Presidents truly lived up to their billing by representing the very best that Georgetown had to offer to the nation and the world at that troubling moment.

In 1938, Yard President E. James Hickey sponsored a Peace Day at Georgetown. As tensions heightened in Europe, Hickey's successors continued and expanded upon his original idea. Accordingly, on May 17, 1939 (Ascension Thursday), Yard President Thomas Gildea served as Chairman of the National Catholic Students' Peace Day. By the following year, the Peace day became a "country-wide celebration...initiated at Georgetown."[39] In a letter to his fellow students about the ceremony, student president Hyland stated, "Every true Georgetown man will attend tonight."[40] Responding to this plea for action from the man they regarded as the embodiment of the Georgetown spirit, hundreds of Hoyas joined Hyland in praying for world peace.

The peace ceremonies that night were held at 225 Catholic schools and universities throughout the nation as a result of a letter that Hyland had sent to the Deans of America's Catholic learning institutions. In that letter, he declared:

In the midst of general intellectual uncertainty, of the ruthless violation of moral obligation and of the unjust appeal to physical force,
our Catholic schools should propose to our fellow citizens the eternal principles of justice and charity in which alone lasting peace can
endure.[41]

This moment, initiated by Yard Presidents, brought national
attention to both Georgetown and the cause of world peace.
The day ended with a reading of a "Peace Credo for Catholic
Youth" in which Georgetown students pledged their allegiance
to the country, to Jesus Christ, and to the "inspired leadership
of Pope Pius XII in the cause of World Peace."[42] It truly was
one of Georgetown's and the Yard Presidency's most glorious
moments.

Unfortunately for Georgetown, the nation, and all of the
world, the United States was drawn into World War II by the
December 7, 1941 Japanese attack on Pearl Harbor. Three days
later, Yard President William V. Finn displayed the leadership
abilities inherent in his office by imploring his fellow students
to attend voluntary Mass to "offer prayers for guidance of our
nations leaders during this war...for special protection of our
alumni and students...called to active service...and for all those
connected with our Alma Mater, Georgetown."[43]

At a December 15, 1941 gathering of the entire faculty, administration, and student body, Finn read a resolution pledging
"the University and its members, both faculty and student
body, to give themselves wholeheartedly to the cause of defending our nation in this time of peril."[44] After passing the resolution unanimously, the students gave President Franklin D.
Roosevelt the same tribute they had given to President Wilson
during World War I, a rousing shout of "Hoya!"

Once again, the Yard President's actions embodied faith, service, and loyalty, the best of Georgetown's ideals.

World War II had a dramatic effect on all of Georgetown, including the Yard Presidency. Student activities ceased to exist,
as an accelerated academic program was put into effect by the
administration. Student Council and *Hoya* records show a gap
of inactivity between the years of 1944 and 1946. Sadly, in 1944,
the fifty-three-year-old tradition of electing a Yard President
was broken. The campus environment at the time was too dis-

ordered and provisional for a student government or a Yard President to be able to function. The war that many Yard Presidents had worked and prayed so hard to avoid claimed their time-honored office, at least for the time being.

After the last Yard election in 1943, Georgetown suffered a wartime crisis. The student body had shrunk to one-third of its prewar size, and those remaining students were burdened with the task of completing their studies in three years or less. The activities traditionally led and supervised by the Yard President, such as freshman hazing, Old North pep rallies, and sports rivalries were put on hold.

In March of 1945, responding to student cries for a return to a more normal college life, the administration helped form a temporary Student Activities Committee. The minutes of its first meeting reflect the provisionary nature of the assemblage. They state that "the purpose of this committee is to be that of functioning as a wartime Student Council inasmuch as there are at present no provisions for elections."[45] Therefore, the membership was nine nonelected student organization leaders with Father Charles J. Foley, S.J., presiding as chairman.

The new organization did provide a number of social activities and opportunities to the wartime students, yet Hoyas longed for the return of the Yard President. The *Hoya* voiced the opinion of many undergraduates when it wrote: "The present Student Activities Committee is doing a splendid job, BUT it does not have the proper authority or the full support of the student body."[46]

As the war came to an end, one of the first changes the students called for was the return of the Yard Presidency. Many felt that with a true student leader, Georgetown could again capture the spirit of its age-old customs and traditions. Echoing these desires, the *Hoya* wrote, "We want a yard officer once more...It is the only way the student body can be represented, organized, and led with any authority...With this will come that 'Old Georgetown Spirit' so long absent from the Hilltop."[47]

After nearly a three-year absence from the Hilltop, Yard elections returned on January 19, 1946, when Charles Hagan became the first Yard President since prewar days. The task of restoring a normal college life at Georgetown that faced Hagan and his successors was an awesome one. But it was one the undergraduates trusted that their Yard Presidents could accomplish. True to the standards of the age-old office, it was a task the Yard Presidents did accomplish.

Although due to his January election Hagan served an abbreviated term of only six months, the *Hoya* saluted his success. The editors wrote of him, "We now possess a tangible head for the student body at the Hilltop. Once again we can look to one of ourselves as our leader."[48] With the return of the Yard Presidency, "evidence of the vivid colorful life which characterized [prewar] Georgetown...[declaimed the Hoya] made itself felt."[49]

Perhaps one of the most important student leaders at Georgetown during the twentieth century was Hagan's successor, Richard M. Keenan. As Yard President during the first complete postwar year at the Hilltop, he labored to reestablish normal student life by promoting a plan that he called "A Platform for a Greater Georgetown." In this four-page document he outlined nine major points with the goal that "students may obtain the greatest possible benefits from their days at Georgetown and that they will enjoy college life in the fullest."[50]

Keenan's plan included student representation on University policy committees, the improvement of campus facilities, and the return of a progressive athletic program. At the same time, he appointed a committee to draft a new Student Council constitution. Labeling the existing one "unclear and inferior,"[51] Keenan believed that "without an adequate Constitution the Council at Georgetown can never hope to become well established and thus derive for the student body and for the University great and lasting benefits."[52]

In a time of uncertainly at the University, Richard M. Keenan made great progress in reinstating the institution of the Yard Presidency. As he left office, the *Hoya* wrote, "It will take extraordinary perseverance and loyalty to the students on the part of [any succeeding Yard President] to equal the astonishing and praiseworthy devotion to Georgetown so consistently and cheerfully displayed by Dick Keenan."[53]

Luckily for Georgetown, Keenan's successors did possess much of the same leadership abilities.

The next several rebuilding years were difficult ones for the Student Council and the Yard Presidency. An impatient student press began to question the worth of a student government that was accomplishing little. At the same time, the University administration delayed approval of the student government constitution written during Keenan's presidency. Without a constitution, the Council lacked authority, legitimacy, and University funding. It had little ability to "provide concrete results for the students...on a shoestring budget...[There was] no chance to do anything on a large scale."[54] The *Hoya* labeled the Council "almost useless to campus life," and continued by "placing the blame for this whole situation...on the President of the Yard."[55]

This challenge and criticism of the Yard Presidency was unprecedented in Georgetown history. Had the *Hoya* used such harsh words in criticism of a president in years past, the editors would have come under fire for an almost treason-like offense. Yet the student body seemed to share the *Hoya*'s views. The Yard elections of 1947 attracted little attention from the students as compared to the excitement of the spirited campaigns of yesteryear. At the 1947 nomination meeting, "the election fights got off to a dull start...which for its lack of interest and poor attendance was unique in Georgetown history."[56]

Through the tireless efforts of the next several Yard Presidents, the Student Council and the Yard Presidency slowly returned to their prewar stature. In 1947, Yard President Larry Corroon initiated a student fund-raising campaign to assist in the construction of McDonough gymnasium. This project united the student body and the alumni community in an effort to improve Georgetown. During the campaign, Corroon presided over a "galaxy of prominent Old Grads" gathered in a Gaston Hall fund-raising rally.[57] This event marked the official return of a ceremonial function and responsibility to the Yard Presidency. Subsequent developments at the Hilltop contributed to the further reinstitutionalization of the Yard Presidency and to the commencement of that office's glory years during the 1950s.

Despite his successes at partially reestablishing the Yard Presidency, Corroon was dissatisfied with the state of student government when he left office. His frustration stemmed from the delay in ratification of the Student Council Constitution by the Dean of the College. Corroon wrote that without the document, "Georgetown has no Student Council...until such time as the Council is allowed to operate in well-defined spheres with definite responsibilities and authority. There is little or no point in continuing our [the Student Council's] efforts."[58] Corroon's comments, student restlessness with the slow rebuilding, and the quality of Corroon's successors reinvigorated the organization. The Yard elections of the following year, 1948, were marked by a voter turnout of over 70%.

In 1950, four years after the office had returned to campus in the students' minds, the administration approved a constitution containing the office of the Yard President, and stating that: "The President of the Yard shall be President of the Student Body and President of the Student Council."[59] The Yard President at the time, Daniel Degnan, issued a statement that more clearly defined the office by adding a sense of historical perspective to it. Degnan wrote:

> The President of the Yard is still responsible for rallies and general support of athletics, and the tradition of the Athletic Association continues in his signing of the G certificate, and his travelling with the team.

> But even more important than these duties is the great tradition of leadership of the student body which has been handed down through the office of the President of the Yard.

> Georgetown's Yard President is more than a Student Council President. He is the leader and representative of the Student Body in all its activities...

> Since 1891 he has been President of the Athletic Association and leader of the student body. Though the Student Council has been weak and at times almost extinct, his office has remained strong.[60]

Degnan's success in ratifying the constitution and in educating the community about the historical importance of the Yard Presidency returned the office to its prewar stature.

The student press, which had been particularly tough on the Yard Presidency during the rebuilding years, recognized the importance of the new constitution. The *Hoya* reported that the document "adds powers and responsibilities never before given to the students of Georgetown."[61] This accomplishment was "the product of tremendous effort expended by...the efforts of every Yard President since the war."[62]

During his tenure, Degnan increased the responsibilities and influence of the office in ways other than through ratification of the constitution. He initiated a regular column in the *Hoya* titled "From the Yard Office," through which he could speak to the student constituency. Among other things, the column enabled him to appeal for support of the athletic teams, a responsibility of Yard Presidents of the past. He also established close ties with the Alumni Association, earning the Yard President an ex-officio seat on the Alumni Board of Governors. Of this organization, Degnan wrote to his fellow students, "A man can't belong to a better organization after college than his own Alumni Association, where he works with men who have the same beliefs, common memories and associations, and a real feeling of friendship and charity for each other."[63] Like Yard Presidents of years past, Degnan set an example for his classmates of the duty-minded and loyal Georgetown gentleman.

Throughout the 1950s, the Yard President enjoyed successes on several fronts. The level of communication with the student body increased with the introduction of "fireside chats" over WGTB by President Richard McCooey in 1951 and by the continuation of regular *Hoya* columns. This high level of communication in turn led to increased support for Yard and Council activities from the students. In 1951, Yard President B.J. Phoenix organized a successful student trip to Miami that had failed for lack of support in past years. The overwhelming response to the 1951 trip caused Phoenix to write a letter of thanks addressed to the "Men of Georgetown." In it he wrote, "The whole venture of the Miami Trip points out so clearly what we can do when we get behind our student leaders 100 percent...we can accomplish much when we work together as a unit, as that of a body of men called Georgetown."[64]

The support of the student body also enabled the Yard Presidents to revive traditions of the past. In 1953, the prewar Old North porch athletic rallies returned when the Yard President staged a "monster rally...followed by a car caravan to Uline

Arena," for a basketball game against George Washington.[65] The Yard President once again presided over these gatherings of Georgetown men, "instilling in each student a spirit of loyalty and honor to Georgetown."[66]

With the return in the importance and respect for this office, the Yard President again truly sat above his classmates. The role was a demanding and sometimes thankless one. For example, after several acts of vandalism on campus, Phoenix wrote to his classmates, "I feel a responsibility, given me by you, to bring this matter to your attention...These acts are a violation of the principles of a Catholic gentleman...We as Georgetown men should be concerned...I ask your cooperation to prevent any further recurrences."[67] The Yard President often fulfilled this role of the moral conscience of the student body.

The Yard President also returned to his role as a representative of Georgetown to the outside world. He was often sent to national conventions, funerals, and gatherings of alumni in this capacity. On occasion, the Student Council passed resolutions directing the Yard President to address an area of local concern. For example, in 1956, the Council voted that "The President of the Yard write a letter to the Editor of the *Washington Post* concerning the adverse coverage which Georgetown has been receiving."[68]

Perhaps the most important factor involved in the return and rise of the Yard Presidency was the legitimacy granted to the office by not only the students, but the entire Georgetown community. Alumni leaders worked closely with the Yard President throughout the 1950s to "discuss and develop ways in which the student body might become more closely integrated with the alumni."[69] These efforts resulted in regular formal gatherings of alumni and students to discuss Georgetown, student involvement in University fund-raising campaigns, alumni screening centers for Georgetown candidates, and alumni assistance in job placement for graduating seniors.

This interaction with the alumni community was invaluable for the students and the school as a whole. The undergraduates obtained a real sense of pride and devotion to Georgetown from their elder brothers. In his Student Report to the Alumni, Yard President Richard McCooey wrote: "I should like to close by again extending my sincere thanks on behalf of the Georgetown student body; and expressing a note of hope that we can prove as generous in the ranks of the Alumni as you, and help in realizing a Greater Georgetown."[70] The Yard Presidents all worked selflessly towards this goal.

In addition to winning support and recognition from the alumni community, the Yard Presidents during this era were successful in dealings with the University administration. Throughout the 1950s, Father McGrath, Father Rock, Father Bunn, and other administrators addressed the Council. Each time they prefaced their remarks with praise and advice for the Council and the Yard President. In fact, Father Yates respected the work and purpose of the Yard President so much that he developed an oath for the incoming officeholder to take. The pledge contained the lines, "I promise faithfully to devote my best efforts to working for the common good of all the students of Georgetown College...to promote in all ways possible and at all times the good name, prestige and interest of my University, Georgetown, our Alma Mater."[71] Following the oath, the Jesuit moderator of the student government bore witness to and prayed God's blessing on the new president.

The Yard President was often able to obtain favorable results in his dealings with administrative officials. Minutes of Council meetings during the 1950s contain repeated instances that support this conclusion. Yard Presidents were able to negotiate anything from an increased number of "late nights" to the establishment of a student lounge, from excused cuts from mandatory Mass to the creation of a Student Union. The Yard President was able to operate effectively because of his close working relationship with the administration. Richard Coleman stressed the importance of this relationship in his notes to his successor. Coleman wrote, "remember throughout the year that the Administration has agreed to let the Yard President know about proposed rule changes before they are promulgated in order that he may present student views on them."[72]

With the Yard Presidency again operating smoothly with the three major constituencies at Georgetown, the students, alumni, and administrators, the student press backed down on the harsh criticism of the immediate postwar days. The Yard Presidency was described as the office from which "student opinion emanates with authority,"[73] whose occupant was "dedicated to the service of the students and to the ideal of a better Georgetown."[74] Finally, the Yard Presidents of this period were credited with a major role in the successful postwar return of Georgetown to a quality institution of higher education. For "the men of the Yard [as was said]...[were] prominent figures in [these] years of progress."[75]

As Georgetown entered the 1960s, the students seemed content with their level of involvement and influence in the decision-making process as manifested in the Yard President. However, that decade was quickly torn apart by escalating civil rights clashes across the nation, the assassination of John F. Kennedy, and the Vietnam War. Students at Berkeley and other schools began the antiestablishment movements on their campuses by revolting against administrative control, curricula, and the lack of student power.

Thrust into this radical environment, Georgetown students responded in a slow, confused manner. Perhaps students did deserve more power. Yet this notion did not harmonize with many students' Catholic beliefs.

The Yard Presidents and presidency of the 1960s reflected this state of confusion and contradiction. Each year the Yard President responded to the increasing unrest throughout the nation and the hidden tension at Georgetown by calling for a student leadership conference. These conferences, chaired by the Yard Presidents, examined areas of student concern at the University and issued reports on their findings.

The 1963 Special Committee on Investigation for the Student Council of Georgetown College identified several problems at the University, including "a lack of pride, thoughtfulness, and responsibility on the part of some students,...stemming from inadequate communication between faculty-administration and students."[76] A later conference, the 1965 Prospect for Georgetown Student Leadership Conference, reaffirmed this complaint but focused mainly on curriculum issues. It stated that "The most serious abuse of students would seem to be in the case of required theology and philosophy courses."[77] The 1966 conference criticized a lack of real student input in the policy process. The report issued that year stated: "Student leaders must have a vote, not just a voice, in the decisions of the Administration that affect the students in a direct way."[78]

Presiding over all of this student frustration was the Yard President. Ever the statesman, each one was able to convince his fellow classmates against radical action while many of the nation's other campuses were under siege. The Yard Presidents, although in difficult positions, continued their efforts to serve Georgetown and to provide ways that would make their fellow students' Georgetown experience more enjoyable. In 1966, the Yard President "successfully expanded activities to include a greater number of students...on the University Traffic Board, the Discipline Board, and admission's committees."[79]

Perhaps the greatest student complaint at the time was the poor state of relationships between the students, faculty, and administration. In the early 1960s, the Yard Presidents began advocating the creation of a faculty senate, which they felt would "have a wholesome effect on student-teacher relations for both the student body in general and for the individual student."[80] The *Hoya* of March 18, 1965, reports that "Yard President Vincent Gallagher...reported on a meeting between the Yard and Father Bunn [Chancellor] concerning the possibilities of a Faculty Senate."[81] The Council then passed a resolution in support of the idea. Later in that week, Gallagher met with Father Gerard S. Campbell, S.J., University President, and Father Thomas Fitzgerald, S.J., Dean of the College, and discussed "various problems of academics, curriculum, and student-faculty—administrative relationships."[82] Soon afterward, Father Campbell appeared before a meeting of the faculty and supported the idea of a faculty senate. Yard President Vincent Gallagher was instrumental in the creation of this important and lasting body.

As the 1960s continued along a turbulent path, Georgetown began to lose some of her oldest traditions. Her Catholic identity itself had changed with the easing of many restrictions and regulations. Social traditions such as hazing and the Rat Race dances also saw their last days. Even academic traditions, such as rhetoric, logic, and Latin, slipped quietly away. Yet in the midst of this time of uncertainty there remained the institution of the Yard Presidency.

On May 12, 1966, the Georgetown community gathered in Gaston Hall to celebrate the seventy-fifth anniversary of the Yard. Although the office had certainly changed since its creation, its core philosophy remained the same. That philosophy involved finding the one man each year who best embodied the true spirit of Georgetown, her ideals, her faith, and her traditions, and presenting him as the model of the Georgetown gentleman.

As traditions and ideals continued to crumble at the University in the late 1960s, the Yard could not escape this tide of change. By 1968, "The student uprisings and discontent that rocked the Nation found expression in a new attitude and posture for the student leaders at Georgetown."[83] The Yard President "steered a sometimes difficult center course attempting to re-evaluate and articulate the motivations and feelings of the University and her students."[84] By the following year, the Yard President could no longer stay on this delicate course.

The University erupted into change. The five undergraduate campuses were united, women were admitted to the College, and the number of campus radicals greatly increased. Tradition was said by many to be in essence an evil, representative of "the establishment." The student opinion of the time can be summed up by a passage in the 1969 yearbook:

> Behind the abrasive voice of protest lies a genuine spirit of dissatisfaction. To the relief of many and the consternation of a few this dissatisfaction has actually erupted into a nihilistic confrontation.[85]

This spirit of confrontation soon led the students to challenge the system of student government known as the Yard and the Student Council. In April of 1969, the student body, true to the spirit of the 1960s, scrapped one of Georgetown's oldest and noblest traditions, the Yard Presidency. In its place, the students created a technocratic office best filled by one with an administrative mind. There was no need for the office-holder to be a Georgetown gentleman, for the Georgetown gentleman no longer existed. He had vanished along with the Yard Presidency.

Notes

1. *College Catalog*, 1891.
2. *Georgetown College Journal* (hereafter *GCJ*), March 1892, p. 136.
3. *GCJ*, March 1892, p. 136.
4. *GCJ*, February 1893, p. 87.
5. *GCJ*, February 1899, p. 237.
6. *GCJ*, December 1898, p. 127.
7. *GCJ*, January 1891, p. 64.
8. *Hoya*, June 1, 1922, p. 4.
9. Ibid.
10. *Hoya*, May 13, 1920, p. 4.
11. *GCJ*, March 1891, p. 104.
12. *Hoya*, September 30, 1920, p. 4.
13. Ibid.
14. Ibid.
15. *Ye Domesday Booke*, 1915 (n.p.).
16. *Hoya*, September 30, 1920, p. 4.
17. *Ye Domesday Booke*, 1923 (n.p.)
18. *Ye Domesday Booke*, 1925, p. 375.
19. *Hoya*, May 24, 1928, p. 2.
20. *Ye Domesday Booke*, 1934, p. 64.
21. *Hoya*, May 13, 1920, p. 4.
22. *Hoya*, May 23, 1929, p. 2.
23. Ibid.
24. *Hoya*, December 21 1928, p. 2.
25. *Hoya*, September 17, 1921, p. 4.
26. *Hoya*, October 11, 1923, p. 4.
27. Ibid.
28. *Ye Domesday Booke*, 1920 (n.p.).
29. *Ye Domesday Booke*, 1924, p. 25.
30. *Ye Domesday Booke*, 1927, p. 51.
31. *Ye Domesday Booke*, 1926, p. 77.
32. *Hoya*, February 12, 1940, p. 2.
33. Ibid.
34. *Hoya*, May 14, 1941, p. 2.
35. *Hoya*, May 3, 1939, p. 2.
36. *Hoya*, March 9, 1932, p. 1.
37. *Hoya*, April 13, 1932, p. 1.
38. *Hoya*, October 28, 1936, p. 7.
39. Public letter from Kiernan Hyland to the Georgetown community, May 1, 1940.

40. Ibid.

41. *Hoya,* May 1, 1940, p. 1.

42. *Peace Credo for Catholic Youth,* May 1, 1940, Georgetown University Archives (hereafter GUA).

43. Minutes of Student Council meeting of December 10, 1941, GUA.

44. *Hoya,* December 17, 1941, p. 6.

45. Minutes of the organizational meeting of the Student Activities Committee, March 9, 1945, GUA.

46. *Hoya,* November 2, 1945, "That Old Georgetown Spirit," p. 4.

47. Ibid.

48. *Hoya,* "The Yard Elections," February 1, 1946, p. 2.

49. Ibid.

50. "Platform for a Greater Georgetown," Richard M. Keenan, 1946, GUA.

51. Richard M. Keenan, Student Council Minutes, October 30, 1946, GUA.

52. *Georgetown University Journal,* Richard M. Keenan, 1946, GUA.

53. Memo, Eugene Stewart, "The Duties of the Yard President," 1947, GUA.

54. *Hoya,* February 20, 1948, p. 2.

55. Ibid., p. 4.

56. *Hoya,* May 16, 1947, p. 1.

57. *Hoya,* December 12, 1947, p. 3.

58. Letter written to the *Hoya* by Lawrence F. Corroon, GUA, 1947.

59. Constitution of the Student Council of Georgetown College, 1950, Article III, Section 2, GUA.

60. Daniel A. Degnan, Report on the President of the Yard as President of the Athletic Association, GUA, 1950.

61. *Hoya,* May 17, 1950, p. 1.

62. Ibid.

63. *Hoya,* February 21, 1950, p. 2.

64. *Hoya,* February 14, 1951, p. 2.

65. *Hoya,* February 26, 1953, p. 1.

66. Richard McCooey, excerpt from a speech given to the Georgetown University College Student Council, Minutes of October 31, 1951, GUA.

67. *Hoya,* February 14, 1951, p. 2.

68. Resolution #108, Georgetown College Student Council of 1956, GUA, 1956.

69. Excerpt from the minutes of a meeting of the Georgetown College Student Council, GUA, December 3, 1953.

70. *Hoya,* December 7, 1951, p. 2.

71. Father Gerard F. Yates, S.J., The Student Council Pledge, GUA, 1957.

72. Richard M. Coleman, Notes to future Yard Presidents, GUA, 1957.

73. *Ye Domesday Booke,* 1953, p. 140.

74. *Ye Domesday Booke,* 1955, p. 87.

75. *Ye Domesday Booke,* 1954, p. 85.

76. The Special Committee on Investigation for the Student Council of Georgetown College, GUA, 1963.

77. Prospect for Georgetown: The Report of the 1965–66 Student Leadership Conference, GUA, 1965.

78. Prospect for Georgetown: The 1966–67 Georgetown University Student Leadership Conference, GUA, 1966.

79. *Ye Domesday Booke,* 1966, p. 153.

80. Prospect for Georgetown: The Report of the 1965–66 Student Leadership Conference, GUA, 1965.

81. *Hoya,* March 18, 1965, p. 3.

82. *Hoya,* March 26, 1965, p. 1.

83. *Ye Domesday Booke,* 1968, p. 123.

74. Ibid.

85. *Ye Domesday Booke,* 1969, p. 21.

Prologue:
A Bad Day for Tradition

Jonathan Bacal

On the evening of March 9, 1969, hundreds of students massed in Georgetown University's Quadrangle. They had gathered to protest the Georgetown "Establishment," and they proceeded to attack its symbols. The protesters burned copies of the weekly *Hoya*, which they saw as both reactionary and unsympathetic. They also burned in effigy "Joe Hoya," the "hated symbol of all Georgetown has become," *The Hoya* reported later that week.[1]

As student government treasurer Larry LaPere noted, "it was a bad day for tradition." It was certainly a bad day for the seventy-eight-year-old "Yard," the student government of Georgetown College. The demonstration in the Quad had been triggered by the resignation of freshman student council representative Bill Doyle and the subsequent withdrawal of all representatives of the class of 1972, the freshman class, from the Yard.[2] The demonstrators saw the Yard as part of the establishment, and they would have none of it. The Yard—perceived as old, white, male, and conservative—embodied Georgetown tradition in the eyes of many students, and tradition was a dangerous thing to be associated with in the turbulent spring of 1969.

Within a few weeks after the Quadrangle demonstration the Yard was dead. The withdrawal of its freshmen representatives had only hastened the demise of an already doomed institution.

The Yard had—as one *Hoya* writer contended somewhat dramatically—lasted "longer, with more continuity and less disruption, than the governments of 93 nations," and had been led by men of the caliber of U.S. Senator Philip Hart ('34) and restauranteur Richard McCooey ('52); but it was unable to survive the turmoil Georgetown, and the nation, underwent in the late 1960s.[3]

The student government that replaced the Yard in 1969 and flourished until the mid-seventies was in style and substance radically different from its predecessor. It was the product of its times, and was in large part the outgrowth of the then blossoming antiwar and student-power movements. Under it, the students of Georgetown's separate undergraduate schools were unified, and student government achieved greater influence and power in the affairs of the university than it had before or has had since. While it benefited from talented leadership, the reasons for its rise and fall have to do largely with outside events, at Georgetown and around the nation and world.

Was this change in student government a good one for Georgetown? This paper is in part an attempt to answer that question, and to offer a history of student government during the late 1960s and early 1970s. The author's answer will be more complicated than a simple yes or no. As spelled out in the conclusion, the philosophy and goals of the new student government were mostly sound and just, its structure contained good and bad elements, and in its wholesale scrapping of Georgetown's tradition, it was both unwise and wrong.

The freshmen who burned Joe Hoya in the Quad would ultimately have a lot for which to answer.

***

Modern student government at Georgetown officially was born on May 2, 1969. On that date James Clark ('70) was elected student body president, becoming the first chosen by students of all five undergraduate schools; and forty students from all five schools were elected to a new student senate.[4]

Before 1969, Georgetown had no less than three distinct undergraduate student governments. Each elected a president and council representatives. The School of Nursing had its own student government. Students in the School of Foreign Service, the Business School and the School of Languages and Linguistics were all represented by the Walsh Area Student Government. And there was the Yard, which represented Georgetown College.[5]

Of the three, the Yard was first among equals, for a number of reasons. The Yard represented Georgetown's oldest and largest undergraduate school. Founded in the 1890s, the Yard was itself one of Georgetown's oldest institutions. Its student council was composed not only of elected representatives, but the leaders of some of Georgetown's largest and most prestigious student activities—groups such as the Philodemic Society and Mask and Bauble—which gave the Yard added legitimacy. Many College men (by the mid 1960s, the College was the only school that remained all-male) regarded their school—with its unique government—as the only authentic "bearer of Georgetown tradition" on the Hilltop.[6]

The College's separation from the other two campuses was not limited to its lack of female students. To a large extent, College and East Campus students took different classes, lived in different dorms, attended different social events, and participated in different extracurricular activities. The case of *The Hoya* is instructive. Although by the mid-sixties *The Hoya* ostensibly served all three campuses equally, the weekly's leadership maintained an unwritten rule that only a College man could be elected editor-in-chief, a rule that was mischievously enforced in 1967 when a talented School of Foreign Service staffer in line for the job was passed over in favor of a College sophomore.[7]

Barriers between the schools had been eroding, however, since before the beginning of the decade; this erosion eventually affected the three student governments. In the late 1950s University President Fr. Edward Bunn, S.J. had ordered an end to the duplication of academic departments; henceforth, each department served all undergraduate schools.[8] The creation of the Faculty Senate in the mid-sixties, which represented faculty from all parts of the university, provided a more concrete model for a unified student government and encouraged its supporters. [9]

In the 1965–66 term, these supporters waged a serious campaign to unite the three student governments, contending that a united government would be able to address student interests more effectively. They put in place a referendum, calling for a constitution based on unification on the March 1966 ballots of all three campuses, and sparked heated College opposition. While 91% of voters in the Nursing School and 74% of the East Campus electorate favored the proposed constitution (although in the latter case with less than the required 40% turnout), fully 87% of College men voting rejected the change—with a sizable 67% turnout.[10]

Opponents of the move carried the day by echoing Fr. Thomas Fitzgerald, S.J., Dean of the College, when he argued in 1965 that for maximum effectiveness student leaders needed to have personal knowledge and contact with large numbers of their constituents. Unity, by expanding the number of constituents, would threaten this "personalization."[11] A *Hoya* advertisement signed by College student leaders stated simply that "it would be destructive to the identity of each school and would be of no benefit to the College student body."[12]

In the two years following the March 1966 vote, student attitudes toward the unification issue and student government in general were to change significantly, influenced by the growing student-power and anti-Vietnam war movements. Before the late sixties, Georgetown students had had a reputation for being primarily conservative in their political or social attitudes. In 1963 and 1965, *Commonweal* magazine observed that "at Georgetown it is a matter of local pride that the school is one of the few student bodies wealthy enough to field a polo team," and went on to note that "sports car ownership is still a major status symbol...The general reaction (to sit-ins and civil rights protests) is one of apathy..."[13] In the fall of 1966 student leaders had mobilized the student body and threatened the administration with a boycott—demanding that Catholic University be added to the Georgetown football schedule.[14]

A 1966 *Hoya* survey had found that 62% of Georgetown students favored the Johnson administration's Vietnam policy, and a whopping 68% thought that stronger military action was needed. These figures were not all that different from the nation as a whole.

Georgetown student attitudes in the next few years progressively moved to the left. As the American death toll in Vietnam continued to increase, the antiwar/student-power movement gained in strength. An early shock to students occurred in the spring of 1967, when the Johnson administration limited student military deferments by giving draft lottery numbers to college males. The prospect of being sent to Vietnam became ever more threatening to Georgetown students.

Meanwhile, the movement to unite the three student governments became stronger. In March 1967 Fr. Royden Davis, S.J., the new Dean of the College, called for a single student government council to represent all five schools. "In this era of change at Georgetown, the student should have a voice...through the vehicle of student government," said Davis in an address given to the College sophomore class.[17]

By early 1968, advocates of unification had gained enough support to place another unification referendum on the College's March 15 ballot. Voters had three options: (1) a unified student government "superseding the authority of the individual councils," (2) closer "cooperation among the three student councils while maintaining the present political system," or (3) maintaining the existing structure.[18]

Opponents of unification once again contended that the proposed change would slight the interests of the College student body. But unification supporters were better organized and prepared than they had been in 1966. In "The Case for Unification: A White Paper," they argued that "the most urgent problems facing us are University-wide problems—not school problems...All students should be able to deal with them at one time...[unification will] give Georgetown students the voice and the influence they must have."[19] In addition, many involved with student government believed that the university administration "played off one student government against another," in the words of the last Yard president, Daniel Hurson; and supporters argued that this would cease with a single government. They contended that one president could gain more student rights and influence than five could, and that distinctions between schools were breaking down.[20] Finally, unification proponents emphasized that "a vote for [unification] is *not* a vote to kill the Yard. There is a definite need to maintain the present functions of the Yard."[21]

Unification advocates were now able to reverse the 1966 results. In a 62% turnout, a plurality of College voters, 38%, favored unification (Proposition 1), with another 33% favoring closer cooperation (Proposition 2). Only 29% voted for the status quo (Proposition 3), a startling drop from two years earlier. The election demonstrated that there was a clear consensus for change in student government.[22]

And there was now a Yard president who did not oppose this growing consensus. On the day of the unification referendum, College voters elected Dan Hurson ('69) as president over unification opponent Andy Hendry ('69) by forty-eight votes. While Hurson's predecessor, 1967–68 Yard President Larry O'Brien ('68) had staunchly opposed any move toward unification, Hurson was much more ambivalent. As he accepted the traditional key to the Yard office in Copley Lounge, he was greeted by supporters chanting, "Change day! change day!"[23]

The chanters were not to be disappointed. By mid-December of 1968, voters from all schools had elected forty delegates to a constitutional convention called by the three undergraduate councils for the following spring. The convention was charged with the task of drafting a structure for a new united student government.[24]

The framework which convention delegates and later the voters of the three campuses approved contained two main provisions. The first provided for a student body president elected by voters from all schools, similar in form to the presidents of the three old student governments, except that now he would be run with a hand-picked vice-presidential candidate. The second provision changed the student nature of student government more profoundly. In place of the three student councils, it created a forty-member senate, five elected from each school and five elected from each class. In the process the class leadership structure that had existed in the previous system was scrapped. No longer was every class to elect its own president, secretary, and treasurer, a feature of the old system which had often strengthened the cohesion of each class.[25]

The new student senate differed from the old school councils in another important respect: it excluded the leaders of student activities. While the concerns of these leaders were sometimes viewed as parochial,[26] they brought a perspective to student government distinct from that of the elected representatives. Club leaders added a certain "power base" (in the words of Royden Davis) to the old governments, in the sense that students who might work twenty to forty hours per week on their activity often identified more strongly with that activity than with their school or class, and thus were better represented by their club leaders.[27]

Hoya ex-editor Casper contends that "with the presidents of clubs like Mask & Bauble and Philodemic on the Yard the whole spectrum of student interest was represented...You knew" that the Yard Council could really speak for students."[28] Supporters of the new system argued that club representation was undemocratic. Judging from the absence of the issue in *The Hoya*'s 1969 coverage of student government changes, they did not meet with much opposition at the time.

Nor, it appears, did the demise of the Yard. Even with unification, the Yard might have conceivably survived by including all undergraduate schools, but it was too redolent of the College and its traditions, most of them crumbling or under siege by the spring of 1969. In Hurson's view, most students were apathetic or ambivalent toward the Yard, while reformers pushed hard to kill it, seeing it as obsolete.[29]

The Yard was also the victim of generational change, a change in attitudes from Georgetown, class to class. Advocates of the spring 1968 unification proposal had felt the need to claim that unification would not kill the Yard, with the spring 1965 unification defeat in the memories of College upperclassmen. It was the withdrawal from the Yard of the class that enrolled in the fall of 1968, the class of '72, that put the final nail in the Yard's coffin.

The growing liberalism—some called it radicalism—of each successive Georgetown class, demonstrated by the March 1969 Quad incident, was the result of continuing national turmoil over American involvement in Vietnam, as well as the related rise of the student power movement, the "counterculture," and the political New Left. The traumatic and tumultuous events of

1968 had clearly played a key role in shaping the attitudes of Georgetown students and setting the stage for the student government changes of 1969. The year 1968 had seen an incumbent president of the United States—Lyndon Johnson—unexpectedly decline to run for reelection, under fire from antiwar protesters while facing stiff challenges from antiwar Senate Democrats Eugene McCarthy and Robert Kennedy. A week later, the preeminent leader of the civil rights movement, Martin Luther King, Jr., was assassinated; Robert Kennedy was himself assassinated in June. The two murders sickened the nation. Late that summer the Democratic National Convention in Chicago degenerated into a state of anarchy on national television, as Mayor Daley's police attacked antiwar protesters outside the convention hall while inside establishment favorite Vice-President Hubert Humphrey battled the insurgent McCarthy and Kennedy forces. Meanwhile, more young American men were coming home from Vietnam in body bags, and the Tet offensive led the public to doubt whether America could or should win the war.

On college campuses nationwide, students were increasingly protesting the war while demanding influence and even control over university decision making. The widespread perception that student protest had forced an American president to quit emboldened student activists to insist on having a greater say in setting academic, curricular, student life, and other policies. "Students around the country were flexing their muscles on campus and off," recalled James Clark (C '70), who, in early 1969, helped draft the new student government constitution.[30]

Georgetown students, led by Clark, would soon begin to assert themselves on the Hilltop. Although 1968 was still a relatively quiet year at Georgetown, it was marked by at least two major events. In the fall of 1968, Georgetown College announced that it would admit fifty women for the 1969–70 academic year, and the last all-male Hilltop bastion fell (the last outside the Jesuit Community).[31] The move to coeducation played a key role in eroding the barriers between the College and the other schools.

At about the same time, University President Fr. Gerard Campbell, S.J., a quiet intellectual who had succeeded Fr. Edward Bunn, S.J. in 1964, announced that he would retire by the end of the year. For the first time in the history of the university, undergraduates were named to the committee charged by the Board of Directors with picking Campbell's successor (Fr. Edward Quain, S.J. served as interim president from December 1968 until June 1969). The selection of the students, the presidents of the three student governments, was of great symbolic significance because it gave the elected student leadership the power to help make one of the most important decisions a university governing board ever makes.[32]

This was only one example of the change in the concerns and priorities of those involved with student government in the late sixties. Paralleling other college campuses, Georgetown student government became concerned with asserting rights and powers and obtaining a role in the governance of the university. By 1969, university governance had become the big issue in student government. Only a few years earlier it had been very different. When Dan Hurson came to the Hilltop in 1965, student government had seemed like "a throwback to the 1950s. It was preoccupied with things like social activities and dances."[33]

That is not to say that prior to the late sixties student government, particularly the Yard, did not have any role or vision beyond the realm of a student's social life. There was, for example, a long tradition of the university president consulting with the president of the Yard on a regular basis, mostly on matters relating to students but sometimes on larger issues as well.[34] Professor Jesse Mann remembers the presidency of the Yard being "an extraordinary important position...He [a Yard president] would on occasion call meetings of the student body in Gaston Hall and nearly every student would attend..."[35] Donald Casper recalls that during the 1965–66 term of Yard President Frank Keating (C '66), University Vice-President for Physical Plant John Patteros was called to account for a particular action he had taken. Patteros' response: "Mr. Keating told me to do it."[36]

Nevertheless, student government interest in issues of university governance was limited until 1969. That year was a watershed for student government and Georgetown as a whole; the events of 1969 set the tone for student government until the mid-1970s and still had an impact in the late 1980s. The structural change in student government that took effect that year has already been mentioned. Three other 1969 events deserve specific attention. On March 20 Georgetown suffered its first real riot (the affair nine days earlier in the Quadrangle had too festive an air to be considered serious protest, and nobody got hurt) when visiting San Francisco Mayor Joseph Alioto was prevented from speaking before a packed Gaston Hall. Students for a Democratic Society (SDS) militants rushed up to the podium, and a scuffle ensued before Alioto was whisked away; a number of people received minor injuries.[37] This incident is probably the greatest single offense against free speech on the Hilltop before or since, and it caused somewhat of a backlash among students against SDS-type tactics.

In that same month the *Georgetown Voice* first appeared. It was founded by a disaffected *Hoya* staff member named Steve Pisinski (C '71), who set out to promote a frankly liberal agenda, "comforting the afflicted and afflicting the comfortable."[38] It was intended to serve as an alternative to the then conservative (under the editorship of Donald Casper) *Hoya*, covering national political issues. Casper's 1968–69 *Hoya* focused almost exclusively on Hilltop events, as it had in previous years. Within a couple of years *The Voice* started to publish weekly; it had already influenced student government substantially. It did so through its endorsement of Mike Thornton in the 1970 student government presidential race, the first such editorial endorsement in Georgetown's history. Thornton won that election narrowly, and credited *The Voice*'s endorsement.[39]

The final event of 1969 that deeply influenced Georgetown and student government was the coming to office of Fr. Robert Henle, S.J. as university president in June. Although Henle's relationships with student government leaders were not particularly close, these leaders and student government as an institution reached the peak of their influence under his presidency.

***

So, the spring of '69 witnessed the passing of a symbol—the Yard presidency—and, when a symbol of long standing crumbles, the tradition of which it was an important feature is itself weakened. At the present moment it appears that the student body desires both the Yard presidency and the tradition to return in their former glory. Only future events will determine to what extent this aspiration is wise. In any case, the events and dreams of the sixties were heady stuff with some good and some not so good results.

Notes

1. *The Hoya*, March 13, 1969, p. 1.

2. Ibid.

3. *The Hoya*, May 1, 1969, p. 13.

4. *The Hoya*, May 8, 1969, p. 1.

5. *The Hoya*, March 7, 1968, p. 1.

6. Interview with Fr. Royden Davis, S.J., January 20, 1988.

7. Interview with Donald Casper (C '70), 1968–69 *Hoya* editor-in-chief, January 22, 1988.

8. Interview with Dr. Jesse Mann, January 20, 1988.

9. Fr. Davis.

10. *The Hoya*, March 10, 1966, p. 1.

11. *The Hoya*, October 14, 1965, p. 1.

12. *The Hoya*, March 3, 1966, p. 13.

13. *Georgetown Today*, January 1970, p. 3.

14. *The Hoya*, October 27, 1966, p. 1.

15. *The Hoya*, February 25, 1966, p. 1.

16. Donald Casper.

17. *The Hoya*, March 9, 1967, p. 1.

18. *The Hoya*, March 7, 1968, p. 1.

19. "The Case for Unification: A White Paper by the Committee for Proposal #1," Student Government Archives, March 1968, p. 1.

20. Interview with Daniel Hurson (C '69), 1968–69 President of the Yard, January 12, 1988.

21. "The Case for Unification: A White Paper by the Committee for Proposal #1," Student Government Archives, March 1968, p. 3.

22. *The Hoya*, March 21, 1968, p. 1.

23. Ibid.

24. *The Hoya*, December 12, 1968, p. 1.

25. *The Hoya*, March 13, p. 3.

26. Hurson.

27. Davis.

28. Casper.

29. Hurson.

30. Interview with James Clark (C '70), 1969–70 Georgetown student government president, January 18, 1988.

31. Ibid.

32. Hurson.

33. Hurson.

34. Casper.

35. Mann.

36. Casper.

37. *The Hoya*, March 20, 1969, p. 1.

38. *Georgetown Voice*.

39. Interview with E. Michael Thornton (C '71), 1970–71 Georgetown student government president, January 21, 1988.

Early Student Customs, Curricula, and Relaxations

William Devaney

To those students eagerly awaiting Georgetown's Bicentennial, the daily life of the late Victorian Georgetown student would seem unbearable and our old Hilltop would appear a gulag.

During this era, morning came rudely in the predawn hours. After rising, the students would proceed down to Old North's basement to the student washroom. The latter was really a euphemism for a long shallow trough split into two small sections by a light rack on top of which the boys kept their tin wash basins, toilet articles, and towels. A barrel of fresh pump water stood in the corner and on many a winter morning it was necessary to break the ice on the barrel before dipping one's bowl. The job of breaking the ice usually fell upon some hapless freshman who had to rise a few minutes before the others to perform this important duty.

Twice a week, fresh linen was issued, and on these days boys took primitive showers by stripping down, soaping up, and then pouring the icy water on top of themselves. Many water fights occurred, especially during the winter months when it was in vogue to dump a barrel of freezing water on some unsuspecting, preferably fully clothed boy.

Bathing in this manner came to a merciful and abrupt end in December 1909, when the washroom was destroyed by fire. Unfortunately, the college library was also damaged in the blaze and several rare, old English manuscripts were destroyed.

After dressing and eating breakfast in the college refectory, the late Victorian student would begin his daily routine. Although he spent many more hours in class than his contemporary counterpart, twenty-seven and one-half hours of course work and twenty-three to twenty-seven hours of study per week, the aim of a Georgetown education remained the same. Then as now, professors sought to provide a broad-based, liberal education. The 1895–96 College Catalogue states:

> The aim of the college education is to train and develop all powers of the mind and will cultivate no one faculty to an exaggerated degree at the expense of the others. It is intended, too, to impart the broadest possible culture together with accuracy in scholarship. To attain this end, the course during the undergraduate period is prescribed and embraces Latin and Greek Classics, English in its various branches and aspects and correlated studies such as Rhetoric, Literature, History, etc. One modern language besides English. Mathematics, including Differential and Integral Calculus, Chemistry, both General and Qualitative Analytical, the elements of Geology, Astronomy, and Mechanics, and a very thorough training in Physics and Rational Philosophy.

Religious instruction, called Christian Doctrine, was also mandatory and all Roman Catholics had to receive the Sacraments at least once a month.

During this period, all classes began at 8:45 A.M. and continued until 12:00 P.M. Classes resumed once again from three until five o'clock. Wednesday and Saturday were half days and Sundays were free although the Mass obligation was necessary for Catholics. A class schedule from this era looked something like this:

Seniors:
9:00 Rational Philosophy
10:00 Natural Sciences
11:00 Calculus
3:00 Rational Philosophy
4:00 Natural Sciences
7:00 Disputations (Tues. & Fri. after Nov. 1)

Juniors:
8:45 Latin
10:00 Latin (Mon., Wed., Fri.) Chemistry (Tue., Thu., Sat.)
11:00 Calculus
3:00 Greek
4:00 English (Mon., Tue., Thu.)

Sophomores:
8:45 Latin
10:00 Latin (Mon., Wed., Fri.)
    Chemistry (Tues.,
    Thurs., Sat.)
11:00 Trigonometry
    Analytic Geometry
3:00 Greek
4:00 English (Mon., Tues.,
    Thurs.)
    Elocution (Fri.)

Freshmen:
8:45 Latin
10:00 Latin (Mon., Wed., Fri.)
    Chemistry (Tues.,
    Thurs., Sat.)
11:00 Higher Algebra
3:00 Greek
4:00 French or German
    (Mon., Tues., Thurs.)
    Elocution (Fri.)

When analyzed more closely, this arrangement of studies reveals some interesting emphases and omissions.

We note first the unexpectedly large amount of time accorded to the positive sciences. Of the five major courses studied by seniors, two were devoted to the sciences, one to Mathematics, and two to Rational Philosophy. Four of the six major examinations at the senior year's end were in the fields of Physics or Mechanics or other natural sciences, while two were devoted to Philosophy.

Notable also was the heavy literary quality of the curriculum for what today we would term the freshman, sophomore, and junior years, as a glance at the class schedule reveals. It is to be remembered also that the much stressed practice of translation from Latin and Greek into English constituted a most valuable exercise in the use of the latter language.

It is evident that the learning of the French and German languages was awarded a place of honor in the curriculum.

On the debit side we perceive a lack of any attention to History, except for the limited employment of that discipline in the study of the classical literature. Nor were any of the other social sciences given any real recognition. The Georgetown students were presented with a rich humanist pabulum of studies which, since it could not do everything, confined itself to doing excellently what it regarded as the most important things.

Discipline was also considered to be of paramount importance at the College, and Georgetown readily admitted that she was stricter than most universities. The Catalogue, however liked to stress that Georgetown was a family institution, and that the rules and regulations set forth by the patronly Jesuits were intended to be benignly despotic in nature. They urged the parents to think of the professors and prefects, who were Jesuits, as older brothers to the boys; older brothers who would help their sons to nurture and grow but would also occasionally have to box their ears to keep them in line. Nevertheless, despite all this talk of family-style discipline, it was fairly easy to be expelled from the College and all boys from foreign countries and distant states had to have an appointed guardian nearby to whom they could go in the event of suspension or dismissal. The Jesuits took no chances. Some examples of those unfortunate enough to be expelled were:

T.O., January 10, 1892—Idle and Boisterous
B.T., November 30, 1894—Rusticated
J.K., March 8, 1908—In a St. Patrick's Day Rumpus
A.X., October 20, 1912—Out Nights

Boys who were in minor trouble were sentenced to the "Jug," a study hall where sinners against the rules would be given busy work such as Latin translations. Students who were frequently in the Jug were eligible for membership in the Jug Rat Society. Not much is known about the activities of this elite organization, but we do know that it was formed sporadically throughout the late nineteenth century and that the members would dress in outlandish clown-like outfits for Society functions. This brief blurb appeared in the Winter, 1892 *Journal*: "Ye ancient order of 'Jug Rats' has been revived. They have patronized the college outfitter, and appear in hideous yellow and green jockey caps. On holiday in the intervals between 'On Post' duty, the reciting of lines, and other et ceteras, they play lacrosse and throw the boomerang."

Tuition, room and board in 1895 was a mere $325.00, but like good car salesmen, the Jesuits added additional charges for several necessary extras such as medical aid, $10.00, and a library fee of $2.00, not to mention a nominal lab fee for those students required to take Chemistry. Students had the choice of living in a traditional dormitory or opting for a private room, complete with heat, light, and attendance for $80.00. The much coveted double rooms were reserved for graduate students only. The charge for piano use was $12.00, and if one wished to take Spanish, German or Italian, the fee was an additional $30.00. The charge for drawing and painting was $50.00, while stenography remained a mere $20.00. Of course, musical instruction on most instruments, including the banjo, was assured for only fifteen extra dollars. By 1910, the flat tuition, room and board rate had been raised to $422.00, but with the completion of Ryan dormitory, a student could be accommodated in a three-bedroom suite, with a bath, for $400.00 per year. The cheapest private rooms on campus were the sixty-dollar accommodations in the Mulledy building.

School vacations during this era were considerably shorter than the ones we enjoy today. Students received only one day of Thanksgiving vacation, eleven days at Christmas, and four days at Easter. Although Spring Break did not exist, the College did get all holy days off and the rector habitually called several unscheduled holidays during the school year. Appropriately, the day after St. Patrick's Day was a good bet for a holiday.

The Social Traditions and Institutions at Georgetown University in the Twentieth Century

Kevin G. Mahoney and Mark C. Corallo

The Glee Club

Since 1851, the Georgetown University Glee Club has been a major force in promoting the name of the university to students, alumni, friends, and the entire Georgetown community. Outside of the athletic teams there has not been a single club or group that has represented Georgetown University more often to more people than has the Glee Club. There is a fundamental difficulty in writing about this organization since most of its history must be caught in the air by your ear through tones and notes. Unfortunately, writing is the only medium left with which to capture it; so we will try our best.[1]

The main reason why people joined the Glee Club was to sing; however, it was not an organization for musical endeavors only. Characterized by its fraternal spirit, and constant enthusiasm, the Club was also a part of a student's education at Georgetown as well as being an important element of the cultural life of the community. It also performed an invaluable service to Georgetown in that it carried on in such a manner as to convey past traditions, present status, and future aims to the younger members of the group as well as to the audiences for whom they performed.[2]

Since the Glee Club is no longer in existence it is difficult for many Georgetown students of today to grasp just how important it was and what it meant to the school. Perhaps one way of doing this would be to list some of the places where it sang, with the heyday of the Glee Club arguably being the very early sixties. At this time the Club appeared on the Ed Sullivan Show, performed with the world famous cellist Pablo Casals, received a key to the city in San Juan, sang at the inauguration of John F. Kennedy, and appeared also on national and international television in 1962 singing German beer drinking songs from the steps of our very own Healy Building.[3]

In the meantime the Glee Club was carrying on as they had done for over a hundred years by entertaining the students of Georgetown in numerous concerts and shows (such as the annual Christmas Show in Gaston Hall). At the same time the Club was entertaining the alumni at concerts put on by the Met Clubs of Washington, Chicago, St. Louis, Boston, and New York.[4] But more than anything else the Club and its concerts were a social institution on the Hilltop and everywhere around town. Just ask any alumnus from the forties, fifties, or sixties where the best place to meet girls was and they will tell you that the Glee Club concerts were as good as any. Whether these concerts were at Georgetown or across town at Trinity, there were one or two things you could count on: tuxedos and plenty of girls.

To trace the decline of the Glee Club is difficult because there was not one reason, something that you can put your finger on. But there is some evidence in the *Hoya* in 1963 as to why they fell out of favor: they sang very sacred music, very old music, and the students of that day preferred more modern types of music. Also there were the Chimes, who not only sang the kind of music that the students wanted to hear but were also better vocalists than were the Glee Club. In a word, student tastes had changed, perhaps not for the better.

So, we witness another Georgetown tradition pass. Since the Glee Club left us there has never really been any one group that has come close to filling its mighty shoes. It survived into the seventies, but with declining health; it has had some successors but, really, no replacements.

The Chimes

"Hoya Saxa Joe"

He will arrive underneath the campus tree at half past five—
He's a-gazin' at John Carroll,
He's not slow in his broken-down V-8,
He's off to go to Visi,
See a G-girl, or Trinity,
See how he runs downtown to have a little fun,
Before the Healy Clock strikes one,
He's a high-falutin' pinball-shootin' Blue and Gray,
From Tehan's College,*
Stork Club Charlie,
Three beer Freddie,
Hoya Saxa Joe—
Joe, Joe, the dog-faced boy,
He makes those checks and his Mass calls too—
Just like his ever-lovin' prefect tells him to,
And he crawls on his belly like a reptile.[5]

Frank Jones (Ephus 1)

*one of the off-campus nearby restaurants

The Georgetown Chimes were founded in 1946 by Frank Jones (L.L.B. '48, L.L.M. '52). He derived the idea from a singing group that he was involved with at Yale. The style of the Chimes is barbershop quartet, with the usual bass, baritone, lead, and tenor parts. Originally, they started off as a sort of sideshow to the Glee Club (i.e., singing a small set at Glee Club shows) but sometime in the early fifties they broke away and became independent. While brotherhood is important to the Chimes, loyalty is their common pledge, and harmony is their bond.[6] At this writing the Chimes have been singing for Georgetown students and alumni for forty-one years and although there is no set number of undergraduates for the group at any one time there are presently twelve active members, including the Ephus, the leader of the active Chimes who presides over all meetings and rehearsals. He is elected as soon as the post is vacated and interestingly enough the name itself is not Latin or Greek; it is a complete fabrication.

In 1949 the Chimes recorded their first record, containing four songs. This was recorded in a garage, since one of the original four Chimes was on academic probation at the time so he had to sneak over the wall on Copley lawn in order to make the sessions. Since that first record, the Chimes have managed to put out eighteen more and a new one is currently in the works.[7]

As you can imagine, there have been over the years many interesting and amusing anecdotes associated with the Chimes. Many of these have to do with their rise and fall in popularity as time went on. This anecdote happened to take place during one of their high points: During the dedication of the Chimes table in the Tombs on December 27, 1962, fifty-six members showed up to celebrate. Consequently, the Tombs became so crowded that they all had to move outside. While outside on Thirty-sixth Street, they continued to sing and attracted such a large crowd that the riot squad from the seventh precinct was called out.[8]

In the early days, when there were no tape recorders, all of the Chimes songs had to be learned at rehearsals, by ear. If this does not sound very impressive, you may consider that each Chime knows an average of one hundred songs. However, tape recorders did not make everything easy for the Chimes; they still had to battle with acceptance and popularity. As we have said, the Chimes' popularity resembles a roller coaster ride, and this was illustrated dramatically in 1973 when six Chimes graduated, leaving just one. Amid this unpopularity, the Chimes had to turn to their very faithful alumni, who responded by showing up to perform the scheduled shows with the lone undergraduate. This is amazing, considering that at the height of their popularity the Chimes performed for the Ed Sullivan show twice, President Eisenhower twice, President Ford once, President Carter once, and they have even sung at the Capitol.[9]

Yet, through forty-one years, one thing has remained constant, and that is that the Chimes will sing once a month in the Tombs no matter how popular or unpopular they may be. In this bond these two institutions have aided each other in withstanding the elements that could have led to their demise. And so, after forty-one years the Chimes have endured, like all great traditions, and the Georgetown of yesterday, today, and tomorrow is much richer for it.

A few years ago the women of the undergraduate schools assembled an all-female singing group called "The Grace Notes," patterned on the Chimes model. They have been extremely successful.

Cabaret

In 1975 a small group of students decided to put together a show of amateur singers, musicians, and comedians. They held the show in the small but available Darnall formal lounge and donated the proceeds of the event to local charities. Twelve years later Cabaret had become perhaps the single most important social event of the year. It has grown so large and the demand for tickets so great that the show is now presented in the Hall of Nations during five nights in April. Cabaret is more than a social event. It is the embodiment of the tradition of high quality social life which Georgetown students have learned to uphold.

Cabaret showcases the best amateur talent at Georgetown. Perhaps the best way to describe it is to go through a night step by step:

7:30 P.M.: The doors to the Hall of Nations open and the students who will be sitting in the audience are greeted by *maître d*s in tuxedos. The students are escorted to candle-lit tables in the hall and presented with a bottle of champagne. Out at the bar freshman bartenders dressed in black tie stand ready to serve beer and soda to the guests. Waitresses serve drinks to those who have been seated. The house begins to fill. There truly is electricity in the air as the excitement builds. Musicians tune their instruments. Performers prepare their voices. Everyone from the singers to the bartenders has the pre-show jitters.

8:15: Everyone has been seated. Waitresses move about the candle-lit hall which has been transformed into a nightclub. The lights go down as the musicians take their places on the stage.

8:30: The lights go out. The keyboard player sounds a note.

The drummer counts out the beat and the band begins to play as the audience erupts into applause. Two Masters of Ceremonies dressed in tuxedos with tails face off against each other in the spotlights. They shake hands and face the audience. "Live from The Hall of Nations at Georgetown University, it's Cabaret!" The band plays the theme from "Late Night with David Letterman," the popular television program. The music ends to cheers from the crowd. After a few jokes that only a Hoya could love (for instance, in Cabaret XII Dennis Roche (CAS '87) and Jeff Markowitz (CAS '87) read off a list of the top ten reasons Father Freeze misses Mass, including "had to quell a food fight in the Jesuit Community."), the Masters of Ceremonies introduce the first singer, who is always a senior girl and who always sings the popular show tune "Cabaret."

From there on the show gains momentum as talented Hoyas sing popular songs, famous show tunes and a few rock and roll anthems. In years past songs have ranged from "Somewhere over the Rainbow," the popular song from the movie "The Wizard of Oz," to Bruce Springsteen's classic rocker "Rosalita." The only two standards in the show are "Cabaret," which always opens the first act, and "My Old School" by the rock group Steely Dan, which always opens the second act and is always dedicated to the senior class.

Throughout the evening guitars strum, organs groan, drums beat and horns blare in a musical extravaganza unparalleled at Georgetown. By the time the lights go down for the second act, the tables and chairs have been cleared away so that the formally dressed Hoyas (who have by now loosened their ties) can dance their way through the end of the show.

1:00 A.M. (or thereabouts): The show ends as the performers take their bows. The lights go up and four hundred happy Hoyas file out the doors still singing the songs from the show. The exhausted performers and workers prepare for the next night.

Cabaret has a mystique all its own which grows every year. It has become a tradition principally due to its volunteer nature and its non-affiliation with the University. All the performers, musicians and workers are volunteers. No one is paid. Cabaret has even managed to have local professional percussionist Larry "Pops" Hicks play with the band for the last eight years. Pops volunteers for the enjoyment of working with the talented and energetic students who are involved with the show.

Cabaret is an event independently organized and produced by Georgetown students for Georgetown students. It is successful due to the simple fact that Georgetown students love a challenge and, moreover, love to succeed. Cabaret is as close to a professional show as can be found anywhere among amateurs. It involves months of planning and rehearsal. As Richard Brereton (SBA '87), one of the three executive producers of Cabaret XII said, "We work all year to lay the best creative foundation we can, and then on opening night everything just rolls. We [the performers] get into it, and the audience responds and becomes a part of the show. Then the roof blows off."[10] Paul McCarthy (SBA'87), another of the executive producers, said, "It's the biggest social event of the year. Cabaret casts a spell over this campus."[11]

Cabaret truly does cast a spell for five nights a year. It has become an institution because it exemplifies how Georgetown students can use all their creative talents and hard work to provide the University community with a social tradition that shines year after year.

The Georgetown University Center Pub

In 1968 the Peter Powers University Center opened in the basement of the Healy Building. Within the center, along with an art gallery and study rooms, was a Coffee House which occupied the largest space in the basement.

The Coffee House quickly became the most popular room in the new center, providing snacks and soft drinks for those who needed a break from their arduous academic tasks. On weekends it provided an arena for campus and local musicians, singers and poets who performed or read to an appreciative audience. The Coffee House also drew students from other area colleges and even local high school students. It became the most popular meeting place on campus.[12]

In 1974, by popular demand, the Pub, as it came to be called, began serving beer and wine. Student waiters, waitresses, bartenders and pizza cooks were hired along with a staff of senior managers.. The University saw fit to let the students serve the students and promised to interfere with the daily business as little as possible. This was viewed at the time as a positive measure to instill a sense of pride and responsibility in the students who would run the business.

The prospect of a familiar place on campus where the beer was cheap and the dancing was free was met with great enthusiasm from the student body. Support for the Pub increased. It became a viable enterprise while at the the same time proving that Georgetown students, when presented with an opportunity, respond to the challenge with spirit and determination.

The Pub has undergone some drastic physical changes. In 1979 a new tile floor replaced the original parquet one (which had to be waxed once a week). This made keeping the Pub clean a much simpler task. In 1982 a new and much larger bar was added with room for a larger variety of beers. In 1974 the Pub served three kinds of beer, Miller, Stroh, and Schlitz. With the installation of the new bar the Pub was able to sell up to twelve different kinds of beer. Also in 1982 the new D.J. (disc jockey) booth was constructed with a new sound system which further enhanced the Pub's appeal as a nightclub.

The Pub has also been a constant source of controversy. It has had its share of public image problems and popularity fluctuated when during a few years the Pub became almost an elitist establishment. Said Jay Maloney (CAS '84), a Pub manager, "Not only did you have to know someone to get hired but you had to know Pub staff members to get in the front door."[13] A satirical essay entitled "The Pub Doorman" by Kevin S. Green appeared in the 1980 *Ye Domesday Booke*. The author humorously depicted this figure as "The Almighty Pub Doorman...a solitary Buddha atop his two-step stool commanding vast powers. Thronging masses await patiently at his feet their chance to enter the sacred portal, Washington's veritable pleasure dome—the Center Pub...A being all powerful, he decides the fate of all those wishing entrance to the soothing pools of alcohol..."[14]

Then, as now, the Pub is truly the only place on campus where students can really cut loose. They drink and dance, sing and laugh, and enjoy a few hours of near Bacchanalean revelry on weekend nights. Bodies are pushed and shoved, beer is spilled, the temperature hovers at about ninety-nine degrees (the air conditioning never seems to be working) and rock-and-roll music blares as young Hoyas make an all-out effort to block out all thoughts of academia.

From one tradition often springs another. In this case the existence of the Pub gave birth to "Pub Scum" (not to mention a 1980s campus band "The Pub Rats"). Pub Scum is the unique brand of slime that magically appears on the Pub floor each night, lustfully devouring scarves and earrings, gloves and jackets, and other assorted articles of clothing. Yet still, the reveling Hoyas dance like mad things on this murky floor despite an occasional shoe lost mid-dance to the tiles. Pub scum, in turn, gave birth to "Pub Wear." No Hoya's wardrobe is complete without a special pair of shoes which are worn only in the Pub. One would never wear good clothing to the Pub, since everything that goes in clean and bright comes out brown and sticky.

The Pub is not always a fun festival. It has also had its more demure moments. After every graduation the Pub staff holds a formal reception for its graduating seniors and their families. In April 1984 the Pub held its fifteenth anniversary party. The black-tie affair was held in the Pub. In attendance were many of the alumni who had worked at the Pub while they were at Georgetown, as well as the then current staff and all the students who worked in Healy Basement. Pub general manager Leighton Waters (SBA '83) presided as master of ceremony.

Despite the crowd, the heat, and the slime, the Pub has remained a late night Mecca for Georgetown students throughout its existence. There is always a reason to go to the Pub on any given night, whether it is to hear a band, have a few beers and hide in the corner or dance until you have sweated off ten pounds. Ask any Hoyas what they are planning for any weekend night and they will list a number of activities; but the list always ends with "and I'll see you in the Pub late night." The Pub is more than just a bar. It is a place where Georgetown students have mixed together, socialized together, rallied together and felt comfortable for almost twenty years. It is a major part of their home away from home.

The Tombs

Isn't there a serious need for a Georgetown equivalent to Maury's? Wouldn't a good eating club, where the Georgetown atmosphere prevailed, be a wonderful asset to our campus?[15]

Fr. Yates

In 1961 the answer to these two questions was yes, and the man with the vision and ability to bring the idea to reality was Richard McCooey (C '52). McCooey, a former president of the Yard, recognized the problem, and being a deeply concerned and lifelong servant of Georgetown, proposed "to fulfill the need for a traditional gathering place of leisure and excellent food for the students, faculty, and alumni of the oldest university in the area."[16]

However, before McCooey was able to proceed with his plan, he faced much opposition from the surrounding residents. In all, thirteen residents objected on four different grounds and before any work could be done to change the former Chinese laundry and Hilltop Cafe into the proposed restaurant, these concerns had to be met. The residents objected for these four reasons:

(1) The restaurant would be a detriment to the area;
(2) That there was no need for such a restaurant;
(3) Because of its proximity to a school and a church;
(4) And the lack of parking facilities.

McCooey countered as follows:

(1) The restaurant would be a "nice place" and a "positive contribution" to the area and the corporation was planning on spending six figures to make sure of this.
(2) The need, he said, could be traced back to Fr. Yates' statements years before, expressing the need for a Georgetown equivalent of Yale's Maury's, a good eating club where the Georgetown atmosphere would prevail.
(3) It would also be a significant distance from the school and the church.
(4) And lastly, there was no need for parking because the restaurant was designed only for Georgetown.

After overcoming these initial obstacles, McCooey proceeded to make The Tombs a "club for everyone" that would be modeled after Maury's at Yale, and the Nassau Tavern at Princeton, and yet be unmistakably Georgetown. The original menu contained hamburgers, onion rings, crab cakes, and a few simple sandwiches. Later on, as the business thrived, pizza was added. All this was served on paper plates and napkins. The Tombs specialized also in offering different types of draught and bottled beer, and the effect of an old English inn was created by the now famous pitchers hanging over the bar.[17]

On July 23, 1962 The Tombs opened its doors to Georgetown with its bare oak tables, so that people may carve their names into them and its three-cent draughts.[18] In building a tradition, McCooey immediately affiliated The Tombs with another Georgetown stand-by, the Chimes. Establishing a place for them to perform on a monthly basis, McCooey also forged a relationship between The Tombs and the Chimes that has lasted for over twenty-five years. The cementing of this relationship occurred on Thursday, September 27, 1962, when fifty-six Chimes gathered to sing at the dedication of their own table, named (not surprisingly) the Chimes Table. Ever since 1962 the Chimes have sung in The Tombs once a month during the academic year, originally on Wednesdays, now on Tuesdays.[19]

The Tombs has endeared itself to the alumni as a social institution that is a constant, and as a place where they are always welcome. In fact, the same World War I recruitment posters and old Georgetown football clips that were hung around the bar in 1962 are still there today.

As McCooey became older, the strain of owning and operating three restaurants started to fatigue him so that he wished to pass on The Tombs, the 1789, and F. Scott's, his adjoining very high-class nightclub. After searching for a group which would act as a servant to Georgetown and as a keeper of tradition, as he had done for so many years, McCooey settled on the Georgetown-based Clyde's Corporation. Many patrons immediately became wary of the new owners, due much to McCooey's very close relationship with many of them and the school, and in 1985 their fears were realized when all three restaurants were closed down for renovations. For the next two weeks there was great trepidation as the workmen moved in and out of the historic building on the corner of Thirty-sixth and Prospect. However, all fears subsided when the "new" Tombs opened on New Year's Eve and much to everyone's delight, it had the old ambiance with minor changes, only cosmetic. It was still the Old Tombs!

One other addition was built in the summer of 1987. The new room, with an entrance beside the fireplace, was designed by none other than Richard McCooey. It added forty new seats to The Tombs. It was called "Sweeps" (the name of the first prize at a crew race). It has helped greatly in alleviating the traditional "Tombs Line."

All in all, much has changed in the past twenty-five years, but, as they say, the more things change, the more they stay the same. This is especially true of The Tombs. Richard McCooey used his talent and determination to complete what has become one of the greatest social institutions to grace Georgetown University. In the past twenty-five years, The Tombs has been the site of more ideas, social and academic conversation, social interaction, and sharing and witnessing of Georgetown tradition and history, among faculty, students, alumni, and administrators than has any other place on campus. And so, after twenty-five years of service, vision, and dedication to Georgetown University, we would like to say thank you to Richard McCooey (C '52), alumnus *par excellence*.

Notes

All our research, with the exception of personal interviews with faculty and alumni, has come from past editions of *The Georgetown College Journal, The Hoya, The Georgetown Voice,* and *Ye Domesday Booke.* Thus, this paper is the work of the many distinguished persons who saw fit to record not only the events which took place during their years at Georgetown but also their perceptions and recollections of their beloved Alma Mater. This, therefore is a continuation and compilation of their work and experience.

1. *Ye Domesday Booke,* 1968, p. 132.
2. Ibid.
3. *The Hoya,* 25 November 1962, p. 5.
4. *The Hoya,* 15 December 1960, p. 1.
5. James Walsh, S.J., 2 December 1987.
6. *Ye Domesday Booke,* 1968, p. 144.

7. John Douglas (CAS '89), 4 December 1987.

8. *The Hoya,* 21 September 1962, p. 1.

9. Interview, John Douglas (CAS '89), 4 December 1987.

10. *The Hoya,* 26 April 1987, p. 4.

11. Ibid.

12. *Ye Domesday Booke,* 1972, p. 116.

13. Interview with Jay Maloney (CAS '84).

14. *Ye Domesday Booke,* 1980, p. 130.

15. *The Hoya,* 21 September 1961, p. 1.

16. Ibid.

17. The Blue and Gray, Holidays 1987, p. 32.

18. *The Hoya,* 21 September 1962, p. 1.

19. *The Hoya,* 27 September 1962, p. 1.

Community Service at Georgetown, A Longstanding Tradition

Jennifer L. Smith

There has always been a long tradition of community service at Georgetown. Today, Georgetown is replete with examples of community service work such as that done by the national service fraternity, Alpha Phi Omega, the Georgetown Emergency Response Medical Service (GERMS), and the Community Action Coalition. However, an abundance of such activities is far from novel at Georgetown, although the names of the organizations that serve, the people who run them, and the types of work they do have changed over the years.

Georgetown's community service tradition began during the last decade of the eighteenth century with the formation of the *Sodality of Our Lady* at Georgetown College. The Sodality, founded by the Fathers of the Society of Jesus, originated in Rome in 1563.[1] The Sodality can be described as a "confraternity," i.e. "a body composed of the faithful—especially those who are not members of a Religious Order or Congregation—canonically erected, governed by a competent ecclesiastical Superior, and aiming at fostering Catholic life by the exercise of certain special works connected with the divine worship or of charity to the neighbor."[2] In the United States, the Sodality was intended primarily for college students, but later it became usual to find Sodalities in congregations such as Trinity Church, Georgetown, and St. Joseph's, Philadelphia.[3] All aspects of the Sodality, from its establishment to its governance and membership practices, are outlined in material covering the Sodality. Mullan says, "its main purpose was the practice of devotion to Our Lady [the Blessed Virgin Mary]...which was accomplished in two ways in the Sodality: namely, by striving after personal perfection and by *apostolic work*."[4]

The beginning of the *Sodality of Our Lady* at Georgetown College is frequently dated as the year 1810, but, as was first pointed out by Fr. E.J. Devitt, S.J., in his May 1913 history of the Sodality, there is evidence that it was organized as early as the last decade of the eighteenth century. In a letter to Fr. Middleton, he cites a quote from the "Diary of Brother Joseph Mobberly": "About the year 1802, a student was taken into the Sodality with me by Bishop Dubourg, who was then a priest and president of this institution."[5] Fr. Devitt, a great archivist, continued to point out that "as to the fact, there can be no doubt, that he was received as a member, and by Bishop Dubourg: but the Bishop ceased his connections with the college in 1799: *ERGO*, we can date the origin of this Sodality to the last decade of the eighteenth century."[6] The Georgetown Sodality held the honor of being the first Sodality established in the United States.

As described by Edward F. Garesché, S.J., "personal holiness,...*the help of the neighbor*, and the defense of the church, in honor of the Blessed Mother and with her protection and assistance, are the three great spheres of Sodality activity."[7] These three areas of Sodality activity are stressed by Garesché, who wrote that "whoever would be a good Sodalist and completely faithful to the duties of his membership must give fair and considerate attention to each of these three departments of endeavor. To slur over any one of them and neglect to cultivate the field it offers is to miss just so much of one's high opportunity as a Sodalist and to fall just so much short of doing all one should for the honor of the Queen of the Sodality."[8]

In the rules of 1587, the Sodalists are recommended "to visit prisons and hospitals, to teach the Christian doctrine, and to perform other good works."[9] This set precedent and demonstrates a tradition of emphasis on corporal works of mercy. However, a writer in the Jesuit Vatican journal, the *Notizie istoriche*, complains that to a great extent "the works of piety have been neglected, *which used to be performed by the members of the*

Sodality."[10] The author complains, but at the same time also admits that there was still work being done: "every Friday still some of the Sodalists served the sick in the hospitals....Some also went every month to serve the prisoners at dinner."[11] The recommendations for corporal works of mercy were reiterated in Sodality writings in the nineteenth century. Father Mullan gives numerous examples of such works performed by Sodalities all over the world, in all the centuries, since the founding of the Sodality movement in Rome in the sixteenth century. For example, in the late nineteenth century, in the Boston Alumni Sodality "about twenty-five members who had already appeared in the lecture field were ready at the call of the Bureau to lecture, free of charge, at any place they may be assigned to. [sic] In one season, these lectures reached no fewer than 10,000 people."[12] It can be concluded therefore, that even though there have been some lapses, as is evident from the previously quoted complaint, they cannot be too harshly criticized, since the corporal works of mercy were continued.

The Georgetown Sodality grew and expanded, as evidenced by the establishment of the Junior Division in the Georgetown Preparatory School on February 12, 1857, and its extension on May 4, 1914 included the Law and Medical Schools and on November 17, 1917 it included the Georgetown Hospital Sodality.[13] However, the material available on community work done by the Georgetown Sodality does not document any such activity earlier than 1920. Father Mullan wrote that members of the Sodality did not usually organize their own projects, but worked through a coexisting St. Vincent de Paul Society.[14] This seems to have been true for the Georgetown Sodality, since in 1910 J.M. Power was a member of the Sodality and at the same time secretary of the St. Vincent de Paul Society, and J.F. Crosby was a member of the Sodality and the head wardrobe keeper for the St. Vincent de Paul Society.[15] Also, because the Sodality had already existed for over one hundred years prior to this date, and in light of its emphasis on corporal works of mercy, it can be assumed that it was active in this regard throughout its existence. Also, Father Durkin noted that although corporal works of mercy have been emphasized in Catholic writings, and even though they may have been performed, they may not have been publicized, because it was a time when many people in society as a whole were still not convinced of their importance.[16]

In the early part of the twentieth century the Sodality took hold and grew. Evidence of this growth is supported by a historical account of the Sodality printed in the *Georgetown College Journal*,[17] which describes an increased fervor and interest in the Sodality as supported by the fact that each of the University Sodalities numbers over one hundred and meets monthly at the college.[18] Organized in June 1920, the Foreign Service section of the Sodality was affiliated with the Catholic Students' Mission Crusade, which aided foreign Catholic missions.[19] The *Journal* reported this affiliation and portrayed the student body's enthusiasm over the idea of helping the foreign missions, as evidenced by their perseverance in collecting large quantities of canceled postage stamps and tin foil, the proceeds of which went to help the struggling missionaries, and by the contribution of $25.00 voted by the Sodality to the Rev. Mark J. McNeal, S.J. for the advancement of Catholic education in Japan.[20] On June 17 of that same year, the Sodality donated $7.50 to the Catholic Students' Mission Crusade.[21] Other efforts of the Sodality include the assumption "of the task of furthering the religious, social, and athletic interests of the Christ Child Society, a Washington organization for the welfare of Catholic boys. The forming of a scout troop, teaching of catechism, coaching of basketball and baseball teams, and other works of zeal"[22] were also among the works done with the boys.

Beginning in 1929, Georgetown's Sodality experienced its greatest growth and change. Until May 1929 its officers consisted of the director, prefect, first assistant, second assistant, secretary, sacristan and the freshman, sophomore, junior, and senior consultants.[23] Then, as of December 1929, due to increased membership, the offices of the Sodality were expanded to include chairmen of the Foreign Missions, Eucharistic, Publicity, Catholic, Literature, Finance, Membership, Programme, Our Lady's, Entertainment, and Social Service Committees.[24] The expansion and restructuring of the administrative positions reflect the Sodality's growth, but more significantly, the addition of a Social Service Committee demonstrates its commitment to corporal works of mercy.

There are many recorded instances of the Georgetown Sodality's social work during this period. An article in the *Washington Star* (20 October 1929) cited the donation of a radio set by the Sodality to the Georgetown room at the University hospital.[25] In 1930, the Sodality raised one thousand dollars to aid the missionary work of Rev. Daniel Sullivan, "Georgetown's own 'adopted' missionary in the Philippines."[26] In the *Journal*'s 125th Sodality Anniversary article, we read, "Georgetown has often been the leader in Catholic movements, which is only fitting and proper since it was the first Catholic college Sodality established." The author relates that the students are proud of the Georgetown Sodality, because of its function as a model in spiritual life and because they are familiar with the service work it is accomplishing.[27] In a later issue (October 1936), the *Journal* lauds the Sodality for its great work off-campus: "the 'Big Brother Committee' is to be commended for its fine accomplishments in leading wayward youth back to the right path and keeping them there. Then, there are the Religious Instructions Committees, who have done fine work in instructing in some of the colored parishes of the city, not only in religion, but in directing them in athletics; Citizenship Committees who have taken an interest in current affairs and the bearing which they have on Catholicism and citizenship; enabling the members of the Sodality to become better informed and better equipped to meet world problems."[28] Another example of the Sodality's work was described in the *Washington Star* (22 December 1940): "The Georgetown Sodality of Our Lady Immaculate performed its usual mission of distributing Christmas cheer among needy families of the neighborhood. Students took up a collection and provided baskets of food and clothing for a number of families."[29] In its article titled "The Sodality of Our Lady Immaculate" (June 1944), the *Journal* wrote: "[This year], as in the past, the Sodality has carried on many great things here at Georgetown....The Sodality has...sponsored many drives throughout the college for various worthy purposes. [One of these] was the Christmas drive for the poor. From this drive enough money was collected to buy baskets for poor families in the Holy Trinity Parish. Another drive was for the promotion of Catholic Literature on campus."[30] Finally, in an interview, Father Joseph T.

Moffitt, its director in 1946, related that the Sodality, in an effort to raise money for missions, on occasion sponsored dances on the campus.[31]

***

In 1888, a group of Georgetown College students formed a "Conference of the Saint Vincent de Paul Society."[32] St. Vincent de Paul conferences were established not only at colleges, but also in parishes around the country. As stated in an article in the June 1891 edition of the *Journal*, "the objects of the Conference are to visit and help poor families and to promote spiritual works and readings among students."[33] The *Journal* in 1890 noted that this essentially charitable organization was composed of students chosen from higher classes of the college and concluded that "the exclusive character of the membership ensures a zeal and responsibility not to be proportionately increased by the addition of members."[34] The conference met weekly under the guidance of a priest. Each meeting began with prayer, followed by reports of officers and committees and discussion of ways and means for promoting the group's aims. At Georgetown College the conference and all other religious organizations were under the guidance of the student counselor, a Jesuit. He was in charge of the areas not under campus ministries, but until 1971 there was only one Jesuit and later a small group of Jesuits who were in charge of counseling, retreats, and groups such as the St. John Berchman's Society (a group which furnished servers for the mass), the St. Vincent de Paul Society, and the Sodality. Traditionally, the offices of the St. Vincent de Paul Society consisted of president, vice-president, secretary, treasurer, the heads of various committees such as the ways and means committee, the emergency relief committee, and the distribution committee, the latter comprising two members with a different person in charge every week. Most interesting of all were the positions of head wardrobe keeper and the assistant wardrobe keeper.[35] Together they were responsible for the collection of clothing for the needy.[36] An article in the November 1890 issue of the *Journal* reports, "an occasional collection of clothes is taken up among the students, who always contribute liberally; these articles find their way into *hundreds of coloured families who are in the extremity of need.*"[37] The *Washington Post* reported, "Twice a year, at Christmas and Easter, the St. Vincent de Paul Society [of Georgetown University], which carries on a year-round program of social welfare activities and charity work, collects bundles of clothes for distribution in Catholic parishes of the city."[38] During Christmas 1936, the G.U. conference's clothing drive was conducted in cooperation with the Seventh Precinct of Georgetown and the clothes were contributed to Holy Trinity Church in Georgetown, the Catholic charities, the District Jail and a Catholic parish at Ridge, Maryland.[39]

The conference in its works was responsible to the General Conference in New York. The secretary's job was to write up and send quarterly reports to the General Conference. For example, the following secretary's report summarizes the conference's work for the quarter ending in June 1890: "Active members on roll, 12; total number of families relieved (including donations of clothes, food, etc.), 28; total number of families visited, 33; active members' weekly offerings, $68.90; and the money value of contributions made to the poor, $50.40. The secretary also noted that [the conference] did its most efficient work during the Christmas and Easter holidays."[40] It supported its corporal works of mercy through a collection from members at each meeting which usually amounted to no more than a few dollars, collections done on campus for clothes, canned food, magazines, etc., such as the 1907 magazine drive performed by a specially appointed "special works committee,"[41] and the alms received from a basket placed in the vestibule of the chapel every Sunday.[42] These collections were an integral part of the conference's work.

Many accounts of corporal works of mercy performed by members of the Georgetown student St. Vincent de Paul Society can be found in volumes of the *Journal* dating from 1890 to roughly 1935. An 1890 article describes members' weekly visits to people in need, including an old lady, blind and dependent. The reporter wrote, "she receives the good Samaritans frequently in her poor and destitute home and listens with an attentive ear to their conversation or the book which they may read [to her]."[43] This same article gave an account of the Society's aid to a twelve-year-old girl: "through its agency an orphan girl...was lately provided for and put into asylum."[44] In 1897 the society established a mission among the soldiers at Fort Meyer, Virginia; once a week some of the members of the conference instructed the soldiers in their religious duties.[45]

Many of the Georgetown College Conference's works are recorded in its minute book which covers the years 1906–1911. For example, it was recorded that the clothes collected through the conference's clothing drives were distributed to hospitals where patients were in need of pajamas and slippers;[46] to jail prisoners about to be discharged;[47] and to individuals referred to the Society. For example, in a February 8, 1907 entry in the minute book, the secretary recorded the distribution committee's gift of one suit of clothes, one pair of underwear, and one shirt to a young man referred to the Georgetown Student Conference by Trinity Church.[48] Other works of the distribution committee included donations in December 1908 of coal and other articles of importance to those found worthy.[49] The Society's work also included entertainment. In the fall of 1909 a committee was appointed to decide upon the ways and means of entertaining the aged at the home of the Little Sisters of the Poor[50] and on December 13, 1909 the entertainment committee performed at the Home for Incurables.[51] Other works of charity which illustrate the diversity of the Society's works include donations of fruit to the Bruen Home (possibly a home of the elderly),[52] a magazine collection on campus for distribution to charitable organizations in D.C.,[53] and work done in support of the Guild of the Little Flower of Jesus. On May 27, 1910 the society sold tickets for a charity affair at Trinity Church given for the benefit of the Guild.[54] Although the St. Vincent de Paul campus organization was not a very large one, it carried on an impressive program of aid to society. It continued its social service into the 1940s, when it worked with the Sodality. In 1941 the Sodality, through the St. Vincent de Paul Society, contributed clothes for distribution through Georgetown and other agencies.[55] The St. Vincent de Paul Society became defunct sometime in the 1940s and in 1959 was reorganized at the college with Father William Kaifer, S.J. as the moderator pro tem.[56] The *Journal* stated the purpose of the reorganized St. Vincent de Paul Society on campus as "relief work and the training of its members in the spirit and methods of the organization."[57]

Much more well known, the Sodality at Georgetown continued its spiritual and apostolic work into the 1960s, but suffered a decline in membership. In the 1930s the Sodality began to change its focus. At the December 1935 annual convention where many schools were represented, the topic of discussion was communism and ways to combat the spread of its atheistic ideology in schools and colleges.[58] The Sodality's concern with political affairs is reflected also in its formation of a citizenship committee which studied political questions affecting the Catholic Church and in 1936 "joined in movements to oppose what might [have been] regarded as inimical legislation in Congress; it also campaigned for decency in movies."[59] In 1938 the Georgetown Sodality sponsored the first May Day celebrations. Their purpose, as described by Kiernan R. Hyland, president of the Yard, was "to focus attention of thoughtful Americans on another source of collegiate opinion besides the one usually dominated by the American Student Union."[60] This was a group primarily composed of Communist party members and sympathizers formed through a merger of the Communist-led National Student League and the student affiliate of the social-democratic League for Industrial Democracy; it began to hold rallies in the 1930s when university campuses first became important centers of radical activity.[61]

From the 1930s through the 1960s the Sodality changed with the changing student population; it seems that the group could not overcome the growing antiestablishment movement of the sixties. Sodalists in the past had seen the work as a means of personal sanctification rather than as an agent solely for the good of others.[62] In the 1960s this type of motivation for doing corporal works of mercy (along with most religious things) was rejected and replaced by strictly humanitarian motivation. It appears from the documents that in the 1960s the Georgetown University Community Action Program (GUCAP) (which was organized by the moderator of the Sodality, Father John C. Haughey, S.J.,[63] and numbered approximately five hundred students during the 1963–1964 academic year),[64] took the Sodality's place on campus as the primary student organization.

***

The Georgetown Sodality, in its works of corporal mercy and through the St. Vincent de Paul Society and the Georgetown Conference of the St. Vincent de Paul Society, set the precedent and laid the foundation for the many organizations on our campus today. Documents of the past prove that the tradition of community service work by Georgetown students is as old as Georgetown itself. It is a tradition that continues today.

Notes

1. Van Meurs and Huonder, in *Sodal. Corr.*, 1897, 61ff, in *The Sodality of Our Lady Studied in the Documents*, 3rd ed., Father Elder Mullan, S.J. (New York: P.J. Kenedy and Sons, 1912), 2.

2. Wernz, *Jus Decrectalium*, III, II, 416, Mullan, 8.

3. E.J. Devitt, S.J., "The Sodality of the Blessed Virgin," *Georgetown College Journal (GCJ)*, June 1913, 634.

4. Mullan, 9.

5. Father Devitt, S.J. to Reverend Father Middleton, S.J., 22 May 1913, University Archives, Sodality, folder 333-1, 2, GUA.

6. Devitt, 3.

7. Edward F. Garesché, S.J., *Sodality Conferences*, 2nd series (New York: Benziger Brothers, 1925), 41.

8. Ibid.

9. Father General Aquavia, *Common Rules of the Sodality*, I, November 1587, 27, #621, Mullan, 154.

10. *Notizie istoriche*, 48, 49, Mullan, 154 (italics added).

11. Ibid., 155.

12. Mullan, 160.

13. Record of dates as copied from Father Barnum's stray notes, University Archives, Sodality, folder 333-1, GUA.

14. Mullan, 157.

15. *Minute Book of the St. Vincent de Paul Society at G.U.*, varia I, box 13, folder 1584, 49–50 and *Program from the Solemn Reception of Candidates into the Sodality*, 21 May 1911, University Archives, Sodality, folder 333-3, GUA.

16. Father Joseph T. Durkin, S.J., interview by author, 5 December 1987.

17. Henceforth referred to as the *Journal*.

18. Edward J. Callahan, '17, "History of the Sodality at Georgetown," *GCJ*, December 1915, 161–64.

19. Day (et al.), "Chronicle," *GCJ*, June 1920, 416–17.

20. Ibid.

21. Receipt for $7.50, folder: *Mission Crusade to the Sodality*, University Archives, Sodality, folder 333-4, GUA.

22. "Sodality Action," *GCJ*, March 1924, 309.

23. *Sodality of Our Lady Immaculate—Solemn Reception of Candidates*, 23 May 1929, University Archives, Sodality, folder 333-4, GUA.

24. *Solemn Reception of Candidates into the Sodality of Our Lady Immaculate*, December 1929, University Archives, Sodality, folder 333-4, GUA.

25. *Washington Star*, 20 October 1929, University Archives, Sodality, folder 333-4, GUA.

26. *Washington Star*, 1930, University Archives, Sodality, folder 333-4, GUA.

27. J. Albano, "Editorial for the Sodality's 125th Anniversary," *GCJ*, December 1935, 176.

28. Cyril Breitenback, "Sodality," *GCJ*, October 1936, 60.

29. *Washington Star*, 22 December 1940, University Archives, Sodality, folder 333-5, GUA.

30. "The Sodality of Our Lady Immaculate," *GCJ*, June 1944, 26–27.

31. Fr. Moffitt, S.J., spiritual director at G.U. in 1946, interview by author, November 1987.

32. James E. Duross, "An Apostle of Charity," *GCJ*, November 1890, 28.

33. "The Georgetown College Conference," *GCJ*, June 1891, 168.

34. Duross, 28.

35. "St. Vincent de Paul Society, Conference of St. Francis de Sales," varia I, box 13, folder 1584, GUA.

36. *Minute Book*, varia I, box 13, folder 1584, 33, GUA.

37. Duross, 28 (italics added).

38. "Students at Georgetown Donate Christmas Cheer," *Washington Post*, 20 December 1936, varia I, box 13, folder 1584, GUA.

39. Ibid.

40. Secretary's Report of the Society of St. Vincent de Paul Societies at G.U., varia I, box 13, folder 1584, 44, GUA.

41. *Minute Book*, 10.

42. *Minute Book*, 44.

43. Duross, 28.

44. Ibid.

45. "Societies," St. Vincent de Paul Conference, *GCJ*, November 1897, 84.

46. *Minute Book*, 22.

47. "Students at Georgetown Donate Christmas Cheer," *Washington Post*, 20 December 1936, varia I, box 13, folder 1584, GUA.

48. *Minute Book*, 7.

49. *Minute Book*, 32.

50. *Minute Book*, 43.

51. *Minute Book*, 46.

52. *Minute Book*, 47.

53. "St. Vincent de Paul Society," *GCJ*, March 1917, 361.

54. *Minute Book*, 49.

55. *Washington Star*, 3 November 1941, University Archives, Sodality, folder 333-5, GUA.

56. Fr. Bunn, S.J. to the Most Rev. Patrick O'Boyle, D.D., varia I, box 5, folder 345, St. Vincent de Paul-misc., GUA.

57. "St. Vincent de Paul Society," *GCJ*, March 1921, 303.

58. *Washington Star*, 7 December 1935, University Archives, Sodality, folder 333-5, GUA.

59. *Washington Post*, 22 November 1936, University Archives, Sodality, folder 333-5, GUA.

60. Kiernan R. Hyland, president of the Yard, to Dean, 12 April 1940, University Archives, Sodality, folder 333-5, GUA.

61. *Dictionary of American History*, vol. VII (New York: Charles Scribner's Sons, 1976), 365b.

62. Mullan, 155.

63. *Blueprint* (vol. XVII, no. 4) December 1964, University Archives, Sodality, box 2, folder-GUCAP, GUA.

64. "Community Action Program Nears 600," *The Hoya* (supplement), 17 December 1964, University Archives, Sodality box 2, folder-GUCAP, GUA.

Sources

Primary Sources

1. Father Bunn, S.J. to the Most Reverend Patrick O'Boyle, D.D., varia I, box 5, folder 345, Saint Vincent de Paul Society-misc., GUA.

2. Father Devitt, S.J. to Reverend Father Middleton, 22 May 1913, University Archives, Sodality, folder 333-1, GUA.

3. Father Joseph T. Durkin, S.J., interview by the author, G.U., 5 December 1987.

4. Father Moffitt, S.J., spiritual director Georgetown College 1946, interview by the author, November 1987.

5. *Georgetown College Journal*.

6. Kiernan R. Hyland, president of the Yard, to Dean, University Archives, Sodality box 2, folder 333-5, GUA.

7. *Washington Post*.

8. Receipt for $7.50, University Archives, Sodality, folder 333-4, folder: Mission Crusade to the Sodality, GUA.

9. Record of dates as copied from Father Barnum's stray notes, University Archives, Sodality, folder 333-1, GUA.

10. "St. Vincent de Paul Society, Conference of Saint Francis de Sales," varia I, box 13, folder 1584, GUA.

11. Secretary's Report of the Society of Saint Vincent de Paul at Georgetown College, varia I, box 13, folder 1584, GUA.

12. Sodality of Our Lady Immaculate—Solemn Reception of Candidates, University Archives, Sodality, May 1911, May 1929, and December 1929, GUA.

13. *Washington Star*.

14. *The Minute Book of the Saint Vincent de Paul Society at Georgetown College.* Washington, D.C.: Georgetown College Conference of the Saint Vincent de Paul Society, varia I, box 13, folder 1584, GUA.

Secondary Sources

1. *Dictionary of American History,* vol. VII (New York: Charles Scribner's Sons, 1976).

2. Garesché, Father Edward, S.J., *Sodality Conferences.* 2nd series (New York: Benziger Brothers, 1925).

3. Mullan, Father Elder, S.J., *The Sodality of Our Lady Studied in the Documents.* 3rd ed. (New York: P.J. Kenedy and Sons, 1912).

The Georgetown College Cadets

John Lombard and Justin Davis

For nearly 140 years, there has been a military presence on the Georgetown University campus. In 1852, a group of Georgetown students began the Georgetown College Cadets, which became the forerunner of the present-day Georgetown University Army Reserve Officers Training Corps (ROTC). Unlike today's G.U. ROTC, the College Cadets were student-run, did not offer scholarships, and required a fee for membership.[1] The volunteer aspect of the College Cadets seemingly reflected a patriotic urge and the historic American preference for civilian reserves rather than a large standing professional army. The College Cadets of the mid-nineteenth century, however, had the liberty to create a military student organization that had a Georgetown flavor. Among its characteristics were: the lack of any links with the U.S. Army, its own set of rules and regulations, a code of gentlemanly conduct, a strong democratic ethos, and limited Jesuit control within the organization.

Even before the College Cadets established themselves on campus, there was a military presence at Georgetown. The early nineteenth century commencement ceremonies had a military aura that contrasts with today's more civilian ceremonies. An August 22, 1808 article in the *National Intelligencer* spoke of a military band that volunteered to play for Georgetown:

The President and Professors of George Town College, return their warmest thanks to the gentlemen of the "Union Light Infantry Band" who politely volunteered their services on the night of their exhibition, and will ever esteem the favor conferred on that occasion amongst the first entitled to their grateful remembrance.[2]

At the 1830 commencement, the military band attached to the U.S. Marine Corps were in attendance, and added greatly to the pleasures of the festivity.[3] Another example of the military contribution at commencement came from an account in the *National Intelligencer* on July 29, 1837:

The public exercises of the students commenced at half past nine o'clock, in the capacious Hall of the College, where the United States flag was seen proudly spreading her glorious stars and stripes to the eye of the beholder. The Marine Band, in their rich uniform, graced the orchestra, and played most delightfully appropriate pieces of music.[4]

The presence of military bands demonstrated, of course, the patriotic character of the earlier commencement exercises.

The early cadet members volunteered their time and had to be approved by a majority of the group.[5] One of the most difficult aspects of studying the early cadets is deciding whether a few very dedicated cadets managed the organization with the vast majority showing little commitment,[6] or whether the majority of those who joined were active participants in it. The minutes were filled with proceedings, motions, and debates but it is still not clear if the meetings were taken seriously by the cadets who are not mentioned in the log book or whether the constitution was actually obeyed and regularly enforced.

Yet, other written documents show a high level of discipline and detail. Perhaps one of the most important documents written by the Georgetown College Cadets, revealing the organization's local character, was the Constitution and By Laws, written in 1852. The document had six main sections: the Preamble, Rules and Regulations, By Laws of the Company Concerning the Arms, a section on meetings, a section on the uniforms, and a section for amendments. This is quite an accomplishment for a student organization and represents a contrast between the College Cadets of the 1850s and today's ROTC cadets, who do not have a formal student-created constitution. Today's ROTC program produces only a handbook, prescribing specific regulations and expectations. The central document issued by the ROTC program is a federal contract, signed by the cadet at the beginning of his or her junior year. Cadets of the mid-1800s did not have such a contract, illustrating the difference between the federal control of today's ROTC and the local initiative of the old College Cadets. The College Cadets could shape their own rules and regulations.

The thirteen-line preamble of the 1852 Cadet Constitution states:

> Whereas the undersigned, anticipating the result of the benefits to be derived from a knowledge and practice of a graceful and manly carriage of the person, and being well aware, that a knowledge of "Military tactics" may be, at some future time beneficial to us, and knowing moreover that these great advantages can only be obtained by our performing the exercise of a soldier, have enrolled ourselves into a Military Company...[7]

The pursuit of military training could be "graceful" and could result in a "manly carriage of the person."[8] The preamble, styled with a beautiful hand, set a clear mission for the College Cadet which included an understanding of military tactics.

The goal of today's ROTC has some similarities, as stated in the 1987–88 ROTC Cadet Handbook, which declares that "The mission of the Army Reserve Officers' Training Corps (ROTC) is to train the future officers in leadership of the United States Army."[9] Specifically, the G.U. ROTC program "...is to instill in each cadet the military skills and leadership required to serve as a commissioned officer in any branch of the United States Army."[10] The Cadet Handbook is prepared by the U.S. Army cadre in Loyola and has little student influence. The similarity of goals between the two groups is that they both wish to have cadets understand military skills. However, the College Cadets could prescribe their own standards, goals, and methods, while the G.U. ROTC must meet federal standards set by the Department of the Army.

After the 1852 Constitution's preamble, there was a section on the rules and regulations of the organization, including the procedures for meetings and drills and the fines for not follow-ing rules. The student-administered fining process was an ex-ample of how the early Cadets were a student-run organization. The fines ranged from the minimum penalty of six and a half cents to a maximum of one dollar.[11] A dollar in 1852 converts to roughly $13.80 in 1988, while six cents would be worth $.82 to-day. The two most serious infractions were for disobeying an order and withdrawing from the group.[12] Article 7 of the 1852 Cadet Constitution states:

> That if any member while on duty in the ranks refuses to obey the command of his superior officer he shall be fined not less than one dollar ($1.00) and on repetition of the offense he shall be expelled from the company.[13]

Disobeying an order in today's Hoya Battalion would proba-bly be strongly reprimanded as it was in the 1850s, but current cadet officers are not allowed to fine fellow cadets.

The College Cadets also had a set of priorities which differed from today's standards. Whereas in 1850, stress was placed on gentlemanly conduct and proper procedure during the meet-ings, today's ROTC places more emphasis on safety and mili-tary competence. Article 3, section I of the 1852 Constitution concerning the arms states:

> Bayonets must never be fixed, except when the Squad or company is actually on drill or Parade or until after the formation of ranks, and must always be unfixed and placed in the scabbard before the squad or company is dismissed under the penalty of 10 cts for each offense.[14]

A mere ten cent fine, which in 1852 would be equivalent to $1.38 today, reflects the low priority given to the proper han-dling of weapons. As declared in Article 8 of the arms section of the 1852 Constitution: "The muskets must never be snapped ex-cept on Drill or Parade when the command 'to fire' is given un-der the penalty of 6 1/4 cts."[15] Firing the weapon at the wrong time is very dangerous but the fine for so doing is dispropor-tionately small compared to the Article 20 fine of fifty cents for speaking without addressing the chairman during a meeting.

Article 20 demands: "That any member wishing to speak, must address the chair; and nothing personal be tolerated under penalty of 50 cents."[16] Thus, proper procedure for speaking at a meeting was placed above the safe handling of a weapon.

The College Cadets had severe restrictions placed on their conduct at the time, suggesting the high priority within the Georgetown community on proper social behavior, as shown in Article 8: "That any member who disturbs a meeting, laughs, talks, or refuses to obey the call to order, be fined 12 1/2 cents."[17] Time was even taken from the monthly meeting for the President (faculty adviser to the College Cadets) to give a short lecture on proper behavior. From the minutes of a February 17, 1853 meeting: "The president spoke of the impropriety of laughing and other freaks unbecoming those calling themselves soldiers."[18] Proper speech, social conduct, and graceful written composition were stressed by the early cadets, reflecting the educational priorities of the mid-nineteenth century. Great emphasis was placed on beautiful penmanship, even for casual records such as the weekly fines. Form and procedures were important to the early cadets. During a February 17, 1853 meeting, the secretary, Patrick Down, wrote: "The company met at 1:00 P.M. Commandant in the chair."[19] Although the Commandant, a university official, was always present at the meetings, the secretary felt the need to write down his presence in a standard form for recording the minutes. At the end of the meeting, Down wrote, "The meeting on motion of Mr. Baintree adjourned."[20] The early cadet meetings were always closed with a vote motion and the secretary felt that it was important to note the motion in his minutes, demonstrating his commitment to form and the group's observance of proper procedure. During a December 13, 1857 meeting, the secretary, Booley, wrote:

> Secretary's minutes of the meeting held on Nov. 22, though reluctantly accepted, accepted [sic], were afterwards contested, and strongly supported by the votes of the Society. Mr. Clance offered five resolutions to the consideration of the Company, which were all accepted. Mr. Ward offered a report on behalf of the committee...appointed for Oct. 24 to which Mr. Clance a member of said committee refused to give his approbation, whereupon a debate ensued in which the majority of the court sustained the report: which

was neither accepted nor rejected...On motion, the Treasurer was empowered to procure the Recording Secretary a new book.[21]

The early cadets noted what today would be considered minute details in their minutes, which again demonstrates the early cadet commitment to form and structure. Also, a motion and then a vote in order to buy a new record book seems to be an act of over-zealous proceduralists.

The early cadets' democratic orientation differs from today's ROTC. In the 1852 Constitution, under the rules of the company, there were set procedures for electing officers, approving new members, and expelling cadets. Early cadet leaders, unlike the ROTC of today, were elected directly from their peers. Article two states:

> That the officers of this company shall be elected by a majority of the number present, and the Commissioned Officers (cadet officers) constitute a standing committee for the regulation of the company.[22]

In the present-day Hoya Battalion, cadet officers are selected by the Professor of Military Science (PMS)—the officer in charge of the G.U. ROTC program—who has the final say in selecting the cadet chain of command. From my personal experience as a cadet, having the PMS select the student leadership is effective because it avoids turning the selection of cadet officers into a popularity contest.

Another example of the democratic nature of the College Cadets was their ability to elect members and expel them. Article 5 of the 1852 Constitution states "That a majority may admit, but 2/3 [of the cadet members' votes] be required in order to expel a member."[23] That a peer vote can approve or expel a fellow member is an example of how the early cadets dominated their organization; but no ROTC program today would ever grant such power to cadets.

To apply to the Loyola program, seniors in high school must be approved by the U.S. Army. The selection panel of three Army cadre members who interview prospective freshmen has no student representation and the decision to award a scholarship has no student input. These important decisions which may affect a student's future are so important that the Army feels the need to have only mature adults participating in the cadet selection process.

There is no ROTC student participation in expelling a fellow cadet. If a cadet has committed an act that would warrant expulsion, a panel of four or five cadre members is selected by the PMS that might also include one cadet. That is not to say that today's cadets have no influence on each other's success in the ROTC. During the junior-year summer ROTC Advance Camp, they evaluate one another in a peer rating system. Each cadet will rank the thirty or forty members in his platoon on ability and leadership. These peer evaluations, as they are commonly called, are then given to an officer who will incorporate this student input with his final rating of the cadet. How seriously student input influences the evaluations officer is unknown, but the ROTC cadets at least have a vehicle for expressing their views of fellow cadets.

A uniquely Georgetown influence on the College Cadets was that of the Jesuits, who were involved in the early cadet organization. Article 3 of the constitution states:

> That the commandant shall be appointed by the Revd. President of the College, and that he shall be one of the community, and shall have control over everything that regards the welfare and prosperity of the Company.[24]

A Jesuit was in the direct chain of command for the college cadets. In Article 9, section 3 of the 1852 Constitution it is prescribed that "The commandant shall preside at every meeting; in his absence, the captain, in the latter's absence the 1st Lient. and according to rank in regular order."[25] It is hard to gauge how much power the commandant actually possessed but, according to the Constitution, he had supreme control. The commandant position was changed to commander-in-chief in the 1858 Junior Cadet Constitution but his powers remained unchanged.[26] The Junior Cadets were an adjunct to the College Cadets formed for the younger members of the unit.

The Jesuit influence was also felt by the College Cadets during their award ceremonies after field training. One such training exercise, called the "target shooting excursion," was followed by Jesuit awards. This exercise consisted of a march of one mile from the Georgetown campus to "Hickory Nut Hill," to conduct a marksmanship contest there, and to march back to the campus.[27] An unnamed newspaper clipping portrays the event:

> At nine o'clock every thing was in readiness, and the Senior and Junior Companies, under their respective officers and headed by the College Band, which under the leadership of the ever-pleasant and accommodating Mr. Chism, discoursed inspiring tones of sweet music, began their march.[28]

After dinner that night the cadets were presented with awards and "...with a few appropriate remarks, presented to the successful contestants by the Rev. Jno. Early, S.J., President of the College."[29] Fr. Early took a special interest in the cadets when he donated the first prize:

> The prizes were, for the Seniors, first a beautiful, heavy gold cross, from Father Early, who ever shows himself ready to forward every thing among the students which tends to make their time in College pass more pleasantly...[30]

Such direct participation by Fr. Early demonstrates the support provided by the Jesuits for the early cadets. The Jesuit influence is still evident today. At the Fr. Meade awards ceremony, during the spring of 1985, one can remember the effect produced by Fr. Healy's presence at the event. His expressed support for the ROTC made a lasting impression.

One of the most colorful episodes in Georgetown military history was the American Civil War era as it related to the College. The strife between the South and the North tore the campus apart. It should be noted that a large majority of the students came from the South and had Confederate sympathies. In 1861, a group of Southern students waited on the President, Fr. Early, to present him with a petition. There were about fifteen of the boys, they were sophomores, and this is the letter that they handed personally to Fr. Early on April 16, 1861:

> We, the undersigned, students of the Philosophy Class of George-

town College,...beg leave to present to you this petition,...requesting you to exert your influence in order to effect...our departure from College...Our presence here any longer would be attended but with little good to us,...while all we hold most dear on earth, our Country [the South] our parents and our brethren call loudly upon our presence at our respective homes.[31]

One of the signers of this document, John Dooley, of Richmond, Virginia, eventually joined the Confederate Army, fought in Pickett's charge at Gettysburg, was captured there, and spent the rest of the war in a federal prison. Returning to Georgetown after the war, he entered the Jesuit novitiate (which was then at the Hilltop) and died a few months before he would have been ordained to the priesthood. It is clear that his life was shortened by the hardships he had undergone during the war. He is buried in the Jesuit cemetery at the University.[32]

From the classes of 1861–1867 inclusive there was a total of 358 Georgetown students in either the Confederate or Union armed forces.[33] The total number of students and alumni in uniform was 1,141, 216 of them fighting for the North and 925 for the South.[34] One hundred seventeen Georgetown students or alumni died either in action or by disease or wounds incurred in the war.[35]

During the war years the number of students left at the Hilltop averaged less than 75.[36]

Georgetown entered the war, so to speak, on May 4, 1861, when the government ordered Fr. Early to prepare quarters on the Hilltop for the 69th regiment, New York's National Guard. By nightfall of the same day more than 1,300 federal soldiers were billetted in the Maguire Building and the student's refectory building. The regimental commander, Colonel Michael Corcoran, took over the recreation room of the Jesuit priests.[37]

Before the end of the conflict, the College buildings had also housed (after the departure of the New York 69th) the 79th New York National Guard, 1,000 men strong; and in the late summer of the following year some other campus facilities were rented by a federal army medical unit, and the Jesuit property at Tenleytown, D.C., occupied by a federal general and his staff in 1862.

During the first battle of Bull Run the faculty and few remaining students could hear the roar of the cannon. "When," recounts one who was on the campus that day, "we saw horsemen over near Arlington galloping like mad toward Washington, and constantly increasing in numbers,...Fr. Early remarked to me, 'The tide of battle tends this way; the Union forces evidently have met with a reverse; they may be here before night; God help the poor sufferers, Northern and Southern; if they come, every bed in the College shall be turned over to the wounded.'"[38]

The Civil War gave a death blow to the College Cadets; the students, having witnessed the real thing, lost their enthusiasm for the make-believe. The next military presence of any importance at the Hilltop would be the government's student army training corps of World War I.

Nevertheless, the Georgetown College Cadets fulfilled, with a flair and the rousing sound of music, a need of its time.

Notes

1. Note that the order of the Georgetown Archive document citation is: document, envelope, file, Georgetown University Archives (hereafter cited as GUA), and page. "Constitution and By Laws of the Georgetown College Cadets," Military Cadets 1855–1856, Military File Undated to 1900, GUA, p. 9. This specific source will henceforth be cited as Constitution [1852].

2. Letter from John C. Haskins, 1808, Commencement File 1800–1846, GUA.

3. Letter from "One of the Spectators," 1830, Commencement File 1800–1846, GUA.

4. Saturday, July 29, 1937 Georgetown College, 1837, Commencement File 1800–1846, GUA.

5. Constitution [1852], p. 2.

6. G.T.C. Cadets 1866–67, Military Roll Call 1860, 1865–75, GUA.

7. Constitution [1852], p. 1.

8. Ibid., p. 1.

9. *Georgetown University Army ROTC Hoya Battalion Handbook 1986–1987*, N.P., Washington, D.C., The Cadre, Georgetown University ROTC Instructor Group, 1986, section 1-1.

10. Ibid.

11. According to the Department of Commerce, which gave the 1988 consumer price index and a formula for dollar historical purchasing power, the 1852 dollar purchasing power would be $13.80 in 1988. For more information see *Historical Statistics of the United States*, part 1, p. 211 or call the U.S. Dept. of

Commerce, Bureau of Census.

12. Constitution [1852], pp. 2–3.

13. Ibid., p. 2.

14. Ibid.

15. Ibid., p. 6.

16. Ibid., p. 3.

17. Ibid., p. 2.

18. Military 1852–1872, Military File Undated to 1900, GUA, Feb. 17, 1853.

19. Ibid.

20. Ibid.

21. Military Cadets 155–56, GUA, Dec. 13, 1857.

22. Constitution [1852], p. 1.

23. Ibid., p. 2.

24. Ibid., p. 1.

25. Ibid., p. 7.

26. Constitution or By Laws of the Georgetown College Junior Cadets, Military Varia 1854–1877 and 1899–1901 423-1, Military File Undated to 1900, GUA, p. 1.

27. "A Field Day at the College," Military Varia 1854–1877 and 1899–1901 423-1, Military File Undated to 1900, GUA, p. 1.

28. Ibid.

29. Ibid.

30. Ibid.

31. J.T. Durkin, S.J., *Georgetown University: The Middle Years (1840–1900)*, Washington, D.C., Georgetown University Press, 1963, pp. 47–48.

32. *John Dooley Confederate Soldier: His War Journal* (ed. J.T. Durkin, S.J.), Washington, D.C., Georgetown University Press, 1945, p. 11.

33. Ibid., p. 53.

34. Ibid., loc cit.

35. Ibid., loc cit.

36. Ibid., p. 48.

37. Ibid., p. 49.

38. Ibid., p. 51.

Coeducation at Georgetown

Margaret Dowley and Jessica Seacor

Women at Georgetown!

We begin this study by exploring the programs designed for women before and after the College of Arts and Sciences became coeducational in 1969. Our questions have led us to all the corners and thoroughfares of undergraduate living—academics, student associations, social life, sports, leadership and admissions. We have met with alumni, spent hours looking through documents in our archives, researched our women's sports programs, polled a portion of our present undergraduate population, and interviewed many people who have participated in the lives of many undergraduates throughout the years. We found ourselves in our own backyard looking at our own opportunities at Georgetown, our playing fields, meeting places, and living situations. By concerning ourselves with the "women's issues" of Georgetown's past we have repeatedly wound up in the present and, hopefully, with a better sense of what the future might hold for women *and* men at this institution. Many of the women we have met had the opportunity to be "firsts" as undergraduates—first College women, first female valedictorians, first female editors, first female organizers and leaders.

The "college girl" at Georgetown in the first half of the twentieth century was a nursing student. Although these students had to use many of the same facilities as many of the College men, their classes were kept separate from the College men for many years. Required courses in theology, philosophy, and English were listed in the course book as either "for Nursing students only" or "for College students only." Nursing students were always housed in separate sections of the campus. Many nurses felt that their curriculum was too practical and lacked a good exploration of the liberal arts. One alumna wrote that there was a definite "lack that I had felt as a student nurse which moved me to borrow the Lit book of one of the male College students because I felt I was missing something that I knew I wanted to be part of my education."[1] The nurses were, and are today, an integral part of Georgetown University Hospital. During the Second World War there was a great demand for nurses Stateside since so many had gone to the war. This prompted the director of the Nursing School, Sr. Joanilla, to request that each student nurse serve six months at the University Hospital after graduation.

It was not until years later that women were invited into another undergraduate school at Georgetown in 1919. The Edmund A. Walsh School of Foreign Service decided to consider the admission of twenty-five female and 150 male applicants. Thus, from its inception it has been coeducational. Fr. Walsh wanted it that way. He had no intention of excluding women from this school constructed to educate future diplomats.[2] The female applicants to the new school were highly competitive. Traditionally, the women who were admitted to the SFS programs scored higher on standardized testing than did a majority of their male counterparts. By 1951 there were 209 women enrolled in the Nursing School, 49 in the Foreign Service School, and 70 in the Institute of Languages and Linguistics (opened to women in 1949).[3]

It is important to note that during this period no men petitioned for enrollment in the Nursing School and the number of men who sought degrees from the Institute of Languages and Linguistics was always substantially dwarfed by the number of women.

It is difficult to assess the relations which arose because of the ratio of men to women. Many male College alumni noted that they enjoyed friendships with women who attended the "other" schools at G.U., but preferred to date women from area schools. One alumna of the Nursing School who was at Georgetown from 1954 to 1958 noted:

> There was no question then, GU was a man's university except for the Schools of Nursing and Foreign Service. This put the few women at a distinct advantage with such a high ratio of men to women. We also experienced excellent friendships with a lot of the male students, some carrying even today—a very positive experience. The few of us who took classes with boys were treated as necessary evils by the teachers—not taken seriously.[4]

Another had this to say about the 1940s:

> We knew most of the Arts and Science, Foreign Service and Medical students, since the schools were smaller in those days. They were great off-duty companions and dates. We would congregate almost daily in either of the two eateries across 36th Street to chat and have a coke.[5]

It is quite clear that the "culture" of G.U. was quite different then. Prior to 1943 any female Georgetown student whom a male student encountered was presumed to be a nurse. When other schools opened up, men were asked to see their female classmates in new roles—as future decision makers, linguists, or translators. Another graduate, Barbara Ryan, who studied Diplomatic and Consular Foreign Service in 1950–51, recalled:

> I had little time for socializing, but found the day-to-day contacts generally straightforward and mutually respectful. The only disdain I felt arose from College-Foreign Service relations. [My gender] was not an issue. Having graduated at the top of my class at a rigorous women's college, I owed no one any apologies.[6]

In order to take care of the special needs of women and help them become acclimated to the Georgetown community, many administrative decisions had to be made. Housing, psychological needs, parietal hours, and proper attire for women became issues the administration concerned themselves with increasingly each year. The "Miss G Goes to Georgetown" guidebook was written as the female answer to the "G Book," the men's handbook. This guidebook, patterned after one of Marquette

University, was supposed to be among the female student's belongings at all times. While the "G Book" introduced the male student to the many traditions of Georgetown and left most of his behavioral decisions to "his own discretion," the "Miss G Book" makes few allusions to the same traditions and adheres to a decidedly rigid attitude in reference to female behavior. The first one, published in 1959 by the Nursing School, went to great lengths to describe academic responsibility, religious conduct, on-campus permission to come and go, and proper attire for each circumstance. The "three lives of women" at G.U.—spiritual, social, and academic—were reinforced throughout the guidebook. In the opening passage of the 1959 "Miss G Book," the author states that the Catholic nature of the University should be readily apparent to the visitor by observing the female students who attend. Students were expected to aspire to standards of life and conduct congenial to the faith. Women were encouraged to attend Mass daily and were required to make a spiritual retreat.

The "norms of conduct extend over and beyond those of purely moral and religious obligation, and include the practice of virtue to a very high degree."[7] In short, the attitude adopted by the administration regarding the women on campus was one of *in loco parentis*. The conduct of the student was measured and discussed through a system of demerits. These were administered for missing Mass on Sundays or holy days of obligation, using profane or indecent language, wearing improper dress, or necking in public places. The latter offense resulted in the highest number of demerits granted for a single violation, fifty. In the first few issues of the "Miss G Book" one notices the authors' concern simultaneously to take firm stands and remain readable. For example, in 1962, the rule concerning necking in public places was thus expressed: "leave neck and neck positions on the front steps to the race horses."[8]

In the section "Miss G Plans her Wardrobe," a student in 1962 would have read:

> Personal pride is an inherent quality of the weaker sex, and while clothing plays an important part in the college co-ed's plans for college, it is well to remember that the "price" wardrobe is not always the wardrobe that is appropriate and best suited for co-eds.[9]

Women were expected to wear dresses and skirts to classes and all social gatherings except for picnics, when bermudas were permissible. One alumna noted that wearing a skirt after it was no longer compulsory would afford her a better grade in some classes. No doubt modesty and neatness were paramount in dress and appearance. With time, the reference made to women as the "weaker sex" was dropped, as was the need to have separate guidebooks for men and women.

Back in the 1940s, women were inspected before going out to a formal function. Those with spaghetti straps or even strapless dresses prayed they would pass the inquisition. "Before we left," recalled Mrs. Carol Powers, "we had to report to the superintendent of Nurses for final approval of our evening attire."[10]

According to graduate student Susan Poulson, "coeducation in the College was first considered in the mid-1960s when Fr. Thomas Fitzgerald, Academic Vice President, and Fr. Royden Davis, the College Dean, began to discuss admitting women."[11] It was necessary to expand the student body in order to cover the rising costs Georgetown was continuously facing because of new academic programs and the building of a new university library. Another factor at work in the decision was that many members of the newly formed Faculty Senate had just won tuition privileges for members of their families and hoped to take advantage of this grant by providing their daughters with a liberal arts degree. It was not until the spring of 1968 that the proposal was brought before the Board of Directors to see if there would be any significant opposition to it. The proposal to admit fifty to one hundred girls was approved by the Executive Faculty.

Small pockets did show signs of resistance to the admission of women. The men in the College, if polled, would probably have voted the measure down, according to Fr. Davis. A committee of one hundred college students wrote a letter to *The Hoya* protesting the decision. But the consensus of the faculty was that it was a decision whose time had come.

When the issue of coeducation in the College came to the forum, most undergraduates asked "Why have we waited so long?" since Georgetown lagged significantly behind other northeastern universities. Many of these institutions had reexamined their aims and goals. Some have said that the greatest irony of the sixties was that men desired to experience everything and open up new horizons, but some men were unhappy when women were allowed to do the same. The decision, notes Susan Poulson, "emerged in the context of changing norms about gender roles in society at large, and these changes in attitude, in assumptions, and in legal norms no doubt influenced the decision made by the Georgetown College administration to admit women."[12] Despite the times and a prevalent "culture of social change," some remained opposed.

The discussions concerning the admission of women went through many channels before becoming policy. Original proposals were given to department meetings, the College Executive Committee was consulted, the President had conceded, and, finally, the Board of Directors had approved. Discussions at each step of the process revolved around the economic well-being of the university, the academic impact of coeducation, the tuition benefits for an increasing population of lay faculty, and the role coeducation would play in the Jesuit educational tradition at Georgetown.

On the theoretical level, what was most deliberated over was the traditional resistance to coeducation within the church and what would be sacrificed in order to incorporate women into the College.

Housing, enrollment, and the special needs of young women were the three most impelling practical concerns of the early 1970s. The solutions to these concerns were provided first in the spring of 1969, when Fr. Davis allowed a few undergraduate women to transfer into the College in an attempt to make the transition smoother. This created a sense of ease for the first class because there would already be upperclass women in the College at the time of the arrival of the first coed freshman class in the College in September.

The traditions of 179 years do not die easily. It is not surprising that the task before the administrators, faculty members, Jesuits and residence assistants seemed overwhelming. How could one assimilate 50 women into a class of 420 men? First, the decision was made to admit to the College 50 women instead of the standard initial enrollment of 25 adopted by the other schools. Both models, the School of Foreign Service and the School of Business Administration, began their coeducational eras by admitting a minute number of highly talented women into their first coed classes. This produced a great deal of strife between men and women in these schools, often because women's scores tended to outshine those of men. These precautions were also made in all three schools (meaning that a fixed number of female positions were opened in addition to a proportionate number of men) so that men would not feel that their places were being given unfairly to women.

When asked what he remembers about the transition, Fr. Royden Davis tells a story of that first year. When he awoke on the first day of spring in his New South dorm room, he found a bouquet of flowers attached to his door with a card which read: "Now aren't you glad you admitted women into the College?" His concerns for that first year were many. Would the women feel at home? Would tensions arise on either side? Could he encourage relations among new students? He received letters and visits from many of the women in the first class during the first year. Many expressed a general excitement coupled with a feeling of isolation.

Many aspects of the transition took place quite naturally. For example, the "animal section" of McDonough Arena, an area where boisterous fans cheered during basketball games, was an all-male tradition. It was first visited by one or two women. The trend continued until by 1974 the section was completely coed.[13]

The climate the first College class of fifty women entered was one of widespread division. East campus was home to those in the School of Foreign Service, central campus was College "turf," and both the Institute for Languages and Linguistics and the Nursing School housed women separately in St. Mary's, on the west end of the campus. Therefore, these separate sections of undergraduate housing, each with its own student representative body, resulted in a great deal of isolation for the women.

No doubt the biggest problem coeducation presented was housing. The men were concerned that women would obtain all the choice rooms. When women were admitted to the College there were no places for them in the traditionally female dorm,

St. Mary's. The Sisters of St. Joseph, who worked in the hospital, once occupied the fourth floor. They were relocated during the early 1950s to make room for the influx of female undergraduates. Concern heightened when many excellent candidates were forced to attend other schools since Georgetown could not provide housing. In 1958, Rev. Joseph Moffitt, S.J., the Assistant Dean and Director of Admissions, wrote to Rev. Brian McGrath, S.J., the Academic Vice-President:

> If we are to continue to take girls, as I presume we will, I think we should plan for some permanent dormitory facilities. I would like to suggest that St. Mary's Hall, the smaller of the nursing dormitories at the hospital, be put aside for the use of the girls attending the School of Foreign Service or the Institute or the School of Business Administration. We have lost many good applicants because we have no dormitory facilities for them.[14]

Plans for the creation of another dorm to house women were underway but the immediate concern was the class arriving in the fall. Assistants to the Dean of Women investigated properties and buildings in and around Georgetown in order to house the students. Included in this search was the acquisition of the famed "haunted" Halcyon House on Prospect Street and a number of area inns and hotels. In the first year the third floor of Copley was designated a women's floor and some years later the fifth was used for the same purpose. This was the first coed dorm; Harbin, New North and New South soon followed. In the 1969 annual report it is easy to see that administrators were hesitant about creating coed living spaces:

> We are aware that a considerable amount of thought and effort must go into the implementation of this [Copley], our first experiment in coeducational housing so that it does not become a feminine ghetto—or a scapegoat.[15]

When Darnall was opened in 1965, it was intended to be a purely female dorm. The location was picked by Dr. Patricia Reuckel and a committee of campus planners including one Jesuit who jokingly remarked, "Why don't you just erect the whole structure on stilts over the Jesuit cemetery—then they really would be here over our dead bodies." It was described at its inauguration as a "streamlined facility where 336 Georgetown coeds can take beauty treatments, prepare snacks, or do laundry, as well as study and play in the $2,850,000 residence..."[16] The dorm was named after Eleanor Darnall Carroll, mother of Archbishop John Carroll, the founder of Georgetown University in 1789. The six floors constructed around common rooms were meant to promote friendship and interaction. Among the women themselves, close bonds of friendship formed; for many it was their first venture away from home. For the university, creating Darnall was a major step in acknowledging and attending to the needs of women students. In the Darnall/St. Mary's complex the women were acutely aware of their numbers.

Women were received into a social arena in which most men spent their time meeting women at other schools. In the "Miss G Book," women were encouraged to engage in the social activities of orientation week and throughout their career at Georgetown. All work and no play will make a dull coed! It was common knowledge within the male community that Trinity, Mount Vernon, Immaculata, Georgetown Visitation, Dumbarton and Marymount were nearby preferred social centers. The men liked to be friends with the women at G.U. who were "fun to talk to," but they sought their romances on other campuses. Some women felt that the atmosphere then, though stressful, was usually conducive to meeting men. Others disagreed; one indicated to Fr. Davis that being a woman in the College made her a "dating anathema." Another alumna expressed a somewhat different concern:

> By the time we were juniors, we had matured so much that our relationships with the fellows on campus by and large became less frequent—they were too immature for us. As a student nurse one grew up fast.[17]

Until the late 1950s, no women (not even the mothers of male students) were allowed "on corridor" unless they were accompanied by a Jesuit. Intervisitation or parietals became the subject of intense debate in the years prior to the College going coed. Student government members placed the right to twenty-four hour parietals high on their priority lists in the fall of 1967.

In one sense, this issue was a barometer of the changing mores on campus and in the greater society outside. Freedom from institutions and freedom to conduct their private adult affairs unhampered by curfews were hallmarks of student protest. At Georgetown during 1967 and 1971 the Student Government and the administrators took opposing positions on the issue. Students felt that, as legal adults, their right to visit members of the opposite sex at any hour should not be denied.

The administration, busily assimilating the first coed classes in the College, were backed into a corner on the issue. As a Catholic institution they could not grant students their wish without some debate. Several "experimental" limited intervisitation hours were granted, such as those from February to April 1968. For the women, the issue of a curfew remained paramount—twenty-four-hour intervisitation was not an issue to those who had to be in by 12:30 A.M. on weekends. In the fall of 1969 a policy whereby a female student was free to come and go as she pleased was implemented for all upperclassmen. In the Annual Report on Women in 1969 a new philosophy was discussed. The authors of this document (members of the Dean of Women's staff) proposed that the ultimate responsibility for the individual's behavior should rest in the hands of the individual. In keeping with the new philosophy, the administration not only adopted the self-determined closing hours but also eliminated the specified dress code. First semester freshmen, however, had to be in by midnight on week nights and by 2 A.M. on weekends.

Students continued to focus their attention on the prospect of twenty-four-hour parietals. In 1970, when Dr. Reuckel, then a newly appointed head of the Office of Student Development, placed a moratorium on parietals, student action was taken. Her intention was to clean up the situation by revoking the privilege. The Student Government passed a bill which claimed their immunity to Reuckel's action. After some debate, however, the Student Government reluctantly repealed this act.

A task force concerning the Quality of Student Life was formed to study the question of unlimited intervisitation. It concluded that it could not restrict these rights. It is interesting to note that a student survey found that more men were in favor of unlimited intervisitation: 90% of the men polled were in favor while 70% of the women felt the same way; and of that 70%, 10% were opposed to unlimited intervisitation. A series of articles discussing all aspects of sexuality appeared in *The Hoya* in 1965. Issues such as relationships, pregnancy, abortion, marriage were discussed clinically and personally. A symposium on sex roles was conducted in April 1969 in order to examine some of the attitudes women were experiencing on campus. The 1969 Annual Report on Women concluded that there was a "need to examine and change some of the subtle attitudes and feelings we have if women students are to be full citizens on our campus."[18]

According to this Annual Report on Women, vestiges of prejudice had manifested themselves in lower rates of scholarships for women, use of a ratio or quota system for admissions, use of the word "female" in some of the University's literature, and lack of career guidance for women students.

Consciousness had been raised by various liberal student groups and publications throughout the sixties. As students left the painful change of the sixties behind, they looked forward to the promise of the "stable seventies." But to many, change was still felt to be necessary. That message was clearest to the women activists of this day. Issues such as the Equal Rights Amendment, equal pay for equal work, reproductive freedom, and protection from rape and other violent crimes against women helped to fuel the fire of national women's organizations. This, too, was translated into campus concern. Its most lasting manifestation was the organization of the Women's Caucus in 1972.

Transfer student Julie Johnson founded the group after discovering that Georgetown had no such organization. In its beginning stages it concentrated on small group meetings. In 1973 the Caucus received its first funding from the University and was able to devote a sizable amount of energy to a conference entitled "Incentive to Action," which was held March 30, 1974. Participation in this day-long affair was open to the general public. Delivering the keynote address was Margaret Sloan, the first chairwoman of the National Black Feminist Organization (the NBFO). Her comments, expressed to the small number who attended, touched issues of equality, reproductive freedom, rape, and the need to educate children about sex roles. She discussed the formation of the NBFO, an organization dedicated to fighting both sexism and racism. Ms. Sloan indicated that one of the forces impeding equality is the internalized anger women feel. In keeping with the theme of the conference she asked her audience to channel that anger into productive and serious work for the advancement of all civil rights. One of her most poignant statements concerned the attitudes of both men and women and the liberation of both sexes. She stated that women's liberation is also a liberation for men—it frees them from the entire economic responsibility to the family and grants them freedom to express themselves.

In 1974 the Caucus opened its office in the New North basement, next to the band practice rooms. The October 18th opening was celebrated with a potluck dinner. In the same year a consciousness-raising group of student writers was formed and the Caucus periodical, *The Junon Journal*, was born. In 1975 the Caucus was responsible for a week-long seminar on careers for women. This was repeated in 1976 by viewing the films "Growing Up Female," "It Happened to Us," and "Women in China," and by reading *The Second Sex* and *Against Our Will*. Here issues such as the ERA, sexuality, the development of a female identity, and abortion were addressed. Members demonstrated in the anti-Hyde Amendment march. This amendment proposed the stoppage of Medicaid funds for abortions, thereby, averred its opponents, discriminating against poor women. Women activists could also be found at the "Motherhood by Choice" march on Mother's Day of that year. In the fall of 1983 they distributed a pamphlet entitled *Health Care for Women: A Guide to Services in the D.C. Metropolitan Area*, which was banned by the University administration on the grounds that it included information as to where a student could get an abortion. By 1986 the "Women's Center," though still supported by a faithful minority, set forth its identity as:

> an organization devoted to providing a forum in which women and men can learn about and discuss issues of gender on campus and in the community. We see our role as an educational one, as well as to provide a vehicle for action and a support group for the entire student body.[19]

Today this group seeks to become involved with the new Women's Studies Program (a minor formed in 1986) at Georgetown by expanding and housing its library; to raise consciousness about date rape and sexuality; and, in a general sense, to educate *men* as well as women about feminist issues. In short, the birth of this group on the Georgetown campus is a further manifestation of the concern aroused by the prejudices outlined in the Annual Report of Women of 1969. The act itself of organizing for discussion illuminates the shadow of misunderstanding, frustration, and lack of assimilation that women were experiencing at the time. By 1979 the number of women in the College was greater than the number of men. This creates a new dynamic to be reckoned with through intelligence and imagination. Many of those experiences can manifest themselves in quite new and sophisticated forms in our lives as undergraduates even today.

In pursuit of Jesuit educational ideals to foster "the development of the entire person," Georgetown chose to admit women into the College of Arts and Sciences in the spring of 1969. As women began to take their places in the classrooms, changes were being implemented in regard to the athletic facilities as well. The presence of women students in all five undergraduate programs began to challenge existing traditions to make room for the increasing diversity of the student body. To complement the academic challenges, athletic programs began to emerge to respond to the needs of the varied population. Since those early days of club organizations, Georgetown now provides fifteen varsity sports for women, twenty-five intramural athletic activities, and numerous instructional and recreational programs. By exploring the athletic programs for women at Georgetown, one can determine to what extent athletics enhances the educational experience for women at a Jesuit institution.

The first women's programs "were organized on a very local and very low key level...with so few women at the University."[20] The catalyst behind the development of athletic programs for women was Natalie Paramskas, athletic director and field hockey coach at the School of Nursing since 1952. By 1960 she was promoted to Director of the Georgetown Women's Athletic Association, where women's basketball, swimming, gymnastics, volleyball, tennis and canoeing became her responsibilities. Continued persistence and concern for the improvement of her programs enabled her to acquire the position of Assistant Athletic Director for Women in 1974, thirteen years after achieving the position of full-time athletic instructor in physical training for women. By 1985 she witnessed the maturing of her efforts with seven sports for women participating in the Big East Championships. Her commitment and dedication to developing the women's programs during her thirty-four years of service to the University cannot be sufficiently praised. Her contribution is, according to Director of Athletics Francis X. Rienzo, "the foundation upon which women's athletics [at Georgetown] will continue to develop."[21]

The transition from a male-dominated sports program to one embracing women's sports was a difficult accomplishment. Many of the men were still adjusting to having women in the classroom. "It was hard," recalls Mrs. Paramskas, "because many men did not feel women should advance to the same level."[22] As the University's academic reputation grew through the early 1970s to unprecedented levels, so too did the athletic programs for both men and women. The latter attracted candidates of varied talents, including athletic stand-outs.

The early 1970s marked the beginning of changed attitudes from earlier biases. Professor Dorothy Brown of the History Department recalled an article in *The Georgetown Voice* which commented on the changes: "All in all it looks like a year [1973] of continued growth and enthusiasm as the women's sports teams set out to prove once again that even in the world of sports brand XX chromosomes are as good as brand XY any day."[23]

As the early 1970s welcomed women's basketball, volleyball, track, cross-country and tennis teams to varsity status, newer programs were encouraged. The encouragement, however, was cautious as Georgetown tried to define itself amid the changes and continued improvements in the quality of the educational experience it offered. For the first time, women began to receive full scholarships for their athletic abilities. By the late 1970s, two women were receiving such scholarships. Abbie Dillon, still the most prolific scorer in Georgetown's history, received a women's basketball scholarship as a member of the Class of 1981. Christine

Mullen, whose records in track still hold, was Georgetown's first All-American and scholarship recipient for the track team.

Of the newer programs trying to break into the growing athletic department, the women's crew found it especially difficult to gain support for their efforts. Around the nation women's crew was beginning to blossom. In the fall of 1975, a group of thirty women organized at Georgetown and decided to form a team. John Courtin, the men's crew coach at the time, recalls meeting with the women: "I was impressed by their enthusiasm. They amounted to a very significant number for an unorganized team."[24] The men's team, however, was not particularly pleased. They believed that a women's team was "never going to happen: Women just do not row!" The women organized nevertheless, headed by a George Washington University rower with just four years' experience, Martha Laradeu. A few "screaming matches on the dock at 6:30 A.M. did not deter the women."[25] They trained at McDonough Gym during the winter. Borrowing equipment from a defunct Howard University club, they practiced at 5:30 A.M., before the men's team. With one boat and a few oars borrowed from the men, they began to be taken seriously. By the fall of 1976, the acting captain, Sharon Courtin, now married to the former men's coach, drafted a letter to the Director of Athletics, Francis X. Rienzo, asking for varsity status. At first not overly supportive, Mr. Rienzo granted the women rowers varsity recognition in name only. Fundraising projects similar to the men's team's efforts enabled the women to develop a program which is today regarded as a dominant one in the nation.

As the late 1970s moved into the early 1980s, Georgetown women's teams such as basketball, volleyball, tennis and track/cross-country had won varsity recognition on the First Team Big East Squad. In a nine-year period from 1974 to 1983, the Lady Hoya volleyball teams won no less than sixteen games per season and gained the respect of other powerhouses in the East. The tennis team, under the guidance of Coach Susan Liebenow and later Kathy Kemper, was powered by Suzanne Kuhlman (C '83), a four-time All-American with 60-0 match record, the Big East singles title and the NCAA Division II National Tournament title. The track/cross-country teams were no less spectacular with runners Pia Palladino, a 1979 All-American cross-country recipient, and Christine Mullen, a 1980 indoor AIAW champion and All-American whose records still hold today. Throughout the 1980s, both women's teams developed national prestige. In 1987 the indoor team won two Big East Championship titles in the 4 x 400m relay and 4 x 800m relay.

Georgetown's nonscholarship women's varsity teams have also fulfilled Natalie Paramskas' vision "to produce highly competitive teams."[26] Full-time head coaches were acquired for the women's basketball, volleyball, field hockey and lacrosse teams. Paramskas remarked, "Women's athletics has come a long way over the years and progress has not come easily, but after this year [1985], I can truly say that the future for women athletes here at Georgetown is bright."[27]

The nonscholarship women's teams which have earned recognition include field hockey, lacrosse, swimming and crew. The field hockey team started to compete against Division I champions such as the University of Maryland at College Park, with the skills of Marianne Sullivan (B '86), a 1983 All-American honorable mention, and Laura Clauson (F '88), a goalkeeper for the First Team South squad at the National Tournament. The lacrosse team also emerged in 1981 and by 1987 was defending its title at the Maryland Colleges Tournament. Suzanne Redden (C '87) became the first player to participate in the prestigious North-South National Tournament after trials for the National Team. Women's swimming is steadily progressing under the direction of Mark Pugliese and is defeating powerhouses such as the University of Connecticut in the Big East and American University, the local foe to whom the Hoyas had lost in 1981 by a score of 119-17. In 1987 the women's crew team won a gold medal in the varsity eight race at the nationally recognized Dad Vails to garner a spot for the boat in the National Women's Collegiate Rowing Championships. Led by the coaching combination of John Devlin, in his tenth year, and Jack Nihil, the team continues to compete with other nationally ranked programs. Field hockey, lacrosse, crew and swimming are not expected to be scholarship programs in the near future but they challenge their scholarship opponents fiercely, a fitting tribute to the commitment and dedication of each team's student-athletes.

Also worthy of recognition is the women's sailing team. "Sailing," affirms the team's official brochure, "was the first sport to award a varsity letter of all the Eastern Schools."[28] The women's team qualified for nationals from 1967 through 1972 and again in 1974. Today the women's boat crews, partly funded by the University and partly by membership dues, travel as a nationally ranked squad.

Athletics for women on an intramural, instructional and recreational level have also proliferated since the early 1970s. With construction of Yates Memorial Field House in 1979, named after Father Gerard F. Yates, who was a priest, counselor, teacher, administrator and friend to Georgetown students and alumni for forty years, twenty-five different activities are offered for students and members. Since the beginning of his career as the Director of Athletics in 1972, Francis X. Rienzo has maintained his philosophy that Georgetown should provide "instruction [for] interested athletes at all levels of competition [with] the desire to make athletics an educational experience."[29] The activities range from racquetball to aerobics to court to free weights. Tom Hunter, the Director of intramurals since Yates opened, tries to motivate students, especially women, to join organized intramurals. Of the 2500 to 3000 people who use the facilities at Yates daily, he notes that the ratio between male and female enthusiasts is even: 50/50. Dormitory floors provide the most teams for the organized intramural activities, according to Mr. Hunter. He sees the challenge of planning future activities as the ability to attract students to use the facilities for recreational purposes, especially with the new drug and alcohol policy in effect. As the activities have improved since 1979, the biggest change has been in the greater knowledge the athletes have about sports and health. Hunter hopes the trend will continue and that more students will choose to use the facilities and instruction offered at Yates.

Another concerned administrator is Patricia Thomas, a member of the Athletic Department since 1975. Now in her second year as Assistant Athletic Director after the retirement of Natalie Paramskas in 1985, Ms. Thomas pursues her "overall objective to continue improving programs, increasing visibility and increasing Georgetown's competitiveness in the Big East."[30] She is responsible for field hockey, volleyball, men's and women's lacrosse, sailing and crew teams. As the Athletic Department continues to provide scholarship and coaching endowments, Ms. Thomas comments that the biggest challenge is to develop the existing programs successfully. Her presence as a female administrator offers a different approach to the athletic programs under her guidance and, as she says, "enables the state of women's programs to be one of continuous growth."[31]

The growth of the athletic programs, however, is in terms of improving quality, not of increasing quantity at the risk of academic compromise. The Athletic Department continues to emphasize academic priorities. Ms. Thomas offers this advice: "Put studies and athletics into perspective. Remember that studies should be a priority. Get to know your coaches and assistant coaches early on—so they can help you."[32] The full-time coaches were added to the department for that specific task—to provide guidance and advice for students on a more consistent level than could be achieved with part-time coaches alone. As Mark Pugliese, coach of the women's swimming team since its inception in 1981, notes, "the strength of any program is shown by keeping people interested all four years."[33]

A recent issue of *Hoya Saxa*, a journal of sports at Georgetown, paid tribute to the commitment of the coaches:

> The dedication of these men and women serves as an inspiration to student-athletes. They prove that in striving for athletic excellence, there is something greater gained than mere achievement. Through their own example, these coaches have shown that the effort is reward in itself.[34]

A measure of the success of the Athletic Department's philosophy, which emphasizes academics over athletics, is the Robert A. Duffy Scholar-Athlete Award. In honor of a 1944 graduate of the College of Arts and Sciences who was killed in Germany in the same year, an award is given annually to an outstanding scholar-athlete of the graduating class. The first woman to receive the honor was Sue Polk, a member of both the swimming team (at that time coed, with a majority of men) and the field hockey team in 1977. In 1980 Mary Jean Ryan received the award as a volleyball player, followed by Abbie Dillon of basketball fame in 1981. Two women received recognition in 1983, Pia Palladino for track, and Suzanne Kuhlman for tennis.

Another measure of success is the support which alumni and administrators alike provide the programs as spectators and contributors. Hoyas Unlimited, in addition to publishing its sports journal *Hoya Saxa*, provides equipment and other necessities through the contributions of alumni to the teams with limited budgets. John Courtin, former director of the Alumni Association, regards the generosity of the former Georgetown student-athletes as a tribute to the overall experience athletics provides them: "they become good alumni because they learned a lot about group commitment. Working through problems with other people in the same boat makes you resolve conflicts and care less for yourself and more for whether the group succeeds."[35] The sense of commitment which Georgetown's Jesuit ideals foster in education is reflected in the words of University President Timothy Healy, S.J. regarding the intimate role athletics plays in the educational experience:

We might well ask what are the "great goods" we seek in sports?...The first has to be our ancient joy in mastery...Sports serve our complex society in a second way. The Greeks taught us that the creation of beauty conditions the soul...In sports we know from experience that beauty is the product of discipline and hard work...A third good which sports offer us is a make-believe world, a place with boundaries that hold, with rules to be kept, and with penalties which are imposed only in terms of the game.

We academicians seek to bring to our grounds the good athletics offer to society. First comes mastery. In undergraduate education we are striving to teach the young some mastery of their society, some grasp of its past, some comfort and competence in its present...Our liberal arts aim at depth and possession, our more practical teaching works at skill and manipulation...We can easily tie together academic and athletic excellence. We know that learning is transferable, but so too is accomplishment...Skill, grace, and energy are components of beauty which have always been, despite our efforts to academize it, part of the base of a liberal education...Athletics help the academic enterprise by providing a beauty we are conditioned to understand and accept, and which the young are comfortable making...Collegiate athletics can also minister to another of our weaknesses...[that] few of our students ever deal with themselves as both body and mind...The men and women who come with both bodies and souls we teach under the deeply platonic assumption that the one "serious" aspect of collegiate life is concerned only with the mind. Once an athletic contest of any intensity and organization begins, we step back into the world of reality and do justice to both, body and mind.[36]

***

A self-examination of the University's conscience with regard to its handling of its women students was performed in a symposium held on the campus in April 1986.

Two hundred fifty alumnae and several members of the faculty and administration engaged in what Dean Anne D. Sullivan (who sponsored the meeting) termed "high gossip," a general letting down of hair, squarely facing the question: How, up to this point of time, have we dealt with our female Hoyas?

One of the brochures advertising the symposium had made the following statement:

The Jesuit vision of the world is in a sense imagination run wild, bursting into action. Through it God is seen in all things. In Jesuit education such a vision is neither male nor female, for it informs and shapes both as it frees the heart and mind in the integrative process of learning. Much has changed in the lives of women since they were first admitted to the College of Arts and Sciences. *New visions and new dreams challenge the imagination.* This anniversary [fifteenth of coeducation in the College] is a time for celebration and reflection, for taking sight of what was, what is, and what might be. It is a joyful and meditative moment, a time to speak, to listen, and to understand.[37]

This theme stressing the need for imaginative thinking by women became the *leit-motif* of the meeting, and was made more explicit by "drafts" presented by Dean Sullivan to the audience:

Draft one:....In the fall of 1969, some fifty young women entered the College of Arts and Sciences. They were, in a sense, pioneers, these women who were the first to enter the previously male preserve. They came to learn, yet they also taught that the Jesuit ideal of education is a vision that is neither male nor female, but one that shapes *human* hearts and minds...

Draft two:...The challenge of Jesuit vision is its constant call for changes and reassessment. Imagination is key to one's steady adaptability without losing sight of what was and what is. So all of us at Georgetown—women and men—must imagine ourselves and the patterns of our lives in the face of living change and abiding traditions and beliefs...

Draft three:...Not many realized in that year that the fifteen years thereafter would be a time of changes and opportunities in the lives of women in this nation and around the world. New visions, new dreams challenged their imaginations as they assumed new roles, new responsibilities...

Draft four:...As the way in which young women imagine themselves and the pattern they wish their lives to take as adults in service to the world, as those ways change and remain unchanging, and as young men are challenged to reimagine themselves in response, the College seeks, as it always has, to offer an undergraduate education that helps to form and enrich the lives of young people in ways that will prove enduring and sustaining in the crucible of human experience...[38]

As with any history, this one is not complete. In the four years that we have been students we have seen a tremendous amount of change on the campus among men and women, within sports teams, and in the dialogue we enter into as undergraduates.

In February of 1988 the existence of an all-male secret society was disclosed. Many of the women on this campus felt slighted and patronized. But they were not the only ones. An outpouring of letters and articles signified that the Georgetown community would no longer be tolerant of this kind of secrecy or exclusivity. Ironically, in the same month the first issue of Georgetown's women's journal, *The New Press*, was published. This group of ten undergraduates headed up by senior Soraya Chemaly hoped to bring women's issues the attention they deserve. The atmosphere surrounding the Steward disclosure was an excellent arena for *The New Press'* birth.

Other efforts are cropping up to meet the needs of women at

Georgetown. The women's studies minor is becoming increasingly popular and has been able to add at least two new courses each semester. A group of undergraduate women are currently meeting to discuss plans for a women's center on campus. Recent attention to the needs of the large number of women who are becoming pregnant at Georgetown each semester has caused the university to acquire membership in the nation-wide Nurturing Network to assist these students. Another group initiated a day-long celebration of women entitled "Unheard Voices."

The face of Georgetown is changing. Women's issues cross disciplinary, racial, ethnic and class boundaries. The experience of women at Georgetown is rich. Growth can take a myriad of shapes, we've learned, not just for the women and men who come to Georgetown, but for Georgetown itself as well.

Notes

1. Personal interview with Carol H. Powers, 27 April 1988.
2. Interview, Fr. Joseph T. Durkin, S.J., 13 October 1987.
3. "Female Students at Georgetown: 1951 through Present." Brochure, University Registrar's Office.
4. Interview, Dawna Groom Obert, December 1987.
5. Powers interview, supra cit.
6. Barbara Ryan, response to "Bicentennial Survey," Bicentennial Committee, October 1987.
7. *Miss G. Goes to Georgetown*, 1959, p. 7. Brochure by Office of Dean of Women.
8. *Miss G. Goes to Georgetown*, 1962, p. 2. Brochure, same publisher.
9. Ibid., p. 3.
10. Powers interview.
11. Susan Poulson, "The Decision to Admit Women to the College Division of Georgetown University," unpublished graduate seminar paper, G.U., n.p. [no page], 1987.
12. Ibid., p. 3.
13. *Georgetown Magazine*, Spring, 1986, p. 10.
14. Fr. Joseph Moffitt, S.J. to Fr. Brian McGrath, S.J., Robert Henle, S.J. files, 1511–17, Georgetown University Archives.
15. Henle files, 1511–17.
16. *Washington Post*, May 28, 1965.
17. Interview, Barbara Ryan, supra cit.
18. "Annual Report on Women," 1969, A Symposium on Sex Roles at G.U., p. 11.
19. *Women's Center Newsletter*, February 1986.

20. *Hoya Saxa, A Journal of Georgetown Sports,* published by Hoyas Unlimited, Office of Alumni and University Relations, 1985, vol. 15, p. 1.

21. Francis X. Rienzo, Director of Athletics, G.U., interviewed in *Hoya Saxa,* vol. 15, 1985, p. 1.

22. Ibid., loc. cit.

23. Prof. Dorothy Brown, address at 1986 Symposium on Women at G.U.

24. Interview with John Courtin, 8 December 1987.

25. Ibid.

26. *Hoya Saxa,* vol. 15, p. 1.

27. Ibid.

28. Georgetown University Sailing Association, pamphlet, 1987, p. 1.

29. Yates Field House, pamphlet, 1987, p. 1.

30. Interview with Patricia Thomas, 10 December 1987.

31. Ibid.

32. Ibid.

33. Interview with women's swimming coach Mark Pugliese, 15 December 1987.

34. *Hoya Saxa,* vol. 15, p. 1.

35. Interview with John Courtin, 8 December 1987.

36. Fr. Timothy Healy administration collection: Box 29, folder 902: 07/20/05 (typescript).

37. Fr. Royden Davis, S.J., speech to women graduates of the College's first years, lecture series celebrating fifteen years of women in the College.

38. The documentation for this last section of the paper is based on the official records of the event, office of Dean Sullivan.

Contributions of, and Benefits Received by Black Students at Georgetown

James Griffin and John Shumake

The proportion of undergraduate black students to whites at Georgetown today (Spring 1989) is approximately ten percent, a ratio which places us among the first ten American undergraduate schools in terms of responsiveness to the higher education needs of our black brothers and sisters. It was this fact that evoked the exclamation "Remarkable!" from New York University president John Bradamas on one of his recent visits to Georgetown. Fourteen percent of the students accepted for the undergraduate freshman class entering in August 1989 are black.[1]

Black students have made important and unique contributions to the cultural life of the campus. Outstanding in this field has been the Black Movements Dance Theater, working together with the Black Theater Ensemble. The latter's production of the play entitled *For Colored Girls...* at the G.U. Bicentennial Intercultural Festival of Performing Arts in February 1989 was declared by the program director to have been "one of the undisputed highlights of the festival."[2] Similar enthusiastic praise came from the Director of Performing Arts, Ronald J. Lignelli,[3] and from a long review in *The Hoya*.[4]

Even more striking evidence of the competence of our black

students in the arts are the separate performances (not in collaboration with the theater) of the Black Movements Dancers.

With no faculty director and no training in choreography before coming to Georgetown, the girls invent their own dances. Input from each individual is their first rule: "We just let ourselves go with the steps we like," as one of them described their method. "We do it again—and we have a dance!"[5] Consciously or not, they are imitating the procedure of the contemporary dance avant-garde. George Balanchine would have approved.

The Black Movements Group expresses the special effectiveness of the loose-structured antilinear African esthetic for dance,[6] and does it superlatively well. Their performance, as they explain it, strikes a happy balance between freedom and control.[7]

Presenting for the Annual Talent Tournament in Gaston Hall a ballet number in each of the two styles, classical and modern, the young black women artists were, in the opinion of campus critics, the unquestioned stars of the show. A solo piece by a black female dancer (not a member of the Movements Group) was also a much-applauded feature of the Bicentennial Gala in the fall of 1988 at Washington's Convention Hall.

Georgetown boasts of many eminent black alumni and alumnae, only some of whom can be mentioned in this paper. Fred Brown (formerly a member of Georgetown's National Champion Basketball Team) is president of the real estate firm of Thompson and Associates; David Green (CAS '85) is a law clerk for the Honorable William Penn, U.S. District Court, and is a member of the Pennsylvania and District of Columbia Bars; Desmona Dallis is a CPA for the accounting firm of Beers and Cutler; Ginger McKnight is a junior associate of the law firm of Simpson, Thatcher, and Bartlett, and a member of the New York State Bar; Kimberly Hanley Glass is an account executive for Sallie Mae, Inc. Mr. Conan Louis, a black graduate of the School of Languages and Linguistics, is now (1989) a member of the University Board of Governors.[8]

To produce the foregoing impressive results, who were the University's administrators and teachers who led the march toward equal treatment of our cherished young black men and women students at Georgetown?

The start was slow and, as in the case of all social reform movements, errors were made and people on both sides became impatient. Some of the impatience—on both sides—was justifiable, and some of it was not so.

The work and courage of the black alumni, since the early 1960s, and the unselfish devotion of faculty members such as Jesse Mann, Raymond Reno, Rocco Porrecco, Charles Deacon, Joseph Pettit, Roger Slakey, Keith Fort, Paul Carducci, Father Richard McSorley and several others, helped to equalize the condition of the black student at Georgetown. The movement may not have progressed as rapidly as its sponsors had hoped but—significantly—it coexisted with a marked increase in the number of black applications for admission to Georgetown. People—especially young people—do not willingly rush to the arms of those whom they believe are not being fair to them.

The usual civil rights apparatus for prospective and actual black college students was installed at the Hilltop in the sixties: the Center for Minority Student Affairs, the College Orientation and Upward Bound Programs, and the Community Scholars Effort. All of these operations were supported by a core group of dedicated lay faculty members.

However, the person who, perhaps more than any other, inspired these enlightened movements was Dean Royden Davis. As this Jesuit would later lead the struggle at Georgetown against discrimination with regard to women applicants, so he fought with equal zeal in the case of black matriculation.

From former black students themselves comes confirmation of the claim that at Georgetown any incipient racism was vanquished by fairness and common sense. Black alumnus Richard Urbino attests that he never felt as an undergraduate at the Hilltop any manifest discrimination, nor did he ever suffer during that time any "negative racial incident," as he phrased it. He expressed his appreciation of the faculty's excellence, and the bringing in of new ideas by the administration. He said that he enjoyed his years at the College and law school; and he believes that in coming to Georgetown he made the right choice.

Miss Sandy Chambley, a black alumna, recalls that at first the black students at Georgetown were like foreign students to whom the white students were polite, but without welcoming them into the mainstream. But Dean Davis and Dean Deacon, she attests, were both receptive and accommodating. While there were protests at Howard, Georgetown's administration made such actions unnecessary. If tension existed between the mainstream student body and black students, it was only minor. The black students differed in social background but shared some common problems and the Georgetown academic challenge.[9]

Black alumnus Clifford Carthan Strong (SFS '89) offers the following:

> I would say the most important gift that the Georgetown experience has offered me has been the honing of my leadership skills. Upon entering the University I felt that I possessed all that was necessary for leadership. But in the course of my stay here I have learned the most invaluable lesson, that the price of leadership is earning the respect of your fellow man.[10]

A witness by deeds is performed by many black alumni and alumnae who continually visit high schools in order to recruit black students for Georgetown. One does not urge one's fellows to come to a school if one believes it is prejudiced against them.

Here are some observations from current undergraduates at Georgetown.

Cybil Cineas, born in Mexico City of Haitian parents, will be a senior in the College in 1989–1990. Her father was formerly Haitian Ambassador to the United States. Due to her parents' diplomatic connections she has traveled to several European countries. She is a graduate of one of the nation's top academic high schools, Walt Whitman, of Bethesda, Maryland.

When asked whether she felt "at home" on the campus, Cybil responded with an emphatic affirmative. She likes Georgetown for its cosmopolitan student population. She would appreciate the addition of black professors to the faculty, and more academic courses specifically tailored to the interests of black students. [11]

In summary, Cybil reveals herself as a decidedly satisfied student. She is representative also of a very satisfying phenomenon, perceptible from even a cursory acquaintance with our black students: the extremely high quality of many of them in intelligence, maturity and attractiveness of character.

Natasha Cadet will graduate from the School of Foreign Service in 1990. She likes her teachers, "has lots of friends on the campus" and, consequently, feels very much "at home" here. She made an interesting remark that she welcomed the challenge of the heavy study load at Georgetown since, as she confided, she "worked better under pressure" and has found that she "always finds more time than I thought I had." She would welcome some black teachers, but is enthusiastic about the teachers whom she has now.[12]

"I am enjoying my days at Georgetown," confided Foreign Service School student Rick Sigfield, "because of my excellent teachers and my contact with various kinds of people which my campus affords."[13] (His father is a lawyer in Atlanta, and his mother a member of the Alabama State Assembly.) When asked what improvements he would like to see on the campus, he echoed the wish expressed by other black students interviewed for this paper: greater representation of blacks on the teaching faculty. He added an interesting benefit which, if this reform were made, would, he believes, be gained by our white students: exposure to black viewpoints and, to some extent, acquaintance with black history and culture which they would not otherwise obtain.

Mr. Sigfield impressed the interviewer as being a young man of extremely attractive personality. He is obviously intelligent. He displays a pleasing self-composure which never suggests conceit. He is another instance of the high quality of black youth gravitating to Georgetown's undergraduate schools. These young men and women—and their eagerness to come to us—may be Georgetown's best answer to any charges that we are neglecting such an important portion of American society.

It is evident to anyone who thinks aright that our civilization would be further enriched by the infusion of African culture. Aware of the need, Father Timothy Healy, in one of his last addresses before his retirement as president of the University, urged that efforts be made to increase the number of black faculty members. He noted that our University's view of the world is Catholic, a theological and philosophical attitude which is, by definition, color-blind. He reminded us that our educational outlook is that of a Jesuit religious order established by men of different nationalities and vowed to respect and serve all races. Georgetown, he recalled, was headed by a black president at a time when, by American civil law, black persons were not accorded equality of treatment in public conveyances.

On behalf of our black brothers and sisters at Georgetown we have done much, but there is much more to be done.

Appendix

Review of *For Colored Girls*
The Hoya, 10 February 1989

"Colored Girls" Share Symbols

by Melissa Blocker
Special to the Hoya

The Black Theater Ensemble's production of *For Colored Girls*, by Ntozake Shange, was nothing less than a spectacular way to begin Black History Month. Sponsored by CMSA and the Bicentennial Committee as part of this month's celebration, the production ran for three sold-out performances in the Hall of Nations.

The "play" is actually a collection of poems that incorporates music and dance into its framework. Shange's style is particularly interesting. Although it is deeply personal, it simultaneously appeals to a diversity of black women. In a powerful fashion, Shange addresses the complex issues surrounding black male/female relationships. Her treatment of such events as domestic violence, a girl's graduation night, and a woman's abortion, portray the black woman as a thinking, feeling, sensual being.

Such scenes make the audience painfully aware of the general disrespect accorded to black women, and describes the difficulties encountered by black women searching for their niche in the world. Despite the turmoil, however, the play is overwhelmingly positive; the desire to love and be loved by the world, their sisters, and themselves are the controlling themes in the play. Shange's characters do not give in to bitterness, but "find God" in themselves.

Critics have accused Shange of glorifying women while unjustly denigrating black men. In *For Colored Girls*, men do not speak for themselves, and invariably come across as violent and manipulative. This attitude is exemplified in "No Assistan" where the Lady in Red rousingly ends her relationship with her man.

However, such criticism is probably of no consequence to Shange, who sees explanations of her work as unnecessary. Her foremost priority seems to be expressing the voices of black women; other concerns must have only secondary importance.

Above all, the production allowed us to enter the psyche of a black woman. Why was this so important to Shange? A clue can be found in the programs distributed for the performances. Shange says that black women must "learn our common symbols, preen them and share them with the world." Shange gives black women a taste of themselves, and asks them to do a bit of self-discovery.

Anyone lucky enough to see the play would agree that Jace Gatewood's direction, while subtle to the point of being invisible, was masterful. The casting was also excellent, as the group was able to attain the cohesion necessary for this type of piece. Individual performances by Margaret Makinde as the Lady in Green, Jennifer Jones (the Lady in Blue), and Chevela Fletcher (the Lady in Red), were particularly outstanding and memorable. Their acting allowed Shange's evocative words to come to life, so that the audience could truly experience what Shange was feeling when she wrote.

The direction, production, cast and crew were of highest quality and delighted audiences all three nights. My only criticism is that the Hall of Nations was chosen as the site: with only three performances, the production could have reached a greater number of people in a larger theater. It didn't seem to bother the ensemble, however, illustrating even more talents of the performers who worked so hard to bring Shange's words to life.

Notes

Editor's Note: The interviews identified by notes 5, 9, 12, 13, and 14 were added by the editor as further documentation of the authors' description of black student cultural contributions.

1. From files of Minority Student Affairs.

2. "After-Images: A Final Report on the Bicentennial Intercultural Festival of Performing Arts," submitted by Roger D. Bensky, Executive and Artistic Director, p. 4.

3. R.J. Lignelli to Jace Gatewood and Trilica Gilmore, February 10, 1989.

4. See Appendix of this essay.

5. Interview with Erica Graham, July 14, 1989.

6. Ibid.

7. Ibid.

8. From files of G.U. Center for Minority Student Affairs.

9. Based on an interview with Chambley, January 12, 1988.

10. Letter of Clifford C. Strong to Mr. William Reed (n.d.).

11. Interview with Cybil Cineas, July 15, 1989.

12. Interview with Natasha Cadet, July 14, 1989.

13. Interview with Rick Sigfield, July 17, 1989.

The History and Influence of Latin American Students at Georgetown University

Laura Clauson

Through the years, hundreds of Latin American students have passed through Georgetown University's Healy Gates. As the oldest Catholic institution of higher learning in the United States, the University has enjoyed considerable prestige throughout predominately Roman Catholic Latin America. Consequently, Georgetown has attracted many of that region's future politicians, leaders, lawyers, doctors and businessmen who came to her for the four-year Jesuit education. It is estimated that one-third to one-half of the world's top positions in politics, business, education and the military will be filled by foreign students attending colleges and universities in the United States. As one of the United States' premier universities, Georgetown will educate its share of these future leaders and has in fact already done so.

Traditionally, those foreign students who pursue higher education in the United States come from the economic and political elites of their respective countries. Georgetown's Latin American students who arrive from South and Central America, Mexico, Puerto Rico and the Caribbean are no exception. Obvious and practical reasons explain why Georgetown's Latin American student population, although rising and falling in numbers through the years, has consistently been drawn from the middle and upper-middle class of Latin American society, just as has the student body population as a whole.

Georgetown's Latin American alumni range from the Mexican Emperor Iturbide's son to the present Brazilian ambassador to the Organization of American States and the former director of Latin American affairs on President Reagan's National Security Council.

Moreover, the general standards of most Latin American high schools are not equal to those in the United States. Financially, the lack of Georgetown scholarships for foreign students translates into the unfortunate reality that only wealthy Latin American students, or those with outside funding, can realistically afford Georgetown tuition.

Add to all this the unstable economies and rampant inflation prevalent in many Latin American nations, and another problem is created for potential Latin American students. Those students whose families do not have bank accounts in dollars are held hostage at the mercy of currency fluctuations.

Similarly, there is a certain correlation between the country-by-country breakdown of the number of foreign students attending Georgetown and the financial situation of each nation. Today, not one Latin American nation is among the top ten nations who send the most students to Georgetown. Georgetown increasingly admits more Japanese students and fewer Mexicans, Brazilians and Argentinians.[1]

Nor is the number of Latin American students affected only by the respective economies of each nation. The political situation plays an influential role as well. The Georgetown Admissions office attributes to Latin America's political problems a considerable disruption over the last ten to fifteen years in the flow of Latin American students to Georgetown. Changing military dictatorships, revolutions and political turmoil create an unstable environment, sometimes causing wealthy families to be driven out of the country and forcing them to relocate under reduced financial circumstances.

Some Jesuit high schools in Latin America have a history of encouraging their students to apply to Georgetown. For example, in Panama, a steady stream of applications flows from the Colegio Xavier, and in Puerto Rico the Colegio San Ignacio regularly sends its graduates to the Hilltop.[2]

Another interesting reaction to North American higher education in general is José DeLarelle's view of the differing mixtures of education and politics in Latin American universities as compared with North American institutions. He graduated from a Jesuit high school in Lima, Peru. "Americans All" states that José "...is surprised to learn that university students who are such a potent political force in Central and South America, exert [in the United States] no influence upon the United States government officials or their policies...."[3]

Puerto Rican students are Latin, but they fit less exactly into the Latin American student mold than do the rest of the Latin Americans. As a generalization, Puerto Rican students tend to come from professional families; their fathers are generally lawyers, doctors and businessmen, and usually quite wealthy. As Puerto Ricans are United States citizens, there is a Georgetown recruitment program in Puerto Rico, a situation not found in the rest of Latin America. Moreover, Puerto Rico has a strong tradition of sending students to Georgetown. The territory is a sharply divided class society, and, strictly speaking, no public high schools in Puerto Rico have yet attained the caliber of education desirable for future students of an American university such as Georgetown.

Yet, Puerto Rican students have long been the most dominant group of Latin American students at Georgetown. This was true throughout the nineteenth century. At the turn of the twentieth century, the majority of all Latin American students originated from Puerto Rico. As they do now, many of these Puerto Rican students returned to their native land to live and work, generally in the professions such as law, medicine, dentistry or politics.

Antonio Gonzalez-Lamat, a LL.B. 1914 graduate and LL.M. graduate of 1915, was a lawyer and a Special Assistant Deputy of State for Puerto Rico. Jesus Gonzalez, a LL.B. 1920 graduate, became Special Assistant U.S. Attorney for the District of Puerto Rico. Ferdinand Turnard, a 1912 graduate, became a lawyer. The Hon. Benigno Fernandez, a LL.B. 1908 graduate, was a lawyer and later served as Insular Representative in the House of Representatives from 1912 to 1914. After graduating in 1913, Leopoldo Venagas y Ortiz became a dentist in San Juan, Puerto Rico. The Hon. Acosta-Velarde, a LL.B. graduate of 1919 and LL.D. graduate of 1921, became a lawyer for the American Railroad Company of Puerto Rico.[4]

As a result of this long tradition of sending students to

Georgetown, Puerto Rico has developed an extremely loyal alumni network. It has one of the most active and supportive alumni chapters in the United States. In fact, two years ago the John Carroll awards ceremonies were held in Puerto Rico.

The Admissions Office would like to attract students from different social and economic classes, but once again the stumbling blocks of financial aid and poor high school preparatory background frustrate this goal. As a result, the office has directed its efforts toward attracting Hispanic students already living in the United States.[5]

Often these students come from less economically privileged backgrounds than does the traditional Latin American student. Of course, many are Mexican-American; a large number originate also from Central America. Generally, their families have come to the United States either to escape political turmoil or to seek a better life, and more specifically, a betterment of their economic status. They do not spring from the economic elite of their country of origin. These Hispanic students have several significant advantages over their economic counterparts who continue to live in Latin America. They are educated in the American public school system, which means that they have received their elementary education in English. Moreover, as American citizens, Hispanic-American applicants are eligible for Georgetown's financial aid program.

Once a foreign student has been accepted at Georgetown, the Office of International Programs (OIP) keeps track of him or her and coordinates activities for the foreign student body as well. Usually, Latin American students coming to the United States face the same types of problems as any other foreign student tossed into a new situation and culture. And many do not complain of any problems at all. As a rule, many of these Latin American students have visited the United States several times before coming to Georgetown or have spent a year studying in an American high school. As a result, they have some idea of what to expect from Georgetown University. In addition, most of the undergraduate Latin American students come from the same middle-class or upper middle-class economic and social backgrounds as do most U.S. Georgetown students, and therefore do not face serious economic difficulties.[6]

There is no university-wide orientation program for graduate students at Georgetown; in their case, the OIP organizes a special three-day orientation program for all foreign graduate students. This orientation focuses on a description of life in an American university, and tells the foreign students what they can expect academically as well as socially and culturally. This orientation program has been going on ever since the inception of the Office of International Programs fourteen years ago.

Many Latin American undergraduates are not used to as much independence as they find at Georgetown. Once they leave for college, most American college students take independence for granted. But, in Latin America, most university students continue to live at home with their families while attending classes at the nearby university. They are accustomed to a family support system. As a result, some of those Latin Americans arriving in the United States for the first time request a "homestay," which means boarding with an American family in Washington. Unfortunately, because Washington is such an international city, there are not enough families willing to accept a foreign student into their home. Foreign students are not such a novelty in Washington, D.C. and they do not attract as much interest as they do in some of the Midwestern states.[7]

One of the complaints raised by Latin Americans is that they find relationships in the United States very superficial. They may have many American friends, but they consider these friendships as a different type of friendship—one which is less close and intimate.

"Americans All" sees a different side to the contrasting North American and Latin American attitudes toward personal relationships. While the article admits that there is a "marked difference between U.S. and 'Spanish American' social customs,"[8] it draws different conclusions from its interview with Georgetown's Latin American students. "Americans All" concludes that

The greatest contrast...is to be found in the comparative familiarity with girls [which] Northerners enjoy. Coming from countries in which girls are held in aloof respect, the Southerners enjoy the way their Northern amigos treat girls as equals. Particularly they like the absence of chaperones on most occasions.[9]

From its interviews, the article concludes that Latin Americans at Georgetown are quite content with the different customs and social situations that they encounter here.

Although it is difficult to find many mentions of Latin American students in the *College Journal*, brief allusions to their presence appeared in the 1970s. In 1972, the *Journal* reported that "December opened propitiously for our skates, the first day of the month giving us, the college pond, two and a half inches of excellent ice, which was immensely enjoyed."[10] Commenting specifically on the fate of their fellow Latin American students, the *Journal* continued to remark,

> A severe test of strength was afforded by its endurance of the bouncing falls of our Spanish American friends, or of such of them as found themselves on ice for the first time.[11]

Fragments of Latin American culture made their way into Georgetown University society and continue to do so. On November 22, 1872, at the celebration of St. Cecilia's Day, Mr. E. de Elia of Buenos Aires, Argentina spoke. The *Journal* wrote a brief description of his address:

> ...its rendition was characterized by that warm and earnest action peculiar to the Castilian school of elocution alone.[12]

A more current example of the Latin American culture enjoyed by the University student body at large is the participation of both the Spanish and Luso-Brazilian clubs in the annual School of Languages and Linguistics Christmas carol contest. Each language club at Georgetown practices and presents Christmas carols in its language in a contest held in Gaston Hall. In 1986, the Spanish Club, one of the largest groups at Georgetown, won the competition. This contest affords a good opportunity for introducing the rest of Georgetown University to Latin American culture as revealed in popular songs and dances.

Mention of Latin American alumni began to appear intermittently in Georgetown's yearbook, *Ye Domesday Booke*, in 1908. In that year, Puerto Rico had been a United States possession for only eight years, and the Puerto Ricans had not even been granted American citizenship. Yet Georgetown's law class of 1908 included Benigno Fernandez from Lukullo, Puerto Rico. The caption underneath Benigno's photograph revealed that:

> Benigno means "kind," and if he is the kind they have in our new possessions, we're strong for Porto Rico. He can't get any quizmaster to explain to him why anybody, not an alien, should not be an American citizen.[13]

The 1914 edition of *Ye Domesday Booke* contains references to a Cuban and a Puerto Rican graduate of the Law School. Interestingly enough, the caption beneath each man's photograph mentioned a potential political career for him, demonstrating the type of Latin American students Georgetown has attracted throughout its history. These captions present interesting anecdotes about life in the United States for the Latin American student. About the San Juan graduate, Antonio Gonzalez-Lamas, the yearbook staff wrote:

> We now present to you the future delegate from Porto Rico, Señor Gonzalez. A deep student of law and an embryonic statesman...Is of the opinion that some of our English words are unnecessarily long, and has suggested that "buzz" be substituted for "buzzsaw."[14]

When discussing the memorable moments of the Cuban graduate Alberto F. Hevia's experiences at Georgetown, they said:

> Not content with the high official dignity in the Cuban diplomatic service, Alberto decided to give "Corpus Juris" a 3-year tussle and he is some gladiator, as evidenced by him during the sweating process about that season of the year when we are taking our "last 3," with perspiration rolling from his manly brow and prayers of mercy from his lips, he sits and writes and prays.[15]

Markedly fewer Cuban students have come to Georgetown since the 1959 Cuban revolution and subsequent Castro years. But this lack of Cuban students has been supplemented by an increase in Cuban-American students. These students are American, because their parents fled Cuba generally in the early 1960s and settled in the United States. Their influence is evidenced by the fact that there is a separate category of "Cuban-American" on the Georgetown admissions application form.

Nicholas and Jean Feurer, brothers, were two of the first foreign students to attend Georgetown from Latin America. Despite the fact that both were of French background, they arrived from either Central America or Mexico (it is not sure which). Nicholas and Jean entered the College of Arts and Sciences in 1792 and left in 1794. Neither brother was a boarder at the University, nor was either employed while a student. Both paid Georgetown's tuition in sugar and coffee, ostensibly brought from their country of origin.[16]

A common thread running through these early Latin American students is their common religion—all were Roman Catholic, which is not very surprising, considering that most of Latin America was and still is primarily of that religious faith. Another point in common is that none of these students appeared to suffer any financial difficulties and none considered it necessary to hold a job while studying at Georgetown.

Only in the last decade has it been possible to obtain more than minimal information about Latin American students at Georgetown. The University registrar's office implemented a new computerized record system in 1977. For the first time, it was possible to obtain a country-by-country and state-by-state breakdown of the Georgetown student body. Moreover, the new system divides Georgetown students into sections consisting of undergraduate, graduate students, and continuing education students. These statistics offer valuable insights into the nature of the Latin American student body at Georgetown.

An interesting point at once emerges: the marked differences which exist in the school-by-school make-up of the Puerto Rican students and the rest of the Latin American student contingent. Not only is the breakdown by school markedly different, but the concentration of students studying at the undergraduate as opposed to the graduate level differs for the rest of the Latin American student body. But, because this is such a recent change, it is difficult to classify definitively the 1985/86 change as a significant new trend in the Latin American student population at the University. Nevertheless, the academic year 1985/

86 marked a significant change in the distribution of students both by country and by school.[17]

In examining the social and academic experiences of Latin American students at Georgetown University, it is helpful to examine the particular histories of current undergraduate students and of active or prominent Latin alumni. A look at the personal motivation of several of the current undergraduate students presents a microcosmic look at the social and academic experiences of the Latin American student body as a whole. Considering that Georgetown primarily has served to educate the elites of Latin America, a brief examination of the postgraduate lives of some of Georgetown's more prominent Latin American alumni is worthwhile.

The experiences of Ramon Kury, president of the Puerto Rican Students Association, are not unusual for a Puerto Rican studying at Georgetown. Puerto Ricans have strong ties to the University. In Ramon Kury's case, both the Kury family and the high school which Ramon attended influenced his decision to study at Georgetown. Georgetown has also been the home and alma mater of Ramon's two older brothers, both of whom obtained their B.A. in the School of Business Administration. The presence of close relatives, along with Georgetown's unique location in our nation's capital, were strong factors in Ramon Kury's decision. Washington, D.C. is an international city and contains unlimited possibilities and opportunities for internships and interesting lecturers for the Georgetown student.

Kury is a sophomore in the School of Business Administration and plans eventually to attend law school either in the continental United States or in Puerto Rico. He has political aspirations in Puerto Rico and does not rule out the possibility of entering politics after he has established himself in the Puerto Rican business community.

The Puerto Rican Association continues to be a very tightly knit group of students, and is so considered both by U.S. students and by other Latin American students. Unlike the Latin American Club or the Cuban Association, the Association limits its membership to Puerto Ricans. It offers social, cultural and educational activities to its members, and opens many of these to the general student body. Currently, there is some debate as to whether the doors of the club should be opened further and membership extended to the rest of the Georgetown community.

Even among Latin American students at Georgetown, there exists the half-serious, half-joking belief that the Puerto Rican students are such a self-contained group that even other Latin American students do not feel totally comfortable at Puerto Rican get-togethers.

The Club performs various functions. Besides the commonplace throwing of parties (parties which have always held quite a lively reputation at Georgetown), the Puerto Rican Association, in conjunction with the Latin American Organization, holds Spanish Masses for those students interested. The Club organizes lectures and movies and gives Puerto Rican dinners featuring Puerto Rican music and food. Lecturers are invited to speak on topics of interest to the Puerto Rican community, such as the continuing and controversial debate surrounding the possible move to statehood for Puerto Rico.

There is a tendency for Latin American students to form their own cliques at Georgetown. This is a natural phenomenon, considering the cultural and linguistic differences which exist between Latin Americans and the rest of the student body. Regarding the large number of Puerto Ricans studying at Georgetown, many of them already know each other before they arrive at the University; those who do not, see each other daily and quickly form a very close-knit group.[18]

The 1945 "Americans All" article directly confronts this issue. It says that because many of Georgetown's students come from South and Central America,

> It is quite understandable that they show a preference for speaking in Spanish, and that they should seek one another's company. But we have had the feeling for a long time now that they should strive to become better acquainted with their North American fellow students and vice versa.[19]

This is practical and necessary because

> The way the world is shrinking these days, friendships formed in school between North Americans and Latin Americans are bound to have a meaning for the future.[20]

On the other hand, the Latin American Club is not limited to Latin American students. It contains a good number of North American members as well. Like the Puerto Rican Association, the Club is well known for its social activities, but also like the Puerto Rican Students Association, it promotes numerous other activities. It has initiated a series of breakfasts with Latin American ambassadors to the United States. In past years, it also sponsored trips to the Organization of American States and to various Latin American embassies in Washington.

The Luso-Brazilian Club, like the Latin American Club, has a membership of Brazilian and Portuguese students, and North Americans also. This year's [1988] president is a North American sophomore in the School of Languages and Linguistics, not even a Brazilian citizen. One of the primary goals of the current Club is to show Portuguese students how exciting Brazil and Brazilian culture are and to increase student awareness of Brazilian culture and life.

The Luso-Brazilian Club's most important activity has always been their huge Carnaval Party held in the spring to coincide with the world-famous carnival that takes place every spring in Brazil. Unfortunately, four years ago, there was a huge problem with the annual carnival party and the Student Activities Commission drastically cut the Club's funding, and prohibited it from continuing to sponsor the party, a yearly campuswide event co-sponsored by the Portuguese Department and the Luso-Brazilian Club and held in the New South Cafeteria. As much as possible, the goal was to emulate an authentic Brazilian carnaval celebration, complete with pulsating samba music.

In addition to selling tickets to students on campus, the Brazilian Embassy and the Brazilian-American Cultural Institute also were permitted to sell tickets to the general public. The result was a completely unexpected and uncontrollable crowd of several thousand people, all trying to go to the party in the New South Cafeteria. Both the District police and firemen arrived on the scene. The Club lost two to three thousand dollars and as a result was put on an austerity budget by the Student Activities Commission, and has just this year recovered fully.

The Luso-Brazilian Club currently has about one hundred

members. It sponsors *fejoada* dinners (the Brazilian national food) twice a year, to which all Portuguese students and club members are invited. Every year, one of the Brazilian Portuguese teachers cooks the *fejoada*. The Club holds "happy hours" addressed by native Portuguese speakers. In conjunction with the Portuguese Department the Club also sponsors lectures; for example, last year the Brazilian ambassador to the United States spoke. The School of Languages and Linguistics holds an annual Christmas caroling contest in Gaston Hall for all foreign language speakers. Every year the Luso-Brazilian Club enters a group of singers to sing Christmas carols in Portuguese. Trips to Brazilian restaurants and to a Catholic Mass held in Portuguese are organized every semester.

Georgetown's earliest prominent Latin American student was famous on account of the identity of his father. Salvadore Iturbide was the son of the dethroned Emperor Iturbide of Mexico. Iturbide entered the College of Arts and Sciences in 1829 and left in 1830. A description of Salvadore after graduation pictured him as

> ...a tiny man, side whiskered, so short that he barely reached the shoulders of the Ladies...there was never anyone like him. He was a Mexican, here in the diplomatic service, and had married Miss Alice Green, daughter of Uriah Forrest.[21]

Apparently, Salvadore Iturbide was, like his father, rather bellicose. At the Marburys' a fight broke out between Iturbide and Baron Bedisco, a Russian minister. The prince called the baron a liar and the baron immediately knocked him down. Then,

> The Little Prince sprang onto a sofa and bounced up and down, shouting over and over again, "He knocked an Iturbide down, he knocked an Iturbide down" as if he expected Mr. Marbury to straightaway haul the Baron off to be beheaded at least.[22]

Needless to say, that was the last party given at the old house for many a day because Mr. Marbury was so upset at being disgraced by his guests.

After four years at Georgetown, life is only beginning for

Georgetown's Latin American graduates. Many alumni return to their native countries and settle down to become important members in their communities. Some stay in the United States.

Georgetown has been the alma mater of some very impressive Latin Americans. A prime example of a Georgetown graduate going on to become a very successful and influential actor in the United States political realm is José Sorzano. Not only did this Georgetown alumnus successfully graduate from the School of Foreign Service in 1965, but he later received his doctorate from the Government Department in 1972. His career is remarkable because he arrived in the United States in 1961, a refugee from Cuba, with only five dollars in his pocket. After his arrival, he took a job as a "deep-fry man in a Marriott Hot Shop."[23] From a penniless Cuban refugee, he rose to become a Georgetown student, then a professor and finally a powerful American politician. His grandfather had graduated from the College of Arts and Sciences in 1899, so the idea of attending Georgetown was firmly implanted in José's mind.

In 1969, Sorzano became an assistant professor, and later an associate professor in the G.U. Government Department. He exhibited great respect for the Jesuit ideal of service to others, when he interrupted his teaching career to assume charge of the Peace Corps in Colombia from 1976 to 1979. Service to his adopted nation followed two years later when his colleague Jeane Kirkpatrick asked Sorzano to serve as her deputy at the United Nations. In 1985, he returned to teach political philosophy at Georgetown. At the same time, he took over as president of the Cuban American National Foundation, a research and advocacy group which represents the Cuban-American community.

Today José Sorzano has risen even further in the Washington political establishment. In 1986, he was appointed Director of Latin American Affairs under then National Security Advisor Frank Carlucci. In a *Washington Post* column in December 1986, Rowland Evans and Robert Novak said that Sorzano's appointment "shifts the NSC's Latin American policy chief from a highly regarded Foreign Service officer dependent on long-term relations with the State Department to a tough intellectual with impeccable Reaganite credentials who is accountable to no one in the bureaucracy."[24]

An example of a Latin American student educated at Georgetown who returned to serve his own country after graduation is F. Cypriano Zegarra, a Peruvian citizen. He entered Georgetown on September 14, 1859 and received his undergraduate degree in 1864, his master of arts in 1865, and finally his LL.D. in 1877. He "...spent several years at Georgetown," says the alumni file, "esteemed by professors and students and was graduated with honors."[25]

After his education, he returned to Peru to serve as Minister Plenipotentiary and Envoy Extraordinary to the United States. During his stint in the United States, he attended the 1889 annual meeting of the Society of Alumni and delivered an address in favor of arbitration of national disputes. It was reported that the address

> will long be remembered because of the learning and force of the argument displayed in the treatment of the subject and the advanced position he took in favor of the peaceful settlement of international disagreements.[26]

Juan Batista Sacasa, a Nicaraguan student from Leon, matriculated at Georgetown on September 10, 1891. After graduation he rose to become dean of the Medical School at the University of Nicaragua and president of the National Board of Health. The 1930 LL.B. graduate, Jaime Benitex-Rexach, served as chancellor of the University of Puerto Rico.

Georgetown has graduated Latin American students who have become leaders, as well as scholars, of their own countries. Galla Playa, an Ecuadorean, who later served as the president of the Republic of Ecuador, arrived at Georgetown on an exchange scholarship program on September 28, 1930.

Luis Muñoz-Marin, another Georgetown graduate, became Governor of Puerto Rico. While at Georgetown Preparatory School between 1911–1914, he made his First Communion, at which his mother and father were present.

Later in life, Muñoz-Marin's name appeared in a 1960 *Time* article describing a dispute he had over the statehood debate. A Catholic bishop, the Brooklyn-born Bishop of Ponce, James McMane, charged that "...Muñoz-Marin by saying repeatedly that Puerto Rico is a 'proud, free, self-governing commonwealth joined to the U.S. by her own choice,' is eloquently 'ignoring the hard historical fact.'"[28] The Bishop concluded that:

> The people of our colonies should be given a fair opportunity to choose between independence or statehood. The present condition in Puerto Rico is that Governor Muñoz-Marin is by his own will imposing upon the people of Puerto Rico and on the Congress of the U.S., an independence which was never granted, and a "voluntary association" which is absurd unless independence has been granted.[29]

Georgetown's Latin American graduates were certainly not uninvolved in controversy. Another of Georgetown's prominent Latin American graduates, Thomas Herran, was born in Bogotá, Colombia, in 1843 but moved as a child with his family to New York City. After receiving from Georgetown three academic degrees, A.B., M.A., and Law, he achieved a brilliant diplomatic career. As an attorney he was a central figure in the negotiations between Colombia and the United States in the matter of the Panama Canal. His extremely valuable papers concerning the latter project he donated to the archives of his alma mater. They still await a definitive use by a competent scholar.

Now, when examining the general influence and the role of Latin American students at Georgetown University, the words written in the 1945 *College Journal* article, "Americans All," hold particular relevance today. This paragraph expresses the importance of the small but integral role these students have played in Georgetown's history. The *Journal* writes:

> ...one general impression seems to emerge. As a group, the boys [and girls] from south of the border are more aware than students from the States that today the Western Hemisphere is almost one country, a new America...More perhaps than we, they realize that Providence has joined their lot in solidarity to ours, and that we must face an uncertain future together.[30]

Undoubtedly, though, the Latin American students

> ...know...that they do not come to us with empty hands. Their music, their painting, their architecture, even their philosophy of life, will, in time, deeply enrich ours.[31]

Latin American students enriched Georgetown in 1945; they enriched the University when they first began arriving at the end of the eighteenth century; and today they, as did their predecessors, continue to make Georgetown a racially and culturally more diverse, and therefore, richer university.

Notes

1. Interview with Dean Deacon, Dean of Admissions, 20 Nov. 1987.
2. Ibid.
3. *Georgetown College Journal* (hereafter, *GCJ*), 73:5.
4. *Alumni Directory of Georgetown University*, (1917–1943), p. 97.
5. Dean Deacon, Interview.
6. Interview with Eric Hyburg, Director, Office of International Programs, 23 Nov. 1987.
7. Interview with Julie Holtzman, Office of International Programs, 24 Nov. 1987.
8. *GCJ*, 73:7.
9. Ibid., loc. cit.
10. *GCJ*, 1 (Dec. 1872):9.
11. Ibid., loc. cit.
12. Ibid., loc. cit.
13. *Ye Domesday Booke* (1914), p. 108.
14. Ibid., loc. cit.
15. Ibid., loc. cit.
16. Fr. Curran's Mss. Register of Students.
17. G.U. Registrar's Files (1977–1987).
18. Interview with Ramon E. Kury, President, Puerto Rican Students Association, 7 Nov. 1989.
19. *GCJ*, 73:5.
20. Ibid., loc. cit.
21. Fr. Curran's Register of Students (unpublished).
22. Ibid.
23. Eric George, "Georgetown's Loss," *The Guardian*, 5 (April 1987), p. 10.
24. Ibid., loc. cit.
25. Alumni Files, Sub: F. Cypriano Zegarra, GUA.
26. Ibid.
27. Alumni Files, Sub: Jaime Benitex-Rexach, GUA.
28. Alumni Files, Sub: Luis Muñoz-Marin, GUA.
29. Ibid.
30. *GCJ*, 73:7–8.
31. Ibid., loc. cit.

Bibliography

Alumni Register of Georgetown University, Washington, D.C., 1917–1924.

Fr. Curran's Mss. Register of Students.

George, Eric, "Georgetown's Loss," *The Guardian,* 5, April 1987.

Georgetown Alumni Files, Georgetown University Archives.

Georgetown College Journal, 1, 5, 73, 50, 26, for years 1873, 1876, 1922–23, 1945, 1975.

Herran Papers, Georgetown University Archives.

Interviews

Interview with Dean Deacon, Dean of Admissions, Georgetown University. 20 Nov. 1987.

Interview with Patricia C. Delaney, President, Luso-Brazilian Club. 8 Nov. 1987.

Interview with Julie Holtzman, Office of International Affairs. 24 Nov. 1987.

Interview with Eric Hyburg, Director, Office of International Affairs. 23 Nov. 1987.

Interview with Ramon E. Kury, President, Puerto Rican Students Association. 7 Nov. 1987.

Interview with Dr. Valenzuela, Director, Latin American Studies Program. 11 Nov. 1987.

IV. Sporting Life

ABOVE: "Crew Member" (from *The Georgetown Journal*, October, 1901).
BELOW: Varsity crew on the Hudson, 1901.

Georgetown Basketball Coach John Thompson.

Georgetown basketball star Patrick Ewing.

"Georgetown Shot Putter" by J.E. Sheridan (from *The Georgetown Journal*, March, 1902).

Pre-Varsity Sports at Georgetown

Joseph Wagner

Before any Hoya lettermen arrived at the University to fight for the Blue and Gray against outside-the-campus athletes, different, more study-oriented kinds of teams prevailed at the Hilltop. These were the young men of the College who, during the first century of Georgetown's existence, organized themselves into athletic clubs intended only for intramural play. Many students involved themselves in an athletic club of their choice, while carefully seeing to it that whatever sport they practiced would be harmonized with and not be an obstruction to their education.

When so-called "varsity" sports were evolving on American college campuses, Georgetown for a long time refused to follow the trend. She was unwilling to have in any sport a single team representing the University as a whole.[1]

A feature—and virtue—of this traditional intramural or campus club athletic plan was that it was, to a large extent, controlled and administered by the students themselves, and not by the University Administration. For example, you and some of your classmates selected nine men, called it a team, gave it a name, and challenged others of your classmates (who had done the same thing) to compete on the College playing fields. The theory was that it was more fun to do it this way, untrammeled by the rules and red tape always present when the College as a whole or any other organized body got into the act.

313

The College authorities were smart enough to catch the point: here was an opportunity to have the students train themselves in self-reliance and self-help, planning and organizing in a project which, if they bungled it, would do no harm and probably teach them a lesson for the future. So, the Jesuits gave the boys a free hand; besides, it gave the Reverend Fathers more time for more important work.[2]

Yet, it soon became evident that if too much organization was stifling, too little of it was confusion. Hence the students set up what they called the Athletic Association, a steering body, an umbrella committee embracing all the scores of campus teams to serve their needs and give at least a minimum of order to their sports activities.[3] The Jesuits felt they were vindicated: the boys, by the boys' own experience, had discovered the necessity of law and reasonable patterning for any human enterprise.

The Association (as by this time the reader may have guessed) was appointed by students, and administered by them.[4]

The advantages of the unification were immediately evident. The gymnasts, for example, who required money for the construction and maintenance of the new gymnasium, benefited from their sharing in the dues paid to the Association. The numerous intramural baseball clubs had at first hesitated to join the Association due to their fear that such an act would lessen their autonomy. But they recognized the financial benefits accruing from membership. The nines could now, for instance, purchase their balls and bats at lower prices by ordering larger quantities.[5]

Yet, in the opinion of many, the Association never really lived up to its potential. From it, however, arose an even more important device for aiding the students in their governance of themselves. Students began to say, "If we have a single body to regulate athletic activities on the campus, why not a similar organization to regulate campus activities that are nonathletic, such as the Debating Society, the Dramatic Society and so forth?" The response to this was the creation of what was called "the Yard," a body with its own president, modeled on the presidency of the Athletic Association.[6]

The latter was indeed a strange sort of constitutional invention. It weakened itself by initiating a program of varsity sports, for the avoidance of which it had been initially founded. And it continued to support the growth of its child, the Yard government, which eventually swallowed up its parent.

Of the two bodies the Yard was, of course, the more important. As we have said, it finally secured control over all realms—athletic and nonathletic—of student activity, so far as the rules established by the University permitted. The Administration did not abdicate, but it practiced a prudent respect for democracy.

***

Intramural sports, athletic contests on the campus engaged in by classmates—this was the staple of the old-time students at the Hilltop during most of the nineteenth century.

Beginning in 1875, a day was annually set aside for "field contests." These consisted mostly of the following, with minor variations from year to year: the mile run, the hurdle race, the hop, skip and jump, the running long jump, the standing long jump, the 100-yard dash, running bases, throwing a stone (later, a hammer), the barrel race, throwing the baseball, vaulting, the three-legged race, the class tug of war, and the greased pig race which, for reasons unknown, unfortunately seems to have disappeared from the events after several years.

The inception of the athletic sports program in 1875 actually covered two days, due to a full day of classes on the first day. (Apparently, the Jesuits were not yet persuaded that the activities of the day merited the students a day outside the classroom.) Nevertheless, after classes on November 4, the campus was filled with spectators from the town along with nearly everyone from the College, including large boys and small, prefects and teachers, and even the President of the College.[7] The College Band opened the day by giving "a selection from their choicest melodies,"[8] and finally, the extremely eager boys, who had signed up for the different events and practiced at every recess, could begin their athletic sports. Or at least they could have done so were it not for the ceremonial cannon which somehow, under the direction of a small boy, "always went off at the wrong time."[9]

As one might guess, the greased pig race highlighted the first day. The *Journal* reported the action and even included an analysis of the greasing: "It was a College Pig, and was too grave to squeal, and too well fed to make any effort to get away....The patience with which it allowed its tail to be shaved and greased was something marvelous of the pig family. The melancholy thought doubtless presented itself to its mind, that it was being 'greased with the lard of a departed comrade.'"[10] The winner of the race was to be the first to catch the pig by its tail. It was rumored that "the pig would become the prize of the captor and be served up at some future day for the particular table to which said captor belonged."[11] This prediction proved to be false, and the victor for his efforts did not receive a pig roast but a toilet case.

The second day of athletic sports proved equally remarkable. In the walking race over the "College Walks," from end to end 4,178 feet, Tom McAndrews made it first in six and three-quarter minutes, but the judges decided that he once or maybe even twice broke momentarily into a trot, and so he was disqualified.[12]

The contestants were blindfolded for the wheelbarrow race, so as to lose all bearing on the true direction. According to the *Journal*, after "the word was given,...each man chose his own direction independent of the location of the finish stake...the Philosophers who took part in it went no more directly to the point than did other people, nor did the geometricians pursue any straighter course than algebraists."[13]

On the morning after the second day, the President of the College awarded prizes to the winners of the athletic sports, and "where the prizes consisted of articles of consumption, the receivers were immediately button-holed by their friends, perhaps to congratulate them."[14]

The *Journal* provided accounts of the athletics sports for the years immediately following the very successful first field day. Most enjoyable are the descriptions of several of the athletic sports events of 1878. In the hurdle race, "one contestant made a graceful finish in the unprecedented time of one second, but unfortunately he made it at the very first hurdle, over which he executed a double somersault."[15] The *Journal* was also quick to poke fun at an unnamed professor of law who, "wishing to show forth the 'strong arm of the law' picked up the twenty-two pounds with the air of a man about to throw it over the fence. His throw did not exactly come up to his expectations; however he managed thereby to clear the extremity of his right foot which was slightly in advance; and taking the size of his foot and the size of the man into consideration, it was not such a bad throw after all."[16] A rather detailed account is also given of the class tug-of-war between Philosophy and Rhetoric: "Kind nature having constructed the Philosophers with the biggest average foot of any class in the house, they were consequently favorites with the bettors, who avowed that they would walk away with Rhetoric. But notwithstanding the natural gifts and human expectations, the Rhetoricians managed to walk away with the Philosophers....But although Rhetoric forced Philosophy over the line, it was in turn afterwards vanquished by Second Humanities who, having also been victors over English, were consequently champions of the yard."[17] Contested prior to the greased pig race, a potato race was involved in the athletic sports for the first time in this same year. Although the race is not explained, the winner was George Oxnard who "displayed his usual agility and skill"[18] in doing whatever he did to the potato to win the event.

The field days of ensuing years did not achieve the excitement and fanfare of the first few, but the novelty was far from exhausted; the College continued to engage in the athletic sports with much enthusiasm and gaiety. In fact, after the successful completion of the sports in the fall of 1881, many students advocated holding the same sports in the spring, thus envisioning the creation of spring athletic sports.[19] Over the winter, the proponents fumbled with the idea, but with the arrival of spring they had not acted. Not until several springs later was the first spring sports held. By this time, the Jesuits had conceded to the students' pleas and granted a holiday for the occasion. The President of the College even went so far as to offer a gold medal to the contestant scoring the greatest number of points.[20]

As the athletic sports became more structured and the scoring more competitive, the evolution into what is now called a track and field meet never became so obtrusive as to eliminate the more ridiculous but most fun events of the day. In this light, the bicycle slow race was introduced in 1884.[21] This event was anything but a contest of speed. Instead, the cyclists paced themselves over the straight and narrow course as slowly as possible while still moving forward and maintaining balance. With hopes of victory by crossing the finish line *last*, three of the four contestants moved slowly enough to win but not swiftly enough to stay balanced atop their two-wheeler, so that the three fell to the ground. The winner and only finisher patiently expended two minutes and thirteen seconds while traveling only ninety yards. These types of events made the day more enjoyable and less athletically competitive while allowing more participation on an equal footing.

***

I believe that the athletic sports, more so than the other sports, truly epitomized the golden mean or the ideal of what college athletics should be. In my mind, these games and the other club sports were better for the *students* than the later varsity teams. The clubs' teams were more spirited and the "average" students more involved. With regard to these latter two points, the varsity version of sport at Georgetown must take second place. In my mind, the club sports represent the real highlight of Georgetown College athletics.

Notes

1. Documentary support for a description of this primeval and extremely unstructured era of Georgetown's athletic history is almost exclusively in the form of reminiscences of students who were at the Hilltop at that time. The limitations of such sources are notorious. The "Sports Archives, Box #1, Athletic Association" of the Georgetown University Archives (hereafter GUA) proved to be disappointing, except for its old *Journal* of the Athletic Association. The best sources for the author's topic are selected articles and news items in the *Georgetown College Journal* (hereafter *GCJ*), on which the author has heavily depended.

2. Sports Archives, Box # 1, supra cit., GUA.

3. *GCJ* 3, no. 9 (1875), p. 104. See also *Journal* of G.U. Athletic Association in Sports Archives, Box 1, GUA.

4. *GCJ* 3, no. 9 (1875), art. cit.
  5. Ibid., loc. cit.
  6. *GCJ* 14, no. 2 (1885), p. 18. See also ibid. 12, no. 1 (1883), p. 8, and ibid. 18, no. 6 (1890), p. 117.
  7. *GCJ* 4, no. 3 (1875), p. 28.
  8. Ibid.
  9. Ibid.
  10. Ibid.
  11. Ibid.
  12. Ibid.
  13. Ibid.
  14. *GCJ* 4, no. 3 (1875), p. 29.
  15. *GCJ* 7, no. 2 (1878), p. 15.
  16. Ibid.
  17. Ibid.
  18. *GCJ* 7, no. 2 (1878), p. 16.
  19. *GCJ* 10, no. 7 (1882), p. 90.
  20. *GCJ* 13, no. 2 (1884), p. 19.
  21. Ibid.

The History of the Georgetown Crew: Guardian of the Blue and Gray

Lawrence H. Cooke

Eight men drift across the still water that flows in front of Washington Harbor and Thompson's Boathouse. It is 5:45 a.m. They are sitting above the river propped up by a long, thin shell. Each drapes his arms over the oar to lace his feet into the sneakers that are fastened to the bottom of the boat. When they are finished tying in, and have checked the wheels attached to the bottom of their seat by sliding back and forth on the tracks mounted to the bottom of the boat, a count begins in the bow and continues up to the last man in the boat who announces "stroke," telling the coxswain the group is ready. Idle chatter and an occasional laugh interrupt the darkness that envelopes a predawn practice.

A man in a tattered, woolen Georgetown jacket arrives in a small motorboat. He shouts the first command: "All right, take it off with arms and bodies." The coxswain repeats this command, adding "at the finish, ready all," the rowers bring the oar to their stomach, leaning back until they hear the next command from the cox: "Row!" Backs straighten, shoulders square, eyes look straight ahead, each focusing on the man in front of him. Almost immediately the eight start to move in near perfect unison. They first push the oar away from their bodies with their hands; their backs follow out until they are stretched and their hands are almost at their feet. Immediately they lift their hands and together the blades instantly fall into the water, leav-

321

ing only a small splash behind the blade where it entered the water. The eight pull together, moving the boat methodically up the river. The coach tells the cox to add quarter, half, three-quarters and then full slide. The cox gives these commands to the rowers and the boat accelerates.

This is the way practice begins for the Georgetown Crew. The scene takes place more than one hundred and ten years after the founding of the Georgetown University Rowing Association. The crew and rowing have changed in many ways since 1876, but in many ways they remain the same. This paper depicts three stages in the history of the Georgetown Crew. The first stage contains the origins and earliest history of the crew. During the first stage, which began in 1876, the crew was learning to row. Their strongest desire was that of not being left behind in the competition among the colleges and universities of the time. They were very careful to conform to the proper forms and procedures of the other rowing associations along the east coast. The second stage of the paper discusses the developments between 1900 and 1910. During this time the crew had its first experience with competition and victory. Unfortunately, as in the first stage, the crew declined because of a lack of funding, the deadliest blow to this expensive sport. The third stage started in 1958 and runs continuously to today. During the sixties the crew had to start over and relearn the lessons of the first two stages. The seventies saw a decline of interest in the crew but never to the point of discontinuing it. The efforts of the crew and the administration beginning in the mid 1970s made the crew an institution and strengthened its ties to the University.

Stage 1

We are not among the timid who look upon the enterprise with doubtful eyes, and, judging by the failure of the past, are fearful lest failure instead of success should be the reward of strenuous endeavors. We are not among those who suspect there is not enough of generosity in our students to contribute their mite towards the accomplishment of this laudable undertaking. We are convinced that though our beginnings be small and our progress moderately rapid, the result will be commensurate with the dignity and proportionate to the high standing of other institutions.[1]

These were the aspirations of the first members of the Georgetown University Rowing Association who came together in 1876 under the leadership of John G. Agar. To report the founding of the crew without deferring to his eloquent words would be a disservice:

> At last, this long projected association is formed, and with every prospect of an active career, if one may judge from the spirit manifested by all concerned. Let it be recorded upon the tablets of time that March 15th, 1876, gave birth at Georgetown to this commendable organization—one that now sets us abreast with other Colleges on the seaboard in the matter of physical sports, as we hope Georgetown is not behind in other matters of more serious importance. On that day, a meeting of the students was called at noon, J.G. Agar in the chair, and a Committee was appointed to draw up a scheme of the organization.[2]

At this first meeting several matters had yet to be decided. The one fact the members of the association were sure of was that Georgetown was not going to be a second class school in any respect to others on the east coast. So, they made sure that they had all the trappings of any fine crew, and published the first Boat Song in May of 1876:

Boat Song
Dip lightly the oar,
To guide the boat o'er
The bright placid breast of the river;
We're gliding along
As we sing our boat-song,
Neath the moon-beams that scatter and quiver.

The light tinkling plash
Of the waves as they dash
On the bow of the boat and are broken,
The eddying whirl
Of the watery curl
Are like words that but one could have spoken.

May our vessel of life
In the turbulent strife
She encounters while sailing Time's river,

E'er find a strong hand
That will guide to the strand
Where we all must be landed forever.[3]

The Association had a large agenda to be addressed during its first year: it must select a crew, buy or borrow boats, and find a place to store those boats. All these problems were solved in the first two years after the founding of the Association.

The Association was more than crew as one would imagine it to be today. Today the Rowing Association consists solely of those athletes who row for the crew. The historic Association was a large group of students and friends of the river. From this group a crew was selected for competition; other members of the Association were not rowers in the crew, but had free use of the facilities. The *College Journal* explained that this practice was not different from the custom of other colleges:

> In other Colleges where such Associations exist, their first step is to select a suitable crew, who then go into training in a gymnasium, are subsequently given their boat—generally a six-oared gig—and after sufficient practice in their different positions, are put in possession of a shell. Then, for the convenience and amusement of the other members of the Association, a number of single boats are purchased, which are free to the members at any time.[4]

The Rowing Association had members whose only connection to racing was that they thought rowing was helpful to the community. Members paid dues as if it were a club. The Association would then select a crew. The Rowing Association was very much concerned with this process:

> The most important matter to be settled is the selection of the crew, and too much stress cannot be laid upon this point—that they be selected for the strength and endurance of the individuals comprising it. Again in order that the benefit of this year's practice may be added to the next, thus placing them in a position to cope with some of the neighboring clubs, the men now selected should be such as can hold their position until June [18]77....The selection of a comrpetent crew cannot receive too much attention.[5]

The result of this decision by members of the Association

meant that J.G. Agar and other members founding the organization were never able to be members of the crew. There were many applicants for the crew as early as May 1876. The Association received assistance from others (non-G.U. people) in the area who were concerned with rowing:

> Mr. Randall, one of the members of the Potomac Boat Club, has kindly volunteered his services in selecting and "coaching up" the crew. About fifteen, in answer to a notice on the bulletin board, have handed in their name to the Secretary as contestants for the honor of being on the crew, and daily the number exercising on the rowing weights in the gymnasium is increasing.[6]

The Potomac Boat Club would allow Georgetown to use its boats to practice in because GURA did not have any of its own.

By June of 1876 a crew had been selected under Mr. Randall and they were practicing in an eight-oared gig. This was done to prevent the previously unexperienced men from flipping into the river. The coach thought that soon these six men could be trusted in a shell. A gig is a rowing boat that is much wider than a shell; many of the early descriptions of gigs describe them as having room for passengers. A shell is only about two feet wide and is very easily tipped over into the water.

The first six members of the Georgetown Crew were E. McCarthy, W.F. Dammann, J. Dolan, T.F. Mallan, M.J. Condon and Jas. Lynch.[7]

The crew contained six members, unlike today, when crews race mostly in eight-man shells and sometimes in four-man shells. American crews raced in sixes without a coxswain because this is a faster boat than an eight with a coxswain. American rowers at this time were able to use these boats because unlike their English counterparts who had to race on very narrow, winding rivers, the rivers that the Americans raced on were generally very large and had buoyed lanes, generally straight, so that no coxswain was needed.[8]

Having thus selected the Crew, the Association advanced toward their second task; they had to find boats for them to row in. First they used Potomac's boats "Every Tuesday and Thursday afternoon during the months of May and June."[9] During the spring of 1876, the crew thought it unwise to seek to purchase a boat because they had collected only $250. In May, they received a generous gift. A letter from the Potomac Boat Club, dated May 4, 1876 arrived. It read, much to the delight of the Rowing Association:

> By a vote last evening; our Club passed a resolution presenting to your Association one of our four-oared shells and oars complete, and which I have to now ask you to accept. Arthur T. Brice, Sec'y P.B.C.[10]

Quickly the Georgetown University Boat Club acted, and on May 6th passed the following resolution:

> Resolved, that a vote of thanks be returned the Potomac Boat Club, for their kind and gratuitous donation of a shell and oars complete.
>
> Resolved, that the above resolution be printed in the *College Journal* and *Washington Capital*.[11]

The GURA was now in possession of its own boat. This was a four-oared shell, which required a minor modification of the crew. The six members were changed to four and two alternates. The story of paring down the crew is accompanied by an interesting anecdote in the *College Journal*, describing a practice. The author complained that there had been no mention of "an accident to the shell and its occupants, of being run into by a tug, without other damage however than wetting of the rowers and a slight straining of the shell; it is said that 'Kaiser' thereupon doubled up his fist and knocked the tug over, and that the owner of the tug has presented his bill to the College for a thousand dollars damages."[12]

Georgetown Rowing realized almost at its inception that it would need outside support to continue its programs. In May of 1876, the crew started its first alumni fund-raising drive. Before the donation of the Potomac Shell, the Association sent out this notice to former students and friends of Georgetown:

> Even this [just buying a modest boat] will tax our resources heavily, and if there are old students who feel disposed to do a generous ac-

tion, or if there be a friend of present students who wishes to encourage their laudable enterprise, let him come forward at once with his donations, and communicate with the Treasurer of the Association, or some other resident of the college.[13]

The Association was fortunate enough to have a shell donated to this laudable cause. It shortly thereafter received word that the Potomac Boat Club was interested in selling an eight-oared barge which Georgetown quickly bought. Moreover, the Analostan Boat Club donated a six-oared gig, named "Lightfoot," to the Association. The immediate problem was to find a place in which to store these shells. A boathouse was the solution.

In the first spring of the Rowing Association, some members were looking for ground that would be suitable for a boathouse. At first, the only land available was across the Key Bridge near the aqueduct piling. In the short run this was unacceptable because the bridge at that time was a toll bridge and the students couldn't afford to pay to get to their boathouse every time they wished to practice. They thought this problem would be alleviated because there was a rumor that Congress was going to buy the bridge and make it available for public use.[14] The Association also realized that they would not be able to buy a boathouse that year because they had accumulated only $250. Much of this problem was solved early in the next school year. By October 1876, a Mr. Shoemaker made a gift of land on the Georgetown side of the river. It was a "short distance above the College" and upon "passing through the tunnel under the canal, one comes immediately upon the spot."[15] This was a perfect location on the river for a boathouse. Shortly afterward Mr. J.L. Smithmeyer designed plans for this construction. The house was to be 60 feet long and 26 feet wide and was almost 15 feet high. The section designed to house the boats was 50 feet long, 6 feet wide.[16] On February 22, the Association proclaimed that the boathouse was completed:

The students of this college, appreciating the inestimable physical advantages to be derived from the excellent and popular exercise of rowing, about one year ago formed themselves into an association for the purpose of organizing a boat club. The work being undertaken at once, was prosecuted with a great deal of zeal; and with the assistance of some friends, but mainly through their own untiring efforts, they succeeded in accumulating a fund large enough to induce them to undertake the erection of a boat house. A suitable site was chosen; and the house, begun several months since, has just been completed, and is now in the possession of the club.[17]

The boathouse was completed by Messrs. Young & Kenenan at a cost of $1100.[18]

The Association had now made the three most important moves necessary to start an organization of this type. There were still several problems to be solved. One question on the mind of at least one prolific student concerned the name of the organization. Georgetown University Rowing Association was not appropriate because Georgetown College had been the name that the students had always used. This writer was afraid that students would lose their identity as collegians if they started calling themselves University students.[19] The members of the club a few years later changed the name of the club for another reason. They wrote: "We must remark that the term 'Rowing Association' used by us, is, out of date. The proper title is 'Georgetown University Boat Club'."[20] These distinctions seem minor now, but the discussions about them took up several pages of the *Journal*. The students who associated themselves with rowing in the 1870s were very much concerned with observing the forms of the craft to which they quickly became apprentices.

No discussion of the Georgetown Crew will ever again be complete without examining its role in the adoption of the Blue and Gray as Georgetown's colors. When J.G. Agar founded the crew, he formed a committee on colors.

During the mid-to-late 1800s colleges across the country were adopting colors that were distinctive of their schools. This happened primarily because of the increasing importance of crew at these schools. Crew races at that time were generally four miles long. Binoculars had yet to be invented and the spectators needed a way to distinguish the crews on the river. Harvard was probably the first to adopt colors; they chose crimson. All the rowers wore scarves around their necks as they rowed so that those on the shore knew for whom to cheer. This obsession with color increased among the colleges. Yale adopted blue and white, Princeton used black and orange to distinguish themselves, Penn used red and blue. The Georgetown committee on colors selected blue and gray "as appropriate colors for the Club and expressive of the feeling of unity that exists between the Northern and Southern Boys of the College."[21] Shortly thereafter the young ladies of Visitation presented the Boat Club with a Blue and Gray pennant. The pennant was half blue and half gray. It was embroidered with the words *Ocior Auro* ("swifter than the wind"). This flag became the informal rallying point of the student body. When it was first presented by the girls, there was an impromptu parade after its unveiling. The next two occasions when the flag was used signaled the acceptance of the colors by the student body of the whole University, and not by the Boat Club alone. When the President of the University left Georgetown in the summer of 1876 to attend the centennial celebration in Philadelphia, the leader of the students ran into the President's office to get the banner and then led the parade that was the Father's send-off. When the seniors of 1876 graduated, two flags flew during the ceremony: the United States flag on one side and the blue and gray on the other.[22]

The college accepted the Boat Club colors as those of the school. The Club then made moves to incorporate the colors into its organization. Within a month the boat song was changed to incorporate the colors. The dedication of the song referring to the colors indicates that this song was more appropriate, because of its reference to blue and gray, than the previous one had been. It also constitutes today a precious relic of American Victorian expression of feelings:

Boat Song
Dedicated to the G.U.B.C. Colors: Blue and Gray

Above the smooth and limpid wave,
Come, speed our boat along,
And as she dashes to the goal
We'll time her with a song

    chorus:
    Give way,—give way,—no man shall say

We're laggards at the oar;
No dame shall flush, nor maiden blush
For Georgetown's honest fame.
Hurrah! then, boys, hurrah! hurrah!
The Blue and Gray forever.

We give to thee, Potomac fair,
—Thou river all our own—
As trim a bark, as blithe a crew
As e'er thy waves have known

    chorus: —Give way, —give way, &c.

Speed—speed her on with stalwart arms,
Cleave—faster cleave the wave!
These storied shores should look alone
Upon the dauntless brave.

    chorus: —Give way, —give way, &c.

She flies: the oars, with rhythmic beat,
Divide the sparkling spray:
She leaps like some gay thing of life,
All eager for the fray.

    chorus: —Give way, —give way, &c.

Still on! The Blue our pennon bears,
To triumph leads the way:
Or, if we fail we still shall hold
To honor with the Gray.

    chorus: —Give way, —give way, &c.

This period in the history of the crew lasted for a few years. During the era there was little mention of any racing done by the boats although they practiced frequently. The only mention of a race is an invitation that was received in 1879 from Albany, New York. It displayed three beautiful challenge cups and announced that they would crown the National Amateur Oarsmen. The *Journal* said that it believed that Georgetown would decline.[23]

The crew relied on the donations of friends of the river during this first period. One way in which the Association was able to keep a crew on the water was through frequent socials. The crew began to hold dances in 1877.[24] They also sponsored poetry readings, concerts and many other functions designed to raise funds for the crew.

The crew disappeared from the *College Journal* after the fall of 1877. A letter of 1891 tells the tragic story:

> Thus it was with our boat-house. Though built on strong piles and warranted to withstand the buffets of a storm or freshet, the boat-house, or a great part of it, never-theless, fell a victim to an extraordinary freshet and went sailing down the lordly Potomac one spring morning.[25]

The crew was still listed in the University Catalogue in 1884 but there was no mention of any of its activities.There were attempts to find another boathouse and restart the crew around 1890, but these ventures were unsuccessful.[26]

Stage 2

Rowing did not stop at the Hilltop with the washing away of the boathouse. The men of Georgetown continued to row when the weather was pleasant in the fall or in the spring. This account appears in the year 1899:

> The river has received more patronage this year than for some years past, owing to the mild weather which has made rowing agreeable. Rowing is enjoyed almost every half holiday,...[27]

Crew did not follow far behind. The support of alumni and friends began what was a very successful era for our rowers. Starting in the school year 1899–1900, rowing was again a team sport at Georgetown:

> Just after Christmas, rowing machines were presented (through the efforts of Mr. [J. Hadley] Doyle) to the Athletic Association and were immediately installed in the old baseball cage. Since that time Frank Kerns, Med., of Worcester Mass., the intermediate sculling

champion, has been busy trying to install the rudimentary ideas of rowing into a squad of earnest and worthwhile candidates.[28]

The crew entered a period of exceptional success in 1900. The coach during this time, Mr. Zappone, would direct its 4:15 P.M. practices from his single shell, rowing abreast of the eights. Practice for the men consisted of daily eight-mile rows starting at Potomac Boat House. The crew trained hard and the rewards were soon to come.

On May 17, 1900, the crew raced against Navy at Annapolis. Georgetown won on the water for the first time in her history. The crew then directed its attention to Poughkeepsie and the nation's prime intercollegiate regatta, where 25,000 to 50,000 witnessed a "thrilling, nerve destroying, heartbreaking experience of the greatest, closest most exciting and one of the fastest boat races ever rowed in this country and probably the world, over a four-mile course."[29] This pace was too much for our tyros, whose boat finished last with a time of twenty minutes nineteen and one fifth seconds. Mr. Zappone expressed the feeling of the boat when he said:

> ...we felt very much like apprentices assuming to enter the class of skilled mechanics, for, up to sixty days before the race, six of the eight never sat in a shell or handled a sweep![30]

The general sentiment was that this was not a real cause for discouragement for the Crew. They knew that if they trained hard they would be able to come back next year and do much better.

During the fall of 1900 Georgetown found another boathouse in which to store its shells. By April of 1901, the Columbia Athletic Club had turned over the keys of their boathouse to the Hoyas, who bought it for $5,000.[31] Father Whitney took this opportunity to recognize rowing as a permanent institution of the College.

In July 1901, the crew again loaded shells for the long trip to Poughkeepsie. This year the results were slightly different. Instead of writers telling Georgetown that they had nothing to be ashamed of, Georgetown was the surprise of the contest. The *Journal* summarized the press' reaction:

No eight in the regatta deserves higher praise than the Georgetown Crew. They went into the race with but one previous contest as experience; half of the men never handled a sweep in a race before, yet Georgetown surprised everyone by holding on to the leaders in grand style. Such a combination of pluck and skill was entirely unlooked for; it was something even for seasoned oarsmen to have finished fourth in such a race, to have defeated the other two contestants, and to have broken an intercollegiate record; but to have done all this with such little preparation and experience is, indeed, a thing to be remembered in the history of athletics at Georgetown.[32]

In this second regatta Georgetown, although not winning, had finished in faster time than the previous world record for a four-mile race.

Georgetown continued to make Poughkeepsie an annual event. In 1902 the Blue and Gray finished last there; they came in second in the 1903 race, their best finish ever. In 1904 came a let-down when they crossed the finish line in fifth place.

In the fall of 1904 Mr. Dempsey became their new coach. Unfortunately, in the spring of 1904 the crew was forced out of their home in the Columbia Boat House on 34th Street. The site was government land and the boathouse was razed. Luckily, Mr. Dempsey had an ice house next to the aqueduct abutment where Georgetown was able to store their shells. While the crew continued to look for a home, Georgetown held a huge track and field contest that was to benefit the Boathouse fund;[33] four thousand people attended.

Despite the large crowds that turned out in support of the crew, the sport itself is amateur. There is no way to charge admission to a regatta because it covers four miles of a public river. The crew was faced with severe financial difficulties in the spring of 1904. It did not have enough money to buy the land for building the boathouse. The crew was not as successful as it had been in the early 1900s. The administration, facing the decision of whether or not to support the crew, decided to maintain it.[34]

However, interest in rowing at Georgetown began to ebb. In 1911 a reference to the crew appears in the scrapbook of Wm. E. Harrington. The note says the University could continue to support the crew if the football team remained successful.[35] After this there were no more references to our rowers until 1941.

Stage 3

The men of Georgetown continued to keep the spirit of rowing alive despite long periods of obscurity. Rowing was not formally part of the university after 1910 but many continued to row as individuals and simply for fun. There is an account of a race between American International College and the Georgetown Rowing Club in the newspapers in 1941. There is a description of Georgetown racing and unfortunately losing to Washington and Lee in May of 1941 and to Penn in July. These students used shells, like many of the first members of the crew in 1876, that were borrowed from the Potomac Boat Club. These races were infrequent and they received little press attention.

The Georgetown Crew embarked upon its current history in 1957.[36] Again rowers used the club format to cultivate interest in the sport. Fr. Bunn, then president of the University, told Mr. Maletz, the coach of the club, that if he could keep students rowing for five years, the University would again adopt the sport officially. The crew continued as a club for a year, then, during the next year Washington rowing got its biggest boost.

In 1959, the Water Sports Center, now known as Thompson's Boat House, was approved on the merits of three advantages proposed by the Washington Rowing Association. This new facility would be a place for public rental and storage of boats, a place for colleges and high schools to store the delicate shells that they used for crew, and for planned intercollegiate regattas.[37] Washington had been the host to four Eastern Sprint Championships, two High School National Championships and, during the summer of 1959, played host to the tryouts for the Pan American Games and as a training site for the Russian National Team. All these factors led to the construction of Thompson's Boathouse, which insured that Georgetown would have a place to store its boats.

The Hoyas began regular workouts with the addition of the Water Sports Center to the shores of the Potomac. In May 1961, the boathouse that Coach Dempsey had built to house the shells at the turn of the century burned down. This was the converted ice house next to the aqueduct abutment.

Georgetown became a serious contender for rowing honors in 1962, when Don Cadle became the head coach. In the year before his arrival the crew had finished third in the Dad Vail Final, the small college national championship regatta. In his first season, Cadle's team was undefeated and then won the Dad Vails. This boat was even considered as a possible Olympic contender. During the next season, the crew defeated all its regular season opponents. The only team it lost to was the World Champion German National Team. The crew came in second in the Vails in 1963. In 1964, it continued its dominance and again won the Dad Vails.

Success guided the crew in the early sixties. Coach Remuzzi finished medical school while directing the crew in 1965. This group of rowers was not as successful as Don Cadle's but they kept rowing alive at the Hilltop. The 1964 Vail winning season prompted many others to join. This also marked the beginning of the long association between the crew and the Tombs restaurant. Many of the 1965 rowers called themselves the Black Velvets because several oarsmen would go to the Tombs to drink a combination of Guinness beer and champagne.

During 1964 Georgetown started its lightweight rowing program. Lightweight boats must average 155 pounds for eight rowers, none of them weighing over 160 pounds. The lightweights rowed in the more competitive Eastern Sprint League, which includes many Ivy League schools. The lightweights did fairly well against the tough competition in the Eastern Sprints, but never won. When the Dad Vail opened its competition to lightweights, Georgetown's crews in this class switched to take advantage of the winning possibilities by competing against schools whose crews were not heavily endowed.

The lean years of the mid-sixties gave way with the 1966 arrival of Tony Johnson, a former Washington and Lee rower who returned to Washington to row with his partner Larry Hough, and competed in rowing internationally. He undertook the coaching job at Georgetown with the understanding that he was to volunteer his coaching services in order to maintain his amateur status. He worked in the Alumni House as assistant fund director. Johnson led by the sterling example he set. He just missed in his attempt to represent the United States in the 1964 Olympics in the straight pair, a race involving two sweep oarsmen without a coxswain. With a new partner and during his years at Georgetown he was undefeated in national and international competition. In 1968 Johnson and Hough went to the Olympics as the favorites but lost by less than a second to the East German team in a hotly contested final.

Tony Johnson was able to translate his personal victories into coaching success. One of his rowers explained that Johnson told his crew what it took to win and had them decide if that was what they wanted to do. To them winning was something that the coach made easy. Almost immediately this style resulted in victory. In 1967 the Hoya heavyweights captured the silver medal at the Dad Vails. In 1968 they recaptured the gold. The same crew then repeated their championship performance in 1969.

In that summer Yale heavily recruited Tony Johnson. After winning the Olympic silver medal he decided to end his amateur career and accepted a lucrative position at New Haven.

He left a group of very talented sophomores at Georgetown. Under the guidance of Frank Bensen they again won the Dad Vail in 1971. This was the last gold medal for the heavyweight crew. The late sixties and seventies were difficult times for the crew. The sport at Georgetown fell victim to the sweeping social changes that were happening both outside and inside Healy gates. Crew became associated with conservatism. It was part of the old school; getting up at 5:45 to row as a unit wasn't popular. Johnson had been able to preserve the dedication of the Hoya crews during his tenure, but shortly after his departure the effects of the nationwide social changes started to emerge.

Success was spotty for Georgetown's crew in the early and mid seventies. Not as many athletes remained committed to the program. There were many good oarsmen but they didn't seem to "get it together." Only recently did the crew start to regularize itself and strengthen its ties with the University. The most important factor in this process was the arrival of Father Healy in 1976.

The new president of Georgetown had long been a strong

supporter of crew, and his work and that of others enabled crew to become a permanent part of Georgetown. During the late seventies and early eighties the crew has grown tremendously. In 1975, Sharon Courtin founded the highly successful women's team.

Currently, over a hundred students row for Georgetown. Starting around 1977, part-time coaches became more permanent, coaching longer than others had done previously. John Forrester was the men's head coach for nine years between 1977 and 1986. He would often use his own money to cover the crew's expenses. John Devlin and Jack Nihill, both former members of the Georgetown Crew, started coaching in 1979 and continue doing so today. The establishment of the crew is most significant in the areas that troubled the crew in the past: funding , coaching and a boathouse.

The crew is currently completing a million-dollar capital campaign. The nearly $900,000 that has been pledged provides assurance that this expensive sport will always be funded. Coaching was regularized further with the hiring of Fred Schoch, the team's first full-time coach. Georgetown is currently attempting to build a boathouse for the crew as the final guarantee of the sport's continued survival at the Hilltop.

The bonding between the crew and the University has brought back the success that the crew was accustomed to in the early 1900s and then again in the early and late 1960s. The freshmen boats, a good indication of talent to come, have won the Dad Vails for two years running. The lightweights earned gold medals in 1986 and 1987, the heavyweights in 1985 and 1986. Last year the varsity boats came closer to former Vail glory. They were all in their respective finals at the championships. The women won the Vails and went on to finish seventh in the nationals held in California. Fred Schoch further augmented the reputation of the crew during the summer when he coached the Junior National Team to a gold medal in the world games held in Germany.

The Georgetown Crew has become a regular part of life at our University. We are celebrating her bicentennial in 1989. Crew has played a major part in the lives of many of our students for the last century. The union of the University and the crew served to protect the crew from withering away. The crew has also served to honor the Potomac's lovely daughter and, in the words of the boat song, has preserved the "Blue and the Gray forever."

Notes

1. *Georgetown College Journal* (hereafter, *GCJ*) 4 (1976):81.
2. Ibid., 80.
3. Ibid., 87.
4. Ibid., 81.
5. Ibid.
6. Ibid., 89.
7. Ibid., 104.
8. This conclusion results from observations of pictures portraying crews in the late nineteenth or early twentieth century.
9. Ibid., 89.
10. Ibid., 104.
11. Ibid., 101.
12. Ibid., 101. This story is an interesting example of the sometimes sarcastic comical nature of certain material in the *Journal*. It never explained which one of the other rowers was nicknamed Kaiser.
13. Ibid., 80–81.
14. Ibid., 104–5.
15. *GCJ* 5:7.
16. Ibid.
17. Ibid., 78.
18. Ibid., 92.
19. *GCJ* 4:112.
20. *GCJ* 5:8.
21. *GCJ* 4:104.
22. Ibid., 118.
23. *GCJ* 7 (1878):30–31.
24. *GCJ* 5:53.
25. *GCJ* 9 (1893):147.
26. *GCJ* 10 (1892):120.
27. *GCJ* 29 (1900):137.
28. *GCJ* 28 (1899):357.
29. This is from a newspaper article in the university archives, in the box labeled Sports 9. The article is titled "Penn wins the race at Poughkeepsie" and is dated July 1, 1900.
30. *GCJ* 29:46.
31. Ibid., 337.
32. Ibid., 479.
33. This is from an article in the *Washington Post*, found in the box Sports 9 in the university archives. The article is dated Sept. 4, 1904 and is titled

"Games on Labor Day."

34. An article in the university archives box Sports 9, from the *Washington Post*. It is dated Sept. 11, 1904.

35. This is from a note in the Sports 9 box in the university archives.

36. This is from a roster dated 1957, in the Sports 9 box in the university archives. There were twenty-four on the roster in 1957–58.

37. This is from a press release from the Washington Rowing Association, dated March 3, 1959. This is in the Sports 9 box in the university archives.

Highlights of Georgetown Track and Field Sports and Baseball

Edward F. McHugh

The highlights of Georgetown's history in track and field sports date from the late nineteenth century.

After some sputtering beginnings with such track and field competitors as "Big George" Mahoney and William E. Fox (reputed also to have hit a baseball from the Hoya diamond into the C & P Canal), Georgetown attained national and even international fame with its two sprinters and middle-distance runners, Bernard Wefers and Arthur Duffey.

From 1895 onward, Wefers achieved the following: he held the world's record for the hundred-yard dash (as it was then termed) and also for the popular 220-yard dash. His best time for the former race was 9-3/5 seconds. The 1963 world's record—when the distance was still being run—was 9.2 seconds. He covered the "220" in 21 seconds flat, not much slower than the 1963 record of 20 seconds.

Wefers once commented on his success: "because I was better trained and in better condition than my competitors." He was regarded by his rivals on and beyond the campus as "that speedy sprinter and good fellow." By his classmates on the Hilltop he was looked on as a leader in other activities besides athletics, and as exemplifying the "Georgetown gentleman."

The turn of the century brought another legendary sprinter to the Hilltop: Arthur Duffey. He ran the fifty-yard dash in 5.2 seconds, two-tenths of a second faster than Wefers. He equalled Wefers' world's record for the hundred-yard dash, covering the distance in 9.6 seconds. This was the first occasion when a man had ever made such time in competition. Wefers' record had been attained only in an exhibition race.

At the Paris Olympic games in 1900, Duffey and his G.U. partners Minihan and Holland were shining stars in the short races.

It might almost be said that Wefers and Duffey were victims of their own success. Both were accused of professionalism, partly on the grounds that they were simply too good to be true amateurs. With the full cooperation of Georgetown University, the allegations were exhaustively probed. Both men were completely exculpated.

No subsequent Hoya track hero has ever equalled the exploits of Wefers and Duffey, but later track and field achievements were not lacking.

The 1920s witnessed the greatest track *team* in Georgetown's history. Bob Legendre, its captain, won the American pentathlon championship. He was first also in the Interallied Games in Paris. His long jump of 25 feet 5.5 inches was a world's amateur record for the era. In the 1920 Olympics at Antwerp, he finished fourth in the pentathlon.

Georgetown won the national track championship in 1925, with the largest point total ever featuring the event up to that time. "Little Emmie" Norton, a student from Georgetown's School of Foreign Service, who starred in the meet, had won the silver medal in the Olympic decathlon. In the 1925 intercollegiate championship meet, Sherill from the University of Pennsylvania was forced to break a world's record to beat Norton in the pole-vault.

Anthony ("Tony") Plansky was another Hoya track and field great of the 1920s. He was dubbed the "Athlete-Scholar-Gentleman" by his classmates. He was indeed an all-round athlete, a star halfback in football, a pinch-hitter and relief pitcher for the baseball team, a gifted golfer, and a winner of the decathlon at the Penn relays.

Georgetown, like her sister college Holy Cross, has frequently excelled in the mile relay event. Throughout the 1920s the Hoyas brilliantly upheld this tradition. The four quarter-milers George Kinally, Vernon Ascher, Paul Herlihy, and Jim Burgess, were the equal of any in the nation and, possibly, in the whole amateur world. Their best time for the mile relay was three minutes 21.8 seconds, remarkable for any period.

The success of the team led to a heartening incident of good sportsmanship. At the 1925 Penn relays all the other teams, overawed by the Georgetown quartet, decided not to participate in the event. This was a great disappointment to the Hoya team since it had hoped to break a world's record, an achievement recognized as legal only if accomplished against competition. The Hoyas were rescued by the unselfish decision of Jake Weber, the coach of the Fordham University runners, to enter his far inferior team against the Georgetown men, who then proceeded to capture the world title.

Another unique athlete at the Hilltop during this same era was an immigrant from Norway, Charles Hoff, who set world's records in pole-vaulting and the broad jump. The fact that he also brought with him a wife does not seem to have precluded his taking courses at Georgetown. He was certainly our only student who could boast of such a double accomplishment.

The twenties may be seen as the second golden age of Georgetown track and field sports.

Much of the credit for bringing together such brilliant athletic programs must be accorded to Fr. McDonough, faculty athletic director at the Hilltop from 1916 to 1932. This priest, after whom McDonough gymnasium was named, did more for Georgetown athletics than was accomplished by any other administrator in GU's history. He was a strict disciplinarian and much feared; yet he was also loved by the students. As an alumnus remarked, "Everybody on the campus was scared stiff of Father Mac, but we also counted on him as a friend who would fight his head off against injustice."

Georgetown's achievements in track and field sports did not cease with the 1920s. In 1941 the Hoya quarter-milers ran the fastest mile relay in the school's history, 3 minutes 19.5 seconds. At the 1932 Olympics, a Georgetown alumnus won a gold medal in the shotput, with a 52-foot 6-3/16 inches throw of the sixteen-pound ball.

It is fitting to conclude this section with a tribute to a Georgetown athlete who, perhaps more than any other, typifies the ideal Georgetown gentleman whose all-round excellence of character transcended even his extraordinary accomplishments in three sports. He was Albert Blozis. He weighed about 245 pounds and was 6-1/2 feet tall, dimensions which in the athletic world of today would be considered only moderately "big." He was urged by professional boxing experts to enter that dubious career, but evinced no interest in the suggestion.

Like many physically strong people, he was, when not competing in sports, a very gentle person. A Jesuit who knew him well recalls the thoughtfulness inducing Al not to disturb the afternoon slumbers of a classmate who was tutoring him academically.

In 1940 and 1941, Blozis was the world's champion shotputter. At Madison Square Garden in the latter year he broke his own world's record by tossing the sixteen-pound shot while merely warming up. In twenty-four meets during his glory years he failed only once to shatter a meet record. He excelled also with the distance, his best cast being a bit over 160 feet.

Nor did he stop here. He is one of Georgetown's two All-American football greats (Augustus "Augie" Lio being the other) for his performance as tackle in the Hoya team of 1937–1940, which went to the Orange Bowl. After graduation he played more football for the professional New York Giants, earning the Rookie of the Year award for 1942.

Albert Blozis volunteered for the army in 1942. In 1945, as a second lieutenant, he was killed in action as he tried to rescue one of his wounded men in a Vosges Mountains engagement in France. It was said at the time that the lieutenant could have legitimately sent some subordinates on this mission, but that he preferred to go himself.

Georgetown's track and field history has by no means ended.

In the autumn of 1989, the Hoyas could boast of winning the Big East tournament, with runner John Trautmann performing brilliantly. In the previous year, Trautmann, with Darron, Ousler, and Miles Irish, had set a world's record in the distance medley relay with a remarkable time of nine minutes 20.96 seconds.

In a companion paper to this one, the impressive athletic achievements of our women Hoyas have been thoroughly recounted.

***

Baseball at Georgetown began with intramural games for pure fun and ended—until recent times—with national championships at the start of the present century.

At first there were the rustic on-campus gambols of the numerous "nines" selected from the various classes of the college. They provide us with incredible scores of 30 to 5, or 25 to 0, pitchers who strike out twenty men in a game, occasional contests with neighboring high schools, and a three-game series with the first professional team representing Washington, D.C. In this fascinating potpourri almost anything was possible. Midway in the meeting with the Washington professionals the latter were so impressed by the GU catcher that they hired him for the final game of the series. The distinguishing features of the sport as practiced at the Hilltop at this time were informality, disorganization, and pure enjoyment. It was not polished but it was good sport in an age of innocence.

Then, beginning in the middle 1890s, Georgetown baseball came of age, or fell from grace, or arrived at greatness; one has various options according to one's viewpoint on this development.

The nine of 1895 should have been a warning to the competition. It beat Navy, 32–1, Yale, 20–5, and, in a split series with Princeton, won the second game, 17–11. Obviously, college pitchers at this stage of the evolution of the national pastime had much to learn.

With the 1899 season the Georgetown team hit its stride. This was the era when baseball was the major sport among American colleges. Football had been discredited on college campuses and in the eyes of the general public, by some tragic deaths (one of them occurring at Georgetown) of college football players. Baseball, for a brief time, filled the vacuum.

Coached by Paul King, a graduate of Princeton, the Hoyas captured the intercollegiate championship with a record of twenty wins, two losses, and one tie. During this carnival of destruction they defeated the teams of Harvard, Yale, Princeton, Penn, Brown, Columbia, and Dartmouth. In the succeeding year Georgetown's baseball record was nineteen wins, one loss. They were second only to Princeton, which won the national college championship in that year. The Hoyas, however, were regarded as firmly on top of the pack of American colleges in the national sport. During the period 1889–1902 they won 101 games against the best teams in the nation, with only twenty-six losses. Even some professional nines were among the victims of the Hoya nines, in exhibition contests.

Georgetown's greatest baseball player was probably "Doc" White, whose first name seems to have escaped the college records, and who later pitched successfully for the Chicago White Sox.

Note

Research comes from newspaper articles in the Georgetown University Archives, the *Georgetown College Journal,* and from the research and publications done by the Sports Information bureau of the Athletic Department of Georgetown University.

Football at Georgetown: Some Highlights

Hugh Golden

Since the first contest was played with Gallaudet College in 1883, the Hoyas' football past has been about 40% mediocre and 60% really great.[1a] This, as things go in the world of sports, is far above the average for non-professional players.

During these 105 years, Georgetown has fielded 84 varsity football teams, yielding 51 winning seasons, 22 losing ones, and 11 seasons in which wins exactly balanced losses. The Hoyas have played, throughout their history, 655 football contests against "outside" teams, winning 379, losing 245 and playing to a tie in 31 games.[1b]

Even before the first intercollegiate games had been played, the Georgetown University Football Association had been formed in 1874. Wrote the *College Journal*:

> The committee of fifteen appointed at the mass meeting of the students, Nov. 1st, subsequently met and appointed the following officers: Mr. M. O'Kane, S.J., President; John G. Agar, V. Pres.; A. Hood, Jr., Sec. and Treas.; E. Dolan and Paul Arnold, Censors. A committee of three was appointed to draw up a code of law, and another committee of ten, to serve as referees. A small monthly collection from the students who wish to take part in the game, suffices for all expenses. The game is played only during the winter months.[1c]

In 1887 the Hoyas played three contests with outside opponents. Here is a section of the *College Journal*'s account of the first of these:

The first was played on the College field with the team of Emerson's school which won the toss and dribbled the ball. A poor pass was made which Hartman, for the College, took advantage of by kicking the ball towards Emerson's goal. Four downs gave the ball to the College and several runs by C. O'Day and Hennessy brought it to the goal. C. O'Day then kicked it and a fumble by Emerson's fullback allowed the ball to roll in goal, where the visitors were forced to touch it down for safety. Shortly afterward Hennessy made the first touchdown for the College.[2]

From here on, Georgetown proceeded to win the game by a score of 46 to 6.

The next two outings of the pioneer Georgetown footballers were scarcely a rousing success. They lost to the eleven of Alexandria High School by a score of 24 to 8, and edged out a close victory over Washington High.

The Georgetown–University of Virginia rivalry in football began in 1888, and would thrive during most of the following twenty-five years. Georgetown started the series with a 34-0 win over the Cavaliers.[3]

This season, spotty though it was in achievement, earned for the Hoyas a rather ambiguous prize called the championship of the District of Columbia.[4]

Until the second decade of the subsequent century, Georgetown football, except for a two-year hiatus soon to be noted, survived in a fair although not consistently vigorous state of health.

The history of this period may be best told in a series of significant events.

A victory of the Hoya Eleven of 1892, if not impressive in substance, is worth recording for the character of the defeated opponent, the Neptune Boat Club! The Neptunes showed up at Georgetown with only ten players, so the Hoyas loaned them a player for the game. The Hoyas won, "by a disgracefully large margin."[5]

During the 1894 season, the greatest tragedy ever to take

place at a Georgetown athletic event occurred. In the last game of the season against the Columbia Athletic Club, the football field became the scene of a street fight. There were players of both teams being knocked out, with much punching and kicking going on after the whistle. Bettors on the sidelines were wagering on who would be knocked out next. Then the most serious injury of the day was inflicted on George "Shorty" Bahen. Reported the *College Journal*:

> But Bahen, Georgetown's plucky little halfback, lay white and motionless on the ground....[He had been hit] by Leet's head planted in his abdomen....It is also said he was struck twice, and then after he was down one of his opponents kicked him in the back, while another jumped on his prostrate form, planting both knees upon his stomach.[6]

Behan lay paralyzed in bed during four months until he died from failing kidneys, the result of his broken back.

It was a week after the fatal injury that Georgetown decided to ban football from the campus. Not until 1898 was the game resumed at the Hilltop.

Finally, in that year, Georgetown decided to reinstate the sport, due largely to the fact that President John D. Whitney, S.J., was an admirer of the game. However, the Hoyas would henceforth not be permitted to compete against athletic clubs, but only against educational institutions.

In the following fall, Bill Church, a former Columbia Athletic Club player and All-American with Princeton, became the football coach at the Hilltop. Now that the Hoyas were no longer playing the Columbia A.C., the game against the University of Virginia was given more attention. The 1899 meeting with this rival resulted in a scoreless tie. The following account from the *College Journal* is a sampling of the enthusiasm—and baroque prose—generated by the contest:

> Georgetown's brilliant offense and impregnable defense, and Virginia's desperate bull-dog pluck in endeavoring to stop the merciless sweep of our backs, caused the bleachers, crowded with all sorts, conditions, and ages of life, to burst out in genuine applause time and time again.[7]

In 1899 Georgetown ran up what was probably the highest score in all her football history—an 84-0 victory over the University of Richmond.

In the summer before the 1905 season, a letter from Georgetown President Jerome Daugherty stated that "in no case will board or lodging in college be given for athletic service." This means that Georgetown wished only "bona fide" students to be on the football team. As a result of this rule, three star players were cut from the team.[8]

The 1905 season was a dismal one for the Hoyas. They won only two of nine games, and suffered a 76-0 loss to Coach "Pop" Warner's Carlisle Indians, the greatest disaster in Georgetown football history. It was said that Warner "ran up " the score because in a 1903 game the Georgetown players had delivered some cheap shots to his boys.[9]

The Hoyas had a 3-2-1 record in the season of 1909. Their star was "Curly" Byrd, a quarterback skilled in throwing a "forward pass," a very new tactic at that date. His favorite receiver was a halfback named "Wild Bill" Corrigan. It is to be noted that credit for introducing the forward pass is usually accorded to players Knute Rockne and Gus Dorais of Notre Dame, who beat a strong Army team with it in 1914. But here is Georgetown's Byrd anticipating them in 1909.

Georgetown football after World War I featured truly great teams coached by Lou Little, former Penn star. From 1923 through 1929 they won 77% of their games, most of them against nationally ranked opponents. Ironically, one of their most impressive showings in this period was a 3-0 loss to a powerful Penn Eleven before a crowd of 34,000 at Philadelphia's Franklin Field.

It was during Little's tenure as coach that for the first time a Georgetown player captured a place on Walter Camp's All-American team—Harry ("Babe") Connaughton, the Hoyas' guard.

The debate still rages as to which was the most stellar team in all Georgetown history, that of 1927–29, or the one under Jack Hagerty of 1937–40.

Frank Leahy, who in the 1940s and 1950s was considered college football's greatest coach, began his coaching career in 1931, as a line coach under Frank Mills. Although the Hoyas line was excellent, led by Capt. "Mush" Dubofsky, Ray Hudson, Tom Carolan and Dick Danner, they finished the season at a dismal 4-5-1. Leahy decided to leave after the 1931 season because he felt that the University wasn't committed to its football program.

After the Hoyas started off the 1932 season with a record of 2-3, Frank Mills resigned as their coach.

Jack Hagerty, the great Georgetown halfback from 1923 to 1925, and also formerly with the New York Giants, was named successor to Mills. He immediately scrapped the Rockne system for a mixture of the Louis Little and "Pop" Warner system.[10] Also, he named "Mush" Dubofsky, the captain of the 1931 team, as one of his assistants.

At the start of the 1933 season, Hagerty added former Hoya teammate George Murtagh to his coaching staff. The Blue and Gray had a lot of spirit that year but lacked ability; their 1-6-1 record proved this.[11]

The 1934 team won its first three games and tied the fourth against a strong NYU team, 0-0. It was apparent that Hagerty's system was gradually taking hold; it was just going to take time.

In the following week, the Hoyas suffered their first defeat of the season when Richmond beat them 14-13, on a last minute desperation pass.[12] They won in the next week and then ended the season on a bad note, losing the last two games.

Although the Hoyas' final record for eight games was just above .500, they still were able to hold opponents to only thirty-three points for the 1934 season.

Hagerty's Hoyas expected to do better than 4-4 in 1935, one source of encouragement being the defensive play. In their four losses, they never lost by more than a touchdown and they gave up an average of only five points a game.

In 1936, the Hoyas were looking like Exendine's and Little's teams of old. They started the season unbeaten in their first six games, winning five and tying NYU 7-7. The seven points that NYU scored were the only ones scored on the Blue and Gray in the first six games. Then in the seventh game, the Hoyas lost their first game of the season to Manhattan 13-0. The following week, the Hoyas avenged Maryland's win of the preceding year, with a 7-6 victory.[13] They were defeated in the final game by Miami 10-6, giving Georgetown a final record of 6-2-1, their best showing in six years.

Great things were expected of the 1937 team, but the expectations were not fulfilled. The Hoyas finished the season winning only two games. One major reason for this was that in a scrimmage with the newly arrived Washington Redskins of the National Professional Football League, three Georgetown players were injured and subsequently out for weeks.[14] The three were Bobby Nolan, Tom Keating, and Elmer Moulin, all from the first team backfield.

The standout of the team was captain "Big Red" Hardy, who played center. The pleasant surprise of the season was Joe Mellendick, who received his shot when the backfield was injured.[15]

Also, the Hoyas lost their last game of the 1937 season to Maryland 12-2. This would be the last time an opponent defeated the Hoyas for nearly three years.

The 1938 team had only nine seniors and was made up predominately of sophomores, which was thought to be a drawback at the time. But once the season started, the sophomores quickly proved that their presence would not only be an asset but the main reason for the team's success.[16] Some of these contributing sophomores were Jim Castiglia, Jules Koshlap, Augie Lio, Joe McFadden, and Lou Ghecas. Two years later, these Hoyas would be ranked with some of the best football players in the country.

The Hoyas beat Hampden-Sydney 51-0 in the first game of the season. This was the beginning of a 23-game unbeaten streak that lasted until the next to the last game of the 1940 season. They finished the season with a 14-7 win over Maryland, ending the season 8-0, undefeated and untied, for the first time in the team's 63-year history.[17]

Five players were named to the All-District first team: Joe Mellendick, halfback; Joe Frank, tackle; Bill Burke, guard; Bob Kercher, end; and Joe McFadden, quarterback. In addition, Mellendick was awarded All-American honorable mention.[18] His success was due in large part to the offense Hagerty had learned while playing for the New York Giants, called the "spread system."[19] This offense worked because it spread the defenders across the field, making the opponent very vulnerable. Although Mellendick had two years of eligibility left, he gave up football after the 1938 season, to play professional baseball.[20]

The first game of the 1939 season was almost the end of the eight-game winning streak which had begun in the previous year. Georgetown and Temple were scoreless through the first three quarters. Then in the final quarter, Temple tackled punter Lou Falcone in the end zone for a safety. With only a few minutes remaining, the Hoyas began their final drive from their own 21-yard line. Ambidextrous passer Jules Koshlap led the Hoyas down the field to the Owls' 3-yard line. But after a few penalties and some bad breaks, the ball ended up on the 24-yard line, with only 35 seconds left. Augie Lio, called upon to attempt the field goal, successfully kicked it, winning the game 3-2 before 15,000.[21] In the third game of the season, the lone blemish of the two undefeated seasons was suffered. Georgetown tied Syracuse 13-13 in an incredible finish. The Blue and Gray had the ball on their 30-yard line, with only a few minutes remaining, down 13-6. Lou Ghecas received the handoff and the rest is history. He raced the 70 yards, leaving every Syracuse defender far behind him.[22] The Hoyas won their next four games and then finished off the season with a victory over NYU 14-0, extending the unbeaten streak to 16 games.

The Hoyas finished the season with a 7-0-1 record and were ranked in the top 20 teams in the country.[23] There were rumors that they would be invited to the Orange Bowl, but this did not come about.

After the 1939 season, the only players on Georgetown's squad honored nationwide were end Mike Kopcik, and guard Augie Lio. Kopcik made the honor roll for the All-American team, while Lio made first team All-East.[24]

The great sophomores of the 1938 team were now the players who were expected to lead the rest of the squad. These seniors of the 1940 team were a talented group. Some were able, even as sophomores, to start on the undefeated team of 1938. The 1940 first team was comprised of all seniors. This was important because that meant that the first team had been playing together for the past three years. The 1940 first team is listed as follows: Joe Lascari, end; Joe Daniels, tackle; Augie Lio, guard; Al Matuza, center; Marc Ostinato, guard; Earl Fullilove, tackle; Bill Wixted, end; Joe McFadden, quarterback; Jim Castiglia, fullback; Lou Ghecas, halfback; and Jules Koshlap, halfback.[25]

The 1940 Hoyas battered their first seven opponents. The victims included Roanoke, Temple, Waynesburg, Virginia Tech, New York University, Syracuse and Maryland. This now put the Hoyas' unbeaten streak at 23 games. Jack Hagerty believed that the Hoyas' defense was the key to their unbeaten streak. He said the reason for the team's success was "based mainly on the ability of his boys to play defensively." He added, "They're smart and aggressive; all I have to do is to teach offense—they take care of the rest."[26]

Their eighth opponent of the season was Boston College. BC was also undefeated and untied in seven games. These two teams were considered among the leaders in scoring and this was being billed as the biggest game of the season in the East.[27] Critics believed that Georgetown would have to beat Boston College in order to receive full recognition of its three-year winning streak.[28]

In comparing the two teams, BC had scored 261 points to Georgetown's 247 points, and defensively, BC had surrendered 27 points to the Hoyas' 22 points. The only basis for a direct comparison was the lone common opponent, Temple. Georgetown defeated the Owls 14-0, while BC slipped by them 22-20. Both of these results seemed to support the belief that Georgetown was a little stronger defensively, while BC was somewhat more powerful in the offensive department.[29] In terms of personnel, Georgetown had the superior front line, so they were expected to gain more first downs on the ground. BC had the better chance to make the big play with All-American Charlie O'Rourke.[30]

On November 16, 1940, 34,000 fans jammed Fenway Park to watch the biggest game to hit Boston since 1928. Within five minutes of the opening kickoff, Georgetown jumped out to an early lead of 10-0, on a Lio field goal and a Koshlap touchdown run. BC scored next on a pass from O'Rourke to Woronicz, but the extra point was not converted, making the score 10-6. When first period ended Hagerty put in his second team. BC scored again on a short run by Holovac and the extra point was added, making the score 13-10, giving the Eagles their first lead of the game. Georgetown came out of the second half and marched 66 yards, with McFadden scoring on a triple reverse; the extra point failed, making the score 16-13, in favor of Georgetown. BC scored on the next series to take the lead for good, 19-16. The Hoyas were able to get to the BC 20-yard line but opted on going for the win and were unable to score. BC took over and stalled for three downs. Then occurred the most famous play in Georgetown football history. Charlie O'Rourke took the ball and "played hide and seek with the mighty linemen," intentionally scoring a safety, which helped to run the clock down. Georgetown did get the ball back, but were unable to score and the score ended BC 19, Georgetown 18.[31] This was undoubtedly the greatest game in Hoya football history.

Here is what some of the sports writers who witnessed the contest had to say:

Grantland Rice: An American football classic...In many ways it was probably the greatest football game ever played by colleges or by the pros. I doubt that any other team could have beaten the other.

Lawrence Robinson (*The New York World Telegram*): One of the great games of football history.

Jack Munhall (*The Washington Post*): A football epic to rank with the most exciting ever played.

Although Georgetown lost the game, it was still recognized nationally as a great football team. It was even said that the loss to BC did more to enhance their future reputation than did the 23-game unbeaten streak.[32]

Georgetown finished the regular season with an 8-0 win over George Washington, bringing their season record to 8-1. They were ranked thirteenth in the country, according to the Associated Press, and were somewhat surprisingly chosen to meet Mississippi State in the 1941 Orange Bowl.

The Hoyas' opponent was slightly favored by the sports writers and the oddsmakers to win the game; however, the American Football Coaches Association picked Georgetown to easily defeat the Maroons, on the ground that the Hoyas were superior material, both in quantity and quality.[33]

The 1941 Orange Bowl drew the largest crowd in its history up to that time, with over 35,000 anxiously awaiting fans, ready to see the Hoyas of Georgetown University take on the Maroons of Mississippi State.

The Maroons got off to an early 7-0 lead, when they blocked Joe Daniels' punt and recovered it in the end zone. In the second period, standout halfback Billy Jefferson of the Maroons plunged over for their second touchdown, making the score 14-0. In the second half, the Hoyas came out inspired. Jules Koshlap hit Big Jim Castiglia for a big gain. Then Lou Ghecas caught a pass and spun his way to the 3-yard line. Koshlap followed with a plunge for a yard and then Castiglia rammed over for the score. Lio kicked the extra point, making the score 14-7, which would unfortunately be the final score. The Hoyas dominated the game in every way except the score. They outrushed the Maroons 122 yards to 109 yards. Also, the Hoyas had more yards through the air, 112 yards to the Maroons' 51 yards.[34] In addition, they had 14 first downs, doubling the Maroons' first downs.

After the game, the Hoyas still felt as though they were the better team. The coach of Mississippi State, Allyn McKeen, said that "Georgetown was the best team we played all year."[35]

At the end of the season there were many who deserved credit for raising Georgetown football to such a high level of competence. There was Augie Lio, the All-American pick who later played with the professional New York Giants; Jim Castiglia, the bruising fullback, selected by the Philadelphia Eagles; Al Matuza, who went to the Chicago Bears; and speedy halfback Lou Ghecas, picked up by the Eagles.[36]

The 1940 Hoyas were successful, not because they were stocked with talent but because the seniors were fast friends and unselfish toward each other. This is Castiglia's expressed opinion.

Castiglia recalled also to the writer that the seniors had decided to come to Georgetown as a group, and not to separate. The believed that if they went to school together they would be more likely to do well. They called themselves the New Jersey group, reminiscent of their family origins. Another thing that attracted them to Georgetown was their admiration of Hagerty as a coach.[37]

Besides the talent and the *esprit de corps* attitude, the Georgetown squad had someone who was the most important ingredient in their team, and that was Jack Hagerty. He is considered by many to be one of the greatest coaches of all time. When asked by the present author, both Augie Lio and Jim Castiglia said that he was the greatest coach they had ever had, including their mentors in the pros. Castiglia said: "The # 1 quality in a coach, I feel, is that the coach be a human being and Jack Hagerty was just a fine human being; I have nothing but the highest esteem for him."[38] Castiglia also said that Hagerty "was very knowledgeable of the game and he had a strong fundamental foundation in instituting a system."[39] Hagerty would prepare his teams both mentally and physically. Although he was a very inspirational coach, he would never say in a game "You gotta win at any cost."[40] He was very fair, and to some extent this led to the loss in the BC game. He was accustomed to giving his substitutes a chance to play after the first quarter. In the BC game he followed this tradition. It was while the substitutes were in the game that BC regained the lead. According to the rule at the time, a player removed from the game could not be allowed back in during the same half in which he was taken out.[41]

This is how the famous sports writer Grantland Rice paid tribute to Jack Hagerty:

> There can be no set system of ranking football coaches....However, in my opinion, Jack Hagerty of Georgetown belongs high up in this list among the very best that football knows....Hagerty is not only the best when it comes to fundamentals and the mechanical side of the game, he is also a fine inspirational type....[42]

With at least nine starters graduating after the 1940 season, much rebuilding was necessary. The team would be built around gigantic Alfred Blozis, a senior who stood 6'6" and weighed 245 pounds. At that time he was also the world record holder in the shotput. Blozis later played professionally for the New York Giants in 1942 and 1943, and then was named to the All-Pro team.[43]

After these accomplishments, it seemed strange that it took Blozis until November of his junior year to get a substantial amount of playing time. Jim Castiglia explained that Blozis had just not had enough experience as a football player to start over one of the more experienced tackles, either Fullilove or Daniels. Castiglia said, "You could see that in a year or two he could be the greatest and what proved this was that he was picked on the all-time All-Giant team, after only playing two years for them."[44]

The 1941 team, with the incredible Al Blozis, finished 5-4. They had victories over Mississippi, George Washington, Maryland, North Carolina State, and Manhattan. Blozis was the standout of the season, breaking up the opposition's offense almost singlehandedly.[45]

The Hoyas were unbeaten in their first four games of the 1942 season. They won over Temple, Mississippi, Manhattan, and Auburn. Then the Hoyas' season took a turn for the worse, and they lost three straight games, to Detroit, Boston College, and North Carolina Preflight. They finished the season on a good note, winning their last two games: North Carolina State and George Washington. In the GW game, possibly the shortest punt in Hoya history was recorded, six inches by Art Hines.[46]

Notes

1a. Georgetown University Archives (hereafter GUA), Lauinger Library, Box 1, Athletics, Football, "Summary"; G.U. Athletic Office, Public Relations files.

1b. Ibid.

1c. *Georgetown College Journal* (hereafter *GCJ*), 3 (November 1874), p. 15.

2. *GCJ* 16 (October 1887), p. 20.

3. Morris Bealle, *The Georgetown Hoyas*, Washington, D.C., Columbia Publishing Co., 1947, p. 17.

4. Ibid., loc cit.

5. *GCJ* 20–22 (November 1892), p. 26.

6. *GCJ* 23–25 (November 1894), pp. 21–22.

7. *GCJ* 28 (December 1899), pp. 157–58.

8. *GCJ* 34 (October 1905), p. 137.

9. *GCJ* 34 (December 1905), p. 159.

10. *The Washington Herald*, December 1, 1932.

11. Bealle, op. cit., p. 143.

12. Ibid., p. 146.

13. Ibid., loc cit.

14. *The Washington Post*, December 13, 1937.

15. Bealle, op. cit., p. 155.

16. *Ye Domesday Booke*, 1939, p. 254.

17. Ibid., loc cit.

18. Bealle, op. cit., p. 161.

19. *Ye Domesday Booke*, 1939, p. 254.

20. Bealle, op. cit., p. 159.

21. *The New York Herald*, September 30, 1939.

22. *The Syracuse Herald*, October 15, 1939.

23. Unidentified newspaper clipping, December 4, 1939, GUA.

24. Unidentified newspaper clipping, November 30, 1939, GUA.

25. *The Washington Post*, December 30, 1940.

26. Unidentified newspaper clipping, October 3, 1940, GUA.

27. Unidentified newspaper clipping, November 7, 1940, GUA.

28. Ibid.

29. Ibid.

30. Ibid.

31. Unidentified newspaper clipping, November 17, 1940, GUA.

32. *The Washington Post*, November 24, 1940.

33. *The Daily News*, December 31, 1940.

34. *Nashville Tennessean*, January 2, 1941.

35. *Miami Daily News*, January 2, 1941.

36. Interview with Jim Castiglia, January 8, 1988.

37. Ibid.

38. Ibid.

39. Ibid.

40. Ibid.

41. Ibid.

42. Grantland Rice, quoted in *The Hoya*, October 22, 1976.

43. *The Hoya*, October 22, 1976, Alumni file, GUA.

44. Interview with Jim Castiglia, January 8, 1988.

45. Bealle, op. cit., p. 169.

46. Bealle, op. cit., p. 175.

Basketball at Georgetown College

Michael Aiken

Georgetown University basketball competition with other schools began in 1907 with the appointment of a coach, Maurice Joyce, and the compilation of a 5-1 winning record against such rivals as Maryland and Virginia, the latter being defeated by the Hoyas twice. Before that time, basketball at the Hilltop had been strictly intramural, with occasional sorties against ragtail teams assembled by neighboring high schools.

This first group of Georgetown hoopsters was not recognized by the executive board of the Athletic Association of the University, which coldly instructed them to find their own source for funding.

On February 27, 1907, the first game was played with George Washington University's team as rival. The scene was the Hoyas' Ryan Gymnasium, then considered—believe it or not—as one of the best athletic arenas in the south.

One is naturally eager to know, for historical reasons, who were the students who comprised our first basketball team ever. But because of a fiendish habit doubtless infused by the demon of inaccuracy, the *Journal* reporters provide us with the players' last names only. These were, from Georgetown: "Rice, Downey, Simon, Shumm, Mullens, Lavelle, Pallen [not Condé Pallen], and Murray."

This initial contest was lost by Georgetown in a fast-paced, down-to-the-wire struggle, with the remarkably low score of 18 to 16. In a return match later that season the Hoyas avenged the loss by a 15-13 win over their cross-town rivals. Shooting from the floor, it seems clear, had not yet been fully developed by either side.

The season concluded for Georgetown with a 2-2 record.

The 1908 team showed that our basketball fortunes were on the march. Encouraged by a sympathetic Jesuit President of the University, Fr. David Buel, the Hoyas were now playing their home games in Washington's Convention Hall against opponents including Penn, Navy, Cornell, Virginia, Columbia and Fordham. The 1909 team was considered to be one of the best in the nation. It did not qualify for the NAAC Tournament, although it was acknowledged to be the undisputed holder of the Southern Collegiate Conference title. Its record for the season was 9-5.

The school's Athletic Association gave up on Georgetown basketball in 1909. The stated reason for the divorce was the team's unpaid debt to the University in the amount of $188.54.

From then on, until the coming of John Thompson in 1972, our basketball record was, with a few brief periods of partial success, nothing to send Hoya fans leaping and shouting, to Wisconsin and M. The team reached the NCAA Tournament first round in 1953 and 1970, but quickly bowed out at that point.

In reviewing this pre-Thompson era of Georgetown basketball, a question occurred to the author: Did students and players of that period derive more fun from the game than the students and players of today, and did a larger proportion of students participate in the fun than is the case now?

With not the slightest intention of depreciating the magnificent achievement of John Thompson, the present writer is forced to answer these two queries affirmatively. His opinion may not be the popular one, but it is sincere. One might ask, is the pressure worth its cost? Does the accompanying commercialization diminish (at least to a degree) the enjoyment?

***

The record of Georgetown basketball under Thompson speaks, nevertheless, for itself, is here summarized, and, admittedly, warms any loyal Hoya heart:

The Thompson Years

1986–87:   Record 29-5
   NCAA Tournament-Southeast Regional Finals
   Big East Tournament and Conference Champions
1985–86:   Record 24-8
   NCAA Tournament–Midwest Regional
1984–85:   Record 35-3
   NCAA Tournament Final Four
   Big East Tournament Champions
1983–84:   Record 34-3
   NCAA Tournament Champions
   Big East Tournament and Conference Champions
1982–83:   Record 22-10
   NCAA Tournament–Midwest Regional
1981–82:   Record 30-7
   NCAA Tournament Final Four
   Big East Tournament Champions
1980–81:   Record 20-12
   NCAA Tournament–East Regional
   Runner up in Big East Conference
1979–80:   Record 26-6
   NCAA East Regional Finals
   Big East Tournament Champions
   Big East regular season Co-Champions
1978–79:   Record 24-5
   ECAC Upstate–Southern Champions
   ECAC Southern Division Champions
1977–78:   Record 23-8
   N.I.T. Semifinals
   ECAC Semifinals
1976–77:   Record 19-9
   N.I.T. First Round
   ECAC Semifinals
1975–76:   Record 21-7
   NCAA West Regional
   ECAC Southern Division Champions

1974–75:   Record 18-10
NCAA Mideast Regional
ECAC Southern Division Champions
1973–74:   Record 13-13
First winning record for Thompson
1972–73:   Record 12-14
Vast improvement for Georgetown basketball in
Thompson's first year[1]

John Thompson had led his team from modest goals in the beginning to a National Championship, three Final Four appearances, five Big East Conference championships, 11 NCAA Tournament appearances, and a total of 350 wins vs. 120 losses. In addition, he had seen 18 of his players drafted in the NBA and—more importantly—51 of 53 of his players graduated from Georgetown.

But Thompson's achievement goes far beyond these successes.

During every minute of his work with his squad he is an educator in the truest sense of that term, as well as a basketball mentor. His record (as of 1988) of 51 graduates out of his 55 senior players is well known.

What is not often recognized, however, is the unusually large proportion of his former players currently holding positions on middle-management or even higher levels in business, industry, and, in a few instances, the professions. Here is the record, with professional basketball positions not included:

Ronnie Highsmith ('88)	Housing Inspector, D.C.
Michael Jackson ('86)	Accepted by John Kennedy School of Government, Harvard University.
Ralph Dalton ('85)	Obtained graduate degree from Georgetown and currently works on Wall Street.
Fred Brown ('84)	Color commentator with Home Team Sports.
Gene Smith ('84)	Currently works for the promotion department of Nike of Atlanta.

Ron Blaylock ('82)   Currently with Paine Webber and a member of Georgetown Board of Regents. Active in charities.

Ed Spriggs ('82)   Strength coach and video coordinator at G.U. Former asst. athletic director at St. Peter's.

Al Dutch ('80)   Currently a supervisor at Georgetown's fieldhouse.

John Duren ('80)   Owns Duren Enterprises, a sporting goods retailer.

Steve Martin ('79)   Former Chief Accountant for the World Fair. Now an administrator for the NBA.

Craig Esherick ('78)   Georgetown Law School graduate. Currently an assistant coach at G.U.

Ed Hopkins ('78)   Currently a U.S. postal worker in Baltimore.

Derrick Jackson ('78)   Currently a minister of religion in the suburbs of Chicago.

Mike Riley ('78)   Former assistant headmaster at Gonzaga H.S. Now assistant for Thompson.

Notes

This article is based on "Athletics," Box 6, covering the period 1887–1910, in the Georgetown University Archives, Lauinger Library; on several issues of the *Georgetown College Journal,* and on information provided by the Georgetown University Athletic Association. Special courtesy and assistance was accorded to the author by Mr. Francis Rienzo and Mr. Craig Esherick. Special thanks also to: T.F. Boyle, "Historical Account of Basketball at Georgetown University," in *Georgetown College Journal* 35 (1906–1907), pp. 199 and passim.

1. Source: *Official Game Program-Georgetown Basketball 1985–86.* G.U. Athletic Department.

V. Books, Buildings, and Test Tubes

"The Museum" in the Healy Building.

Chemistry laboratory in the Healy Building.

The Classics at Georgetown

Matthew M. Yaeger

"Hoya Saxa!" This, one of the most distinctive sports "cheers" on the campus at Georgetown University, is a reminder of the prominent place occupied during the late nineteenth century by the study of the ancient Latin and Greek languages at the school.

The phrase's origin is said to have been a more or less spontaneous exclamation of admiration by student spectators at a Hoya football game. "Hoya" was a bastardization of the Greek word for "Oh!," or "Hooray," and "Saxa" was the Latin word for rocks. The intimation was that, on the occasion, the Georgetown team was presenting to the attacks of their opponents a rock-like defense.

In 1870 "Horace Academy" was established at the College, a volunteer group of students devoted to doing extra readings in the verses of the Roman poet, and to translating some of them into English. What were to be considered the best of these latter would be published in the newly founded (1872) *Georgetown College Journal.*

During the following decades until approximately World War I, many such English versions of selected odes and epodes appeared in the campus publication. While obviously not professional work, the literary quality of most of the translations is surprisingly high—which emboldens the present writer to let his readers in on what has been hitherto a well-kept secret.

This ode, "To Pyrrha," became the subject of a great number of translations.

Liber I Carmen I

Quis multa gracilis te puer in rosa
perfusus liquidis urget odoribus
　　grato, Pyrrha, sub antro?
　　　　cui flavam religas comam

simplex munditiis? Heu quotiens fidem
mutatosque deos flebit et aspera
　　nigris aequora vestris
　　　　emirabitur insolens

qui nunc te fruitur credulus aurea
qui semper vacuam, semper amabilem
　　sperat, nescius aurae
　　　　fallacis; miseri, quibus

intemptata nites; me tabula sacer
votiva paries indicat uvida
　　suspendisse potenta
　　　　vestimenta maris deo.

The following translation appeared in issue 1 of volume 11 of the *Journal.*

Ad Pyrrham

Come, Pyrrha, I would know
Your newest lover, e'en the pretty boy
Who dallies near thee now
The scented youth that oft disports with thee
In rosy bowers

For whom those golden tresses all unbound
Free, unconfined

In beauty unadorned the sport of every wind?
How many a time and often he will bewail
An altered fortune and thy broken vow,
And, fearful, wonder at the unfriendly gale
By many a one, alas, ere now
Experienced in sorrow!

And he, poor love-sick boy,
Nor dreams of thee as aught save mistress true,
His own forever, ever-loving Pyrrha!
Soon he'll know thee as thou art,
Sweet of tongue but false in heart;
The summer breezes not so fickle as Pyrrha.

Ah, destined his to be a wretched life,
Whose path of duty thou shall e'er illume
With one of those bright smiles that Father Jove
Paints maiden faces with to show that all
is pure within!

For me, my votive offering
Too plainly tells the tale of shipwrecked love;
My sea-drenched garments all,
Now dedicated to the Power above
That rules the ocean's rise and fall,
May warning be
To the many: beware the siren glance of Pyrrha.[1]

The succeeding issue of the *Journal* printed another translation of the same ode.

To Pyrrha

Well, my fair Pyrrha, tell us, pray,
What comely lad, with perfumes showered
Is pressing now his ardent suit
Upon you 'mid your roses bowered
That golden crest lies on whose breast,
Luxurious simplicity?

    Ah, his what tears for broken vows—
    What fears for fate's duplicity!

    How will he—used to skies that smile—
    Stand awe-struck when the furious wind
        Drags black clouds o'er the roughening waves—
    Soft fool, who clasps thee now all kind—

    Hopes thee to proves aye worthy love,
    Aye loving—thee capricious breeze!
        Ill-fated they who meet unwarned
    They smile—the storm calm of the seas!

    For me—the temple's walls declare
    Thy guileful charms, thy frown's alarms
        Are past; my wrecked heart's hanging there
    And toga, vowed the God of storms.[2]

These two attempts at translating the Pyrrha ode are both admirable and in some ways each should be commended. The Georgetown students who produced them were both introspective and innovative in their use of the English language to convey Horace's Latin ideas. The translations, however, are hardly similar, thus confirming the value of translation as an intellectual tool. It forces the student to think, to manipulate his own language in order to better express the ancient one and to make educated choices in his interpretation of the original. These two works exemplify the choices and thinking that must go into any translation. The first might be called more modernistic while the second is a more traditional rendering of the poem.

The first of the attempts at translating Ode I.5 is what I have termed more "modernistic," for several reasons. First and foremost is the actual structure of the student's translation. He is rather free in imagining the manner in which he thinks Horace might have written the poem in English. In dividing the verse into stanzas he digresses from Horace's use of four and instead uses five. Also, the original Latin poem was composed in what is called an Asclepiad meter. This particular one is called Asclepiad(d). It consists of two Asclepiad lines, each having twelve syllables; a pherecratean, with seven syllables; and a glyconic, with eight. This form is followed in each of the four stanzas. G.'s translation, however, does not attempt to preserve any of this structure. The five stanzas vary in length from five to eight lines and the lines themselves range anywhere from four to thirteen syllables. The poem also combines some rhyming couplets with a curious *bc bc* rhyme scheme in certain stanzas. Another stanza makes no attempt at rhyme. The seeming haphazardness of the whole endeavor might lead one to wonder exactly how diligent the translator was in his analysis. However, certain things must draw the reader to a different conclusion.

The translation is very carefully crafted. In choosing to change the original drastically for dramatic purposes, G. is treading in difficult waters. However, he comes out very nicely. The surprising rhyme scheme adds an emphasis not possible with a traditional rhythm achieved in either Latin or English poetry. When a particular couplet is rhymed effectively, it brings instant recognition and attention to it in the context of the stanza.

Therefore, the "bewail/gale" rhyme in the third and fifth lines of the end stanza and the "art/heart" rhyme in the fourth and fifth lines of the third stanza are marked by a particular power. It is clear what G. wants to warn the reader about: the unbounded passion of Pyrrha knows no shame. Horace apparently has also been charmed by Pyrrha's wiles and he is warning the reader. However, it is here that the translation is lacking. The student has compensated well for many of the images presented earlier and encompasses much of the feeling of unrequited love from the original. His error, however, arises from his adding to the translation. He produces the bold statement in the last line to "beware the siren glance of Pyrrha." Horace's subtlety in his own last stanza is overlooked. He admits his own shipwrecked love and, I think, leaves the preaching he has already done open-ended. He knows how powerful the attraction to Pyrrha can be and perhaps knows that this youth, too, will be unable to resist her advances. Perhaps every young boy should go through what Horace did. The point added by G. is either self-evident or one that Horace himself did not intend to make. Overall, though, the translation fares well. Since G. chooses to depart so markedly from the original style and structure, an intimate analysis of the original text, although helpful, is better left to the next translation.

In this latter one, a much more "traditional" attempt is made. Consequently, an understanding of the Latin text is helpful in showing how it serves as an inspiration for the translator. He tries to maintain the rhythm achieved through regular meter in Horace's ode by himself instituting a regular meter in his translation. The original Asclepiad meter would be very difficult to match in English, so our author chooses a simple, repeated eight-syllable line. Since English is not inflected, it is difficult to determine what R.'s intention might have been for individual accents.

By attempting to maintain more of the original's flavor, this second translation has actually glossed over a few minor points that could drastically change the meaning of the poem. Before examining these, one should note that the first translator retains for the most part the original grammatical structure. His changes are made by the addition of qualifiers to explain himself. The second effort clearly mistranslates parts of the poem. First, the rendering of *cui* in line four is inaccurate. The translator interprets it as a genitive or ablative structure, transposing it into "on whose breast." Clearly, however, the words in the original have a dative sense. An action is implied by Pyrrha for the boy. She, then, is courting him. The young boy is the receiver of the action performed by Pyrrha. Addressing Pyrrha, the line reads, "For whom do you bind back your golden hair." Pyrrha actively seeks her lovers and then later discards them. This, although a minor correction, can change the whole interpretation of the poem. It also attains the eventual goal in translating—the achievement of more precision in meaning and more clarity in expression than was in the original itself.

Overall, the poem could be described as *simplex munditiis*, just as Horace describes Pyrrha: "simple in its elegances" or "luxurious simplicity," as R. phrases it. The translation is basic in its statement and avoids the preaching that marred the other poem. The statement is a powerful one and I think may be closer to the intent of the original poem. Certainly, we have a warning, but one not necessarily for consumption by the youth. The poem is for Pyrrha and Horace directly addresses her in the first stanza. She is older now, her lover being characterized as *gracilis puer*, "comely lad." Perhaps it is time for Pyrrha to settle down. Horace himself got over his shipwreck at Pyrrha's hand and he gives no indication that he doesn't think this boy will do likewise. I have noted before that I didn't think the earlier translation should have added the warning. This translation confirms my view.

Both these poems have weak and strong points. It is difficult to determine which is better and, hence, which best summarizes the poet's original feeling. However, as translations, both succeed.They are original pieces and epitomize the original thought inherent in a strong translation. Certainly, each sees Horace and his poetry differently but this is a mere by-product of the judgment that must go into a translation. As the translator chooses to express certain ideas, naturally other ideas are closed off. Therefore, vastly disparate translations can both be termed effective. This is the case with these two, only proving that great minds don's necessarily think alike, they just think.

The period following the turn of the century was a weak one for classical studies at Georgetown, as it was for many areas in academic life at the University. To come to this conclusion, I have followed the *Journal*'s development and production during this and later times. I have found that this gives the best account of the state of academia at any given time. Certainly, work produced by students is the best indicator of how well they are being taught and the work produced and printed in the *Journal* from 1900 to 1920 was not up to the high standards set in earlier or later periods. This somewhat stagnant state lingered until after the First World War.

After 1919, however, a great number of translations appeared in the *Journal*. It seems that with the prestige afforded by the awarding of the Horace Medal, more students were willing to try their hand at translating Rome's great lyric poet. This unfortunately led to a proliferation of bad translations, many of which weighed down the pages of the *Journal*. Here is an excerpt from one such:

I.4

Solvitur acris hiems grata vice veris et Favoni
trahuntque siccas machinae carinas
ac neque iam stabulis gaudet pecus aurator igni
nec prata canis albicant pruinis;

iam Cytherea choros ducit Venus imminente Luna,
iunctaeque Nymphis Gratiae decentes
alterno terram quatiunt pede, dum gravis Cyclopum
Volcanus ordens visit officinas

Nunc decet aut viridi nitidum caput impedine myrto
aut flore, terrae quem ferunt solutae;
nunc et in umbrosis Fauno decet immolare lucis,
seu poscat agna sive malit haedo,

pallida Mors aequo pulsat pede pauperum tabernas
regumque turris: o Beate Sesti,
vitae summa brevis spem nos vetat inchoare longam;
iam te premet nox fabulae que manes

et domus exilis Plutonia; quo simul mearis
nec regna vini sortiere talis
nec tenerum Lycidan mirabere, quo calet iuventus
nunc omnis et mox virgines tepebunt.

The translation begins…

I.4. *"Ad Libitum"*

When Winter's chains at last were worn,
  And gentle Spring again is born,
The kiels once more plough brine deep
And o'er the meads come bleating sheep.
etc.

The short lines and simple rhyme scheme here give the idea
of a carnival jingle. The poem, however, is a serious commen-

tary that Horace is making on youth and death. The image of Spring coming with death not far behind is a very powerful one. Horace encourages everyone to enjoy life while he can, for death is always lurking. The translation, however, leaves the reader with no real image, but only a series of failed rhymes.

The present author has attempted to improve the translation and here are his results:

I.4

The biting winter dissolves away with the welcome breath
    of spring,
  And the wind brings out all those dried out hulls of ships.
The sheep happily bound from the barn and the farmer from
    the hearth,
  as the meadows turn their white frost to green.
Venus now leads the dance under a leaning moon,
  This seemly group of Nymphs and Graces
Shakes the ground with their rhythmic beat,
  while red-hot Vulcan goes to his Cyclops' forges.

It's time again, to cover your glowing head
  with a sprig of Myrtle or a flower which Mother Nature
    alone begets;
And now it's time to sacrifice to Faunus under
  the shadowy trees, a lamb or a kid will do.

But pale Death pounds his knuckles with the same force
  on the poorest hut or the prince's palace: and Sertius,
even your money won't make this short life any longer;
  soon the night will be upon you...
Exiled to Hades
  You'll no longer see the toast
Or gape at delicate Lycidas, now the favorite
  of all the boys, soon of all the girls.

The translation, although certainly not perfect, captures better, its author trusts, the mood of the poem. Spring is coming but at the same time Death waits right around the corner. So enjoy life while you're young. Someday you won't be able to enjoy things as they are now, so grab what life you can! This certainly was not very well conveyed by the earlier effort which brought forth a jingly optimism not really in the original Latin. Horace realizes everyone's fate and could actually be termed somewhat pessimistic, at least moderately so. His poem celebrates new life but it also focuses very much on death. And so it must be translated with more balance, which the present author attempts to do.

Following the downswing of the educational system and intellectualism at Georgetown was an era in which the Classics and education in general flourished. Beginning during the First World War, this revival of the earlier great period lasted into the Second World War. The renaissance began with an increase in the number of essays published in the *Journal*. The Classics were still a frequent topic among these, although in general there was a much broader range of subjects.

The classical program began to pick up at this time, with the students again turning to some classical concerns. An essay on epic poetry delved into a definition of that genre: "Poetry is the art which has for its object the creation of intellectual delights by means of passionate and imaginative expression."[3] The students again were willing to tackle weighty problems and to make definitive judgments. This example of epic poetry is one, but there are many others during this time. As the war approached and great changes were occurring in every aspect of life, an increasing number of essays appeared, covering a broad focus from economics to history and literature. The emergence of specialization and subspecialization can be viewed in these essays. The students were making real stands on real issues that affected a wide range of ideas and systems. Editorials during this time went beyond what was immediately visible on the Georgetown campus. This orientation still dominates the educative process today. At this former time, a great deal of original literary work also appeared, along with an increased amount of the short fiction that would later dominate the *Journal*.

As the war ground to a halt and was placed at the back of people's minds, the *Journal* again changed focus to more literary concerns. However, it is indebted to this war for the great era of intellectual vigor that followed. The students, spurred on by the problems they faced, dealt with them in a fairly sophisticated way. When these problems were solved, student attention turned to other pursuits. One avenue avidly pursued was the Classics. The era of peace and prosperity was perfect for classical studies. It seems that classicism thrives best in an era of idealism such as that following World War I. After World War II, however, this idealism never returned and by the same token, neither has an intense interest in the Classics.

However, the Classics made a comeback during the 1920s. In volume 51 of the *Journal*, one particular writer, Bernard M. Wagner (later to become a distinguished teacher of English literature at Georgetown) was dominant as a translator of some of the Classics. Here is an excerpt from his translation of Liber II Carmen XII of Horace:

> quam nec ferre pedem dedecuit choris
> nec certare ioco nec dare bracchia
> ludentem nitidis virginibus sacro
>   Dianae celebris die.

> The most beautiful of all in the rhythmic flower-
>   strewn dance,
> Her wit is like tossed coins that glint and glance.
> She is the fairest of the maidens when the sacred
>   rite
> Of Diana's festival is done—airy and light
> She trips, a Queen, before the gazing throng.
> To her I raise my song.[4]

This is what a translation should be. Wagner obviously is a master of his own English language and effectively uses its rhythms to create a solid bit of poetry. He always adds something to the original, a little extra bit of style that Horace himself didn't achieve, a rhythm and rhyme that were perhaps not possible in Latin, and occasionally a better statement of point or emotion than that originally conveyed by Horace. In the same translations, Wagner is able to preserve a feel for the totality of image that Horace gives us. In short, he comes as close as anyone who has appeared in the *Journal* to rendering Horace beautifully into English. It is no surprise, then, that he is easily the most prolific writer in general during his student days at Georgetown. He produced over half the articles, translations and other literary material that appeared in volume 51 of the *Journal*. The natural assumption, then, is that his rich classical background benefited his other work. This is true. Consistently, the best writers are also the students able to render translations through good judgment and sound thinking.

Notes

1. *Georgetown College Journal* (hereafter *GCJ*) 11 (1883):1.
2. *GCJ* 11 (1883):15.
3. William Ratzenberger, "On Epic Poetry," *GCJ* 38 (1909):160.
4. Bernard Wagner, *GCJ* 51 (1923):199.

Bibliography

Durkin, Joseph T. 1963. *Georgetown University: The Middle Years*. Washington, D.C.: Georgetown University Press.

Gusdorf, Georges. 1973. *L'Avénement des Sciences Humanes au Siècle des Lumières*. Paris: Payot.

Georgetown College Catalogue, 1845–1965.

The Georgetown College Journal, vols. 1–81, 1872–1953.

Record Book of the Prefect of Studies, 1878. GUA 462.23.

Steiner, George. 1975. *After Babel: Aspects of Language and Translation*. New York: Oxford University Press.

Gaston Hall:
The Making of History

Eileen D. Roberts

What I have learned at Georgetown, in the three short years that I have been here, is a lesson which will affect my perception for the rest of my life. I have learned that I exist in the 1980s and the 1980s exist in me. I have learned that every event in my life and every piece of myself that I leave here is a piece of living history, history of myself and history of this age. I have learned that being the bearer of my own history is a great responsibility. I am the recipient of every age that has gone before me and I must share the story of what has gone before me with future generations. My age, my culture, my time is not a vacuum; it is a living, breathing entity, connected through time to every other age. It is I and I am it.

This was made most apparent to me during a trip I took in October of this year. The trip was to a place long and far away and right under my nose. Actually, it was above my nose. Father Durkin took me to the farthest corner of the University, to the top of Healy tower. I took with me a piece of my heart, a small scrap of metal from the reconstruction of my old dormitory, New North, a building which now houses offices instead of freshmen. On this small metal slug, I left a message:

> This is from the reconstruction of
> New North, my home.
> Left here on October 7, 1987
> By Eileen Roberts, Class of 1989.

When I was two stories above the face of the clock, among the dead pigeons and lost graffiti, I left the piece of my history. It became very clear to me as I reached up to place it on a window sill that one hundred years from now, I will be an artifact, a piece of history, someone a Georgetown student will wonder about and try to connect with.

I also remember the first time I had an inkling of this realization. It was during freshman orientation, in Gaston Hall, six stories below the window sill where my piece of history now lies. I looked around at the brand-new class of 1989 and at the frescoed walls which students eighty-eight years before had first seen and I felt an incredible tie to all of those students who had come here before me. Here, in Gaston Hall, was "history," I thought. Here was where generations of students would identify themselves with their past. Here was where the true history of the students lies.

It is in this light that I wish to confront Gaston Hall: as a piece of art, but more importantly, as a piece of history. As a piece of history which united my class and my age to the ages which have come before me. And to leave this piece of history, my interpretation, along with my small piece of metal, to the future generations.

The history of Gaston Hall begins with the Healy Building, in which it is located. Before the Healy Building made its appearance on Georgetown's campus, the university had an almost rural setting. The Georgian Colonial buildings on the grounds served all the functions of the university; there was no great auditorium nor separate housing facilities. Georgetown was becoming far too cramped in the nineteenth century for its growing reputation.

Father Patrick Healy, president of the university from 1873–1882, saw the need for a large building on campus which would serve the needs of the students. He planned it to be a complete student complex; Georgetown men would live on the top two floors, attend classes on the lower levels, and relax in the recreational facilities in the basement. This way, the university could truly develop a campus, with adequate room for all facets of university life.

The architects Father Healy chose for this undertaking were the firm of Smithmeyer and Pelz. John L. Smithmeyer and Paul Pelz, who later built the Library of Congress, chose to design the Healy Building in the Flemish Romanesque style.[1] This style is one of the many types used during the Victorian period in American architecture, a period known for its eclecticism. The Flemish Romanesque style, here in its revival form, has many characteristics present in the building; the stonework is the most obvious. The heavy masonry of the building is what gives it its strength and power. Some of the great stones, in various shades of gray, are local materials. Too heavy to be transported over long distances, they were quarried in Virginia, a few miles from the university.[2] These stones not only lend the Healy Building its historical spirit, relating it to the pure Romanesque structures of A.D. 800–1200,[3] but also point the building toward the future, grounding it permanently for the coming twentieth century.

Other Flemish Romanesque features animate the facade of the building. The numerous small windows and the high pitched roof refer to the snowy climate of the Northern European countries.[4] The rounded arches of the doorways and windows, as opposed to the pointed arches of many Gothic cathedrals, are a purely Romanesque form. But it is the spires and towers of the Flemish Romanesque style which make the Healy Building readily identifiable. The clock tower in the center of the building is Georgetown's most recognizable landmark, its finials reaching high above the surrounding campus. It is not surprising that Smithmeyer and Pelz planned the Healy Building in this style. Due to the influence of architect Henry Hobson Richardson, the Romanesque style was one of the most popular forms in later nineteenth century American architecture. His use of heavy stonework and rounded arches gave rise to the term "Richardsonian Romanesque." His Trinity Church in Boston (c. 1875) is a massive Romanesque building, articulated by low rounded arches, a high, octagonal tower and polychromatic stonework. Richardson moved from this Boston commission to work on Harvard's campus, constructing such buildings as Sever Hall in 1878–1880. His work would have definitely influenced Smithmeyer and Pelz, his Washington, D.C. contemporaries.

The Healy Building, massive in its weighty stonework, and embellished with its Romanesque forms, was completed in 1879. It was a work representative of Georgetown, the locally quarried stones set by some of the student themselves.[5] But the construction had been long and arduous. Funding was difficult to come by, and only by a final donation from Daniel O'Connor, father of a Georgetown Jesuit, was the building completed. This left no money for the decoration of the large auditorium space on the third floor of the building. The hall was left a large open "barn-like" space when the Healy Building opened.[6] There was a need for the auditorium as there was no other space on campus adequately large for plays or other campus functions, but the funding was not available. For years, when the room was in use, the high ceilings were concealed by decorations and draperies.[7] It was not until 1900, with the hiring of artist Brother Francis Schroen, S.J., nearly twenty years after the completion of the Healy Building, that Gaston Hall as we know it came into being.

Francis C. Schroen was born in Bavaria in 1857 and emigrated with his family to Baltimore while still a child. His family was a large, poor Catholic one and it became necessary for Schroen to begin work at an early age.[8] He was apprenticed as a tailor, his father's trade, while still a young boy. But Schroen was an artistic child and not at all interested in being a tailor. He asked his parents for drawing lessons, yet permission was denied because such things were an extravagance which they could not afford.[9] However, Schroen was so determined not to become a tailor that he left the trade and became a housepainter at the age of twenty. His work as a housepainter included decorating, which soon became his specialty. His employers, the firm of Emmart and Quarterly, recognized his unique talent and prompted the young artist to study drawing at the Maryland Institute in Baltimore.[10]

At the age of twenty-two, Schroen married Mary E. Meldick, a converted Catholic. The couple had three daughters. In quick succession, Schroen lost his two eldest daughters to diphtheria and his wife died in childbirth. Left with only his youngest daughter, Margaret Mary, Schroen moved in with a married sister and eventually placed his daughter in a boarding school.[11]

Devastated by the deaths of his wife and children and crushed by a series of financial losses,[12] Schroen became involved with spiritism and the occult. According to his own account, he created a ouija board for himself and fancied that he was communicating with his deceased wife.[13] Soon afterwards, Schroen began to work with a pencil and tablet, asking questions in his mind and watching his hand write automatically with the pencil.[14] The project began to take up most of his time and even while working on decorating jobs, Schroen would experiment with the occult. It began to take on a sinister nature as the answers he received to his silent questions became "obscene blasphemous and shocking."[15]

Patrick J. Cormican, Schroen's biographer, explains the final incident in Schroen's experimentation:

He grew impatient and asked in the name of God who was communicating. The answer came in the shape of an unintelligible scrawl. Finally, he said: "I adjure you in the name of the living God to tell me who you are." Then with painful squirming, the operating intelligence slowly wrote the single word "Beelzebub"...[16]

Schroen, without questioning the incident, truly believed himself to be possessed. As the story is told by Cormican, he immediately went to his old Catholic church, St. Michael's in Baltimore, and, begging salvation, decided to enter the priesthood.[17] Placing his daughter in a Visitation academy near Baltimore, he entered the Jesuit novitiate on June 21, 1898.[18] He decided, because of his skills as a decorator and an artist, to become a laybrother of the order rather than a priest. In this way, "he could use his skill for decorating churches to the edification of the faithful and to the glory of God."[19] It is not surprising, due to the curious circumstances surrounding Schroen's conversion, that he so ardently took up the task of decorating the churches, chapels, libraries and halls to which he was sent by his order. Evidence of his work is found in churches in Boston, New Orleans, Baltimore and Jamaica. But it is his work in Washington, D.C., his first great commission as a Jesuit laybrother, which graces the Healy Building.

During the years of 1897–1899, Paul Pelz kept in contact with the new university president, Father J. Havens Richards, concerning the completion of Gaston Hall. Apparently, the new president had been accepting designs from different artists for the decoration of the hall so that everything would be ready when enough money was raised to finish work on the auditorium. Pelz was adamant that the decoration of the great hall should do his architecture justice. Upon seeing certain plans for decoration, he was appalled that they did not fit with his own work and refused to suffer the humiliation of seeing his work in the hands of those who clearly did not appreciate it.[20] So, Gaston Hall remained undecorated while its walls and ceilings were paneled in beautiful Florida pine with money raised from alumni donations. According to a newspaper account of October 1889:

> Within a week, the scaffolding (in Gaston Hall) will be taken down, showing the most beautiful ceiling in the city. It is paneled in white Florida pine, with massive polished girders, and an elaborate metal cornice of beautiful design in Gothic arches and brackets finished in bronze. The walls are plastered with white sand finish, the light-tinted coloring contrasting well with the dark ceiling, making a very beautiful and striking effect.[21]

However, in 1900, the work of Brother Francis Schroen came to the attention of Father Richards in Georgetown. Schroen was assigned to decorate the ceilings and walls of the Healy Building and to design a great mural for Gaston Hall.

Schroen's work in the entrance hall of the Healy Building, on the first floor, is a wonderful example of his skills as a decorator. The artist used the motif of the foliage of Georgetown to adorn the hallway. Winding across the ceiling are the leaves of the most predominant species at Georgetown: the beech, the oak, the sycamore and the chestnut.[22] Rather than using a stencil to execute these forms, Schroen painted them all free-hand. Each leaf is a unique unit, as it is found in nature.[23] Cormican cites a "contemporary Washington newspaper" which discussed Schroen's method:

> ...the surface is first covered with a composition of the consistency of a thick batter which is worked up into a stippled and repped ground; and on this, while in a plaster state, the design is executed free hand by means of a spatula, with a gliding motion...[24]

Schroen then went on to decorate the parlors on either side of the reception hall in much the same way, using flowers as the motif, rather than leaves. Each parlor is embellished with a different flower: the rose, the magnolia, the chrysanthemum, the daisy and the hollyhock.[25] One can imagine the arduous task of executing each leaf and flower, without a stencil or pattern, presumably while the artist was upside-down on the scaffolding. Yet, each figure is perfect in size and form. The Georgetown community raved over Schroen's work at the time. The *Georgetown College Journal* noted that although before the parlors had been in a sad state, now they were "classic bowers."[26]

> no mere conventional flowers are they, no perfunctory work of the mechanic; the truth to nature, the perfection of each leaf and fibre, the harmony of the tones of color, mark the talent and conscience of the genuine artist.[27]

Schroen continued to work his way up in the Healy Building, concentrating next on the philodemic room and the hallway outside the president's office on the second floor. In the philodemic room, he employed a simple yet befitting theme; he garnished the ceiling with golden vines which surround the names of the great debaters of the century. The names of Abraham Lincoln and Stephen Douglas share the ceiling with the likes of Wendell Phillips and Charles Sumner. The ceiling outside the president's office looks much like the philodemic room, but here Schroen ensconced the Latin titles of Georgetown's areas of study: theologica, mathematica, rhetorica, poesis, chimia, etc. But it was Gaston Hall which became the artist's crowning glory.

He intended his work in Gaston Hall, particularly the mural over the auditorium stage, to be symbolic of the religious beliefs he held so fervently. Each figure he created would stand for an "abstract truth."[28] Schroen explained this intention in an interview with the *Boston Sunday Post*, years later:

> Very few people have known how much study, scheming and planning are required to carry out the ideas in ecclesiastical decorating. I have always planned to have every figure mean something. It must be symbolical even to the smallest scroll. Without this, in my

opinion, the whole attractiveness, purpose and beauty of decoration are lost.[29]

Because the work was a form of religious devotion and philosophical expression for the artist, he refused to accept pay for it.[30] Although the Alumni Association had planned to pay him $4,000.00, the total bill came to only $827.50, which must have been the fee for Schroen's few assistants and for the materials.[31] The artist worked mostly on his own in the great hall while his daughter, Margaret Mary, an accomplished musician, played the harp.[32]

Schroen's work in Gaston Hall begins with the seals of each of the prominent Jesuit colleges and universities in the United States and abroad. The emblems, a popular Jesuit art, served to put Georgetown University in a worldwide setting. It is no accident that the emblem of Georgetown occupies the central position in Gaston Hall. In union with the other university seals, it shows our roots and our fellowship, but it also asserts our strength as a major institution. It is the continuation of Father Patrick Healy's vision to have Georgetown gain universal recognition.

With the assistance of Father John Whitney, S.J. (Father Richards' successor), Brother Schroen received sketches, pencil rubbings and ink drawings of the emblems of each major Jesuit college. Many of these came with congratulatory letters, as word of Schroen's work spread to the other universities. From St. Louis:

> I am delighted to hear that your grand building and splendid hall are nearing completion and that everything is being done on a scale befitting the most splendid college building I have ever seen.[33]

Carefully, the artist copied each emblem, with exact renderings of figures and colors, onto the walls of Gaston Hall. Alphabetically arranged according to location, they make a beautiful border around the room. Other emblems of importance, such as the emblem of the Alumni Association and the various areas of study at Georgetown, adorn the wall under the string of university seals.

However, it is Brother Schroen's great murals behind the stage of Gaston Hall which are the focus of the great auditorium. It is here that we truly see his plan to paint symbolic art, art which conveyed his deepest beliefs. The mural is composed of two pieces: "Art, Alma Mater, Science" and "Morality, Faith, Patriotism." The two pieces, each containing three figures, exist side by side on the west wall of Gaston Hall.

"Art, Alma Mater, Science" is a rendering of three classically garbed figures which resemble Roman goddesses. They wear flowing white robes with luxurious capes draped around their shoulders. The figure of Alma Mater stands on a pedestal in the center of the composition. A laurel wreath encircles her head. Serenely, she looks straight ahead, holding in her hands two similar wreaths with which she is crowning the kneeling figures of Art and Science. The figure of Art kneels at the feet of Alma Mater with three objects, a palette, a lyre and a book. Across from her, also kneeling, is the figure of Science, who carries with her books and a globe.

"Morality, Faith, Patriotism," the companion piece, has three similarly garbed figures. In the center, the figure of Faith is seated on a throne. While Schroen's other figures appear very secular, Faith bears a resemblance to the Virgin Mary, as she is typically depicted. A cloak is draped over her head and shoulders. In her hand, she holds an open book which shows the symbols of the Alpha and the Omega. It has been suggested by Dr. Hubert Cloke that this figure is a possible reference to the funerary statue executed by St. Gaudens for the wife of Henry Adams. The statue, in Rock Creek Cemetery, caused a great deal of distress at the time because the figure was so foreboding. Instead of looking up, as Schroen's figure does, St. Gaudens' figure, clothed and seated in the exact same manner, hides her face in despair. The hopelessness and melancholy nature of the funerary monument made the statue an unpopular one. It is possible that the figure of Faith is an attempt, on the part of Schroen, to redeem the figure, as her halo would seem to indicate. On either side of this figure stand Morality and Patriotism. Morality, her hand over her heart, holds the tablet of the ten commandments. She gazes upwards, toward heaven. Across from her stands Patriotism, holding a sword and shield. She stands erect and fixes her eyes defiantly ahead.

Without a doubt, Brother Schroen has rendered here the philosophy of the university: dedicated to art, science, our nation and the ideals of our faith. Yet, one finds it necessary to question Schroen's style. Why, in 1901, do we find classically garbed figures and ideals? The figures are, first of all, not entirely in keeping with the architecture of the Healy Building. Although the building uses Romanesque arches, its eclecticism and the period in which it was built give it the spirit of a High Victorian Gothic structure. Granted, the austerity of the figures complements the massive building, but in such an elaborate building, one does not expect the simplicity and rationality of classical figures. Romantic figures and natural forms, such as the foliage Schroen paints in the entrance hall, would be more in keeping with the style of the building.

It may be argued that what these classical figures represent, artistically, is a regression in style. The artists and architects of America had worked their way through the classical mode which best represented the ideals of the new democracy. Thomas Jefferson's Monticello and Virginia State Capitol are prime examples of this. But, then artists had moved on, working in Gothic forms in the nineteenth century which best exemplified the ideals of the romantic transcendentalist philosophers such as Emerson and Thoreau. Here, instead of progressing into another style, appropriate for the twentieth century, Francis Schroen turns back the clock. Why? What happened in the years between the construction of the Healy Building and the completion of Gaston Hall which would cause such a drastic reversal in style?

To answer this question, it is necessary to look at one of the most important cultural events of the nineteenth century: the Columbian Exposition of 1893, or, as it was commonly called, the Chicago World's Fair. The nineteenth century experienced a remarkable craze for World's Fairs, each one dedicated to exhibiting the fantastic new inventions of the day. They were "festivals of machine-age capitalism in which nation after nation showed off its industrial strength and the breadth of its colonial resources."[34] The Chicago World's Fair of 1893 was specifically designed to express the strength and power of America on the four hundredth anniversary of her discovery.

Architect Daniel Burnham was chosen to lead a team of the

most illustrious American architects in the designing of the fair. Included among the planners of the fair was Frederic Law Olmsted, whose job it was to design the plan for the grounds of the exposition. The area chosen for the fair was, at the time, open swamp land. Olmsted's plan included the dredging and restructuring of the area to make it possible for buildings to be constructed on the land. Olmsted included room for great monuments and buildings, but also for a series of lagoons and basins to add to the aesthetic view of the fair. Walkways encircled the area and opened up onto a great central waterway on which the main buildings were located.

Burnham and his staff of architects chose to create the fair as a great classical city; every building would be done in a classical style, using Greek and Roman forms. This style was chosen, not only because each architect was well versed in the classical forms, but because it was thought to embody the ideals of the American democracy. By creating Roman structures, the buildings were automatically related, in the mind of the viewer, to the buildings of the original Roman Republic. After the American Revolution, this was the most popular form of architecture in the United States. Since the Chicago World's Fair was intended to be a celebration of Columbus' discovery of America, the architects thought there was no better style in which to build.

The string of white temple-like structures which encompassed the central "Court of Honor" gave rise to the nickname, "The White City." Viewers came by the hundreds of thousands to see the Columbian Exposition during the year in which it was held. One critic called it "a vision of beauty,"[35] another referred to it as "a sight unparalleled since Rome."[36] Although the Great White City was constructed to be torn down in a year's time, built mostly of plaster and staff,[37] America was enraptured by the vision of the fair.

The effects of the Columbian Exposition in America were phenomenal. The carefully designed plan of Frederic Law Olmsted was noted by city planners and landscapers nationwide. It was the beginning of the "City Beautiful" movement in America, which would lead to rationally ordered and planned cities, creating scenic areas of nature and buildings which related to each other and to the land.[38]

The Chicago World's Fair, which spearheaded the American Renaissance, was also the cause of a great change in American architecture. Due to the success of the fair, architects who previously worked in Gothic forms now turned back to the classical mode of architecture. Daniel Burnham went on to work in the American Renaissance style which had gained him notoriety at his fair. He created Union Station, a huge white classical structure, in Washington, D.C. from 1903–1908, after his work on the planning commission for the Federal Mall. McKim, Mead and White, architects of the fair, gained national prominence for their work in the classical style.

There was, however, one architect, who was not working in the American Renaissance style of the fair. Louis Sullivan was the one architect of the Columbia Exposition who refused to work with his colleagues in the classical mode. No building of Sullivan's is seen on the Court of Honor. Instead, he designed the elaborate "Transportation Building" of the fair, unlike any of its other structures. It is a celebration of modernism and ornamentation rather than of rational severity. Sullivan, unlike the other architects, did not believe the classical forms to be appropriate for the time. In his opinion, the American Renaissance style was elitist and did not relate to the people.[39] It was more important to create a building which was modern and reflected the present age, not the past ideals. Just as America had reached the "dawn of a new age" with the construction of tall office buildings, the fair pulled the nation back a mere twenty years later.[40] As Sullivan explained:

> [the crowd] departed [the fair] joyously, carriers of contagion, unaware that what they beheld and believed to be truth was to prove, in historical fact, an appalling calamity.[41]

In other words, by accepting this style as truly appropriate and representative of America, and by carrying the vision of that style throughout the nation, Americans pulled themselves back (stylistically) fifty years. Instead of creating new forms for the twentieth century which would be appropriate for the inventions displayed at the fair, Americans grounded themselves in the old forms and retarded their own cultural growth.

Francis Schroen himself was part of this "contagion-carrying" crowd. His figures represent what he believes to be the highest form of art; it is symbolic and democratic. They are typical of those which grew out of the American Renaissance. The Brooklyn Museum's 1979 American Renaissance exhibition catalog cites three cultural currents which pervaded the style: nationalism, idealism and cosmopolitanism.[42] Nationalism, a political as well as social factor, was almost certainly associated with the Centennial. Cass Gilbert, a prominent architect of the period, noted that the state had a duty to satisfy man's "national craving" for art, and thereby secure "patriotism and good citizenship."[43] Here, in the public's clamor for art which promotes good citizenship, we find Schroen's figure of "Patriotism" on the walls of Gaston Hall. Idealism, and what the Brooklyn Museum calls "the genteel tradition,"[44] were upheld by the elite artists of the day. "Charles Eliot Norton, professor of art history at Harvard, observed that the 'highest achievements in the arts' were...the expressions of a nation's 'faith,' 'loftiness of spirit' and the 'embodiment of its ideals.'"[45] Here, in this tradition, lie Schroen's figures of Morality and Faith. His art truly reconciles with the popular artistic traditions of the day. He follows, letter for letter, the instructions of the artistic proponents of the American Renaissance.

Artists and public alike embraced the classical figures of the American Renaissance precisely because of the values the style upheld. Schroen and the other Renaissance artists felt that the answers to the questions raised by the forthcoming twentieth century were to be found in these forms. Nationalism, idealism and cosmopolitanism were more than social movements, they represented a personal and religious philosophy to these artists. The absolutes referred to in the style were ones which provided a sense of cohesiveness in a changing world; men were to be upstanding and genteel, following the old moral codes. They were to uphold the values of democracy and liberty, reminded by the art that "all men are created equal." They were to assert America's strength and national unity. By reworking the art of the Ancient Republic, the American Renaissance artists were, in essence, saying "Here is what we believe; these values represented the greatest society in all history and these values represented America, the new Great Republic."

However, I agree with Louis Sullivan that as popular as it may have been, this form of art was detrimental to Americans. It was anachronistic; it did not represent what was really happening in their culture and their time, it merely represented past ideals and Republican myths. This would, as Sullivan said, prove to be "an appalling calamity."

The world from 1900 to 1902, when Schroen was working on Gaston Hall, must be remembered as a distinctly modern world. Speed had become the passion of Americans. Now, in the twentieth century, they could not only rush to their destinations by train, but also by automobile. Trains had greatly affected the perception of men in the nineteenth century. Turner's famous painting "Rain, Steam and Speed" shows a train rushing through a country field in a rain storm. A twentieth century eye can easily make out the different parts of the train. But to the nineteenth century, this vision was entirely new; Turner's painting depicts the train as a gray slash, a blur. That ability to "see" speed was something entirely new and exciting. Trains dashed across the United States, bringing together the four corners of the nation. But it was automobiles which made speed such a great part of American culture. The appearance of Henry Ford's cars, in 1893, would take America bustling down the highways and into the cities. Rural America was quickly disappearing and the glamor, speed and hustle of city life took America by storm. The emergence of skyscrapers in the cities of Chicago and New York also brought America into the modern age. With the necessary inventions of the elevator, the steel cage system of building and new fireproofing techniques, the first skyscrapers rose in Chicago in the early 1880s. In the short span of twenty years, hundreds of corporations and businesses occupied tall office buildings. Skyscrapers, creating mountainous skylines in the major cities, became a symbol of the modern corporate age.

Within these skyscrapers, as within many American homes, were the inventions of the late nineteenth century, "the modern conveniences." Thomas Alva Edison invented the phonograph in 1877, and, two years later, the lightbulb. The Kodak camera was invented in 1888, Ford's automobile in 1893 and X-rays were discovered by Roentgen in 1895.[46] Americans were racing into the twentieth century. The Wright brothers were flying in;

their first powered flight occurred one year after Francis Schroen finished Gaston Hall, in 1903. These changes "amounted to the greatest alteration in man's view of the universe since Isaac Newton."[47] Gaston Hall itself employed the wonderful invention of electric lighting. The *Georgetown Journal* noted the effect of this:

> the Hall in its new garb was a beautiful sight, the magnificent pictures, the rich carpets...and over all, the soft glow of electric lights made it a veritable fairy bower.[48]

The world of art was changing just as drastically. Paul Cézanne, the French post-Impressionist who is considered to be the father of modern abstract art, brought a new vision to painting. He brought a new relativeness to seeing during the 1890s until his death in 1906.[49] Rather than painting figures: grass and rocks, he painted the relationships between grass and rock.[50] His art, influenced by speed, motion and the new modern vision, introduced "a new process of seeing, [the] adding up and weighing of choices."[51] Rather than putting a painting before a viewer to question: What is this? Does this connect with my perception of art? Does this connect with my perception of reality? Rather than stating "This is what I see," Cézanne asks: "Is this what I see?"[52] As art critic Robert Hughes explains, "doubt becomes part of the painting's subject."[53] This new process of seeing, of taking part and confronting the world, questioning it and doubting it, was taken up eventually by Pablo Picasso, Georges Braque and other cubists.

It was the cubists' philosophy that it was necessary to take our world apart, confront it piece by piece, inch by inch, then put it back together, showing all parts and components, on the canvas. As in Cézanne's work, the viewer is asked to become part of the painting, to question it, to take it apart and put it together in his own way. Only by doing this, can we understand our world and truly represent it.

It is Hughes' theory that the Eiffel Tower, built for the Paris World's Fair of 1889, is partly responsible for this changed sense of perception. At the time of its construction, it was the tallest man-made object on earth, "meant to illustrate the triumph of the present over the past, the victory of industrial over landed wealth."[54] This steel-constructed tower promised the victory of technology in the approaching twentieth century. What the Eiffel Tower also did was to offer a new vision of Paris:

> Nearly a million people rode its lifts to the top platform; and there they saw what modern travellers see every time they fly—the earth on which we live seen flat, as pattern, from above. [Paris became] a map of itself, a new type of landscape began to seep into popular awareness. It was based on frontality and pattern, rather than on perspective recession and depth...this way of seeing was one of the pivots in human consciousness.[55]

This pivot of human consciousness, the force behind cubism, found its way into the American consciousness also, particularly in the architecture of Frank Lloyd Wright, whose vision was of an architecture which would relate to nature, extend horizontally with the land, and provide a new unity of space, based on the movement of those who dwelled inside the buildings. His vision became known as "the Prairie Style." These homes, like the paintings of Cézanne, required confrontation and questioning. They demand the viewer's participation.

In short, the world during 1901 was a world concerned with speed and motion. It was a world which had acquired a new vision of itself, demanding confrontation with reality and participation in the interpretation. It was a world which was racing into the twentieth century, in love with technology and industrialization. It was a world which was beginning to take apart and put back together life as they knew it, creating new forms and new realities faster than they could reach the top of the Eiffel Tower. This is the world in which Schroen chose to paint the didactic, classical murals of Gaston Hall.

His reasons for choosing this style are obvious. The American Renaissance style was based on the Greek ideal of ultimate order in the universe; beauty was to be found in rational geometry and evenness of form. Well-ordered art would have been very appealing to Schroen with his deep, religious convictions. To him, it would have been a work suited to the glorification of God who gave the ultimate order to the universe. The elegant figures stood for the perfection of the Christian ideals. The even, balanced forms which represented the highest ideals of the American democracy (all parts and members being equal) and the universal order promoted by Schroen's religion, would have been attractive in the chaotic twentieth century. The forms would have also been favored by his patrons, the Georgetown Jesuits and Alumni, just as they were heralded at the fair. For these reasons, neither Schroen's choice of style nor the praise it received at the time—or down to our own day—are at all surprising.

It is interesting to note, however, the artistic styles which were beginning to be practiced in Europe at the same time as Gaston Hall was painted. Picasso's *Demoiselles d'Avignon*, an early cubist painting done only five years after Gaston Hall, represents five women, their bodies distorted and broken. Picasso gives us all sides of the figures at once, showing them as he perceived them in reality. Two wear ancient African masks, as African art was, for Picasso, "inseparably involved with its apparent freedom to distort."[56]

While it is perhaps not entirely appropriate to compare the work of Brother Francis Schroen, an American artist working for a specific patron, to Picasso, a European genius working for the joy of his own imagination, the questions posed by the two artists offer an interesting contrast. While Picasso's work impels the viewer to work on the painting for a while and attempt to understand it, Schroen's work poses no questions. By choosing the American Renaissance style, the most popular style of his day, Schroen chose a style which completely displayed its philosophy on the canvas. It is obvious that the new European style being developed had doubt as its overriding theme, a theme very appropriate for the twentieth century. But the American Renaissance style offers absolutes rather than doubts. Artists such as Schroen who embraced this style had no doubts about what they were painting. Schroen presents only one side: one side of his figures in the mural and one side of his philosophy. One cannot go inside of, or beyond this art. While Gaston Hall may beautifully represent the extreme faith of Brother Schroen and the ideals of the American democracy, the style does not represent what was actually occurring in his culture at that time, the exciting changes of modernism.

The classical figures are of an age which no longer existed and which would have little to do with the lives of the Georgetown students who would graduate beneath them. The figure of Alma Mater crowns a robed, ideal figure of Art, her palette and lyre at her side. But with the likes of Paul Cézanne and Frank Lloyd Wright, this Renaissance conception of Art seems outdated, a stubborn refusal to recognize the world of modernism. Science, who receives the other crown from Alma Mater, carries with her books and a globe. She represents the science of theory and exploration. Yet, the most important science at the turn of the century was the science of electricity, cars, trains, telephones, gramophones, x-rays and elevators. The Science of the American Renaissance does not represent the modern age because it is a style concerned with representing the ideal rather than the actual. The figures of Morality and Patriotism are direct results of the philosophy behind the World's Fair and could appear in any work of art in America as these are timeless themes. But where is the presentation of the modern problems posed by morality and patriotism: the problems brought about by a world newly concerned with corporate power? How did the style of Schroen's murals fit in with what was actually happening in the world at the time, the world in which Georgetown students would be a driving force?

The Education of Henry Adams, Adams's autobiography, may be helpful in understanding this problem. Adams, one of a long line of great American leaders, expresses his confusion over the quickly approaching twentieth century after visiting the Chicago World's Fair in 1893. He speaks of his experiences inside the buildings of the fair, seeing the amazing new inventions which were to bring America fully into the modern age. Once inside the Hall of Machinery, Adams is overwhelmed by the buzzing and whirring activity around him. He is surrounded by machines, each one moving faster than the other. Unable to take it all in, he lies down on the floor of the exhibition hall in order to see as much of it as he can at one time. Still, it is impossible.

Here, Henry Adams has a revelation. He discovers that there is a new force at work in the modern age: the force of the dynamo. The dynamo, the driving force of machinery, would become the new idol. Adams saw that men would worship this technological force because it would give rise to their entire civilization. He compared it to the life force he had known in his premodern world, the Virgin. For it is the figure of the Virgin Mary, and her fertility, which pretwentieth century men worshipped. Natural growth and fertility perpetuated their civilization, their culture and their faith. Men found their roots in the worship of this force. But now there was a new force at play, one as strong as the force of the Virgin, but one able to move into the technological modern age as the force of the Virgin could not. Speed and Power were the new engines of civilization.

Although Adams clearly favored the spiritual force of the Virgin, he saw the need to confront the dynamo because it was a force which could not be stopped. Man would have to come to terms with it if he were to be part of the new century. Adams noted how difficult this would be for men like himself who could not see, much less comprehend, all of the new inventions of the day. Being completely overwhelmed, Adams held on to the spiritual force of the Virgin. He needed it because he could not understand the force of the dynamo. He stood in fearful awe of the dynamo, but clung to his old ways in order to understand his culture.

It may be said, then, that Gaston Hall is Schroen's Virgin in the midst of the Dynamo. Using the most popular style of the day, a style which made sense to him and made the world whole to him, was his way of clinging to the old-world structure and method of understanding in the midst of the rapidly changing world. As this style asks no questions of the viewers, the artist is free from asking questions of himself. He presents his art as he presents his faith: solid, lasting, unquestioning, unfaltering. His painting, showing no struggle with the new currents in his culture, is his way of spiritually coping and comprehending the modern world. While this may have been necessary and appropriate for the artist at the time, it does a disservice to the students of Georgetown whose legacy this art is. The American Renaissance style grounded itself in the old ideals and forms which became popular in the late nineteenth century and thus happily ignores the modern world. What students today view as the art which connects them to the students who have come before them to the university, actually does not stand for those students. The art only connects us to a vision of an ideal world, to a style and to a philosophy which refused to confront the modern world. If the artist had attempted to incorporate modernity, either in philosophy or form into the murals, it would have left a more meaningful representation of the time. Instead the style leaves the class of 1902 not fully present in the Hall.

What we must ask ourselves is this: knowing what we now know about Gaston Hall, can the same be said for us? Are we leaving a correct vision of ourselves here on campus for future generations? Are we remembering that we must strive to leave an art and architecture which not only is beautiful in its structure, but which truly represents us as a community, particularly a community of students? Does our art represent our times and our philosophies? Does it represent the currents in our culture?

When I look at the Intercultural Center, built on campus in 1982, I am proud that this is the legacy we leave of the eighties. This is a building which represents what I want to be known of students of my age. Georgetown students one hundred years from now, on the three-hundredth anniversary of our founding, will look at the Intercultural Center and know that we were concerned with energy and the world's resources. They will know that we wanted to find new ways to collect and distribute power so that our children and grandchildren will grow up in a world as safe and comfortable as ours. They will know that we are concerned with world peace, and nations coming together as a universal community. They will know that we desire communication over arms. They will know that these beliefs were an intrinsic part of our Georgetown education and our personal philosophy. Here is art which stands for us and our age.

I must ask myself the same questions about the Leavey Center as it is being constructed because this, too, will be a legacy of my age. Does this building represent the students of the day, our beliefs and our world? What message does it leave for the future generations about my fellow students and myself? The answers I come up with are disturbing.

To me, the building is massive, almost fortress-like. Yet, it does not have the appeal of the equally massive Healy Building.

It seems closed and alienating. When I imagine the Healy Building, the first images which come to mind are the delicate artistic touches: the emblems, the gargoyles and the colored tiles on the roof. I remember its history, and how it was a labor of love for the president of the university; the focus of the building was to be a powerful symbol to the world, but a symbol of how much the students were to be cared for and educated.

When I imagine the Leavey Center, my mind does not reach beyond the bricks, the millions of bricks which make up and enclose this building. Its size, particularly because its size is its main point of reference on a campus screaming for open space, makes the building unapproachable. Symbolically, this represents the strength and size of the university as an administrative body, but does not quietly, artistically, open itself up to the community of students. It speaks loudly of our money and our power, but not of our souls and our minds.

The inclusion of a hotel within the complex adds to my reservations about the building. Not only does the facade of the building appear inaccessible to the students, but the actual use of one of the major parts of the building will have little to do with us. Many students already speak of the lack of community felt within the Village C dormitory because of its hotel-like construction; the addition of a campus hotel serves only to increase this feeling of alienation on campus.

However, members of the Georgetown community one hundred years from now will understand this building to be representative of my age. They will understand me by the art of my time just as I (mistakenly) understand the class of 1902 by the art of theirs. If the Leavey Center does represent me and my age, it is saying that I am closed and unapproachable. It is saying that I am extremely concerned with money and exhibiting my wealth. It is saying that it is more important to me to appear impressive than to serve the immediate needs of my community. I do not feel that this is what I am about, and I hope it is not what my fellow students are about.

For there is an important lesson to be learned from Gaston Hall, a lesson which is a timely one for the Bicentennial of this university. We need to examine our past to discover ourselves and our ideals, and so it is necessary to look into our history.

But we cannot lock ourselves in that history. We must always remember to look into our future. The statement that we make of ourselves today will be read for hundreds of years to come. It must be a statement which we will be proud to point to, a statement which fully represents ourselves. We have the responsibility to question ourselves, to discover what our beliefs are and what we ultimately stand for, and then to find the way in which we can best represent those beliefs. We have a responsibility to examine our culture and accurately portray our times. If we neglect this, as the American Renaissance artists seemed to do, we leave our future generations with an incomplete sense of who we are and what can be learned from us.

Notes

1. Nicholas Natasi, "The Construction and Architectural Origins of the Healy Building" (term paper, Georgetown University, 7 March 1962), p. 11.

2. Ibid., pp. 10–11.

3. Ibid., p. 10.

4. Ibid., p. 11.

5. Ibid.

6. "Gaston Hall," 1934. Box 316, Georgetown University Archives (henceforth indicated as GUA).

7. Ibid.

8. Patrick J. Cormican, S.J., *A Brand Snatched from the Burning: A Sketch of Brother Francis C. Schroen, S.J.* (Lackawanna, N.Y., The Victorian Press, n.d.), p. 3.

9. Ibid.

10. Ibid.

11. Ibid., p. 4.

12. Ibid., p. 43.

13. Ibid.

14. Ibid., p. 43.

15. Ibid.

16. Ibid.

17. Ibid., p. 23.

18. Ibid., p. 24.

19. Ibid.

20. Letter to Father J. Havens Richards, from Paul Pelz, Architect, 11 March 1898 (GUA "Gaston Hall," Box 316).

21. Description of Gaston Hall from unknown newspaper clipping, 1889 (GUA, "Gaston Hall," Box 316).

22. Uncited newspaper article in: Cormican, *A Brand Snatched*, p. 32.

23. Ibid., p. 31.

24. Ibid.

25. Ibid., p. 32.

26. *Georgetown College Journal* (henceforth indicated as *GCJ*) 29, no. 1, 1900–1901, p. 39.

27. Ibid.

28. Cormican, *A Brand Snatched*, p. 33.

29. Ibid., p. 31.

30. *GCJ* 29, no. 1, 1900–1901, p. 40.

31. *GCJ* 29, no. 10, 1900—1901, p. 483.

32. Cormican, *A Brand Snatched*, p. 27.

33. Letter to Father Shandelle, S.J. from St. Louis University, 24 April 1901 (GUA, "Gaston Hall," Box 316).

34. Robert Hughes, *Shock of the New* (New York: Alfred A. Knopf, 1987), p. 9.

35. Daniel Burnham in M. Schuyler, "Last Words about the World's Fair," *American Architecture and Other Writings*, vol. 2, 1961, p. 571.

36. Mariana Griswold Van Rennsalier, "The Artistic Triumph of the Fair Builders," *The Century Magazine*, 1893, p. 528.

37. Class Notes of Author from Professor Elizabeth Prelinger, Georgetown University, "19th and 20th Century American Architecture," 9 September 1987.

38. Ibid., 28 September 1987.

39. Ibid., 9 September 1987.

40. Louis Sullivan, *The Autobiography of an Idea* (New York: Dover Publications, 1956), p. 325.

41. Ibid., p. 321.

42. The Brooklyn Museum, *American Renaissance 1876–1917* (Brooklyn Museum, 1979), p. 28.

43. Ibid., p. 29.

44. Ibid., p. 28.

45. Ibid., p. 29.

46. Hughes, *Shock of the New*, p. 15.

47. Ibid.

48. *GCJ* 30, no. 2, 1901–1902, p. 99.

49. Hughes, *Shock of the New*, p. 18.

50. Ibid.

51. Ibid.

52. Ibid.

53. Ibid.

54. Ibid., p. 10.

55. Ibid., p. 14.

56. Ibid., p. 21.

The Healy Building: Instilling a Belief in Georgetown University

Jeffrey Renzulli

The new Georgetown College Building, now being completed, is a stone beauty worthy of its commanding position, visible for many miles, a formidable competitor in magnificence with the government buildings and probably the finest educational building in the country.—*The Georgetown College Journal*, vol. 8, p. 5 (from *Baltimore Sun*).

The Construction of the New Building

The Georgetown University of the early 1870s was a "college." The school, situated on a hill overlooking the shipping area of Georgetown, was attended by both high school and college students. The campus consisted of a few buildings separated by a water pump. A wall was built around the property to discourage students from venturing into the undesirable town.

Since the Civil War ended less than a decade earlier, the nation and the capital struggled to regain respect. Although prejudices had subsided quickly after the war, Georgetown's position was uncomfortable. Nine hundred of her eleven hundred students fought on the side of the Confederacy and, unlike today, the school was definitely not considered "northern." Students wanted normalcy to return, as they gladly traded in rifles and uniforms for books and debates.

Like many of his time, Fr. Healy wanted to repair the damage caused by war. He was an educator who believed that Georgetown needed to upgrade its curriculum, especially in the sciences, in order to compete with the more prestigious northern schools like Harvard and Yale. He also believed that both students and the "College" needed a large building to house classes and provide living quarters to improve the school.

Fr. Healy's idea of building such a structure on campus was initially ridiculed by students. *The College Journal*, in 1877, began offering a section entitled "The New Building." The editors sought to monitor the progress made on this supposedly mammoth structure about to be built.

"Our fellows view all these operations with languid interest," they wrote in 1878, "having seen similar proceedings before, or heard of them from their predecessors: and they smile derisively, as if the whole thing were gotten up to impose on their credulity."[1] Later, in a following issue, with not much progress to report, they caustically remark that "we adhere to this [new section] because we promised it in the day of incredulity: but, of course, the building has yet to rise."[2]

Yet, in two years, its exterior had been completed, despite legal problems and shortage of funds. The *Journal* writers, who only a year and a half earlier had treated the building with disrespectful sarcasm, were shocked. In 1879 they wrote with praise that "The College has not only made a new beginning, it has almost completed a most extensive, elegant and massive building. The new structure is, within and without, a source of astonishment and admiration to every one who has seen it."[3]

Imagine the excitement! The campus had consisted of the North Building, the South Building, and a few others designed for utility's sake. It was now symmetrically united by a building 312 feet long made of two million bricks, three thousand cubic yards of stone, three hundred fifty thousand feet of timber and two hundred thousand feet of lumber.[4]

Healy Building, or "the new building," nearly doubled the square feet of available floor area on campus. Prior to completion, Georgetown had only about 125,000 square feet of space.

Now there was an additional 110,000 square feet. To put this into perspective, with today's amount of floor area, the new Leavey Center would have to be the size of about fifteen Healy Buildings just to equal the proportionate increase in space created when the new building was completed in 1879.[5]

There was a prevailing sense of pride and excitement when the building was completed. Students and outsiders alike knew that this recently constructed edifice, with its spires and turrets almost two hundred feet tall, was impressive. Barnham Carter toured the building on October 20, 1880, and remarked that it was more beautiful than even the Eiffel Tower.[6]

The following tour of the building, originally published in an 1879 edition of the *College Journal*, begins at the northern end of the basement:

> ...Here we come in view of the grand corridor, running the entire length of the building, the numerous arches and the softened light from the windows opening on the area to the west, serving to magnify its length, so that a grown man at the farther end appears to be a small boy. Passing south on this corridor we meet first on our left the main staircase (of blue stone, all the way) that leads to the upper stories and gives access finally to the great hall; next on our left are two long rooms designed, one for a Recreation Room one for a Reading Room; then we reach the transverse corridor under the central tower, then two more large rooms about thirty feet wide and forty feet long that will be Recreation and Billiard Rooms; then we come to the Laboratory. Here will be the chemical classroom, which on three sides is arched over. The classroom will occupy the open space, while along the walls and in the alcoves the experiment tables, chemicals and all the apparatus will be kept.
>
> At the southern end of the corridor, we reach the stone staircase in the south tower; we turn to the right and an ascent of half a dozen steps brings us to a wide arched doorway looking towards the Infirmary: but following the steps by easy flights and comfortable platforms, we reach the first floor and look into the Scientific Lecture room...when completed, the room will seat about three hundred persons. For the purposes to which it will be devoted, it will have no equal in this country, and will in itself furnish the College just occasion for pride. Leaving the Lecture Room and following the corridor of this story [floor], we pass on the right four

large classrooms corresponding to the Recreation rooms below...The main corridors are all lighted from spacious windows opening onto the court. At the north end of this corridor, on the left, is the Treasury's Room, [currently Campus Ministries Office] with its great vault walled in by solid masonry three feet thick. Opposite the Treasurer's room is the visitor's Drawing Room, a large and lofty apartment, twenty feet wide and forty feet long. At the end of the corridor, we come to the transverse corridor of the north pavilion, opening out at the east on the main entrance for visitors. While the public drawing room is on the left of this entrance, six small parlors for individual parties of visitors range along to the right.

Facing the main entrance, and at the extremity of this short corridor, is a wide stairway leading to the President's room, the Museum and the Debating Hall on the floor above...In the Museum, we are struck by its splendid dimensions, its massive girders and beautifully turned wooden columns and brackets, the bay oak and Georgia pine showing in beautiful contrast to one other. The Museum occupies the whole east front of the north Pavilion. Just outside of the Museum and to the right (the north), is the Debating Hall, and opposite to that is the President's room, the entrance to which is on the main corridor. The beautiful Ohio stone corbels in the President's room are works of art...Again on the main corridor [now the second story] we come first to the main stairway and then to four large classrooms corresponding to those of the floor below. At the far southern end we reach the doors by which part of the audience will have access to the seats in the Scientific Lecture room. These seats are on such an incline that from each row the person can see over the heads of those in front, and the lecturer and his table will be in full view from all parts of the hall.

Just beyond, we ascend the winding stair of the south tower, all together with the platforms, made of the famous blue stone flagging from the Hudson River. Arriving on the third floor, the first door on our right leads into the Library, a grand room forty-two feet by sixty, in which will be stored the 30,000 books of the present library with room to spare for four times as many more...The ceiling will be nearly thirty feet from the floor. With its lofty windows, nineteen feet high, from which a prospect is presented to the eye that cannot be surpassed on the continent, the new Library will be the most splendid in all our country. On this third floor, the corridor is changed to the middle of the building, so as to allow on each side the arranging of rooms for the use of such students that may desire privacy...At the northerly end of the corridor on the third floor, we enter the Aula Maxima, the noble proportions of which strike the beholder with genuine admiration, its lofty ceiling, its magnificent corridors with their carved mullions and caps, the hanging gallery, the oriel outlook, all combining to make it a finer Hall than any other institution can boast. The Hall is capable of giving ample room to fifteen hundred people, a number which but a few churches and fewer theatres can hold...The Library and the Hall occupy the height of two stories, in all thirty-two feet.[7]

Georgetown's enrollment was reduced to less than twenty students during the Civil War, and the institution was now, almost overnight, claiming to be one of the great schools in the country.

Style of the New Building: Instilling Greatness through a Philosophy of Architecture

A college must have buildings...because there must be something to give the public a pledge of the permanence of the institution—and something that will be the center of attachment for its members.—From *The American Literary Magazine*, 1847.[8]

Contrary to popular belief, Georgetown's New Building was not unusual compared to buildings on other college campuses. By the middle of the nineteenth century, American colleges and universities sought the same recognition as English schools. They had existed just long enough to desire this but not long enough to demand it. Schools like Oxford and Cambridge had been in existence for over five hundred years. Most American schools were not even one century old.

Philosophy of architecture reflected a change in social norms. Schools that cared about utility and simplicity now valued competition, elegance and permanence. Each school wanted to emphasize its tradition and importance.

"In the mid 1830's," writes Paul Venable Turner, "a new type of building appeared at the American college: the astronomical observatory...Sometimes the observatory was built close to the other college buildings but often, as at Georgetown College, it was set well apart...to observe the universe in an inspiring scene of unspoiled nature."[9] Williams College, in western Massachusetts, was the first to build an observatory, in 1837, and Georgetown followed suit within a decade, as did several other competitive schools.

Georgetown constructed its beautiful observatory in 1844. Collegians were going out of their way to incorporate nature in their studies and even the most urban schools chose to display themselves in a pastoral setting.[10]

Georgetown, too, emphasized its association with the country: the campus was often photographed from the rear, to include rolling hills, grazing animals and wild trees.[11] Seldom does one witness a picture of the campus during this era from the rows of townhouses looking up at the campus. This was in keeping with the general trend towards interest in the natural sciences.

Styles and philosophies at one school affected others. The most popular style of architecture was Gothic. Variations on this theme were common, with the medieval Romanesque style, first used in 1852 at Antioch College, also used at Georgetown. [12]

First proposed but never implemented for a quadrangular system at Columbia in 1813, Medieval Revival architecture gradually gained national importance.[13] By 1850, it was commonly used at colleges and with its inherent beauty, gave the impression of age, stability, permanence and, of course, prestige. [14]

"Normally," Turner continues, "the [Revival architecture] was used to support the collegiate ideal of a community of scholars, living as a family, perpetuating the traditional curriculum and united by a religious creed." Clearly, this was the goal that Fr. Healy had in mind when he commissioned the construction of the New Building.

Also influencing the style of the New Building was the historical setting in which it was built. The Civil War made a general feeling of insecurity prevail and educational institutions, along with the rest of the nation, had to reestablish stability. The hope was that the new structure would instill confidence into those still unsure about the permanency and venerability of the school:

> This desire that college architecture be "venerable" and "substantial," laden with "associations" and to testify to an "old and honored" institution became common in the mid and late 19th century. [15]

Therefore, given the emergence of Revival architecture on collegiate campuses and, given the unique historical setting in which Fr. Healy found himself, the style and philosophy behind the New Building is more easily understood.

Georgetown was a "college," and like other "colleges" across the country, there was a push to become a better known institution. Many schools were constructing expansive buildings in a similar style to achieve this purpose. Fr. Healy did not want Georgetown to be left behind. Despite weak financial support and a community still shaken by the traumatic war experience, he commissioned J.L. Smithmyer of Washington, D.C., who had been honored for submitting the winning design for the initial building of the Library of Congress, to undertake the job. Putting the building up was one thing; making people believe in it was another. Yet, both alumni and students had roles in this effort.

The building's cost of three hundred thousand dollars nearly bankrupted the school. In April 1879, when Fr. Healy was in San Francisco, the university virtually ran out of money. The thought of halting further construction of the tower was seriously considered.[16] Healy, when reached by telegram with this proposal, would have none of it and instead ordered the building to be completed, as designed, in full.

As a consequence, the school incurred a substantial debt. It was at this point that a most important movement was stirred within the Georgetown community: alumni, recognizing the need to unite, formed their own association. In the Society of Alumni, as it became known, for the first time former students gathered and pledged financial support to the administration. R.T. Merrick declared:

> The college which nurtured us in youth should now in its need receive some reciprocation in the way of aid from the gathered strength of our manhood. This cooperation, then [will bring] this venerated institution into successful competition with the most favored Universities of our English-speaking people.[17]

The New Building, with a meeting hall designed for use by alumni, inspired the former students' increased consciousness of their role in the University. By helping with their payment of part of the burdensome debt, they put into practice their philosophy, which had also been instrumental in the construction of the building.

Students began to think of Georgetown as a great university, too. No longer did they mock the Jesuits for proposing such an ambitious structure; they now applauded its existence on campus. In early 1879, a *Journal* writer wrote what he believed the essential element of a great university to be:

> The present position and influence—indeed the continued existence—of Oxford, Cambridge and other [great schools] founded between the thirteenth and sixteenth centuries are in great part due to the permanent character of their respective edifices. A building, constructed for the purposes of a University should be of the most enduring plan and the architect should, in its interior and exterior and all its parts create a structure of the character to repel the idea of change because...there is associated with the idea of the strength and durability of the buildings of a University that of the permanency in the history and the traditions of the University itself...[18]

Alumni and students now believed, because of the New Building, that Georgetown was a school that warranted national, and even international, recognition.

Style of the New Building: Instilling Greatness through a Philosophy of Education

> We believe that the first qualification of the true gentleman is elevation of character. It may be found in the humblest as well as in the most exalted...[but] where learning and refinement are joined to a heart full of affection and a character of unswerving integrity, we find the highest type of gentleman.—*The Georgetown College Journal*, April 1878.[19]

In the days when the New Building was being constructed, only young men matriculated at Georgetown. A primary goal of the educational experience, then, was to inculcate in the student a sense of what it meant to be a true gentleman.

The educational philosophy and purpose behind Fr. Healy's great building is embodied in this statement. Not only did he want Georgetown to provide the best possible experience in the classroom; he stressed also the need for the development of the individual moral character.

The "refinement" mentioned in this excerpt included excellence in oratory. With two debating societies—the Philodemic and the Philonomosian—as well as by a securely fostered education in the classics, the Georgetown student of that time had to be an eloquent orator.

It was not uncommon for debates to occur quite often. For instance, students held weekly jousts that were argued before judges who decided winners and losers. Decorum was an important consideration as well; no student could effectively argue without possessing proper ideals of etiquette. Medals were given out annually to the brightest stars of such efforts. It can be said that these accolades made the benefactor a highly esteemed class member.

In fact, the *College Journal* shows that students joined with Fr. Healy in stressing the necessity of debate. One *Journal* writer remarked that

> it will, no doubt, be admitted by all, that the greatest achievements of modern times have been the results of properly directed eloquence. Many excellent examples suggest themselves, and among these, may I mention the securing of our National Independence, which may be traced to the...statesmen and orators of that period. It was through their instrumentality that we were incited to that lawful Revolution which resulted so gloriously for us as a people. In view of these facts, then, I must conclude that the cultivation of this function is of primary importance.[20]

Typically, there were annual events, scheduled either on the society's birthdate (February 23 for the Philodemic) or commencement for the undergraduates. Many honored alumni and family members were invited to these affairs, which often lasted three hours or more. With radio and television still more than half a century away, listening to a properly conceived argument provided lively entertainment. The "Debating Hall" was placed outside and directly to the right of the President's office to underline the importance of the tradition.

Many educators felt that the sciences, especially chemistry, were not given sufficient emphasis, and needed to be upgraded in quality, a view shared by Fr. Healy.[21] Accordingly, the southern end of the basement was designed to accommodate the chemistry classroom. Similarly, the physics lecture hall, situated directly above, demonstrated this new emphasis as well. With a seating capacity of three hundred students, the hall was a visible and honored representation of the place of science in daily campus life.

Another value, regarded highly by Fr. Healy (but probably not by his fellow Jesuits), was the opportunity for older students to live in their own rooms. Until the time of the New Building, students lived in a barracks-style system, sharing space with several other students.

Fr. Healy believed that the older collegiate students should live alone so that they could study more easily by themselves. He felt the student would appreciate the increase in freedom away from the prefect's watchful eye.[22]

The third and fourth floors of the building had rooms for student lodgers. There were twenty-six rooms on each floor, each measuring twelve by sixteen feet and all made safe from fire. A new material called "Limeofteil," which was fire- and waterproof, was used to divide the rooms. And, for additional protection, builders installed fire plugs, water pipes and circular iron fire escapes.

Upon opening in 1881, wrote the *College Journal*, the rooms were "elegant in their simplicity and admirably suited to the purpose for which they have been constructed." The editors did not , however, disguise their concern that this change in philosophy might prove unsuccessful: "The occupancy of these apartments," they wrote, "is an experiment, the wisdom and fitness of which must be judged by the effect that will be made on scholarship and discipline in college."[23]

In addition, what is today known as Gaston Hall inspired a great infusion of time, money and interest back into the university community on the part of the alumni. Georgetown until this time had never officially accepted donations and had never sought an endowment. The Jesuit fathers believed that it was their responsibility, and not that of alumni, to provide for the students' needs.

Yet, when the New Building was constructed, it became clear

that money from outside would be necessary to complete the several halls. The Jesuits only reluctantly agreed but students believed that it was time for their elder brothers to share the burden.

In April 1879, months after the building had been finished, the *Journal* wrote a sharply critical piece on the lack of alumni support in financing the debt:

> Georgetown University, unlike all of its Protestant contemporaries, owes its progress and success to Heaven itself alone, for though its children are counted among the rich and powerful of our country, yet no bounty from their hands has up to this time helped to pay for one stone or one brick upon the fabric which should be a standing monument of their zeal for the cause of education...No word of reproach has been heard from any members of the devoted Society under whose management the College has grown to be one of the brightest institutions of American education. Now is the time for these heartless ones to redeem themselves![24]

In devotion to a highly valued institution, Georgetown students demanded of their alumni an even higher standard than the Jesuits would demand: contributions to finance the debt.

At the first meeting of the Alumni Society in 1881, this request was answered. Sitting in a barren "Memorial Hall," which looked more like a barn than a gathering place, the Society officially committed itself to the project of financing the debt. "This hall is unfinished," it was said on June 23 of that year, "[and] it is to be especially appropriated to the Society of Alumni. The Society should accept, then, as its position of duty in connection with these buildings, the need of meeting the expense of furnishing...these bare walls...that look down on us. We...should now unite in a common effort...to make it a memorial Hall worthy as a meeting place of the society of the former students of the college."[25] By creating such a large room, then, Fr. Healy, for the first time, brought the alumni back to campus. This stirred their interest and encouraged them to open their pocketbooks. Finally, by having administrative offices, debating halls, science labs, dormitory rooms, the library and a large gathering space for alumni and commencement exercises under one roof, the New Building was truly instrumental in uniting the university.

Conclusion

There is one thing that Georgetown holds most precious. That is her treasury of traditions. They are zealously guarded from generation to generation and reverenced by all of us. In modern days when great universities can spring into existence overnight and, nurtured with tremendous endowments, vie with each other in their efforts at turning out the hugest number of possible graduates, it is well to remember that neither greatness of wealth nor quantity of students can take the place of traditions.—*The Hoya*, September 16, 1925

As Georgetown embarks on her third century of molding and teaching young minds, the Healy Building remains as the symbolic, if not the actual, center of campus. It represents Georgetown's basic philosophy: a true education in a simple learning environment.

The Chemistry Department was sorely lacking, so a new laboratory was built. Physics needed more classroom space so a lecture hall was built. Debaters needed a place to argue so a hall was built for them. In every instance and in every way, the Healy Building strives to attain only one ideal: perfecting the educational experience.

In 1979, as the University celebrated the one hundredth anniversary of the building's completion, Rev. Timothy S. Healy, S.J., Georgetown's president, praised his predecessor's commitment to the educational experience:

Father Patrick Healy worried about the integrity of the university as an intellectual and scholarly enterprise. The Healy Building itself was built as a statement about that integrity. He wanted...to make his students more independent, more self-starting in their studies and their living. He understood the need for a large library, for good laboratories and ample classrooms. He wanted to house his college with dignity, and he wanted above all to measure everything by the scope and generosity a developing university demanded...What is at stake in these, our times, is not so much the unity of knowledge of which scholars in Fr. Patrick Healy's time were wont to speak, but the oneness of the university's being.[26]

Today, Fr. Timothy Healy has guided the construction of the

great building that his era as president will forever be remembered by: the $48 million Leavey Center. The similarities between his effort and that of Patrick Healy over a century ago are striking. Both presidents sought to unite Georgetown University. Both drained its financial resources. Both buildings were begun about a decade after wars that caused American social upheaval and, finally, both men encountered debilitating legal hassles with the District of Columbia Government.

Yet, equally visible are the differences. Where the Healy Building sought to expand educational capacities, the Leavey Center provides for no classroom or faculty office space. Where the Healy Building offered students new living arrangements, the Leavey Center offers a four-star hotel for guests. And, finally, where the Healy Building offered a debating hall, the Leavey Center has created fast food restaurants and an underground parking garage. In short, while Patrick Healy sought to *improve* Georgetown, Timothy Healy is seeking only to *accommodate* it.

The fault of Fr. Timothy Healy? Clearly not, for the times we live in demand such a building. This, therefore , is not a criticism of the man but of the philosophy of our time. We seem to have forgotten that bigger is better *only when* better is more important than bigger. The Healy Building was big; indeed, it is still big. However, it endeavored to make Georgetown distinctive and exemplary. The Leavey Center, on the other hand, is distinctive solely because it is big.

That is why, historically speaking, the Healy Building has continually been proven to be above reproach. Times have changed, needs have changed and the campus has changed; but that stone structure has retained its character.

In 1913, a former student wrote a letter to the *College Journal*, lamenting the lack of a proper memorial to the late Patrick Healy. "It is greatly hoped," he wrote, "that some day an adequate eulogy will be written of Fr. [Patrick] Healy—not for his sake because he did not covet praise—but for the benefit of others. It would include a description of his remarkable personality, distinguished in any gathering by its grace and impressiveness, without assumption or affectation."[27]

That letter was not answered then but I shall answer it now. Sir, that eulogy has been written, not by my hands or the hands of one who knew him, but by Fr. Patrick Healy himself. He chose the words and molded the sentences. His belief in God and the unbreakable will of God's determined children lives on in the building he created.

It stands alone today, a lovely icon from the past amid the surroundings of modern times. People do not live there, chemistry and physics are not taught there, and students no longer study there. However, reminding us now and forever of the spirit that built Georgetown, the Healy Building will always be the place that answers the call of those who have wondered how Georgetown became one of the great Catholic schools in the United States of America.

Notes

1. The *Georgetown College Journal*, 6 (1878), p. 8. (Henceforth, this periodical will be indicated by *GCJ*.)

2. Ibid., 6 (1878), p. 32.

3. Ibid., 7 (1879), p. 7.

4. Ibid., 29 (1910), pp. 38–40.

5. Office of the Vice President of Administration and Facilities of Georgetown University, "*Campus Plan: 1983–2000 AD and beyond*," December 1982.

6. Collection of material on the Healy Building, Georgetown University Archives.

7. *GCJ* 7 (1879), pp. 18–20.

8. Paul Venable Turner, *Campus: A Collegiate Tradition*, San Francisco, 1984, p. 116.

9. Ibid., p. 117.

10. Ibid., loc. cit.

11. Ibid., loc. cit.

12. Ibid., p. 117.

13. Ibid., p. 110.

14. Ibid., p. 116.

15. Ibid., p. 117.

16. Fr. Joseph T. Durkin, S.J., "Healy Hall: Harbinger of Change," in *Annual Report of Georgetown University*, 1979, p. 3.

17. *The Proceedings of the Society of Alumni of Georgetown College*, Washington, D.C., R. Beresford Printer, 1881, p. 7.

18. *GCJ* 7 (1879), p. 8.

19. Ibid., 6 (1878), p. 78.

20. Ibid., 7 (1879), p. 8.

21. Turner, p. 163.

22. Ibid., loc. cit.

23. *GCJ* 9 (1881), p. 3.

24. Ibid., 7 (1879), p. 61.

25. *Proceedings of the Society of Alumni*, p. 8.

26. Fr. Timothy S. Healy, S.J., "President's Message," in *Annual Report of Georgetown University*, 1979, p. 2.

27. *GCJ* 41 (1913), p. 226.

The History of Chemistry at Georgetown University (1789–1900)

Liam S. Donohue

Introduction

We seek "the improvement of youth in the three important branches of Physical, Moral and Literary education."[1] This goal was set forth by Georgetown University's first board of directors in 1797. Since then, Moral education has been refined to philosophy and theology; Literary education has blossomed into English and Fine Arts; and Physical education is found in the course catalog as Chemistry and Physics. In this paper, I will focus on how well and to what extent Georgetown has succeeded in the latter area. I will show that for two hundred years young men and women have benefited from Georgetown's efforts to seek "improvement in the important branch of Physical education," in particular, chemical education.[2]

The chronology of Georgetown's growth as a university and chemistry's growth as a legitimate field of study overlap in several areas. Georgetown was founded at the time when chemistry was changing from alchemical traditions to a more serious endeavor. By the time *Dalton's Atomic Theory*, which revolutionized the field of chemistry, was introduced in the 1820s, Georgetown was established as a university.[3] Chemistry was always included in the curriculum so no major changes were ever required. The program could expand without upsetting any university traditions.

The Early Years

Since its founding, Georgetown University has recognized the importance of scientific and chemical study. Wedged in between classes in Latin, Greek and Rhetoric there was always some study of "Natural Philosophy." School records show that for the first two decades of the University's existence, every student at Georgetown spent some time studying some form of Natural Philosophy.[4] Lectures were given weekly on the general sciences. There was always a mix between physics and chemistry. Although courses focused on physics, students also had courses in chemistry. Chemistry of this era was qualitative at best; evidence suggests that students observed some colorful reactions with little or no explanation. This apparently cursory treatment was adequate at a time when chemistry was still a primitive and unsophisticated subject, but the Georgetown graduate had at least some familiarity with chemical phenomena.[5]

Father John Grassi, S.J., president of Georgetown from 1813 to 1820, initiated the first effort to strengthen the science program. In a letter to the board of directors in 1813, he outlined the University's new approach to Natural Philosophy (physics and chemistry): "Regular lectures will be given in Natural and Experimental Philosophy, but to defray the cost ordinarily attending such lectures, an additional charge will be made if required."[6]

Grassi's wishes were quickly fulfilled. On April 11, 1814 Rev. James Wallace, S.J. arrived at Georgetown. He was billed as "Professor of Mathematics, Natural Philosophy and Chemistry."[7] From that day until now Georgetown has always had a professor of chemistry on its faculty. When, in 1833, a professor was unavailable, a guest teacher was invited to lecture: "Dr. Aiken gave a course of lectures in Chemistry for which he charged four dollars."[8]

One of the first chemistry professors was Fr. Thomas Mulledy, who taught in the 1828–1829 school year. Just a few years after he left his teaching position, Fr. Mulledy became president of Georgetown University. It is unclear what bias he had toward Natural Philosophy and/or chemistry but he experienced a growing commitment to the study of chemistry during his tenure as president. As the University expanded, graduation became contingent upon several requirements, including chemistry. Although every class coming through Georgetown to this point had heard lectures in Natural Philosophy with its chemistry component, it became necessary under Fr. Mulledy that a concrete requirement be fulfilled. According to the course catalog of 1837, "It is required for a graduate that he be well acquainted with all above branches to wit: Latin, Greek, French, Moral and Natural Philosophy."[9] To insure that every student meet these requirements, after matriculation "he passes on in regular succession to the end of Moral and Natural Philosophy."[10]

By the 1830s Georgetown was genuinely committed to chemistry. Courses were offered and students were required to take them; and the administration fully supported the faculty. What were chemistry courses like in the nineteenth century?

Much of the earliest chemistry was a matter of watching colored reactions and qualitative analysis. "Alum mixed with red cabbage water produce a brilliant purple solution."[11] By today's standards, these were not very sophisticated observations. In the early nineteenth century students rarely engaged in laboratory work. Usually, the professor performed an experiment in front of the class to illustrate his point. In these demonstrations there was little or no student participation.[12]

Yet, although difficult to believe, chemistry was one of the most popular subjects of the time. Every year as part of the graduation ceremony, chemical experiments were performed in front of large audiences. These "Annual Exhibitions" began as early as 1812 and continued well into the 1890s.[13] The students loved them so much that in 1844 the Prefect of Discipline could get his way with the students by threatening to cancel the exhibition. The students, in fear of this threat, improved their behavior.[14]

Beyond entertainment and simple classroom purposes, it is likely, but not definite, that the early Georgetown students were treated to a more sophisticated chemistry course than was usually taught at the time. There is a good chance that some aspects of quantitative chemistry were taught before the 1850s. Two factors support this claim. First, starting in 1814, every teacher of chemistry was also an instructor of "high mathematics" at one time or another. If quantitative chemistry was not officially part of the curriculum, at least the mathematical resources for its investigation were available to the students.[15] Second, when general Natural Philosophy officially separated into its component chemistry and physics courses, the chemistry was very strongly quantitative analysis. This suggests an existing tradition predisposed to quantitative techniques.[16]

The texture and content of chemistry courses at Georgetown during the first thirty years of the nineteenth century changed with every new teacher. One teacher might emphasize only qualitative techniques while the next might explore quantitative aspects of the subject. With the unique approach of each new teacher and the frequent change of faculty (see Table 1), it is difficult to characterize the exact nature of the courses. In 1834 stability was finally achieved. That was the first teaching year of Fr. James Curley. For the next half-century chemistry and all other sciences at Georgetown were taught or heavily influenced by this man.

Table 1. *Chemistry Teachers at Georgetown.*

1. Fr. James Wallace, S.J.	(1814–1818)
2. Fr. J. Marshall, S.J.	(1819–1821)
3. Fr. T. Levin, S.J.	(1821–1825)
4. Fr. Samuel Newton, S.J.	(1825–1826)
5. Fr. (?) Neill, S.J.	(1827–1828)
6. Fr. Thomas Mulledy, S.J.	(1828–1830)
7. Guest Teachers (inc. Dr. Aiken)	(1830–1834)
8. Fr. James Curley, S.J.	(1834–1870s)
9. Fr. James Clark, S.J.	(1847–1848)
10. Fr. Felix Ciampi, S.J.	(1850–1851)
11. Dr. Kelly	(1874–1880)
12. Fr. Henry T.B. Tarr, S.J.	(1880–1884)
13. Fr. John W. Fox, S.J.	(1884–1887)
14. Fr. James J. Deck, S.J.	(1887–1890)
15. Fr. Barry Smith, S.J.	(1890–1895)

The Father Curley Years

Father Curley is best remembered for his work in astronomy. He was responsible for the establishment in 1841 of Georgetown's observatory, one of the best university observatories of the time. He lobbied hard for funds and equipment for it. His best method of persuasion was taking fellow professors and administrators up the hill to see astronomical phenomena. He was so successful in his efforts and so ingenious in his work that the Georgetown University observatory became a model for other university observatories. In fact, a delegation of engineers and astronomers from Harvard came to see Georgetown's observatory before building their own. Curley's method of mounting and positioning the telescope was especially noteworthy.[17] He received letters from Jesuits all over the world, most of whom were asking for advice and supplies to improve their own observatories. One of the most popular requests was for "spider lines." These lines served to stabilize and position the telescope properly and everybody seemed to want them.[18]

Fr. Curley was also the observatory's best patron. He devoted about half of his time to the use of the observatory. He used the telescope to assign the exact latitude and longitude coordinates to all the Federal buildings. His diary is filed with notepaper on which each building and its newly assigned coordinates are listed. These same coordinates are used to this day. From the looks of these lists, Fr. Curley must have assigned coordinates to every single landmark in the telescope's view.[19]

In addition to his love for astronomy, Fr. Curley was very interested in chemistry. He taught the subject at Georgetown almost constantly for thirty-three years (1834–1867) and even after his replacement, he still influenced the way in which the subject was taught.

Fr. Curley was an able and knowledgeable chemist. He combined the educational and entertaining aspects of chemistry with his wide knowledge and he put together an interesting technical course. He often used chemistry to entertain. In the front of his chemical notebook, he had an index of chemical reactions which produced colors. He had at least one reaction for every color in the spectrum:

White—Mix Acetate of lead with Zinc Sulfate
Blue—Sulfate of iron and "Prussiate of Potash"
Red—Red cabbage water and a few drops of muriatic acid
etc....[20]

These experiments were not difficult or even relevant, but they were certainly enough to interest a student in the subject.

In the thirty-year period during which Fr. Curley taught, there was a gradual shift from a predominately qualitative to a predominately quantitative approach. From the early years of the "Curley Reign" at Georgetown, qualitative analysis was the focus, as evidenced by the color experiments. In the "recipes" there was no numeric reference to quantity or concentration. Simple precipitations were studied by Curley's students. One experiment was designed for this purpose: Mixing silver nitrate with muriatic acid (hydrochloric acid), "if you dip a small bunch of corn broom fiber in strongly diluted muriatic acid and then into the nitrate of silver, you will get a beautiful example of precipitate."[21] Although primitive, this is a very effective qualitative method. Fr. Curley at some point in the 1850s also added flame tests to his repertoire. His notebook contains a short but thorough list of the various colors produced by various compounds. Judging from the organization of this chart, the flame color was used to suggest or confirm the presence of a substance in an unknown compound.[22] This means that there was some quantitative analytical study in addition to strict observational chemistry. It is not out of the question that Georgetown students of the 1840s were capable of identifying simple unknowns.

No qualitative study is complete without some laboratory work. Starting in 1834, it became mandatory for every Georgetown student to take a laboratory course along with his Natural Philosophy study. "In Natural Philosophy the lectures are given in English. Once every month the students of this department will have public exercises to test their improvement."[23] These exercises were similar to the lab-practical given today: a combination of lecture knowledge and laboratory technique. Weekly laboratory sessions were up to date with the laboratory techniques of the time. The equipment available in the 1840s was some combination of bought, adapted and fabricated apparatus. Most qualitative experiments were probably done in simple glassware.

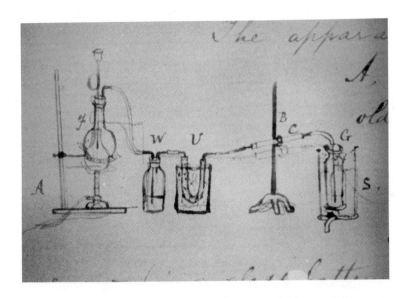

A Sketch of Apparatus from Fr. Curley's Diary (c.1850)

Safety in the laboratory was neglected. Fr. Curley tells about an accident in the lab. In 1869, James Inglehart, a graduate of 1845, paid him a visit. During the meeting Fr. Curley recollected that "at some experiment a glass vessel with hydrogen and air in it, exploded at class and a particle of glass struck his eye, but he never could see with it since."[24]

A student in Fr. Curley's laboratory had to be wary of many dangers. In a series of laboratory sessions on galvanic cells he decided to give a graphic demonstration of how they worked. He used "two galvanic cups to give power to the small shocking coil one of whose handles were laid in the water basin. A twenty dollar gold piece laid at the bottom, many tried to take out the piece of gold by holding it in the left hand [and the coil in the right]....No one succeeded because the shock was too great."[25] The Georgetown chemistry lab in the 1800s was not the safest place to be.

In the mid 1800s the study of chemistry had advanced so that only two approaches to the subject were possible: the qualitative and quantitative analysis of chemical reactions. Fr. Curley taught a predominantly qualitative course; the students analyzed compounds and noted their qualities. For such study a small supply of crude and simple apparatus was adequate. Exact measurements weren't required so approximations were usually good enough for observing phenomena and trends. The pursuit of quantitative techniques, on the other hand, demanded a stock of equipment that was much more precise. The only thing that stood between Georgetown and the pursuit of quantitative analysis was an insufficient supply of quantitative-grade equipment. This shortage was not at all unusual for the time. A survey of the forty major American universities of 1820 found that only half of them taught chemistry and of those not all offered laboratory time or facilities.[26] In addition, quantitative analysis techniques were not well known in the United States; they had only trickled in from the great European universities, where they were still being developed and refined. Most of the country suffered a shortage of quantitative equipment, technique and knowledge. In the early and even late 1800s, Europe was the only source of quality apparatus and technique.[27]

The influence of European techniques and equipment on the growth of chemistry at Georgetown is important. The tradition of scientific exchange began early. In 1913, Fr. Grassi demanded that the Natural Philosophy classes get "physical apparatus according to the latest improvements and discoveries as such as an intercourse with Europe will permit."[28] This blessing from the administration opened the door for the purchase and use of the most modern equipment. Stockroom records and descriptions of laboratory cabinets show a steady accumulation of new and better apparatus.[29] Father Curley was quick to see the value of European equipment and he avidly acquired many pieces of apparatus for the chemistry program. In his diary he enthusiastically noted each time he received a new instrument from Europe. Paris seemed to be the source of most of Georgetown's equipment. One such acquisition was a "French apparatus containing a 41 cup galvanic cell" which was "lit" on June 17, 1871 in honor of the election of a new Pope.[30] One Jesuit writes to Curley in 1859: "I am very glad to hear of the progress of you and your grip [flu]; and the valuable acquisitions you are making."[31]

The acquisition of equipment from Europe was simple in

practice; anyone could order something from a European supply house. The difficulty was in knowing what to order and how to use it once it was received. Often the technique and understanding of how to use a European machine was more valuable than the actual object.

A chemist at Georgetown was fortunate. As a Jesuit university, Georgetown was also a part of the Catholic Church which was and still is centered in Europe. It provided a communication system for quickly and accurately exchanging ideas, so that European ideas were readily available to the priests and teachers at Georgetown. A chemistry teacher would have only to ask and he could have an update on European discoveries from fellow priests in southern Italy or northern Germany. Since Georgetown's roots were in Europe, the transfer of information from there was much quicker and certainly more consistent than at the average American university.[32]

Fr. Curley was an active correspondent in the Catholic communication system. He received letters from Jesuits all over the world. In addition to trivial news, there was always interesting scientific information. Jesuit scientists wrote with findings, advice, new techniques and requests from places such as Cuba, Baltimore, Rome, Guatemala, and Rio de Janeiro. One priest from French Guyana sent Fr. Curley coconuts and local plant seeds in return for "spider lines."[33] A Jesuit at a college in Havana, Cuba informed him about a chemistry lab there: "There is a fine and almost complete collection of physical instruments. The chemistry implements and ingredients come from Paris, which is daily increasing."[34] Each letter from abroad expanded Fr. Curley's scientific knowledge.

In addition to written communication with Europe, the Society of Jesus also provided a mechanism through which people and not just ideas could be exchanged. In a period when chemistry in Europe was significantly more advanced than it was in the United States, anyone schooled in European techniques and practice brought further knowledge to Georgetown. Fr. Felix Ciampi, S.J. was just such a person. At the request of Fr. Curley, he arrived at Georgetown to teach mathematics and chemistry in the 1850–1851 school year. Having learned chemistry in Rome and having a mathematical inclination, Ciampi helped transform the chemistry education at Georgetown to a more quantitative system. This claim is supported by Fr. Ciampi's high regard for sophisticated chemical apparatus.[35] In fact, it was during his first year at the university that Georgetown began collecting a five-dollar fee from each student to pay for "physical and astronomical equipment."[36] This amounts to about six percent of the total tuition cost.

Chemistry at Georgetown changed between 1830 and 1870. Through European influences, chemistry had become a serious science. New apparatus, techniques and personalities advanced the discipline from an observational study to a more quantifiable and theoretical discipline. Fr. Curley was representative of those who demonstrated that chemistry deserved a place in Georgetown's liberal arts curriculum. "Whosoever is not a stranger...to above courses...of [Natural] Philosophy, will not hesitate to consider it essential to a scientific education, the object of which is to prepare the students for any literary profession, that he may afterward embrace."[37]

By 1870, chemistry was a legitimate and integral part of the Georgetown curriculum. The chemistry course with its "hands-on" laboratory had been required study for seniors since 1834. There were several graduates of Georgetown by 1870 who had earned degrees in science. As early as 1817, there were graduates specially trained in chemistry: "Charles and George Dennis of New York (A.B. 1817) studied chemistry and physics."[38] Since the 1853–1854 academic year a student was annually awarded a prize for the best performance in the field of chemistry.[39]

Georgetown as a National University (1870–1890)

From 1870 to the turn of the century, the chemistry program became one of the strongest undergraduate programs in the country.

For example, in 1875, every sophomore and junior student was required to take a chemistry course that included laboratory work. The curriculum had been expanded to include both qualitative and quantitative aspects of inorganic and organic chemistry.[40]

For the first time, a textbook was used as a general course outline. *Blaxaum's Chemistry*, the text of 1875, was devoted almost exclusively to experiments. The author briefly explained a theory or concept and then illustrated it by an appropriate experiment. For example, the section on acid-base neutralizations contains a brief description of acids and bases, then offers an experiment using sodium hydroxide and hydrochloric acid. The book progresses from the basic inorganic to basic organic chemistry. In the last chapters, the author presents advanced topics in both organic and inorganic chemistry. In the first year the course work covered basic organic and inorganic chemistry followed, in the second year, by a look at advanced inorganic concepts. [41]

This textbook complemented a program of qualitative analysis, heavily based in experiment. The laboratory was an integral part of the course. A chemistry student read about a concept and then observed a reaction designed to prove the notion by example. The laboratory served as an illustration for the textbook. Quantitative analysis was taught exclusively in the laboratory.

Experiments required using the European equipment. Since it was delicate and just about irreplaceable, its use had restrictions. Fr. Curley comments:

I find it best not to let the students attempt in the lab any experiment that needs large and expensive apparatus from the cabinet.[42]

To remedy this situation teachers designed simple experiments using simple equipment. These experiments usually involved product preparation, measuring the boiling point, massing a precipitate and specific gravity analysis.[43]

The more pragmatic areas of chemistry were not ignored. In 1875, by request of an administrator, Fr. Ryan, hygiene was introduced as part of the chemistry course. These lectures were given every other week for two hours. Students from the sophomore, junior, and senior class were required to attend.[44]

There is even evidence of interest in chemical research. Stockroom reports show an increased number of small orders for more exotic chemicals. "One small bottle of Uraine the new fluorescent substance" was purchased in 1883 for a modest sum of

50 cents. At the same time new glass-blowing equipment was acquired.[45] This suggests that glassware was made as needed for specific experiments. Although there were no official graduate students at the time, any upper level student who wished certainly had the resources at his disposal to conduct his own chemical research under the guidance of Fr. Curley or his associates.

According to United States Government reports, Georgetown's chemistry program was held in high esteem by 1880. In fact, the undergraduate chemical education at Georgetown University was considered one of the best in the country.[46]

In the early 1880s, the state of chemistry and other sciences at American universities was frequently discussed. Many institutions judged their educational prowess by the strength of their science departments. The first shot in this small war was fired by Mr. Barnard, the president of Columbia College in New York. In a March 1879 interview with *Scientific American*, Mr. Barnard went to great lengths to establish Columbia's superiority. He bragged that his school had recently established a mandatory one-year chemistry course for sophomores. The course consisted of one lecture a week for thirty working weeks a year. Compared to Harvard, which required only twenty lectures; Yale, which required only one half year; and Williams, which demanded only one third of a year, Columbia was the king of the Ivies in required undergraduate chemistry courses.[47] Mr. Barnard must not have been aware of the program at Georgetown when he made this claim.

As we have already seen, Georgetown required much more of its undergraduates than a one-year course without laboratory! At Georgetown, two years of chemistry with complementary laboratory sessions had been the requirement since 1873.[48] Georgetown's course also met three times a week for thirty-five working weeks per academic year. Without question a student from Georgetown was exposed to more chemistry than the average Ivy Leaguer.

Many indicators can be used to compare chemistry programs. Length of existence is one gauge often used to establish superiority. By this marker, Georgetown ranks in the first third. The University of Pennsylvania (1769), Harvard (1782), Princeton (1795), Yale (1802) and Brown (1811) all taught a chemistry course before Georgetown (1813). However, most American colleges, including the University of North Carolina (1818), Massachusetts Institute of Technology (1885), and Notre Dame (after 1880) had not set up chemistry courses until after Georgetown had done so in 1813.[49] The advance of scientific education in the United States during the first half of the nineteenth century was not significant enough to allow an early start to make a big difference.

The quality of undergraduate chemistry education can also be evaluated by noting the number of advanced courses offered each year. In this category, Georgetown did fall short. Although a mandatory two-year course in inorganic and organic chemistry was a rarity in most colleges in the 1880s, it does not compare with the specialized courses offered at schools like Johns Hopkins, Harvard or Cornell. Harvard taught elementary courses in organic, inorganic, qualitative and analytical quantitative chemistry, and even research by undergraduates was recognized. Cornell, on the other hand, had many practical courses taught as part of the agriculture school.[50] Georgetown did not normally offer such courses. The Jesuit philosophy of a well-rounded liberal education was not quite ready to produce students with such specialized training. Georgetown's strength was in providing all its students with a good background in chemistry.

In 1880 there was only one official chemistry teacher, Fr. Henry T.B. Tarr, S.J. Although Fr. Curley was active in the program, he was not teaching either of the undergraduate courses. Most other schools in the country were lucky to have any kind of chemistry teacher at all; Georgetown had a faculty of one and a "half." Yale and Brown each had only one teacher for their comparatively smaller programs. The multiple chemistry instructors at the University of Pennsylvania, Harvard and Cornell were there to teach one of the school's specialized courses of chemistry.[51] For those courses offered at Georgetown, one full-time faculty member was sufficient; in fact, it may have been the very best solution. Schedules were simplified; there was a smooth flow of instruction from lecture to laboratory and the lessons from one year could be built upon in the next.

Georgetown surpassed its competition by insisting upon laboratory practice. Not one of the Ivy League schools required all of its undergraduates to take a lab. So, while Columbia boasted about its mandatory chemistry class, Georgetown students were entering their fiftieth year of laboratory work.[52]

Today it is common knowledge that laboratory experience is necessary in any good chemistry course; this was not so well known in 1881. At that time:

> Two schools of scientific writers are in opposition;...on the one hand it is believed that a full course of didactic instruction should precede the admission of students to the laboratory...On the other hand it is held that laboratory and classroom work should go side-by-side from the beginning.[53]

The government study from which this came

> holds strongly to the latter opinion, and believes that much teaching of science preliminary to laboratory practice is like lectures upon swimming before the pupil enters the pool.[54]

Georgetown required every one of its undergraduates to get involved in the laboratory. Teachers demonstrated the more difficult procedures, but most experiments were done by the students themselves.[55]

Georgetown went to great trouble to support student involvement. Having an entire class at one time in the lab created logistical problems, so as class sizes grew toward the end of the nineteenth century, Georgetown had to make a difficult choice: either to drop the laboratory requirement or to expand the laboratory work area. The administration unhesitatingly enlarged the laboratory which resulted in one of the most complete undergraduate facilities of the time.[56]

The opening of the new Main Building, now the Healy Building, in 1883 quickly offered a solution to the problem of inadequate space. The new lab could easily accommodate fifty to sixty boys in a class. It was specifically designed "for the future accommodations of the chemistry classes on a scale that may be termed munificent."[57] The room was 41 by 62 feet, two stories high and specially fireproofed. Furthermore, additional supports were installed in areas where heavy apparatus might be used. "Each of the forty desks is fitted with drawers and lockers, separate drainage and water supply, and gas for both heating and illuminating."[58] It was well worth the considerable expense of building this new lab. What was once this chemistry laboratory is now another great Georgetown tradition: the Pub.[59]

The new laboratory solved many but not all logistical problems. Space was plentiful but equipment was still inadequate. Fr. Curley, still involved with the program, solved the problem in his own way. One day he "began the trial of a new method in laboratory practice." Since he could not provide each student with his own lab table, he had students rotate between equipment tables. This technique was not successful because it did not give a clear idea of their progress. Students eventually worked in pairs, using apparatus for a single experiment and then exchanging it for equipment needed for the next exercise.[60] Georgetown's concern for enhancing its laboratory program was a certain benefit to the students.

Ira Remsen, whose laboratory technique established the educational standard of the late nineteenth century,[61] is responsible for introducing the most advanced quantitative analysis techniques from Germany to chemists in the United States. Remsen was taught by the great analytical chemist Justus Liebig. The techniques that Remsen learned were the result of years of research and practice, for it was in Germany that "science had attained its highest developments." In the United States, Remsen was practically begged by the founders of Johns Hopkins University to head their new chemistry department. His success at that institution was widely recognized. His techniques were the best to be found in the United States.[62]

Georgetown began to use Remsen's general chemistry textbook and laboratory manual in the first year of its publication. The chemistry students at Georgetown were among the first in the country—even before Harvard—instructed by Remsen's techniques, which were incorporated into the sophomore year chemistry course. Perhaps other schools were biased toward using the textbooks written by members of their own faculty.[63]

In conjunction with the introduction of modern techniques,

the laboratory was refitted and enlarged during the 1890–1891 school year. During the renovation the chemistry lecture room was also expanded to accommodate a growing student body.[64]

Chemistry at Georgetown came into its own in the 1890s. Over that decade, chemistry established a foothold in the University which it has never lost. No longer was it merely a required subject. It began to play a multifunctional role.

The role of chemistry courses in the liberal arts curriculum was redefined and clarified. Chemistry and its sister course, physics, were hailed as integral parts of the Georgetown student's education:

> As soon as the development of the mind would admit of its being pursued in a systematic and really scientific way...to discipline the reasoning faculties by the study of Logic, Metaphysics and Ethics and by higher studies of mathematics and Natural Sciences.[65]

The administration enthusiastically supported the teaching of chemistry:

> Whatever is important in Natural Science is made a part of the curriculum and is taught with a philosophical analysis intended to guard the student against the confounding of mere information with learning which is the danger of modern education. Physics, Mechanics,...General and analytical chemistry all form important parts of regular obligatory series of studies.[66]

Chemistry was taught primarily to convey a scientific way of thinking.

Chemistry in the 1890s became a serious area of study. In 1891, Georgetown accepted its first graduate students and, the following year, a chemistry department was established. At this time all chemistry courses were still taught by one teacher, Fr. Barry Smith, S.J. The chemistry department was given charge of the Coleman Science Museum, to which "access...is allowed to students in the prosecution of their scientific studies."[67] With the formation of this department, students could focus on the study of the subject.

The study of chemistry also became an extracurricular activity. The Toner Scientific Circle, established in 1876, provided a structured organization for students to study chemistry outside of the classroom. The Toner Scientific Circle was the equivalent of a general science club, established in memory of Dr. Joseph Toner, who was a great scientific enthusiast at Georgetown. Dr. Toner enjoyed studying nature through scientific inquiry. In this tradition, members of the Society wrote papers on scientific subjects of their choosing. These papers were read aloud and discussed at group meetings. Some students chose chemistry as their topic.[68] The Scientific Circle was important in that it provided support for science and scientists at Georgetown.

The first director of the Toner Scientific Society and the man partially responsible for the growth of chemistry during the 1890s is J. Havens Richards, S.J. Fr. Richards was president of Georgetown during the decade of growth (1888–1898). Although he never taught chemistry or physics, there is no doubt that he was a key factor in developing the chemistry department. As evidence of his interest in science he was co-founder of the Toner Society. He later showed his commitment by either initiating or somehow supporting the formation of the chemistry department and masters program.

Fr. J. Havens Richards' final act of support came in the pleas he made throughout the 1890s for a new "Scientific School" at Georgetown. Every year he would appeal to alumni and friends:

Chief among the wants of the College are the following:
A Scientific School which would include the present classes of Natural Science, and would add to them the technical courses long contemplated. For the Establishment of such classes, particularly in Engineering, the present time is particularly opportune.

Applications are constantly received from students who desire instruction in these branches; and professors of the highest degree of competence are ready to undertake the task.

What is still needed is someone possessed of sufficient means and impressed with the value of scientific education, who should make this exalted purpose his own. A suitable structure could be erected for a sum not less than $30,000 to $40,000. For apparatus and equipment a like sum would be required.[69]

Every year for the next ten years this request drew few replies. Although this request was never met in full, Georgetown's chemistry department has continued to blossom and develop as an integral part of the University.

Notes

1. Proceedings from Board of Directors Meeting in 1979. *Georgetown Prospectus.*

2. Letter from Fr. Grassi. *Georgetown Prospectus,* p. 64, c.1813.

3. Frank W. Clark, S.J., *A Report on the Teaching of Chemistry and Physics in the United States* (Washington, D.C., Bureau of Education, 1880), p. 90.

4. *Georgetown Prospectus,* c.1815.

5. Ibid., c.1815.

6. Letter from Fr. Grassi. *Georgetown Prospectus,* p. 64, c.1813.

7. *Georgetown Prospectus,* 1815.

8. *Georgetown Course Catalog,* 1833.

9. Ibid., 1838.

10. Ibid., 1838.

11. *Fr. Curley's Diaries,* c.1840, Georgetown University Archives (hereafter GUA).

12. Ibid., c.1830.

13. *The McElroy Diaries,* August 12, 1813, GUA.

14. "The Case of the Knife Fight," *Record of the Prefect.*

15. *Georgetown Course Catalogs,* 1800–1850.

16. Ibid., c.1850.

17. Fr. Francis Heyden, S.J., *The Beginning and End of a Jesuit Observatory, 1841–1872,* c.p.17.

18. Letters to Fr. Curley in Archives.

19. *Fr. Curley's Notebooks and Diary,* GUA.

20. Ibid., c.1840.

21. Ibid., c.1840.

22. Ibid., c.1847.

23. *Georgetown Course Catalog,* 1850–1851.

24. *Fr. Curley's Diary,* April 1869, GUA.

25. Ibid., March 15, 1869.

26. "Chemical Education in America in 1820," *Journal of Chemical Education,* vol. 9 (1932), pp. 677–680.

27. Heilbron, J.L., *Elements of Early Modern Physics* (Berkeley: University of California Press, 1982).

28. *Georgetown Prospectus,* letter from Fr. Grassi, c.1813, p. 64.

29. *Georgetown Course Catalog,* c.1850.

30. *Fr. Curley's Diary,* June 17, 1871, GUA.

31. *Elements of Early Modern Physics,* p. 93.

32. Ibid., p. 95.

33. Letters to Fr. Curley in Archives.

34. Letter to Fr. Curley from Fr. Felix Ciampi, 1859.

35. Ibid.

36. *Georgetown Course Catalog,* 1850.

37. Ibid., c.1860.

38. *Georgetown Prospectus,* 1817–1818, p. 35.

39. *Georgetown Course Catalog,* 1853–1854.

40. Ibid., 1875–1876.

41. Ibid., and the textbook itself.

42. *Fr. Curley's Chemistry/Physics Notebook,* 1883.

43. Ibid.

44. *Exam Record of the Prefect of Studies,* 1875.

45. *Fr. Curley's Diary* and Curley's Laboratory Stockroom Report, c.1875.

46. *Report on the Teaching of Chemistry and Physics,* 1880.

47. *Scientific American,* March 15, 1879.

48. *Georgetown Course Catalog,* c.1873.

49. *Report on the Teaching of Chemistry and Physics,* Appendix I, 1880.

50. Ibid.

51. Ibid.

52. Ibid.

53. Ibid.

54. Ibid.

55. *Fr. Curley's Chemistry/Physics Notebook,* c.1870.

56. *Report on the Teaching of Chemistry and Physics,* 1880.

57. "Scientific Studies at Georgetown," *Georgetown College Journal,* May 1879, p. 78.

58. *Georgetown Course Catalog,* 1892.

59. This was confirmed by G.U.'s chief archivists.

60. *Fr. Curley's Chemistry/Physics Notebook,* 1883.

61. J. Getman, *The Life of Ira Remsen,* c.1970.

62. Ibid., confirmed by Dr. Catherine Olesko.

63. *Georgetown Course Catalog* ,1890–1891.

64. Ibid.

65. Ibid.

66. Ibid.

67. Ibid., 1892.

68. Ibid.

69. Ibid.

The Chemo-Medical Research Institute of Georgetown University (1931–ca. 1960)

Antoinette Wannebo

One of the major events in the history of science at Georgetown University was the project of establishing a "Chemo-Medical Research Institute" undertaken by Rev. George L. Coyle, S.J.

George L. Coyle was born in Philadelphia, Pennsylvania, on December 11, 1869. Having graduated from La Salle College he entered the Society of Jesus on December 31, 1887, and was ordained in 1903. In 1894, he was appointed instructor of chemistry at Gonzaga College, Washington, D.C. From 1897 to 1905 he was professor of chemistry at Woodstock College, the Jesuit seminary in Woodstock, Maryland. In 1906, he began graduate work in organic chemistry in Göttingen, Germany, where he obtained his Ph.D. in 1907. On his return to the United States, he became professor of chemistry and head of the department of chemistry at Holy Cross College, Worcester, Massachusetts, where he remained until 1923. While at Holy Cross, Father Coyle reorganized the Department, added three new laboratory courses, developed a course of Qualitative Analysis, and, in 1922, published his laboratory manual "Basic, Acid and Dry Analysis," which was reedited four times. He also conducted research on acid analysis, salts, fermentation, and heart-stimulating drugs.[1,2,3]

In addition to teaching and research, Father Coyle was an active member of the scientific community. During the First World War, he obtained information on German processes for manufacturing dyes, and passed it on to both the American and Canadian governments.[4] Until that time dyestuffs had been imported from Germany.

Father Coyle had been a member of the Northeastern Section of the American Chemical Society since 1908 and had served as that section's representative to the national society. In 1925, he was named representative of the American Chemical Society to the National Research Council. He acted as Chairman of the NRC committee on "The Construction and Equipment of Chemical Laboratories" and was editor-in-chief of its publication.

Father Coyle joined the Georgetown University faculty in 1923, when he was appointed chairman of the chemistry department and professor of organic chemistry. He devoted the greater part of the last eight years of his life to the establishment of a research institute which would apply chemistry to medicine. Today, this is hardly an unusual concept, with institutions such as the National Institutes of Health well established, but it was indeed a progressive idea in the first quarter of this century.

Coyle began work on this project in 1925. A few years later, a committee of the American Chemical Society investigated the possibility of establishing a "Chemo-Medical Research Institute" at Georgetown. The basic purpose of this center, according to a brochure describing the project,[5] was to work:

> towards the goals of prolonging life, preserving health and vanquishing disease...The discovery of specific remedies to check or completely rout tuberculosis, cancer, pneumonia and other major agents of death is promised in such an attack. Many new antitoxins to vanquish germ poisons are sure to be discovered: the surgeon must be aided by further chemical advances in anaesthesia and the secrets of the all important gland secretions will be probed with enormous benefit to humanity. Natural drugs will be freed from their harmful ingredients, or synthetic compounds formed which will hit the mark and nothing else...

The pamphlet continued with the following:

Following the guidance of their [the ACS committee] Report and in full accordance with it, Georgetown University wishes to meet its obligations of national service to the present age and to generations yet unborn. It proposes to erect a chemical laboratory which, while supplying needed facilities for its Arts and Science Schools, will at the same time contain a completely separate Institute of Chemo-Medical Research...We are confronted with this high duty, since it is agreed that the nation must look to private institutions rather than to industrial or governmental laboratories to perform it.

Washington, claimed the pamphlet, is an ideal research center, with a vast array of government laboratories and scientific libraries, such as the Library of Congress and the Library of the Army and Navy Medical Museum.

The pamphlet reported that clearly the "kind of institution envisioned was one of considerable cost." The ACS committee estimated this to be approximately $10,400,000 (in 1927). Georgetown University, whose income was derived almost exclusively from tuition, would be unable to fund this project. The University, however, was already equipped with grounds, a hospital for clinical material and a Medical School. The University estimated that the institute could be started with only $3,680,000 endowment. The concluding page of the pamphlet called for a donation from the reader for the Institute of Chemo-Medical Research.

During the late 1920s Father Coyle traveled throughout the United States to raise the endowment needed to establish the Institute. Unfortunately, by 1929 many of those who might have contributed to the institution had been bankrupted by the stock market crash. Nonetheless, by 1931, Coyle had managed to raise $252,000. (This would be equivalent to about thirty million 1988 dollars). Interest amounted to $26,000 a year. A certain Mr. Maloney was the major donor,[6] contributing over $200,000. In addition, the "Chemical Foundation of New York" promised a contribution of $14,000 a year for three years.

In February of 1931, the Chemo-Medical Institute was opened in temporary quarters in the Georgetown University Hospital (now the Loyola Building) with a three-person staff, including Michael X. Sullivan and Walter Hess. The institute undertook a search for an early diagnosis of cancer and a study of Bright's disease. Father Coyle died suddenly in New York on January 16, 1932, during a campaign to raise funds for the Institute.

In 1933, the White-Gravenor Building was completed. With the concurrence of Mr. Maloney, $147,000 of the endowment for the Chemo-Medical Institute was used to equip laboratories, leaving about $150,000 as remaining endowment for the Institute. The interest on this sum was not sufficient to maintain the Institute. Principal was used for some expenses.

A particularly influential figure for Georgetown chemistry was Michael X. Sullivan. He was born in Fall River, Massachusetts, did his undergraduate work at Harvard, and received his Ph.D. at Brown University. He worked for many years as a biochemist at a government laboratory in Washington.[7]

In 1931, when Father Coyle was the head of the Georgetown Chemistry Department, Sullivan was hired as first (and only) director of the Chemo-Medical Research Institute. Not until 1934 was M.X. Sullivan listed in the catalog as being an official part of the faculty of Georgetown University. His title then was "Research Professor of Chemistry," under "Officers of the Administration." He was pictured with the faculty in *Ye Domesday Booke* in 1939, under the title "Director of the Chemo-Medical Research Institute."

M.X. Sullivan published 217 items during his career, including sixty-eight which were under his name only. He presented papers regularly at the American Chemical Society's annual meetings. A few samples give some idea of his interests: "Synthetic Culture Media and the Biochemistry of Bacterial Pigments" (*Journal of Medical Research*), "Biochemical Studies of the Saliva in Pellagra" (United States Public Health Service Pamphlet, 1919), "Significance of the Cystine Content of Finger Nails in Arthritics" (*The American Journal of Surgery*, 1932).

In an address to Georgetown's "Secchi Academy," an organization devoted to "the appreciation of the cultural value of the sciences," in December 1940, M.X. Sullivan is quoted as saying:

> the science of chemistry had become as integral to man's life as breathing, and its influence was growing. Since the natural world man finds himself in, and as man himself is, composed of chemicals, chemistry is in fact the study of man's existence on this earth,

his actions, the mechanics of this existence, and the things, living and inanimate around him. The foreknowledge of the products, by-products and process of a reaction lead to its control and the ability to procure the product at will in specific quantities. An example of this procedure on a large scale is industrialization, upon which are dependent the economies, politics and cultures of modern nations.[8]

Sullivan held that "...the understanding of the wonders of our environment, the glory of the myriad of harmonious reactions going on in the body and the purposefulness of these reactions going in the body will give thrills of pleasure to a supposedly humdrum existence and will add dignity and honor to man's days on earth."

"The prime notion a scientist must keep in mind is that nothing in experimentation is definite, that all is relative and that basically all a scientist can do is marvel at the natural world and speculate on its mechanics." "...in chemical research—especially in biological Chemistry, a field in which I work, attention is paid to fundamental causes in so far as the mind of man can comprehend them."

Dr. Sullivan directed the Chemo-Medical Institute until well into the 1950s.[9] He supervised the Chemistry graduate program which prospered with the development of government laboratories in the Washington area during World War II and thereafter, directing about one hundred Ph.D. theses. His three main lines of research were sulphur metabolism in health and disease, the study of trace constituents in the urine of cancer patients (for early diagnosis of cancer), and the development of more specific tests for amino-acids and other biologically important constituents of body fluids and excretions. He continued to be active, publishing scientific papers until his death in 1963. After his death, the "Chemo-Medical Research Institute" ceased to exist. The Institute had been quite successful in gaining Georgetown a respectable place in research in the specific areas of its interest, and it provided a base for further developments in science at Georgetown.

Notes

1. *Holy Cross Alumnus*, February 1932.

2. *Industrial and Engineering Chemistry*, Necrology, 10 February 1932.

3. *Journal of Chemical Education*, vol. 9, no. 4, April 1932.

4. Seaverns, J.A., "An Expert on Dyestuffs," Georgetown University Archives (hereafter GUA).

5. Chemistry Department file, 1891–1953, GUA.

6. The archivist of the Catholic University of America reports that Martin Moloney (born 1846), a "capitalist and philanthropist" of Scranton, Pennsylvania, was a main benefactor of the "Moloney Chemistry Building" at the Catholic University, dedicated in 1917.

7. "The M.X. Sullivan Papers 1905–1941," GUA.

8. "The M.X. Sullivan Papers, Folder 1, Chemo-Medical Research Institute, July 1, 1932 to June 30, 1933," GUA.

9. Joseph F. Cohalen, S.J. (Treasurer of the University), Office Memorandum to Father Rector, May 14, 1954, GUA.